Web Design & Desktop Publishing For Dummies®

Color, Costs, and Control: How Web and Print Publishing Differ

- Color on the Web is "free."
- Scanned photographs do not increase costs on the Web.
- Web costs don't increase when the amount of information increases.
- You have much less control over the appearance of headline and body copy type on the Web.
- Control over typography is available on the Web if you're willing to greatly increase your site's downloading time.
- Large photos and other graphics take significantly more time to download than small graphics.
- In print, your message is delivered in a tangible format that can be saved, shared, and referred to later.
- The Web is a flexible medium: Your message can be easily and inexpensively changed as often as needed or desired.
- Tangible print pieces are more likely to be at least skimmed by your target audience, to whom you can control mailing and distribution; you can't tell for certain if your target audience is visiting your Web site, and your site is more easily abandoned if conditions are not "right."
- Most of your prospects can read print materials anywhere at anytime, but many may not have access to a computer connected to the World Wide Web.

Content Counts: How Web and Print Publishing Are the Same

- Success is proportional to the amount and quality of your planning.
- [illegible]

- [illegible] your audience can immediately prioritize each part of your message.
- You can use typography to "voice" your publication.
- Visuals such as charts, tables, illustrations, and other graphics often communicate better and faster than text.
- You can use color as a tool to add selective emphasis, highlight important information, code parts of your message, and project a desired image.
- Color works best when used with restraint.
- Your audience is in a hurry, more likely to skim your words than to read them unless the benefits are clearly presented.
- Make your message as easy to understand as possible.
- Success comes from chunking — dividing long messages into bite-sized pieces, introduced with catchy subheads.

Web Design & Desktop Publishing For Dummies®

Look at the difference 10 simple design improvements can make!

Before

This column needs help!

Effective desktop publishing publication design and production is based on your willingness to pay lots of disciplined attention to detail. It's the little things that count. Even outstandingly beautiful publication layouts can be sabotaged by failure to pay attention to detail. No matter how masterful the publication designer's intent, if the type is too large or too small, or the lines of type are too closely spaced, or hyphenation is inadvertently omitted, the page will be difficult to read and readers will pass it by.

Likewise, text will not be read if paragraph spacing is off or--worse yet--the wrong punctuation characters are used! Master the details in order to master the page!

After

Notice the dramatic improvement that takes place when you pay attention to details!

EFFECTIVE DESKTOP PUBLISHING publication design and production is based on your willingness to pay lots of disciplined attention to detail. It's the little things that count. Even outstandingly beautiful publication layouts can be sabotaged by failure to pay attention to detail. No matter how masterful the publication designer's intent, if the type is too large or too small, or the lines of type are too closely spaced, or hyphenation is inadvertently omitted, the page will be difficult to read and readers will pass it by.
Likewise, text will not be read if paragraph spacing is off or—worse yet—the wrong punctuation characters are used! Master the details in order to master the page!

Changes made...

1. Default line spacing was replaced by a measurement more suitable for the typeface, type size, and column width.
2. The larger initial cap now looks deliberate instead of accidental.
3. The bottom of the initial cap now aligns with the third line of the paragraph.
4. The text was wrapped as closely as possible to the initial cap, and the first line of text is set in small caps to form a transition between the initial cap and the text that follows.
5. By splitting words over two lines, word spacing was made more consistent.
6. Letter spacing appears more natural because normal tracking was used.
7. Word spacing was fine-tuned by reducing the amount of possible variation between closely spaced words and widely spaced words.
8. The large horizontal band of white space between the two paragraphs, created by pressing the Enter/Return key twice after each paragraph, was replaced by the minimal amount of space necessary to indicate a new paragraph.
9. The first-line indent was eliminated.
10. The two hyphens introducing the parenthetical expression were replaced by the typographically correct em dash.

(See Chapter 9 for an explanation of why these changes were made.)

Cheat Sheet $2.95 value. Item 0139-9.
For more information about IDG Books, call 1-800-762-2974.

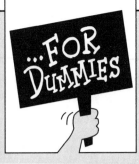

WEB DESIGN & DESKTOP PUBLISHING FOR DUMMIES®

WEB DESIGN & DESKTOP PUBLISHING FOR DUMMIES®

by Roger C. Parker

IDG Books Worldwide, Inc.
An International Data Group Company

Foster City, CA ♦ Chicago, IL ♦ Indianapolis, IN ♦ Southlake, TX

Web Design & Desktop Publishing For Dummies ®

Published by
IDG Books Worldwide, Inc.
An International Data Group Company
919 E. Hillsdale Blvd.
Suite 400
Foster City, CA 94404
www.idgbooks.com (IDG Books Worldwide Web site)
www.dummies.com (Dummies Press Web site)

Library of Congress Catalog Card No.: 97-70742

ISBN: 0-7645-0139-9

Printed in the United States of America

10 9 8 7 6 5 4 3 2 1

1B/QV/RS/ZX/IN

Distributed in the United States by IDG Books Worldwide, Inc.

Distributed by Macmillan Canada for Canada; by Transworld Publishers Limited in the United Kingdom; by IDG Norge Books for Norway; by IDG Sweden Books for Sweden; by Woodslane Pty. Ltd. for Australia; by Woodslane Enterprises Ltd. for New Zealand; by Longman Singapore Publishers Ltd. for Singapore, Malaysia, Thailand, and Indonesia; by Simron Pty. Ltd. for South Africa; by Toppan Company Ltd. for Japan; by Distribuidora Cuspide for Argentina; by Livraria Cultura for Brazil; by Ediciencia S.A. for Ecuador; by Addison-Wesley Publishing Company for Korea; by Ediciones ZETA S.C.R. Ltda. for Peru; by WS Computer Publishing Corporation, Inc., for the Philippines; by Unalis Corporation for Taiwan; by Contemporanea de Ediciones for Venezuela; by Computer Book & Magazine Store for Puerto Rico; by Express Computer Distributors for the Caribbean and West Indies. Authorized Sales Agent: Anthony Rudkin Associates for the Middle East and North Africa.

For general information on IDG Books Worldwide's books in the U.S., please call our Consumer Customer Service department at 800-762-2974. For reseller information, including discounts and premium sales, please call our Reseller Customer Service department at 800-434-3422.

For information on where to purchase IDG Books Worldwide's books outside the U.S., please contact our International Sales department at 415-655-3200 or fax 415-655-3295.

For information on foreign language translations, please contact our Foreign & Subsidiary Rights department at 415-655-3021 or fax 415-655-3281.

For sales inquiries and special prices for bulk quantities, please contact our Sales department at 415-655-3200 or write to the address above.

For information on using IDG Books Worldwide's books in the classroom or for ordering examination copies, please contact our Educational Sales department at 800-434-2086 or fax 817-251-8174.

For press review copies, author interviews, or other publicity information, please contact our Public Relations department at 415-655-3000 or fax 415-655-3299.

For authorization to photocopy items for corporate, personal, or educational use, please contact Copyright Clearance Center, 222 Rosewood Drive, Danvers, MA 01923, or fax 508-750-4470.

About the Author

Roger C. Parker has been called "the nation's leading guru of desktop publishing design excellence." Over one million readers in over thirty countries throughout the world own copies of his 24 books, which include the bestselling *Microsoft Office For Windows For Dummies* series and *Desktop Publishing and Design For Dummies.*

Roger has conducted hundreds of design seminars around the world, including the Magazine Publishing Association's Folio Conference in New York. Roger regularly contributes to numerous print and online publications, including Microsoft SmallBiz. He is a member of the Microsoft Small Business Council and a consultant to numerous firms. He is a member of the International Design Association.

For free additional print and Web design ideas, visit Roger C. Parker's Meaningful Content Web site at www.rcparker.com.

Dedication

This book is dedicated to the memory of my parents, Glynn and Hazel Parker, who encouraged my love of the printed word from the start.

Author's Acknowledgments

Books are not written by authors, they're created by teams.

On this project, I enjoyed the support of an especially strong team, starting with its "captain," Kathy Cox, one of the most professional editors I have ever worked with. Kathy's patience and unfailing encouragement kept this book going. In her efforts, Kathy was ably assisted by copy editors Michael Bolinger, Jennifer Davies, Tina Sims, Diane Smith, Joe Jansen, and Kim Darosett, and a diligent production and graphics staff comprised of Regina Snyder, Jane Martin, Drew R. Moore, and Christine Berman.

I'd also like to acknowledge the support of my family; my wife, Betsy and my three sons, Christopher, Zachary, and Ryan. Zachary's midnight visits to my office helped maintain my enthusiasm and always provided a burst of energy when the going got rough.

Special thanks to my agent, Margot Maley of Waterside Productions whose enthusiasm and assistance always comes at just the right point. I am also indebted to Ken Oyer, one of my favorite designers and fellow authors, for his assistance preparing several illustrations.

Publisher's Acknowledgments

We're proud of this book; please register your comments through our IDG Books Worldwide Online Registration Form located at `http://my2cents.dummies.com`.

Some of the people who helped bring this book to market include the following:

Acquisitions, Development, and Editorial

Project Editor: Kathleen M. Cox

Acquisitions Editor: Michael Kelly

Copy Editors: Michael Bolinger, Tamara S. Castleman, Jennifer Davies, Joe Jansen, Tina Sims, Diane Smith

Technical Editor: Jim Alley

Editorial Manager: Mary C. Corder

Editorial Assistant: Donna Love

Production

Project Coordinator: Regina Snyder

Layout and Graphics: Lou Boudreau, Angela F. Hunckler, Jane E. Martin, Drew R. Moore, Anna Rohrer, Brent Savage

Proofreaders: Sally Burton, Christine Berman, Rebecca Senninger

Indexer: Liz Cunningham

Special Help

Colleen Rainsberger, Editorial Manager; Richard Graves, Product Development Administrator

General and Administrative

IDG Books Worldwide, Inc.: John Kilcullen, CEO; Steven Berkowitz, President and Publisher

IDG Books Technology Publishing: Brenda McLaughlin, Senior Vice President and Group Publisher

Dummies Technology Press and Dummies Editorial: Diane Graves Steele, Vice President and Associate Publisher; Mary Bednarek, Acquisitions and Product Development Director; Kristin A. Cocks, Editorial Director

Dummies Trade Press: Kathleen A. Welton, Vice President and Publisher; Kevin Thornton, Acquisitions Manager; Maureen F. Kelly, Editorial Coordinator

IDG Books Production for Dummies Press: Beth Jenkins, Production Director; Cindy L. Phipps, Manager of Project Coordination, Production Proofreading, and Indexing; Kathie S. Schutte, Supervisor of Page Layout; Shelley Lea, Supervisor of Graphics and Design; Debbie J. Gates, Production Systems Specialist; Robert Springer, Supervisor of Proofreading; Debbie Stailey, Special Projects Coordinator; Tony Augsburger, Supervisor of Reprints and Bluelines; Leslie Popplewell, Media Archive Coordinator

Dummies Packaging and Book Design: Patti Crane, Packaging Specialist; Lance Kayser, Packaging Assistant; Kavish + Kavish, Cover Design

♦

The publisher would like to give special thanks to Patrick J. McGovern, without whom this book would not have been possible.

♦

Contents at a Glance

Cartoons at a Glance

By Rich Tennant

The 5th Wave
By Rich Tennant
©RICHTENNANT

"THE FUNNY THING IS, I NEVER KNEW THEY HAD DESKTOP PUBLISHING SOFTWARE FOR PAPER SHREDDERS."

page 5

The 5th Wave By Rich Tennant

"You know, I've asked you a dozen times not to animate the torches on our Web page!"

page 309

The 5th Wave
By Rich Tennant
©RICHTENNANT
Well, there's your Web page, Crypto. Designed like you asked. But personally, I think it has too many spinning spirals and blinking lights. It makes...hard reading. Make...tired... look...at...lose...all... con...cen...tra...tion...
Perfect!
CRYPTO THE HYPNOTIST

page 63

The 5th Wave
By Rich Tennant
©RICHTENNANT

"Of course graphics are important to your project, Eddy, but I think it would've been better to scan a picture of your worm collection."

page 225

The 5th Wave
By Rich Tennant
©RICHTENNANT

"I APPRECIATE YOUR COMPUTER HAS 256 COLORS, I JUST DON'T THINK THEY ALL HAD TO BE USED IN ONE BOOK REPORT."

page 121

Fax: 508-546-7747 • *E-mail:* the5wave@tiac.net

Table of Contents

Part II: Web Marketing and Design 63

Introduction

The introduction of a new generation of publishing software, designed for the creation of Web pages, continues the communications revolution that began in the mid-1980s when Adobe introduced PostScript, Apple introduced the original Macintosh computer and LaserWriter, and Paul Brainerd introduced Aldus (now Adobe) PageMaker.

Times change!

Within a few years, desktop publishing replaced typesetters and printers. Graphic designers had to adapt to electronic production or leave the business (for all practical purposes) and — most important — everyone could become a publisher. The power of the press was no longer limited to the press. Previously impractical, limited-circulation newsletters and niche publications were now feasible, and consultants, entrepreneurs, and a new breed of self-employed professionals could produce their own marketing materials, brochures, newsletters, and price sheets.

Web Publishing Enters the Mix

Since the appearance of the original *Desktop Publishing & Design For Dummies,* the Internet has increasingly become a practical part of our everyday lives.

Until very recently, the Internet — like typesetting — was the province of a few lucky and highly trained people willing to master the intricacies of HTML programming. Now, everything's changed. A new generation of programs makes it as easy to create good-looking Web sites as a previous generation of desktop publishing programs made it possible to create good-looking brochures and newsletters. As a result, owners and managers of even the smallest businesses can create a Web presence, *even if they don't know anything about design!*

This rush to Web publish is precisely today's problem: Just as the first generation of desktop publishing programs ushered in a generation of ugly documents, completed with 42 different fonts per page, the new easy-to-use Web authoring programs are causing an explosion of slow-loading, hard-to-read Web sites — Web sites that often do more damage than good.

I wrote this book so you can look good in print and on the Web.

Who Do I Think You Are?

I wrote *Web Design & Desktop Publishing For Dummies* for three audiences. One of these audiences probably defines your needs.

- **Experienced desktop publishers.** I wrote this book to help those with desktop publishing experience make the transition to Web design. Important similarities and differences exist between designing for paper and designing for the Web. This book can help you apply what you already know about print design to designing for the Web, so you can make a smooth and painless transition.
- **Newcomers to desktop publishing.** This book is intended to be a single-source reference guide for those who are just getting started creating their own print marketing materials — their own ads, brochures, newsletters, and training materials. This book provides the basic information you need to look good in print from the start.
- **Newcomers to Web design.** Many entrepreneurs are creating their own Web sites as their first design projects. Personal and family Web sites are also becoming increasingly popular, helping people keep in touch with distant friends and relatives. This book provides the basic design and software information you need to create good-looking Web sites, even if you have had no previous experience or interest in print communications.

How This Book Is Organized

How you should read this book depends precisely on what you want to do today!

- If you're *just getting started* in desktop publishing and have recently purchased a "do everything" software program that can prepare print communications as well as Web documents, start with Chapter 1 and read this book in a linear fashion (or at least as linearly as you need for what you'll be doing). The four chapters in Part I are of major importance in providing you with the ground rules for successful print and online design.
- If you have had *some previous desktop publishing experience* and are familiar with the basics of print design, you can go directly to Part III to see how to maximize the impact of your print designs. You can also see Part IV for information on color and other refinements.

  As a bonus, I've added a condensed "Newsletters For Dummies" at the end of Chapter 10 to serve as a primer and a guide to better newsletter designs.

- If you want to *immediately get started creating a Web site*, turn directly to Part II and start reading. These chapters help you establish realistic expectations and introduce the tools that you work with — as well as the challenges that you must master. If you're interested in previewing advanced tools and techniques, sneak a peek at Chapter 18.

Finish your journey by checking out Part V for a review of the most important ideas contained in the previous chapters and some good advice.

Icons Used in This Book

Here are the icons you'll encounter in *Web Design & Desktop Publishing For Dummies.* Graphics can often say things better and faster. These tiny graphics highlight information that makes a difference in how you approach your designing tasks.

This icon flags text that contains an important design principle that you can dress up nicely and attach to your refrigerator door (or your computer screen).

This icon highlights design tips that are specific to the online world. Don't try these in print.

This icon indicates a shortcut you can use to make your life (or someone else's life) easier.

Some stuff bears repeating so you remember it well; this icon marks the spot.

This icon lets you know that you're entering deeper waters than most non-designers care to swim in. It's for those who want to become Graduate Designers sooner or later.

This icon points out specific software programs to ease the work of online and print design.

There are few things you can really do wrong in design other than waste your time and money (or your client's money), or your audience's time. This icon steers you clear of the most potentially damaging mistakes.

The More Things Change . . .

When looking back at the past ten or so years and all that has transpired since the Apple Macintosh and PageMaker changed the world, it's interesting to note how little has changed.

The basics remain, and one of the joys of writing this book has been the opportunity to look back and see how little has changed, even though the tools are so different.

We now routinely work with computer hardware that, a few years ago, only huge firms and government agencies such as NASA had access to. We use 200 MHz Pentium processors and big-screen monitors. We have inexpensive and instant access to tens of thousands of typeface designs.

Yet our basic goals as designers and communicators, both in print and online, remain the same:

- To make our message as *simple and easy to understand* as possible.
- To *attract attention and maintain reader or Web site visitor interest* at a time of information overload.
- To fine-tune the way we develop *our communications* as well as the content and the overall design of our projects.

Conclusion

Whether you're a newcomer to desktop publishing and Web design or an experienced designer making the transition to Web communications, I hope that you enjoy the journey that begins in these pages.

Part I
Perspective: Design as Marketing

"THE FUNNY THING IS, I NEVER KNEW THEY HAD DESKTOP PUBLISHING SOFTWARE FOR PAPER SHREDDERS."

In this part . . .

Part I starts at the beginning, with an overview of design principles and how they relate to successful marketing efforts online and in print, whether for your company, your nonprofit organization, or yourself. Throughout this part, you see the important role that design can play in the success of your communications as well as your career growth — whether you're a full-time designer or design is just a minor part of your job description (or serendipitous add-on).

Chapter 1

The Dollars and Sense of Good Design

In This Chapter

- The importance of design in the age of MTV
- How design contributes to readability
- Design as personality and unity
- How design can contribute to your success
- The emotional rewards of good design

Good design makes sense. . . and dollars too! In this overcommunicated world, design is a necessity, not a luxury. The constant barrage of communications and a rising standard of design literacy make the need for effective design greater today than ever before.

The spread of desktop publishing and word processing software, coupled with the availability of numerous typeface options and low-cost inkjet and laser printers, have produced a spurt of design innovations and abominations that have made readers more sensitive to the advantages of effective design. As a result, people today notice and respond to design blunders that they used to tolerate. Bad design not only devalues your message by burying it in babble; bad design also insults your readers who perceive a lack of regard indicated by careless design and production.

In this chapter, I analyze the design process and then look at ways that design can make your words and your images more meaningful.

What Is Design?

Design is a process, not an event.

- Design is the process of taking responsibility for the appearance, as well as the content, of your message.
- Design is the process of asking questions about your audience and implementing the answers most appropriate to your medium and your message.
- Design is placement and proportion, balance and imbalance, shadow and light, contrast and unity, subtlety and surprise.

Good design is not so much the result of a burst of creative activity as it is an analytical "try it and see; if it works — make it better; if it doesn't — make it work!" process.

Effective design is the result of planning before acting, and effective planning involves these four aspects:

- **Audience:** Start by analyzing your audience. Ask yourself: "Who are they?" "What are their expectations?" "How much do they know?" "How interested in my message are they likely to be?" Try to focus on one person who represents your audience ideal.

  Consider the recent anniversaries of various World War II events. A message for teenagers who never experienced war would need to be crafted differently from one directed at senior citizens who had lived through the war. Whose interest level would you expect to be higher? How can you compensate for a lower level of natural interest?

- **Message:** What is the purpose of your message and what obstacles must you overcome if your message is to succeed? Ask questions, like: What action do you want the audience to take? How much convincing is likely to be required?

  It helps to prioritize your message. If the reader can come away with only one idea, what idea should that be?

- **Environment:** Determine the environment in which your message will appear. Environment includes where your audience is likely to encounter the communication, how motivated you expect the audience to be, and how much time the audience can spend absorbing your message.
- **Competition:** Finally, analyze the other messages that compete for your audience's attention. You don't want to show up at a party wearing exactly the same outfit as your best friend, do you? Well, it's the same principle — your document must be distinctive for readers to notice it.

For example, many designers today use oversize paper to distinguish their messages from the bulk of ordinary-sized paper that comes across people's desks. Have you noticed how large the Publisher's Clearinghouse Sweepstakes solicitation is? Hard to miss, isn't it?

Only after you prepare the groundwork is it time for you to pick up your pencil and paper and start doodling a design. And only after you identify several possible solutions should you even think about turning on your computer. (Unless, of course, you've binary code in your blood and wouldn't think of starting off on a design effort without your cybertools at hand.) My point is to think first — plan first — and let your design flow from that planning.

Six steps to success

Regardless whether you're designing a yard sale flyer to hang at the local library or an annual report for a Fortune 500 firm, successful designs result from following the same six-step procedure:

1. **Establish goals and organize your material.**

   Start by analyzing your message and your audience. Don't even begin to think about what you want your publication to look like until you have answer the who, what, where, when, and why questions. (Check out Chapter 2 to get the scoop on what these questions entail.)

2. **Choose an appropriate format and page layout.**

   What do you want the overall *look* of your publication to be? How large do you want it to be? How many columns of type are you going to use? How many colors do you want? What color, weight, and texture of paper do you want to print it on? What graphic accents can you use to direct the reader's eyes to the appropriate places?

3. **Make appropriate typeface, type size, and spacing decisions.**

   Although it's a picture-oriented world, the majority of your message appears as headlines and body copy — even on a Web page. Your job is to walk the fine line between creating titles and headlines that attract attention and body copy type that doesn't interfere with your reader's ability to quickly understand your message. Not an easy task!

4. **Add and manipulate visuals.**

   Words alone cannot, and should not, tell the whole story. After all, reading is harder than looking, and, for better or worse, it's an MTV-influenced world. Whenever possible, replace words with visuals — photographs, illustrations, charts, graphs, tables, organizational charts, flow charts, and timelines. Each type of illustration has its advantages and disadvantages, and each type requires careful placement on the page. I talk more about using visuals in Chapter 15.

5. **Build momentum into your pages.**

   Words and visuals require organization. You achieve this organization by *chunking,* in which you break up large amounts of material into manageable, bite-sized chunks by using organizational devices such as subheads, pull quotes, and sidebars. Another approach is *layering,* in which you present information that readers can read on an "as needed" or "as wanted" basis. For instance, on the reader's first pass through your publication, they can read the primary layer of information. On subsequent passes, or if your publication piques their interest, they can read the secondary and tertiary layers, or dialog.

6. **Refine and fine-tune till you drop (or at least until you've reached the point of diminishing returns).**

   Successful pages are the result of incremental refinements. Seldom can you isolate a single element, command, or software feature that is the *one thing* responsible for a perfect page. Perfect *wholes,* in other words, are the result of perfect details, and perfect details are the result of breaking a project down into its component parts and fine-tuning each part. A single blast of a tuba is enough to destroy an otherwise perfectly played string quartet. Likewise, a single glaring error can undermine the credibility and readability of your entire document.

What about creativity?

Experienced designers know that they're not going to get it right the first time, so you shouldn't expect to get it right the first time, either. Just about everyone enjoys the thrill of a burst of creative clarity — the instantly obvious solution or "Ah-ha" experience, as the psychologist William James defined it. But those creative moments cannot be legislated. All you can do is prepare the ground work for creative bursts by trying out and rejecting alternative solutions. So that when the right solution suddenly presents itself, you are ready to notice it. But even when you come up with the perfect design solution, the more you nit-pick the details, the more you find things that need fixin'. And, the more you fine-tune details, the better your design will be.

How Design Adds Value to Your Ideas

Although design sometimes takes place before you write any words, in most cases the starting point is working with the words already written. Design adds value to these words in ten ways, which I explain further in this section:

- Design attracts attention.
- Design adds value to your message.
- Design enhances readership.
- Design simplifies.
- Design provides selective emphasis.
- Design provides organization.
- Design creates unity.
- Design sets your message apart.
- Design speeds production.
- Design saves money.

If design doesn't add value to the words, then you may as well distribute those words as a typewritten manuscript or word-processed file, which readers can read on their computer screens! (Unfortunately, in some cases, typewritten manuscripts are easier to read than poorly designed desktop-published documents.) But design does add value in a number of important ways.

Design attracts attention

Design helps your message get noticed in an overcommunicated world, where millions of messages are competing for your audience's attention. Newspapers are filled with ads, mailboxes are stuffed with direct-mail flyers and newsletters, and more businesses are promoting themselves on the Internet every day. In order to compete, it's vital that your message gets noticed. The effective use of design tools like color, type, and white space can help your message attract attention — even in the most crowded environments.

One of the best ways to understand the power of design is to go to a bookstore or newsstand with a large display of magazine covers. Notice how some covers attract your eyes' attention while others sit passively in the background. Take a few moments to note some of the characteristics that the attention-getting covers have in common. This simple exercise can be a turning point in your marketing and design career!

Design adds value to your message

People make immediate assumptions about the value of your words based on the appearance of your pages. Effective design presells readers on the importance of your words by simultaneously making your words appear more valuable and easier to read.

Design projects images, which operate on nonverbal levels. A well-designed page projects a spirit of optimism and an atmosphere of professionalism. A cluttered, poorly organized page indicates that you didn't care enough about your words to take the time to present them as neatly as possible. And, if the person who prepares the document doesn't care about the document, why should the reader?

Design images are based on subtle clues like white space, borders, type, and colors. Fortunately, these are all elements that you have under your control! And guess what? You can find out about all these tools in this book.

Design enhances readership

Good design makes your words easier to read. Long lines of small type, for example, discourage readers because the page just looks so darn hard to read. Check out Figure 1-1; which version do you want to read? A good designer makes readability a priority.

Readership studies document the amazing impact that design has on readership. Colin Wheildon conducted the most recent study in Australia and reported the results in his recent book *Communicating in Print — Or How Type and Layout Can Get Your Message Across — Or Get In The Way* (Berkeley, CA: Strathmoor Press, 1995). Colin's research indicates that:

- Changes in headline typography can increase readership from 57 percent to 92 percent. The worst possible combination of typefaces reduces legibility to a mere 3 percent — hardly worth the effort of turning on your computer.
- Body copy comprehension can jump from 12 percent to 67 percent when you use a more readable typeface.
- Subtle changes in line spacing typically can increase body copy comprehension from 77 percent to 98 percent.
- Setting body copy against a background screen can reduce comprehension from 70 percent to 3 percent, depending on the grayness of the background.
- Headline colors can reduce the comprehension of adjacent type from 67 percent to 17 percent.

One of the best ways you can improve your design skills is to create a paragraph or two of text which you can use for various examples. Keeping the content of your test paragraphs similar forces you or your readers to concentrate on the typographic and layout differences you are illustrating, rather than the content of your samples.
By exploring your software's power, by experimenting with the various commands located under the different menus, you'll be amazed at the major differences that the same text paragraph can project when typeface, type size, line spacing, letter spacing, alignment, hyphenation and paragraph spacing are manipulated. Just be sure you only experiment with one variable at a time and you identify the change that you illustrating and you identify the settings of each example.

One of the best ways you can improve your design skills is to create a paragraph or two of text which you can use for various examples. Keeping the content of your test paragraphs similar forces you or your readers to concentrate on the typographic and layout differences you are illustrating, rather than the content of your samples.
By exploring your software's power, by experimenting with the various commands located under the different menus, you'll be amazed at the major differences that the same text paragraph can project when typeface, type size, line spacing, letter spacing, alignment, hyphenation and paragraph spacing are manipulated. Just be sure you only experiment with one variable at a time and you identify the change that you illustrating and you identify the settings of each example.

Figure 1-1: Which typeface and line length looks easier to read?

Design simplifies

Design can simplify your message by breaking long batches of text into manageable, bite-sized chunks. Subheads (mini heads that briefly convey the point of the text that follows) are the most obvious use of design as a simplification tool. By inserting subheads into long columns of text, you can increase readership of even the longest message. By adding white space and by using a different typeface, you can make sure that each subhead adds visual contrast to your message, replacing boredom with interest. Each subhead provides an additional entry point for the reader to begin reading your message.

Design also simplifies by communicating at a glance. A design can make comparisons, relationships, and trends come alive if you replace text paragraphs with visuals such as pie charts, flow charts, organization charts, and tables. Design makes complicated messages easier to understand. Remember, if you bury information deep within a paragraph, it's harder for the reader to understand than if the same information appears as a visual.

Design provides selective emphasis

Design communicates a clearly defined hierarchy of information, which helps readers quickly separate the important from the less important. Design helps your audience avoid information overload and makes it easy to quickly locate the information they desire.

You can visually signal levels of importance by using headlines of different size as well as by separating secondary topics from long articles by creating sidebars (self-contained but related information set off to the side in a separate graphic treatment). Headlines of equal size imply stories of equal size. By making one headline (or photograph) significantly larger than the others, you nonverbally communicate different levels of importance.

Design provides organization

How does your audience know where your message begins and ends? Is it easy to find? The top of Figure 1-2 presents a confusing mishmash of articles. Where should you start?

Design organizes your message by permitting you to visually signal elements of message architecture. Large chapter numbers and titles clearly indicate new chapters, for example. A foreword set in italics indicates a brief conversational aside to the reader. Tips introduced by warning icons visually signal their importance. A different page layout for the information at the back of a book separates appendix, glossary, and index information from the main body of a book.

The study I discuss in the "Design enhances readership" section of this chapter shows that revising a page's layout can increase readership from 32 percent to 67 percent, which doubles the impact of your message without you changing a single word or increasing printing and postage costs one red cent! (Excuse me, Fidel.)

Design provides unity

Design multiplies your printing communication dollars by creating unity both within and between your publications. Within a single document, design can create a *whole* out of a series of pages. The elements of unity include consistent margins, column placement, graphic accents, typeface, type size, and color choices.

More importantly, when you use design properly, you create a one-plus-one-equals-three synergy out of all of your association's or firm's print communications. Design can also create a whole out of a series of individual brochures or newsletters. The term *corporate identity* says it all. When a firm has a well-established corporate identity, you see an obvious family resemblance between its advertising, correspondence, faxes, brochures, price lists, and newsletters.

Techniques as simple as consistent margins and the consistent use of a few well-chosen typefaces can create a welcome familiarity. A series of newsletters with a consistent column layout become old friends rather than strangers when they arrive. Consider Figure 1-3. Although each advertisement in the figure illustrates a different project, each is obviously part of a series. You can see an underlying unity because the advertisements are more similar than different. The framework, graphic accents, and typographic tools remain consistent, even though the content differs.

This page looks like a lot of trouble to read, and it is.

There is no clearly-defined starting oint for your eyes nor is there a logical and immediately obvious hierarchy of content. Nor is there any visual contrast on the page. You, and your readers, are presented with a solid gray mass of text. There's nothing to grab your eye, or your reader or web site visitor's eye.

Which paragraphs do you read first?

What is the most important message?

Where are important supporting facts located?

The answers to these, and other questions, are carefully camouflaged in the contents of this page.

Readers are in a hurry.

Remember that readers are in a hurry. They are not going to take the time to puzzle-out the meaning of your print and online documents. They want immediate access to your information. Readers are always looking for an excuse not to read. Your goal is to cajole, modivate and tease them into reading. Anything you can do to make their job easier will be repaid in higher readership and repeat visits to your web site.

Headlines are important.

Headlines are like road signs that attract readers into your pages. A strong headline, or title, acts like a billboard along a highway enticing readers into reading the text that follows. The stronger your treatment of headlines, the greater your page readership.

You can increase the effectiveness of your headlines by setting them in a contrasting type face, type size or type style. For example, if you are using a serif typeface for body copy, consider using a bold or Extra Heavy (i.e. extra thick) sans serif typeface for your headlines. Make your headlines significantly larger than the body copy so they clearly stand out.

This page looks easier to read, and it is.

There is no clearly-defined starting point for your eyes nor is there a logical and immediately obvious hierarchy of content. Nor is there any visual contrast on the page. You, and your readers, are presented with a solid gray mass of text. There's nothing to grab your eye, or your reader or web site visitor's eye.

Which paragraphs do you read first?

What is the most important message?

Where are important supporting facts located?

The answers to these, and other questions, are carefully camouflaged in the contents of this page.

Readers are in a hurry.

Remember that readers are in a hurry. They are not going to take the time to puzzle-out the meaning of your print and on-line documents. They want immediate access to your information. Readers are always looking for an excuse not to read. Your goal is to cajole, motivate and tease them into reading. Anything you can do to make their job easier will be repaid in higher readership and repeat visits to your web site.

Headlines are important.

Headlines are like road signs that attract readers into your pages. A strong headline, or title, acts like a billboard along a highway enticing readers into reading the text that follows. The stronger your treatment of headlines, the greater your page readership.

You can increase the effectiveness of your headlines by setting them in a contrasting type face, type size or type style. For example, if you are using a serif typeface for body copy, consider using a bold or Extra Heavy (i.e. extra thick) sans serif typeface for your headlines. Make your headlines significantly larger than the body copy so they clearly stand out.

Figure 1-2: When documents lack a clearly defined starting point, readers don't know where to start.

Compare those advertisements to the ones shown in Figure 1-4. These examples lack unity of layout, accents, and typography. Although the firm paying the bill is the same in each case, the lack of a consistent approach undermines any possible synergy the ads may have generated. It's almost as if four different firms ran the four advertisements.

Let us find you a new home for your home or business!

Commercial real estate makes a great investment

Suburban office condos

Never been a better time to invest in an office that can serve both downtown and suburban markets. Adjacent to local highways and strip malls, beautifully landscaped. Two, three and seven office units available.

$750,000

Downtown splendor

The view from this six room office is so great you just might not want to go home at night! 24-hour elevator service, plenty of parking plus a bonded security service.

$ 177,000

Get a free office

Invest in this three unit office building and keep one unit for yourself, rent the others. The income will more than pay for your office. Hot and cold running water, completely electrified. New roof and ceiling.

$ 299.000

Donald T will be jealous

This downtown office building will put you and your business on the map for years to come. Prestige address, previous home of numerous venture capital-backed enterprises. If only the walls could talk!

$1,999.500

RCP

603-742-9673
e-mail: rcpcom@aol.com
http://www.rcparker.com

Roger C. Parker's Realty Superstore
Real Estate and Development
PO Box 697 — Dover, NH — 03820

Let us find you a new home for your home or business!

Year-round vacation homes for today's lifestyles

Ski in winter, fish in summer

This home in the Deliverance Valley will provide you and your family with hours of endless entertainment. Friendly neighbors, local stores stock plenty of ammunition and survival gear. Meet today's new type of rugged outdoorsmen!

$149,500

Raft from your back yard!

This cabin is so close to the river that you'll be able to raft from your back porch several months of the year. Additional amenities include talking to campers and hikers walking the many trails that cross your property. Sleeps 4 intimately, 2 privately.

$ 99,000

Rocky mountain high in NJ

This chalet-type residence has everything for the serious rock climbing enthusiast. Close to 50-foot railroad embankment and adjacent to abandoned granite quarry. Great swimming for the kids!

$ 79.000

Outer island dream escape

For the year-round swimming enthusiast seeking solitude. Pending plans to discontinue ferry service means freedom from tourists and relatives. Sleeps five and one-half.

$69.500

RCP

603-742-9673
e-mail: rcpcom@aol.com
http://www.rcparker.com

Let us find you a new home for your home or business!

Handy with tools?

Want a fixer-upper?

Firemen gone, ready for you

This beautiful turn-of-the-century gem had a little bad luck, but you can turn it to good fortune with a little work. 4 bedroom masterpiece ready for your sweat equity, foundation and driveway remain in good shape.

$13,000

Flood's over!

If you can handle a little dampness and mildew, this contemporary might be just the thing for you. Upper floors remain intact, built-in swimming pool.

$ 135,000

Join the landed gentry

This neighborhood is just crying out for gentrification. Located in the busiest police precinct in the city, just minutes from the hospital. Current occupants ready to move at a moment's notice.

$ 19.000

Be a landlord, not a renter

This multi-family dwelling requires just a bit of work (roof, walls, floors and basement) before it can start earning money for you. Investment in your retirement before prices go up!

$59.999

RCP

603-742-9673
e-mail: rcpcom@aol.com
http://www.rcparker.com

Roger C. Parker's Realty Superstore
Real Estate and Development
PO Box 697 — Dover, NH — 03820

Let us find you a new home for your home or business!

Looking to buy or sell a farm?

48-acre retreat

Gentleman farmer's retreat. Pristine river-bottom farmland, drained and fenced, with 36-stall barn and six bedroom home. Garage has space for several Porsches, Jaguars and Land-Rovers.

$139,000

Bring your horses!

200 acre ranch just minutes from 42nd Street. All the amenitities from home, located on busy Metro-North commuter line. Stalls for 48 horses, indoor riding ring.

$ 1,500,000

Great starter farm

Get ready to start earning money raising hay and beef cattle with this 6 acre farm, located just minutes from the nearest source of water. Guaranteed free from flooding. Complete with 2 bedroom home.

$ 199.000

A little bit of Montana in NJ

Start your new farming career with this Delaware-sized acreage just minutes from the George Washington Bridge. Over 200 carefully-manicured acres, cross-fenced, complete with burglar alarm and windmill. Home extra.

$599.00

Roger C. Parker's Realty Superstore
Real Estate and Development
PO Box 697 — Dover, NH — 03820

Figure 1-3: Although each advertises different products, these ads all reinforce the firm's identity in the reader's mind through use of consistent unifying elements.

Design helps set your message apart

Design can create a personality for your business. Just as your clothing and facial expressions reflect your values and your approach to life, design helps you differentiate yourself or firm from the competition.

Design allows you to choose the image that you want to project to your audience. Do you want to appear conservative or contemporary, expensive or inexpensive, high-tech or back-to-nature? You can tap all of these deep emotional reservoirs in your audience by choosing typography, page layout, and colors appropriate to the image you want to project.

People often take image for granted, with much of image being instinctive and based on cultural conditioning. Consider the samples shown in Figures 1-5 and 1-6. Something is wrong about them; what is it? How would the typefaces work if they switched figures — the delicate for the wine, and the slab for the wrecker?

Specially-priced farms and acreage for quick sale

48-ACRE RETREAT
Gentleman farmer's retreat. Pristine river-bottom farmland, drained and fenced, with 36-stall barn and six bedroom home. Garage has space for several Porsches, Jaguars and Land-Rovers.
$139,000

BRING YOUR HORSES!
200 acre ranch just minutes from 42nd Street. All the amenities from home, located on busy Metro-North commuter line. Stalls for 48 horses, indoor riding ring.
$ 1,500,000

GREAT STARTER FARM
Get ready to start earning money raising hay and beef cattle with this 6 acre farm, located just minutes from the nearest source of water. Guaranteed free from flooding. Complete with 2 bedroom home.
$ 199,000

A LITTLE BIT OF MONTANA IN NJ
Start your new farming career with this Delaware-sized acreage just minutes from the George Washington Bridge. Over 200 carefully-manicured acres, cross-fenced, complete with burglar alarm and windmill. Home extra.
$599,00

RCP
Roger C. Parker's Realty Superstore
Real Estate and Development
PO Box 697 — Dover, NH — 03820
603-742-9673
e-mail: rcpcom@aol.com
http://www.rcparker.com

latest listings from
Roger C. Parker's Realty Superstore

Handy with tools?

FIREMEN GONE. READY FOR YOU
This beautiful turn-of-the-century gem had a little bad luck, but you can turn it to good fortune with a little work. 4 bedroom masterpiece ready for your sweat equity, foundation and driveway remain in good shape.
$13,000

FLOOD'S OVER!
If you can handle a little dampness and mildew, this contemporary might be just the thing for you. Upper floors remain intact, built-in swimming pool.
$ 135,000

JOIN THE LANDED GENTRY
This neighborhood is just crying out for gentrification. Located in the busiest police precinct in the city, just minutes from the hospital. Current occupants ready to move at a moment's notice.
$ 19,000

BE A LANDLORD. NOT A RENTER
This multi-family dwelling requires just a bit of work (roof, walls, floors and basement) before it can start earning money for you. Investment in your retirement before prices go up!
$59,999

Real Estate and Development
PO Box 697 — Dover, NH — 03820
603-742-9673
e-mail: rcpcom@aol.com
http://www.rcparker.com

Commercial real estate

SUBURBAN OFFICE CONDOS
Never been a better time to invest in an office that can serve both downtown and suburban markets. Adjacent to local highways and strip malls, beautifully landscaped. Two, three and seven office units available.
$750,000

DOWNTOWN SPLENDOR
The view from this six room office is so great you just might not want to go home at night! 24-hour elevator service, plenty of parking plus a bonded security service.
$ 177,000

GET A FREE OFFICE
Invest in this three unit office building and keep one unit for yourself, rent the others. The income will more than pay for your office. Hot and cold running water, completely electrified. New roof and ceiling.
$ 299,000

DONALD T WILL BE JEALOUS
This downtown office building will put you and your business on the map for years to come. Prestige address, previous home of numerous venture capital-backed enterprises. If only the walls could talk!
$1,999,500

Call 603-742-9673 for information

RCP
ROGER C. PARKER'S REALTY SUPERSTORE

Year-round vacation homes for today's lifestyles

Ski in winter, fish in summer
This home in the Deliverance Valley will provide you and your family with hours of endless entertainment. Friendly neighbors, local stores stock plenty of ammunition and survival gear. Meet today's new type of rugged outdoorsmen!
$149,500

Raft from your back yard!
This cabin is so close to the river that you'll be able to raft from your back porch several months of the year. Additional amenities include talking to campers and hikers walking the many trails that cross your property. Sleeps 4 intimately, 2 privately.
$ 99,000

Rocky mountain high in NJ
This chalet-type residence has everything for the serious rock climbing enthusiast. Close to 50-foot railroad embankment and adjacent to abandoned granite quarry. Great swimming for the kids!
$ 79,000

Outer island dream escape
For the year-round swimming enthusiast seeking solitude. Pending plans to discontinue ferry service means freedom from tourists and relatives. Sleeps five and one-half.
$69,500

RCP

Roger C. Parker's Realty Superstore
Real Estate and Development
PO Box 697 — Dover, NH — 03820
603-742-9673
e-mail: rcpcom@aol.com
http://www.rcparker.com

Figure 1-4: A hodgepodge of styles in these four ads from the same company costs this company a consistent, unified image.

Figure 1-5: You don't expect to see delicate script typefaces for an auto wrecker.

Rocky's

24-hour
auto wrecking,
towing and salvage

You wreck'um, we tow'um
1-800-MISTAEK

Figure 1-6: Heavy square typefaces don't fit the elegance you expect of wine.

Chateau Bellevue

Vintage wines with a light, delicate bouquet. A difference you can taste.

Effective design equals emotion and allows instant recognition. Think about it. Driving down the highway at 75 miles per hour, you can instantly recognize a Mobil station as distinct from a Texaco gas station even if you're a mile away. (And, equally instantly, you can decide which of your credit cards is still valid!) Think of the dollar value of that instant visual recognition.

Design creates familiarity. Most readers prefer the familiar to the unfamiliar. By creating a coherent corporate identity for your association, firm, or your own developing business, you're establishing an image that can provide a powerful competitive edge.

Design speeds production

Design not only earns money, but it also saves time by eliminating the need to reinvent the wheel each time you start a new project. The creation of a visual identity for your firm means you don't have to make typeface, type size, margin, color, and paper decisions every time you start a new project.

Design tools such as styles and templates eliminate the need to start from scratch for each new publication. Not only do styles and templates make it easy to project a consistently unique image, but they also make it easy to produce your message. Here's how:

- **Styles** permit you to apply multiple formatting options with the click of a mouse. With styles, you don't have to apply typeface, type size, type style, letter spacing, line spacing, paragraph spacing, color, and hyphenation decisions each time you change from body copy to subhead, and back again. Instead, you can create a named style, which allows you to reapply the exact same formatting options each time you select subhead or body copy from the Style menu.
- **Templates** are collections of styles and page layouts, which contain *placeholders,* or sample text, for headlines and body copy. Instead of starting with a blank screen, templates contain margins and column layouts that you can complete by importing the specific text and graphics you need for your publication.

Styles and templates not only save time, they also ensure consistency between your publications. The design process often involves replacing production time with up-front time. By creating a family of templates and styles, you not only make your own job easier, but you improve the efficiency of your clients and coworkers as well.

By circulating a style library for correspondence, newsletters, and price lists, for example, you ensure that everyone's correspondence reflects your firm's corporate identity. Plus, you save your coworkers from the trouble of opening the font menu and making typeface, type size, and other decisions every time they begin to write a letter.

Design saves money

Design doesn't cost money — design makes money and it saves money. Design helps you make the most of your printing and distribution budget. It doesn't cost any more money to print and mail a publication that people read than it costs to print and mail a publication that people immediately discard. But a publication that's read can bring in money.

Think about the impact that increased readership can have. Increased readership means you have fewer ads to run and fewer direct-mail pieces to send, which results in less waste and more productivity all around.

Image equals reality. When you present your words with care, those words gain more respect. You can charge more for them. Whether you're an entrepreneur, a consultant, or a writer, people treat your message with more respect when it looks valuable and well thought out.

Design, income, and job security

Today, it's not enough to be just a writer. To succeed in most jobs, you must take responsibility for the appearance, as well as the content, of your message. If you work in a corporate environment or are starting out on your own, this dual responsibility is especially true.

A glance at the help wanted pages of any metropolitan Sunday newspaper illustrates my point. If you take a look, chances are you'll see several ads for marketing or copywriting positions that also specify: "Knowledge of PageMaker and/or PageMill desirable."

In these penny-pinching days, your income and job security increase to the extent that you can effectively wear more than one hat. If you're a writer/designer or marketer/designer, you can command a higher salary and enjoy more job security than a one-dimensional person whose skills can be replaced by outsourcing.

Design and personal satisfaction

Many people go through life without experiencing the joy of creative satisfaction, or the joy of starting with nothing and ending up with something totally unique, totally right. But that joy can be yours.

Few things are as satisfying as conceiving and creating a perfect document, be it an advertisement, brochure, newsletter, or Web page — even preparing a good-looking letter or fax can be rewarding. Desktop publishing provides everything you need to enjoy the creative rewards that an art director at a fancy New York advertising agency enjoys. You can afford to experiment with type, white space, and color, and you can create a logo instead of hiring someone else to do it.

Few of people enjoy the opportunity of being well paid while doing things that please them. Web design and desktop publishing are exceptions to the rule. By enhancing your design skills and becoming a more efficient desktop publisher, you can experience the joys of creativity, effectively spread your corporate message, and be well paid for your efforts.

Chapter 2

The Universal Tools of Design

In This Chapter

- Recognizing the commonalties between print and Web design
- Using mental as well as mechanical design tools
- Appreciating the importance of white space
- Making hardware and software decisions

Whether you design for paper printing or on-screen viewing, you work with the same basic tools. By *tools* I mean not only your hardware and software but also your mental attitudes, goals, and design techniques. Although the emphasis on the various design tools may change as you move between print and Web design, the basics remain the same.

Some of the tools have been around for centuries; other tools are being developed and refined as you read this book. Some tools — like computers, software, and fonts — you have to buy, but the most important tools rely solely on the gray matter between your ears and your design approach. I call these the "artistic tools."

As I mention in this chapter and throughout the book, although some media-specific limitations and tradeoffs exist for both print and Web design, the basic principles work the same for both media. For example, much of the design power that you enjoy when you create paper-based communications, such as printed brochures and newsletters, disappears when you design for the Web. You have other advantages with Web design, however.

The following sections describe the universal tools of design you use with both paper-based and on-screen publications.

Think First!

As I explain in Chapter 1, planning is the most important but often least appreciated design tool. To plan correctly, you must take the time to analyze the six major elements of the communication process.

- **Message:** What is your goal? What type of information do you want to communicate? What is the action you want your readers or Web site visitors to take?
- **Information hierarchy:** What is the single most important idea you're trying to communicate? How many arguments or much information can you provide to support that idea? What are the other points you want to communicate? You must prioritize your ideas and decide which points are more important than others.
- **Audience:** Who are your readers or Web site visitors? What are their characteristics and expectations? How much do they know? How motivated are they?
- **Obstacles:** What obstacles stand in the way of your audience's acceptance of your ideas? What must change before your audience accepts your ideas?
- **Environment:** Where does your audience encounter your message — at home, at work, or on the screen of their computer? What restraints do the environment or communications media place on your message? How can you work around these limitations?
- **Competition:** What other ideas compete for your audience's attention? How can you make your message appear easier to read and more attractive?

To the extent that you take the time to answer these basic questions, the range of solutions to your design challenges will become apparent.

Give Me Space

White space — the absence of text and graphics — is the most important universal design tool and the one most often misused by beginning designers. Whether online or on paper, the space that surrounds important text and graphic elements can attract your reader's eyes like a magnet: too much space and the information can float out of sight; too little, and text relationships are not clear, and the eye tires of making the attempt. White space gives the eye "wiggle room" so it knows where to go and can rest a bit when it gets there. More than any other design element, control over white space determines the success or failure of your communications.

Of course, the space doesn't have to be white. If you're printing your project on purple paper, your white space would be purple — but you get the idea.

Printed space

In print documents, you can control white space in the following locations:

- **Margins:** The white space at the top, bottom, and left and right edges of each page. White space at page margins emphasizes and frames the text and graphics that each page contains. The size of your margins also influences how "friendly" your page appears to the reader.
- **Leading:** The white space between lines of type, often called line spacing in desktop publishing and word processing programs. Leading plays a major role in determining how easy it is to read headlines and text.
- **Paragraph spacing:** The white space between paragraphs. Proper paragraph spacing influences the overall appearance and readability of text columns.
- **Letter spacing:** The white space between letters. Letter spacing plays a major role in the appearance of headlines and body copy and determines how easy it is to read the text. Pages with little space between columns present a darker, or grayer, image than pages with wider column spacing.
- **Gutters:** The white space between columns in multi-column layout. Gutters influence the overall "color" of a page.
- **Surrounding text and visuals:** The white space above and/or around headlines, subheads, pull quotes, and visuals. White space around text and visuals acts as a frame and attracts the reader's eyes.
- **Separations:** The amount of white space separating visuals from captions. Separations help determine your message's overall impression on readers and assure that the caption and its visual are seen as a pair.

I discuss these points in more detail in Chapter 9.

Online space

Although the use of white space to create attractive, easy-to-read messages and to focus your audience's eyes on important elements is equally important in Web design and print design, your options for controlling white space in Web design, at present, are far more limited and less precise.

Here are some of the major areas where you *can* control white space online:

- **Margins:** White space to the left and right of headlines and text reduces line length and creates attractive, easy-to-read Web publications.
- **Surrounding text and visuals:** You can add white space above and/or around headlines, subheads, pull quotes, and visuals to emphasize them. But you can't yet control the amount of white space as precisely as you can in print.
- **Paragraph spacing:** You can insert extra space between paragraphs and above subheads to emphasize them, although with less precise control than in print.

Adding white space to Web documents used to be very difficult. Today, most word-processing and Web-authoring programs let you create Web pages that are based on tables, which you can use to carefully position text and graphics. Both Adobe PageMill and Microsoft FrontPage 98 make it easy to use tables to position text and graphic elements. Figure 2-1 shows a typical table format grid. Figure 2-2 shows the finished product, with each block precisely placed.

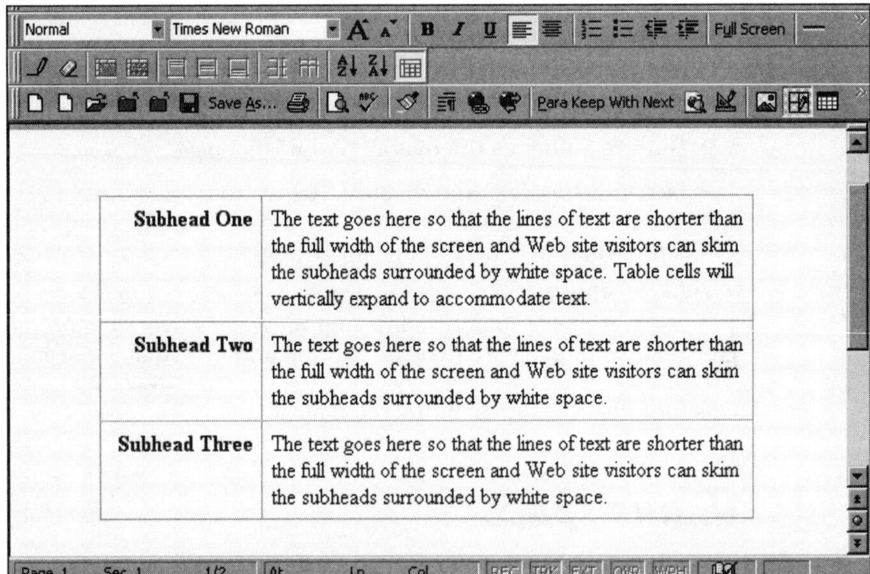

Subhead One	The text goes here so that the lines of text are shorter than the full width of the screen and Web site visitors can skim the subheads surrounded by white space. Table cells will vertically expand to accommodate text.
Subhead Two	The text goes here so that the lines of text are shorter than the full width of the screen and Web site visitors can skim the subheads surrounded by white space.
Subhead Three	The text goes here so that the lines of text are shorter than the full width of the screen and Web site visitors can skim the subheads surrounded by white space.

Figure 2-1: A table format grid.

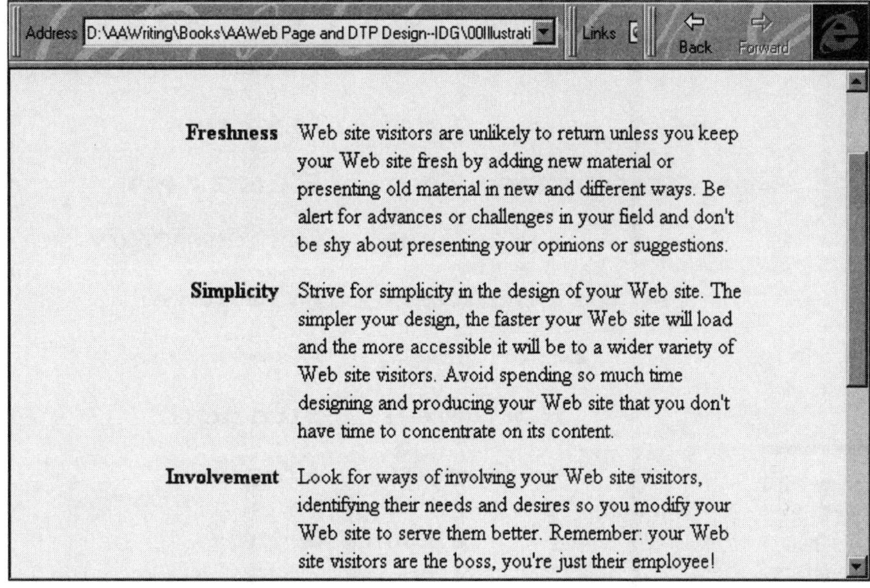

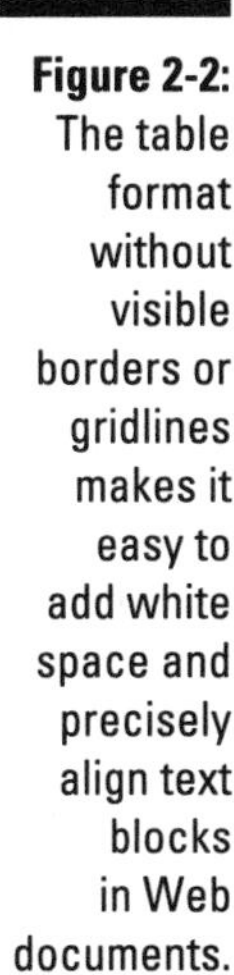
Figure 2-2: The table format without visible borders or gridlines makes it easy to add white space and precisely align text blocks in Web documents.

What Type Are You?

When dealing with print communications, type — the sizes and shapes of the individual letters and symbols used in your message — is one of your most powerful design tools. The ability to choose different typeface designs enables you to visually "voice" your documents with exactly the right tone. I discuss the use of type in more detail in Chapters 9 and 19.

Each typeface visually creates a unique mental image, similar to the nuances of an individual's voice, that your audience will use when they "play back" your message (see Figure 2-3). Some typefaces project an elegant image, some a robust image, and others a trendy image. Successful design comes from choosing the typeface most appropriate for the image you want to project.

Type is available from a number of sources. You can even get basic typefaces (individual designs) for free from the following sources:

- Apple Macintosh and Microsoft Windows operating systems
- Ink-jet and laser printers
- Software programs like Microsoft Publisher 97
- Web sites, like `www.microsoft.com`, which offer typefaces designed specifically for easy online reading

Typeface	Characteristic
Caslon	Classic, academic
Arial	No Frills
COPPERPLATE	ELEGANT
Quay Sans	Contemporary
Arial rounded	Friendly
Brush Script	Handwritten
Rockwell	Strength
Ransom	Trendy
Tetsuo	Grunge
Tekton	Architectural
Sanvito	Informal yet classy

Figure 2-3: Each typeface projects a different image.

Tens of thousands of additional typeface designs are available for sale from digital typeface foundries (who design type for use on computers) such as Adobe, Bitstream, Galapagos Design, Monotype, and from retail firms like Image Club, FontHaus, and Precision Type. Today, most people purchase individual typeface designs from locked CD-ROMs, which are often distributed for free with many software programs or at a very low cost. Type can also be purchased online from firms like the International Typeface Corporation, whose site can be viewed at `www.esselte.com/itc`.

Type is one of the few areas where you see significant differences between print and Web publishing. When you desktop publish a brochure or newsletter for paper printing, you have total control over the typeface, type size, line length, line spacing, and letter spacing. You lose a great deal of this power when you publish on the Web, however.

How your Web site's typeface appears depends on the visitor. In most cases, it is the visitor's computer as well as the default typeface and type size of the visitor's chosen browser software, usually either Microsoft Internet Explorer or Netscape Navigator, that determines the typeface of your message. (You can, however, specify bold and italics style.)

The only way you can be positive that all your Web visitors view the typeface you choose is to set the type as a graphic, which I discuss in Chapter 19. By setting type as a graphic you increase downloading time, however.

Color

Color is a useful tool both online and in print, but color online is a more flexible and powerful design tool.

Color operates on both conscious and subconscious levels. On the conscious level, color provides an easy way to add noticeable emphasis to headlines and visuals. A black-and-white stop sign isn't nearly as effective as a red stop sign. On a subconscious level, color provides emotional clues, which are often based as much on cultural habits as they are on the physiology of the human eye.

- *Warm colors,* like reds and oranges, subconsciously increase excitement and stress levels. *Cool colors,* like greens and blues, are relaxing and reduce stress levels because they affect different parts of the eye. That's why the prominent colors in doctors' waiting rooms are usually blues and greens, whereas fast food restaurants, which want you to "eat and run," often use bright colors, like reds and oranges.
- Colors also carry strong emotional overtones that send a message as powerful as the words you use to communicate your ideas. Red, for example, is universally recognized to indicate "danger" (or "warning"), yellow as a happy color, green for spring, and purple for sophisticated or elegant. Other colors, such as black and gray, imply expensive. Pastels indicate youth: the familiar pink for girl babies and blue for boy babies.

We live in a world of color. Black and white has its moments (as in classic films and art gallery photography), but think how much more fun the Sunday comics are than the same comic strips in black and white during the week! Think of how much you take color for granted on television and in the movies. Color is so important that many classic movies are being colorized to breathe new life into them for television viewing (often to their detriment).

Printed color

As anyone who has ever had dealt with a commercial printer knows, printed color is expensive. Adding a second color to a brochure or newsletter can increase printing costs 50 percent. A third color costs even more. And I'm just talking about *spot colors:* a second or third ink color you use in addition to the basic black of most print publications. Not only do your printing costs go up, but production and set-up costs are likely to increase when you add a second and/or third color to your print publication. (I discuss the specifics of printed color in Chapter 16.)

Four-color *process color* is the most demanding and expensive of all. You have to go to four-color printing if you want to include color photographs in your brochure or newsletter. Four basic inks are mixed in precise amounts on the printing press to re-create the full rainbow spectrum needed to reproduce color photographs. Not only are printing costs higher, but you have to prepare color *separations,* which require four layers, or negatives, for each page.

Color printing also requires that you use a higher quality paper. You can print most black-and-white publications on a wide variety of papers, but color printing needs paper that is specially treated to hold the inks and not allow the color on one side of a page to bleed through so that it shows on the other side of the page. This adds to the expense.

Color on the Web

On the Web, color is free, however. Posting a multicolored Web site doesn't cost a penny more than it does to post the same site in black and white. The only penalty for using color on the Web is that scanned color photographs contain more information than black-and-white photographs and thus take longer to download. And you also have to make sure that you use colors that will look good when viewed on computers running both the Apple Macintosh and Microsoft Windows operating systems.

So color — a tool that is often an expensive luxury in print — is available for free on the Web and can be used with more freedom and greater impact. Because Web color can be so powerful, however, you need to be more careful with your design to avoid creating a colorful chaos. You get more information about the use of color on the Web in Chapter 15.

Visuals: Those Thousand-Word Pictures

Your message improves in print and online to the extent that you can use visuals to replace or supplement text. Human beings used sight long before they invented an alphabet and learned to read; therefore, photographs, drawings, and graphical representations can communicate at a glance. The key to success is choosing the right type of visual at the right time for the right reason. I discuss more about communicating visually in Chapter 14. Here are some guidelines:

- Use illustrations when you want to communicate mood or image. Illustrations are also helpful when you need to show fine details that are difficult to see in a photograph. An illustration of a "hidden system," such as the human body's circulation system, communicates better than a photograph that cannot penetrate the individual's skin.
- Use photograph*s* when you want to communicate specifics, for instance, when you want to show a specific person.
- Use charts and graphs when you want to communicate numerical relationships or trends. Use pie charts to show part-versus-whole relationships, line charts to show trends, and organizational charts to show hierarchy. Use flow charts to communicate sequence or cause-and-effect relationships. See Chapter 15 for more about charts and graphs.

The primary difference visuals make online is that they usually increase downloading time. On the other hand, visuals don't influence costs the way they do in print.

Graphic accents

In print and online, you can enhance the appearance of your message in a variety of ways. Here are some of the graphic tools available to you:

- **Reverses:** Instead of setting black type against a white background, as usual, you can set white type against a black background. By using a reverse you emphasize the text, but often at the expense of readability.
- **Screens:** Instead of setting text against a totally black background, you can set the background in various shades of gray. You can set black type against a light gray background or white type against a dark gray background.
- **Gradients:** Backgrounds don't have to be solid. Gradient backgrounds occur when the background makes a smooth transition between the light and dark shades of a single color or between two different colors.
- **Textured backgrounds:** Textured backgrounds also avoid the homogeneity of a solid background. You can choose nature textures, like stones or wheat, from man-made objects, like fabrics, or from a repeating graphic, such as your firm's logo.
- **Rules and bars:** Rules and bars consist of lines of different thickness. You can use rules and bars to emphasize separation or to draw the reader's eyes to a new topic. Asterisks, bullets, ballot-boxes, ornaments and end-of-text marks are yet another category of graphic accents that, when used consistently, reinforce a publication's image and style.

Simplicity

Remember the old dictum: Less is more. Simplicity involves the conscious elimination of unnecessary text and visual elements. Just as you improve your writing by eliminating unnecessary words, you improve your design skills by eliminating unnecessary visual elements.

Try to get rid of any rules, boxes, backgrounds, shadow boxes, and any other graphic elements that make the page look too busy and distract the eye. For example, you often see vertical rules between text columns that are added out of habit rather than necessity — the gutter width itself should be sufficient to mark the column. Strive to make as few marks on the paper as possible, and have every mark matter.

You also enhance your design skills when you strive for consistency and eliminate unnecessary change. Look at the number of times you change typefaces, sizes, and styles in your design. Are all the changes necessary? See if you can reduce the number of changes, using change only when you have a deliberate need to attract attention or signify specific types of material, as in this book when the typeface changes for sidebars and headings. See Chapter 19 for a more detailed discussion of the use of type.

Contrast

Contrast refers to a significant difference from one area to the next that attracts the reader's attention. Examples include changing from a large type size to a small type size, or changing from black type against a white background to white type against a black (or colored) background — a technique known as a reverse. The use of contrast is equally powerful online and in print. Contrast is both an aesthetic and a functional tool. Aesthetically, change adds beauty and interest to a page. Functionally, you use change to emphasize important text and graphic elements.

Use contrast to add visual interest to your publication or Web page, transforming blandness into excitement and projecting a more professional image.

Contrast can make your document easier to read and more visually inviting. Using contrast works equally well in print and on the Web, but you do have more control over contrast in print design. Contrast techniques can be used individually or in combination with each other. These tools work with both text and visuals.

Here are ten ways you can add contrast to your online and print communications:

- **Shape:** When referring to type, shape usually means the *purposeful change* between serif or sans serif type. Tiny finishing strokes that connect the letters characterize serif, and sans serif type is simpler and lacks these finishing strokes. With illustrations, you can contrast large and small photographs with each other, or you contrast square or rectangular photographs with silhouetted, or outlined, photographs.
- **Size:** Publications become more attractive and easier to read to the extent you employ appropriate size contrast. Size needs to be proportional to importance; the more important a text or visual element is to your message, the larger it must appear.
- **Style:** You can add visual interest and selective emphasis by contrasting regular, or Roman, text with bold, italic, or bold-italic text.
- **Color:** You can set important headlines or short text passages in a different color than you normally use. You can also print important visuals in color.
- **Foreground/background:** You can emphasize important text by placing it against a different colored background, or reversing it.
- **Weight:** You can add impact beyond bold to important text by using a heavier typeface, such as a black or heavy weight of the sans serif typeface you use for headlines.
- **Case:** You can set short text passages in uppercase letters, but use this technique with restraint.
- **Position:** You can emphasize text or a visual element by its position on the page. Photographs that bleed, or extend, to the page edges appear more important than photographs you align with the adjacent text.
- **Graphic accents:** You can add borders and backgrounds to important text or visual elements stand out.
- **Format:** You can add impact to important ideas by reformatting text into charts and graphs, information graphics, tables, illustrated diagrams, or flow charts.

Once you put your artistic design tools to good use to come up with a concept and a plan, you need today's computer hardware and software tools so you can explore your design ideas and see how they work. The better your tools, the faster you are able to work and the easier it is to make the constant changes necessary to get things just right. The following sections describe the types of hardware and software you need to consider.

Computer Hardware: What Do You Need?

Although hardware represents a significant investment, don't let the cost scare you away. The minimum hardware you need to create a newsletter or a Web site is a computer, a monitor, a modem, and a printer (so you can proof your work).

Don't trap yourself into inefficient working habits by using the wrong or outdated hardware. Buy the best you can afford and make sure it's upgradeable. Because of the nature of the computer industry, computing power keeps getting cheaper and cheaper. Today's $1,500 computers are more powerful than last year's $3,000 computers or three-year-old $5,000 computers.

Computer

The minimum computer you want to consider for desktop publishing or Web publishing is either an Apple PowerMac or an Intel-based 486 — or, better, a Pentium computer running Microsoft Windows 95. Either platform is capable of great results. When you choose between them, be guided by which computers your clients, co-workers, and friends are using. Choosing the system your clients and co-workers use will make it easy to share and submit your work and get assistance from friends when needed.

Desktop publishing and graphics software is tremendously processor-intensive. That is, in contrast to number crunching with a spreadsheet or manipulating words with a word processor, you need more computing horsepower when working with a variety of typefaces, type sizes, and graphic images. The added demands mean that you need a fast processor with as much memory as you can comfortably afford.

Plan on upgrading your computer every two or three years because your productivity (make that, earning power) depends on speed, and the productivity you'll gain from the speed advances that occur every few years will more than offset the costs of upgrading. The differences are that great!

Monitor

The monitor is your computer screen; the larger your monitor, the faster and better you are able to work because you have more screen space and so can see more of the screen at a given time without strain. For serious desktop publishing and Web development, a 17-inch (diagonal measure) monitor offers serious advantages over the 14- or 15-inch monitors that come with most new computers — and a 20-inch monitor is even better. If you spend a few hundred extra dollars now on a larger monitor, you will be rewarded with greater productivity over the course of many years:

- You are able to work at actual size, rather than constantly zooming in to work on details and zooming out to get a view of your project as a whole.
- Large monitors provide space for you to leave toolbars and palettes on-screen, so you don't have to constantly open and close them (to see what's behind them).
- Large monitors permit you to work on two-page spreads — seeing both the left- and right-hand pages together — rather than working on just one page at a time.

The better color monitors also offer better color accuracy, necessary for fine-tuning photographs. Some can even be calibrated to exactly reproduce specific ink colors.

Computers become obsolete faster than monitors. You can replace your computer but continue to use the same monitor if you bought wisely in the first place.

Modem

A modem connects your computer to your telephone to enable you to send computer files from your desktop all over the world using telephone lines. You need a modem in order to transfer — or upload — the files containing your Web pages from your computer to the server (or big computer) where visitors can access those files. You can also send your print publication files via modem to service bureaus or imagesetters. Your Internet Service Provider (for more information, see the "Internet Service Provider" section in this chapter) generally provides you with the files you need in order to upload your Web site. Today most computers have built in modems; the minimum modem speed you want to consider is 28.8K. Modem speed is also increasing, however; the faster the modem, the less time you spend waiting for your graphics to upload. You also need a modem, of course, to surf the Web and see what others' — such as your competitors' or your client's competitors' — Web sites look like. The faster the modem, the more research you can do in less time.

Desktop printer

Most desktop publishers use a black-and-white laser printer for creating artwork, which they take to a commercial printer for quantity duplication. Three levels of output quality are available:

- 300 dots per inch
- 600 dots per inch
- 1,200 dots per inch

Laser printers create type and graphic images by placing tiny particles of toner on the paper you're printing on. Resolution, or sharpness, increases as the number of dots per inch increases.

The higher the output resolution, the crisper, more defined the text is. The quality of black-and-white photographs also increases. If you want to create camera-ready artwork on your printer, be sure your printer is at least 600 dpi. If you only want to proof files that you send to a service bureau, you can get by with a low-resolution printer (see the section on service bureaus later in this chapter).

Print hard copies of all your documents because it's difficult to notice mistakes on your computer screen.

Consider purchasing a color printer. Even a low-cost ($200-range) color ink-jet printer can make a major contribution to your productivity, especially if you're creating Web pages. Nothing can replace the added enthusiasm your client will have for your project when you show them what it will look like in color, rather than showing them a black-and-white proof and saying, "This here is red, that's blue, and this is yellow!"

If you are going to be serious about desktop publishing, be wary of choosing a deceptively inexpensive color printer. Although cheaper in the long run, the printer's slow speed and high operating cost may frustrate you. A faster, more expensive color printer may make more sense, especially if there is a chance you might someday need to prepare color overhead transparencies.

Other useful hardware devices

Many desktop and Web publishers invest in a variety of other hardware to increase their design capabilities. I describe the most useful devices in the next two sections.

Storage and backup devices

The bigger and faster your hard disk, the easier and faster your work proceeds. Desktop and Web publishing create significantly larger files than word processing does. The hard disk you've been working with for a long time may well prove inadequate for your desktop and Web publishing needs.

Removable storage media, such as hard disks that you can insert and remove just like big floppy disks, are making life easier for desktop publishers and Web designers. These storage containers operate nearly as fast as the hard disk in your computer, but you can remove them for backup or to archive files that you use infrequently.

Hard disks are prone to failure. Tape backups permit you to restore your working environment — your programs and your settings — as well as store important data. Tape backups copy the contents of your computer's hard disk onto cassettes. If something goes wrong with the hard disk, you can restore everything up to the point of your last backup by "playing back" the tape onto your repaired hard drive.

Removable storage media, like the original SyQuest drives or the popular Iomega Zip Drive, offer another form of protection. These are similar to oversize floppy diskettes, except they contain almost as much storage capacity as your hard disk. These are best used for backing up specific documents and for archiving, or putting into temporary storage, projects you don't currently need.

You should be aware of an important distinction: You cannot work off of a tape backup; that is, you have to copy the material back onto your hard disk. The information on a tape backup has been compressed and is unusable until it is decompressed. But, you can work off of a Zip Drive.

Scanners and digital cameras

A scanner converts photographs, 35mm slides, or photographic negatives to digital files that you can store on your hard disk, allowing you to resize them and manipulate them in a number of ways — such as removing annoying telephone poles or adding Grandma's face next to President Clinton's at the White House. Once a photograph has been scanned, it can be easily inserted into your document or on your Web page. Scanners also permit you to make a digital file of artwork, such as your firm's logo, so you can use it in the background of your Web page.

Rather than scanning conventional photographs, more and more desktop publishers and Web developers are using digital cameras. These eliminate film and store the photographic image directly as an electronic file that you can download immediately to your computer. You save money and time, and you eliminate the need to scan the image.

Software: Putting Words and Pictures Together

The complexity of the documents you want to prepare influences what software you choose to create your pages. Basically, the more graphics you intend to use, the more sophisticated the software you need to acquire. For design purposes, your basic software includes a word processing program, such as Microsoft Word, which can also be used for simple Web page design, a page layout program like Adobe PageMaker or Quark XPress for designing print pieces, drawing programs like Novell CorelDraw to create illustrations, and Web authoring software like Microsoft Font Page or Adobe PageMill for more complex Web page design. For Web design, you also need a Web browser. I discuss each of these briefly in the sections that follow.

Word processing programs

Most current word processors, such as Microsoft Word 97 and Novell WordPerfect, have so much design power that you can use them to create Web pages as well as print materials. Word processing programs are your most basic software and work best, as you would expect, in manipulating text.

For simple designs, word processors can take the place of desktop publishing programs for print pieces or Web authoring programs for Web pages. You can tell if your word processor can easily create Web pages by opening the file menu and seeing if `Save as HTML` shows up. If your Web message or printed report consists primarily of text, you may not need to invest in a dedicated Web authoring or page layout program.

Page layout and Web authoring programs

Page layout and Web authoring programs offer more robust capabilities than word processing programs. Integration of text and visuals is central to their design, not added onto text editing and formatting (choosing the right words and finding the right typeface and type size to display them). Page layout programs give you such capabilities as wrapping text around the shape of a photo, rotating graphics, formatting columns and special text more easily, and other features that make for snazzier, more precise layouts in less time.

Web authoring programs such as PageMill or NetObjects Fusion are page-layout programs for the Web, enabling you to easily blend text and graphics on a Web page, add and subtract hotlinks, and even use sound and animation. The more sophisticated the Web authoring program, the easier it is to maintain your Web site and check it for proper operation. Site management programs such as Adobe SiteMill offer the most power for integrating pages that you create with word processing or page layout programs. These management programs also make it easy to insert links as well as check that the links are operating correctly.

Drawing programs

Adobe Illustrator, Macromedia Freehand, Microsoft WordArt, Novell CorelDRAW, and Corel Xara! are examples of programs that work hand in hand with your word processor or page layout program. You can use drawing programs to create special effects, such as shaded or shadowed text or to create imaginative combinations of text and graphics. There are two types of drawing programs: vector-based and bitmap-based. Vector-based programs such as Adobe Illustrator and Macromedia Freehand tend to offer more precise control of type. Most important, the images they create can be increased or decreased in size without loss of quality. A file containing a logo created with Adobe Illustrator, for example, can be reduced for use on a business card or increased to make a sign for the side of a truck without loss of quality.

Bitmap, or painting, programs often permit more precise control over color. They are often used in conjunction with drawing programs. Their drawback is that you cannot increase or decrease image size after you save the file.

Web browser

A browser is a software program that you use to access Web sites as well as preview your own work as you prepare your own site. You can download the latest versions of many Web browsers for free, but you need to be online using commercial services such as America Online or CompuServe, for example, to download these free Web browsers. Many computers today come loaded with Web browsing software such as Netscape Navigator in Microsoft Internet Explorer or AT&T WorldNet, and many suite programs (word processor, spreadsheet, database, arts, and communications programs packaged together) also include a Web browser.

Image editors: Give Grandma a beard!

Print and Web design doesn't require image-editing programs such as Adobe Photoshop or Corel PHOTO-PAINT because some page-layout programs have image-editing capabilities. (For instance, Publisher 97 has Microsoft Word Art, and Microsoft Image Composer comes with Microsoft Front Page.) However, you make quickly tire of their limitations. Image editing is the ability to significantly change an image by adding or subtracting detail, distorting the image, layering images, and so on. You may want to invest in an image-editing program anyway because they offer far more capacity to create and modify text and graphic images for the Web.

Extra added attractions

Although not strictly software, the following services can help you produce the best print pieces or distribute and manage your Web site most effectively.

Service bureaus and commercial printers

Service bureaus can create better artwork for the printing press than desktop laser printers can. Service bureaus output artwork at a resolution of 2,500 or higher dots per inch, compared with the 1,200 dots that the best office printer is capable of. You need this higher output to obtain the optimum reproduction of photographs as well as crisper, better detailed type.

The drawbacks of working with a service bureau include the time they take to output your job (typically one to three days, although overnight "rush" service is usually available) and the costs and hassles involved. Service bureaus typically charge by both the page and the time required to output each page; pages containing complex graphics take more time to output and, hence, cost more to output. You also face the hassles involved in transmitting files to the service bureau and making sure that they have the same fonts, or typefaces, installed that you do. Often, you have to bring copies of your fonts along with your files. (Service bureaus are honor-bound to erase the fonts after they finish your job.)

Internet Service Provider (ISP)

Few people with their own Web site host it on their own computers hooked up by modem to the Internet. Instead, most rely on Internet Service Providers (ISP), which are independent businesses that have multiple high-speed computers (called servers) and multiple high-speed phone lines. These ISPs rent space on their computers to customers, and most Internet Service Providers can also assist you in posting your completed Web page online.

Internet Service Providers can also maintain, or update, your Web site for you, or help you if you encounter problems updating your Web site. They are also available for assistance on topics like keeping track of the number of "hits," or visitors to your Web site. They can also help you promote your Web site, by registering it with the various Web search services and promoting it on their own site.

The better ISPs can also help you compile lists of visitors to your Web site who register, that is, provide you with their name and address and keep track of survey information, like "How did you locate our Web site?"

Publications and Web sites with class

Check out the following resources to help improve your own eye for design. Each of these can serve as a class in design for anyone interested in developing that art.

Adobe Magazine (www.adobemag.com). The online version of Adobe Magazine is as helpful in both design and software-specific areas is as the print version. You can select articles from back issues by author, subject, or title.

Before and After (www.pagelab.com). This site contains an excellent example of the creative use of color plus information about subscribing to one of the most truly helpful newsletters available.

Design Masters (www.commarts.com) This is the Web site of *Communication Arts,* one of the oldest and most respected design publications.

Print Magazine (www.printmag.com) This outstandingly designed site offers links to the Graphic Design Bookstore as well as numerous articles and excerpts from their yearly regional design issues.

Publish (www.publish.com) *Publish* magazine's Web site balances technical information with portfolios illustrating the latest print and design techniques.

Meaningful Content (www.rcparker.com) Among other content, my personal Web site contains a constantly updated list of the latest design and electronic publishing books and resources.

Ideas and More (www.ideabook.com). Chuck Green wrote *ClipArt Crazy* and the *Desktop Publishing Idea Book.* Where do you think he got his site's title?

Design and Publishing Center (www.graphic-design.com). Fred Showker's site contains both design and technique-specific information plus an on-line newsletter to which you can subscribe.

Idea Exchange (www.warrenideaexchange.com). S. D. Warren is one of the leading paper printers in the world; this site offers an informative look at the various papers available and makes it easy to request samples.

Sametz Blackstone (www.sametz.com) This site from a Boston design firm features numerous sources of Web design inspiration, ranging from the academic and classic to high-tech and latest issues of the day.

Interactive Bureau (www.iab.com) This site contains a portfolio of work by Roger Black's team at The Interactive Bureau. Roger Black is one of the world's most respected designers. If you've been reading Rolling Stone over the past twenty years, you're already familiar with his work.

Newsletter Clearing House (www. newsletter-clearing hse.com)This site contains numerous sample newsletters and allows you to examine the winners of each year's Newsletter Design competition.

Daniel Will-Harris (www.will-harris.com)This site provides an eclectic look at type and design from one of the most popular and entertaining writers of our day.

This list is just a starting point for investigating the numerous Web sites available on the Web devoted to design and publishing Issues. Use your favorite Web search engine (such as Yahoo!, AltaVista, or some other) for more.

Keep on Moving and Grooving

Sound and movement are becoming more and more common on the Web. Although most Web-authoring programs include some pre-done animations — such as spinning globes and letters being slipped into envelopes — it is becoming increasingly easy to add customized sound and movement to your Web site.

You can include video clips of your facilities, for example, or display a time-lapse series of photographs of your company headquarters (for example, a 45-second "sunrise to sunset" view of your office that day). You can also include recorded narration or, in the case of family Web sites, baby's first words. Realtors, for example, frequently include recorded driving instructions to homes listed on their Web sites.

Clearly, the line between television and the Web is closing. Soon, Web sites will be as action-packed as Nick at Nite!

Chapter 3

Web versus Print Publishing: A New War of the Worlds?

In This Chapter

- Looking at the differences between Web publishing and print publishing
- Looking at the similarities of Web publishing and print publishing
- Choosing between print and the Web publishing
- Finding out how the media and format affect the reception and perception of your message
- Weighing the pluses and minuses of various media choices

With the current explosion of interest in the Internet, you may be tempted to focus on the Internet and neglect or eliminate use of traditional media such as print and broadcasting. An effective marketing program must be based on the needs of your audience and your message, which most often requires a combination of new (online) and traditional (on-paper and over-the-airwaves) media. This approach means carefully balancing your time, budget, and staff resources and working hard to plan and implement a communications program that publishes both print and Web materials for your audience.

Web versus Print — Which Is Better?

Contrary to what you may hear, no conflict exists between Web and traditional print media as far as their importance to your business or personal goals are concerned. Both have a place. Putting all your eggs in a Web basket is as inadvisable as spending all your advertising money in the newspaper and omitting customer follow-up or vice versa. You need traditional print media as well as the Web to succeed — now and in the foreseeable future.

Table 3-1 lists some of the major differences between print and Web publishing, which I discuss in the sections that follow.

Table 3-1 Characteristics of Print versus Web Communications

Characteristic	*Print Media*	*Web*
Tangibility	Yes, brochures and newsletters can be saved, shared, and reread.	No, except pages that are printed.
Photographs	Expensive. Each photograph usually increases preparation and printing costs.	Free. No penalty (except downloading time).
Color	Expensive. Color printing greatly increases project cost.	Free. Use as much as you want.
Amount of information	Limited by type size and size and number of pages. Additional pages cost more to print and to mail.	Unlimited. Web sites can be as large as needed without greatly increasing costs.
Flexibility	None. Once it's printed, it can't be changed. Printing additional copies can be expensive if you run out.	Total. Web sites can be updated in minutes without charge.
Distribution costs	High. Costs increase as you print and mail additional copies.	Low, usually just monthly cost of maintaining site at Internet Service Provider (typically $30–$100).
Reader comfort	High. Can be read when and where readers want. Low eye fatigue when correct paper and typeface choices are made.	Low. Reading information on screen can be very fatiguing because of brightness of projected light and relative coarseness of text.

Characteristic	Print Media	Web
Control over appearance	Total. You choose the size, texture, and color of the paper on which your message is printed. You also enjoy total control over the typeface, type size, and line spacing of your document.	Very little (but growing). Visitors to your Web site use screens of different sizes and colorcasts (influenced by room lighting). Visitors can usually control the typeface and type size used to communicate your message.
Control over distribution	Total. Hand or deliver your message only to those whom you want to receive it.	Very little. You can't force people to visit your Web site.

Advantages of traditional media

Not everyone is Internet savvy, and not everybody wants to be. Omitting print media from your marketing program is likely to cut off a significant portion of your audience.

Traditional media refers to ads, brochures, flyers, newsletters, proposals, and support materials (such as applications and instructions) printed on paper. The primary advantages of paper-based media are *familiarity, tangibility,* and *availability.*

- Paper-based marketing succeeds because your customers and prospects are *familiar* with it. They expect it. They know how to use it. Paper-based marketing also gives you the most control over the appearance and delivery of your message.
- *Tangibility* refers to the fact that you can hold a printed document, save it, or carry it around with you. It can go where you go, and it's usually designed to withstand some normal wear and tear.

  If your publication contains meaningful information and is easy to read, the brochure that you handed out last month or the newsletter that you mailed two months ago may still be in your audience's hands. People can reread it at their leisure, referring to important details. They can read and discuss the material at home, at work, at the beach, or in their dentist's waiting room.

- Print materials are almost *universally available:* You have many possible distribution points where your audience can obtain your message, such as direct mail, billboards, and handouts. Anywhere that people go, you can make your print materials available. In contrast, your Web site is available only to those who have access to a computer and who know how to reach your Web site.

Print is also a very focused medium. You can identify your various audiences, such as your best customers and prospects, and you can efficiently target your message to them. There's little waste circulation. You can deliver your brochures only to those who are interested in your product or service and who have visited your place of business. Mail the right message to the right 100 people, and you're likely to sell your product or service to a significant number of them.

Disadvantages of print

No medium is perfect. Print suffers from high preparation and delivery costs — costs that inevitably increase over time. For example:

- Paper costs can rise or fall depending on market forces. A recent shortage of paper that increased costs was followed by increased paper production that lowered them, but costs can climb again.
- Commercial printing is labor-intensive; printers need a lot of time and training to transform your computer files into plates for the printing press, and printers must carefully monitor the presses while printing your job. As labor costs rise, your printing costs rise with them.
- Distribution costs are high; for example, postal rates are a significant expense and are likely to increase.

Getting your message printed also takes more time than showing it on the Web. Imaging and outputting computer files, creating negatives for the printing press, running the presses, applying address labels, and delivering your publication all take time. Experienced newsletter editors routinely work 90 days ahead of the time they want their readers to read their message — and even that schedule is cutting it close.

By way of contrast, the Web site you created this afternoon, or updated this evening, can be updated in minutes!

In addition, print is a "fixed" medium; you do not have unlimited space. A direct correlation exists between the number of words in a printed communication and the number of pages required. When brochure or newsletter space runs short, you must reduce the amount of information you communicate or add pages. And you can't just add a page or two as needed; in most cases, you must add a group of 4, 8, or 16 pages (called a *signature*). Adding pages not only increases your printing costs, it also increases your distribution costs. More pages mean bigger envelopes and higher postal rates.

Make a typographical error in a brochure or newsletter, and you must live with it until you reprint your brochure or until the next issue of the newsletter appears. Compare this situation to the Web, where the material that you decide to correct at midnight is posted and available to readers at 12:01 a.m.

Advantages of the Web

The chief advantages of the World Wide Web are timeliness and interactivity. Unlike print, you can update your Web page almost instantaneously. As information changes or new products and services are added, you can replace the old with the new that same day — maybe even that same minute — with no cost.

And you can include a link that lets your readers or customers send you their thoughts as they access your site. You can use your site for sales and marketing, for surveys and promotions, for customer service — all instantaneously without extra charge.

In addition, the World Wide Web is a highly visual medium that enables you to get the full power of images and color instantly and cheaply. The extra cost of color in print means that the tremendous emotional power of printed color is simply beyond the reach of many firms and organizations. Color is integral to the Web, however, and if you can put up a Web site, you can get the full power of color at no extra charge.

Using photographs is another added expense when producing print documents, especially color photographs. On the Web, however, the only expense is in the time it takes your audience to download the photograph. You can include as many photographs as you like and make them as large as you like (within reason, however, as Chapter 19 points out).

You can add sound and animation to your Web site, and readers can control the flow of information by clicking on links. You can layer your message and vary its treatment depending on the character and depth of the information presented.

Information density, or the amount of information you can deliver in a communication, also differs between print and Web documents. Unlike printed publications, which have limited space, Web space is relatively free. Within reason, you can add as many pages to a Web document as needed because your document only exists as a computer file. Most Internet Service Providers (ISPs) provide 5 or 10 megabytes of space, enough for at least 50 to 100 pages of text and graphics; as long as you're below their maximum size permitted at a given price level, they don't care if you come in with 18 pages or 80 pages.

Disadvantages of Web communications

The primary disadvantage of Web communications is that not everybody has access to them. Not everyone is computer literate — or wants to be. So if you concentrate too much of your communication efforts on the Web, you may miss out on a lot of people who would find your message appealing. Other problems include:

- People who own computers that operate at slower speeds or that have slow modems are likely to become quickly disenchanted with the Web and won't stick around while your message downloads. (Pages that are visually complicated, such as those with large graphic images, can take 2 to 5 minutes or more to download with a 28.8 Kbps modem, even more (as many as 10 to 20 minutes!) if the user is using an older, slower, 14.4 modem.)
- Differences in monitor size can affect the impact and visibility of your Web design. Although professional Web designers typically have 17- or 20-inch monitors to design the Web page, most users view the Web page on a 14- or 15-inch monitor. This means type and graphics may be reproduced much smaller than the designer intended.
- The type of Web browser used can limit monitor *real estate* — the amount of your screen that can be used to convey your message. For example, when visitors access your Web site through some browsers (such as the one included with America Online), they see only a slice of your page instead of the full rectangle.

Lurking in the background is the problem of Web capacity. Although the infrastructure of the Web seems to be holding up well, the chance always exists that the system will become overloaded when everyone tries to access the Web at once, say to proclaim Elvis Day. Sporadic outages do occur, and at certain times of the day — typically, in the early evening — getting online is difficult due to heavy traffic. If you rely solely on the Web to get the word out, you're putting yourself at the mercy of your local ISP or online service.

Another problem concerns on-screen reading. The ugly truth is that, given a choice between reading words printed on paper or words projected on-screen, few people choose the on-screen option (though many will print out your message with the intent of reading it later on good-old-fashioned-paper). Computer screen text is simply not as sharp as printed text. Reading text on a monitor is just not fun, and it's more visually tiring because you're looking at words and images created by light projected at your eyes rather than words and images created by light reflecting off paper. On-screen reading is sort of like looking into the lens of a slide projector.

Navigation — the act of getting from one page to another — is also more difficult on the Web. Instead of simply turning a page, Web readers must read with the mouse in hand to click or scroll their way through a document. This further stresses the already overworked wrists of most computer users.

Finally, no central Yellow Pages directory is available for the Web. Although you can register your Web site with the various Web search services (for example, Yahoo! and AltaVista) that are used to find sites that deal with specific information, you have no guarantee that your target audience will be able to locate your Web site when necessary — or will even know about it without some printed or broadcast communication that includes your site name. That's why your choice of domain address, also known as a URL or Uniform Resource Locator, is crucial to making it easy for prospective readers to locate and remember your Web site (see Chapter 5).

Choosing Print or Web

Both traditional and Web publishing succeed to the extent that they reflect the following characteristics:

- **Hierarchy:** The most important ideas in your document should be immediately obvious, as should the ideas that are merely supportive.
- **Clarity:** Design succeeds on-screen and in print to the extent it is transparent, focusing on the message, not the messenger (such as typeface or color) or the medium (adding useless animations or sound).
- **Chunking:** Communication is enhanced when subheads and other devices are used to break long messages into manageable, bite-sized chunks.
- **Speed:** Readers are in a hurry; communication improves when readers can quickly grasp your ideas and move on.
- **Image:** Both print and Web communications benefit when colors and typography reinforce message content by arousing an appropriate response.

These issues are closely related, as described throughout this book. So how do you know whether to deliver your message in print or on the Web? Before you can make a decision, you must answer the following questions:

- Where in the "decision-making cycle" are prospects going to encounter your message? Whether you're selling or telling, your audience at any given time is at various points of what in sales is called the *purchase cycle* — which involves perception of need, information gathering, comparison shopping, and the final decision to make the purchase or act upon the information.

- What are you "selling," who are your customers, and where are they located? Whether you're trying to get people to buy a car or use their seatbelts, you must think like a salesperson and focus on your main goal.
- How much information do you need to communicate?
- How timely is your information?

The following sections cover these points in more detail.

The "purchase" or decision-making cycle

Your choice between print and online communications should begin with an analysis of where your customer or prospect is in the purchase cycle — a cycle that begins with "I think it would be fun to drive a Jaguar!" and continues to "Should I buy from Jones Motors or Jaguar City?"

For many organizations, the Web serves best as an introduction to your business or service. It enables you to presell your competence, your selection, and your approach to doing business to prospects you've never met. The Web requires very little investment by anyone; you don't have to spend money printing and mailing a brochure to strangers, and strangers don't have to invest in gasoline and automobile wear and tear visiting you, only to find that you're not right for them. At low cost, you can communicate a lot of information, and prospects can check you out, without commitment, from the privacy of their home or office.

As decision-making approaches, however, print communications become more important. Print communications are tangible; people can read, reread, and analyze your arguments and share them with others.

Who and where is your audience?

The number and location of your audience should also play a role in whether you use print or Web communications. Are they in your same city or in another country? Are they likely to have computers and be Internet-savvy? Are they in big cities or small towns?

You should also consider the degree of involvement that you want to have with your customers (which is often a factor of the price of the product or service you're selling) — do you want to call them by their first names? Will you see them again — or ever? If you want to sell many relatively low-priced items to strangers who may or may not buy again from you, for example, using the Web makes a lot of sense because it requires less personal attention.

Print often works better when you're selling a relatively expensive, high-margin, personalized service to a smaller universe of buyers. In that case, sending a newsletter to maintain your visibility with your target market makes sense. Communicating health issues where you want to develop a trust relationship with your audience is an example of public service information that works well in a print format.

Consider two examples at opposite sides of the spectrum: a financial analyst selling investment services to millionaires versus a business informing employees about changes in how to file for health care benefits:

- The financial analyst can benefit from an expensively printed brochure in an impressive envelope or presentation folder because the analyst's goal is to build a close personal relationship with a stranger, which can lead to "big money."
- But an internal Web, or *intranet,* message makes sense for dispensing procedural information to employees about health care claims. The employees are already "sold," and the cost of printing a brochure just increases the cost of doing business.

Amount of information

The amount of information to be communicated is also a factor when deciding whether to use printed material or the Web. Printing and distribution costs for paper-based messages quickly rise as the amount of information increases. Each page costs more money, especially because pages are usually available only in signatures of four.

Yet, on the Web, you can communicate as much information as necessary to "sell" your message without incurring additional printing or distribution costs. This advantage makes the Web a cost-effective media for communicating complicated ideas to broad audiences, without concern for the "waste" circulation of those unlikely to be interested.

Timeliness

The Web is ideal for communicating late-breaking news. Like radio and television, the Web is a "plastic" medium in a constant state of flux. It takes just seconds to revise a file and post updated information on the Web.

This feature contrasts with printed publications, which are set in stone once they've been printed. Print a catalog, and you have to live with those prices until your inventory and prices are so out-of-date that you're *forced* to print a new catalog.

But the Web permits you to communicate in near real time with your audience. For example, the Washington State Department of Transportation has cameras along the interstate highways in Seattle. From anywhere in the country, you can use your computer to visually check out traffic conditions that are only *one-minute old* by clicking on the camera of your choice. This provides far more information than going to a local newsstand and buying a newspaper which couldn't possibly have information about road conditions that haven't occurred yet! (You can check out the current Seattle traffic conditions at `www.wsdot.wa.gov/regions/northwest/NWFLOW/camera/vidframe.htm`.)

Deciding whether to publish on paper or on the Web is not an either/or situation. Both Web and print have their place. Your job is simply to choose the right media at the right time, choosing a media appropriate for your market, the length of your message, and the timeliness of the information.

Table 3-2 provides a quick comparison of the best uses for print and online communications.

Table 3-2 Choosing between Print and Web Publishing

Media	*Pros*	*Cons*
Web	Immediate; low cost; lots of information and color.	Potential difficulty ensuring that prospects will visit your sites.
Print newsletters	Tangible, relatively low cost; hard to overlook; project an "editorial" as opposed to an "advertising" look; two- or three-month shelf-life.	Relatively long lead times for production, printing, and mailing.
Brochures	Long shelf life; good for communicating unchanging information.	Long lead times for production, printing, and mailing; inflexible, hard to build in immediate incentives to act; usually requires quality production to be cost-effective.
Advertisements	Tangible; permits active buyers to comparison-shop your business with others.	Clutter; it's hard to make your ad stand out; even small ads can be expensive; little room to communicate much information.

Media	Pros	Cons
Proposals and reports	Targeted to active buyers at decision making time; can be revised at the last minute.	Size, paper, and color options are limited — stores don't carry nearly the selection of papers that commercial printers carry; slow to print in quantity, especially when using color inkjet printers.
Back-up materials (instructions, applications, and so on)	Reach very important people at relatively low cost (employees and customers who create future business through referrals). Every form and memo communicates an image of the firm, enhancing its credibility or silently communicating a "you don't count" message.	Often viewed as "overhead expense" rather than marketing opportunity; no direct and immediate relation to new business

Media and the Perception of Your Message

A great deal of your success in communicating with various audiences, including customers and prospects, is based on their frame of mind when they encounter your message. Here are a few observations on this topic:

- **Popularity and trendiness:** The Web is quickly becoming a mass medium. Under-$200 boxes that connect the Web to a television set are becoming increasingly popular. If you are marketing to today's "hip" buyers and professionals, you may be perceived as old-fashioned and out of the loop if you do not have a Web presence and are unavailable for previewing when Web-savvy prospects make their "first cut," checking out the Web sites of firms selling the product or service they're interested in.
- **Control and image:** Because the Web gives you less control over the delivery of your message than a print document does, establishing an emotionally charged image based on color, texture, and typography can be challenging.

- The online user can change the colors and may not have the right monitor or fastest modem to see your visuals in all their glory.
- The computer screen itself seems cold and unemotional. People can't read a computer in bed or at the beach — unless they have a laptop, of course, but that's not warm and fuzzy.
- Your message on the screen of a computer has no weight or texture. The same message beautifully printed on a thick, glossy paper, bound between heavy covers with an embossed logo and varnish applied to the photographs, presents a far different image. A finely-printed brochure reflects a tangible commitment that even the most appropriately laid-out and colored Web sites cannot equal.

- **Comfort:** Readers are likely to be more comfortable reading a print communication in their hand than staring at a computer screen. This factor is likely to influence their acceptance of your ideas. Readers are more likely to be accepting when they're comfortable, especially if the communication "feels right" and they can view quality photographs without waiting for them to download.
- **Printed versus printed-out:** Web site visitors can always, of course, print out your documents, but this is rarely satisfying. Backgrounds are typically not printed when you print Web sites. Color and image quality on Web sites are unlikely to be as impressive as a printed page, and strange things can happen — such as type disappearing from one side of the page for no reason. People usually print out home and office Web pages on inexpensive paper, which further degrades the quality of the document compared to a professionally bound publication. Finally, most home and small office color inkjet printers are extremely slow, and supply costs are high.

In short, print communications work best when your market is presold and when quality, image and the ability to direct your message to a few key prospects are more important than timliness and the amount of information you want to communicate.

When the Web works best

For most businesses, the Web works best for preselling customers and prospects. The Web is ideal as a low-cost way of introducing yourself and establishing your competence and professionalism to large audiences that you may not otherwise be able to reach. The Web provides an excellent introductory media because you can communicate in color and employ photographs, as well as sound and movement. Here are examples of business uses for the Web:

- **Architects** can profile staff's qualifications and show photographs of completed buildings.
- **Consultants** can describe previous case studies and offer valuable free information that establishes their credibility.
- **Retail stores** can promote their selection, product guarantees, and service capabilities.
- **Service businesses,** such as advertising agencies and public relations firms, can introduce their key staff and describe their philosophy.
- **Government organizations,** like parks and recreational facilities, can post directions, fees, hours of operation, rules and regulations.

The Web also can help businesses and organizations maintain close links with customers and others by offering a low-cost, basically free way of instantaneously communicating the latest information. Businesses can post their latest inventory and prices on the Web and include enough information so that visitors to the site can judge for themselves the product specifications or your qualifications; they may also see recommendations from past customers if your site has a forum for that information.

The role of e-mail

E-mail should play a major role in your marketing efforts.

Consider e-mail the glue that ties print and the Web together — your Web site should provide you with the names and mailing addresses of prospects who want follow-up print communications (such as brochures, proposals, and detailed information). Your Web site should include frequent e-mail links to you, making it easy for Web site visitors to establish a dialog with you so that you can better identify their needs and consider how you can best satisfy those needs.

Forms, described in Chapter 17, make it easy for Web site visitors to indicate their concerns and describe the products or services they're interested in. By analyzing the forms your Web site generates, you can identify patterns of interest as well as fine-tune your Web site's content.

E-mail helps you identify your prospects and establish close relationships with them — relationships that you can follow up by using traditional print media as you deepen the relationship.

Chapter 4
Image-ination

In This Chapter

- Understanding the elements that determine image
- Choosing the right image
- Creating and organizing text and visual files for use online and in print

The awful truth is, for the most part, you care more about your message than your audience does. Your audience can choose from many messages and pick those that interest them or that appear rewarding in some way. Your audience members are often busy, self-interested (naturally, so are you!), and overwhelmed by the amount of information thrust at them each day. As a result, you have to work doubly hard to get your message read in the shortest amount of time while appealing to your readers' interests and emotions. And that's precisely where design enters the picture — creating and reinforcing the image that goes with your message in order to appeal to the audience whose needs are the best match.

Projecting an Appropriate Image

Everything you do and say projects an image of some sort. The key to successful design is identifying and controlling the image that you project by examining your message, your audience, and your competition. Once you know what image you want to project, you can choose words and graphics to reflect that image in your message.

The power of your message results from content (text and graphics) plus image.

Next time you're at your friendly, neighborhood newsstand, take a look at *The Wall Street Journal* and *USA Today*. The one has a serious, no-nonsense look with small type, gray-looking pages, long articles, few photos, and no color. The other is a riot of color with mostly short, self-contained articles, large headlines, lots of photos and snazzy graphics, and small chunks of information that look like they could be devoured in seconds. Do these publications convey the same image?

Image involves nonverbal communication and operates on an emotional level below the surface of your consciousness. Here are some things that image communicates:

- **Competence (or the lack thereof):** Potential clients, customers, and supporters make assumptions about your ability to satisfy their needs from the image your online and print publications communicate. If your message reflects a crude, amateurish execution, then the assumption is that your products and services are of similar quality.
- **Audience identification:** The image, or look, your documents project allows potential clients and customers to determine the presumed emotional fit, or comfort level, between you and them. If you are selling sneakers to the MTV generation, projecting a monotone, conservative, expensive image is a surefire sales killer. Likewise, trying to market mutual funds by projecting an MTV image won't work either (at least, not until Generation Xers become interested in future security).
- **Competition:** The right image not only tells readers about you, it also differentiates you from others who provide the same products or services. After you decide on the image most appropriate for your organization, your message, and your audience, take care that the image you choose is distinctly different from your competition. After all, you don't want readers to confuse your message with your competitor's message, and you don't want your hard-earned marketing dollars spent promoting your competitors' products and services!

Successful images are so important that many organizations trademark them as a protection from competitors who may try to copy that image in an attempt to appeal to the same audience.

Creating the right image

Both online and in print, several design elements combine to create an image:

- The typeface you use
- The way you place type on the page
- The colors you use
- The visuals you choose and the way you place them on the page

The combination of these elements determines image more than any one specific element by itself. But making generalizations about image is difficult because you can find an exception for just about any statement. In general, however, the following observations are correct more often than incorrect.

- **Typeface:** Each typeface has its own personality, which should be evident when you look at it. Serif typefaces like the one in this book (see Chapter 9 for more about typefaces) usually communicate a quiet, classic, or conservative image. Sans serif typefaces (like the one used for the sidebars in this book) project a more youthful, avant garde, or contemporary look. (*Poor pun alert:* Avant Garde is also the name of a popular sans serif typeface designed to project a "trendy" image. I apologize.)
- **Type size:** Documents (Web pages and print publications) set in a relatively small (for example, 8 point) type size with relatively few size and style changes project a quieter, more upscale image than publications that use several sizes of type with the body type set in a large size (such as 12 point). Justified type (lines of equal length) with centered headlines and subheads generally project a more conservative image than text set informally flush-left (also called ragged-right, referring to text lines of different lengths that align on the left) with unusually varied headline sizes and irregular placement.
- **Letter spacing:** Letter spacing also plays a role in image-setting. Consistent letter spacing communicates a quiet, ordered look. By varying word, line, and letter spacing, you communicate a more creative, youthful, and energetic image.
- **Color:** Colors play a major role in determining the image your online and print communications project. Deep blues and maroons against a gray or ivory background project a rich, elegant impression. Bright colors like yellows, greens, and reds against a bright white background project an exciting, youthful image. Deep greens and browns against a tan background project an outdoorsy image. See Part IV and the special color section for more about color.
- **Placement:** How you position text and graphics on a page is another image component. Symmetrical, evenly balanced designs project a low-key, traditional image. Asymmetrical designs project more energy and movement associated with youth and risk-taking.
- **Visuals:** The style of illustration and the way you treat photographs project an immediate image. Heavily stylized photographs such as extreme close-ups project a youthful image; simple, quiet illustrations project a peaceful, conservative image. Straight lines and right angles project order and solidity; curves are fluid and liberating; acute angles project tension and urgency. And the overall effect of your visuals in combination with the text and with each other can give a variety of powerful, subliminal messages.

In print, the paper, size, and sometimes shape you choose to deliver your message are important factors in creating your image. Brochures and upscale magazines, for example, are usually printed on fine, glossy (or smooth) papers to project elegance and richness. For more about paper, see Chapter 13.

On the Web, the addition of animation, sound, and video as well as the number and quality of the links to other sites and other pages of your own site contribute to the image you want to project. Although I don't cover animation and sound in this book, I give you some things to consider when making the decision in Chapter 17.

Analyzing your image

Look at the following figures. Notice how quickly you pick up the appropriateness or dissonance (or conflict) between message and image in Figure 4-1. Does the headline type reflect quiet, dignity, and privacy? Or does it make you want to party?

Look at Figure 4-2 for an example of image and message coming together.

Long after your audience forgets the specifics, the image you present will live in your customer's or reader's mind.

Figure 4-1: Oh yeah? Somehow I don't believe it. (Headline: "Quiet, dignity, and privacy.")

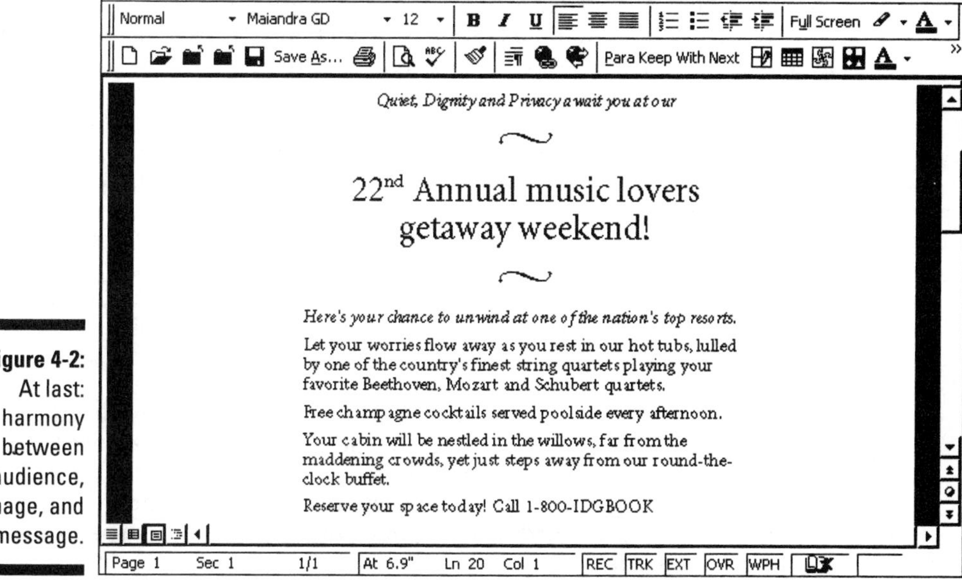

Figure 4-2: At last: harmony between audience, image, and message.

Repurposing Your Message

Repurposing is the reuse of materials meant for one medium in another, as when you reuse the text and graphics that are on your Web site for your print publications, such as brochures and newsletters, or when you create a version of your print publications for use on the Web.

Repurposing is necessary because you can't simply stick the typical print newsletter or brochure up on the Web and expect people to read it — especially if you base your original print publication on a multicolumn format.

Also, repurposing material helps you keep your image and message consistent from one medium to the next, if that's your goal. (Some folks jazz up their image for a Web site in keeping with the often "off the wall" nature of the Internet.)

Paper-design on the Web

When reading a two- or three-column print newsletter, readers don't have much trouble moving from the bottom of one column to the top of the next because the entire page is visible, so readers can easily scan the page and search for subheads of interest.

Moreover, because the entire publication has been delivered at one time, readers can easily turn the page and even continue articles that jump to the next or another page; they can easily return to the first page later.

The Web is different, however. Web visitors don't see an entire page at one time. Instead, they encounter a horizontal slice of the page! In most cases, if you present them with the electronic equivalent of an 8½-x-11-inch page, they can only view an area equal to the top horizontal half of the page, approximately 8½ x 5 inches! So readers have to scroll down to read the bottom half of the first column, then scroll up to continue reading the text at the top of the second column, and then scroll down again to read the bottom half of the column, as shown in Figure 4-3! All this takes its toll on the reader's patience.

In addition, Web delivery of new pages is much slower than the simple process of turning from page to page in a print publication. Because the Web is slower in delivering new pages, readers aren't likely to skim through a publication jumping from page to page and returning to the front cover for a second round. Instead, readers want the information that promises them the most benefit up front.

The Web-document look

To get key information up front fast, Web documents have a different look than print counterparts. Whereas the front cover of a print newsletter is likely to contain one or more articles plus a tiny table of contents, the Home

Address C:\WINDOWS\TEMP\pub-131391.8\index.html
Links
Today's
Back
Creating easy-to-read Web documents
Often, techniques that work in print fail when translated to the Web.
Multi-column documents, containing text that snakes from the bottom of one column to the top of the next are an example of this.
Problems associated with snaking columns
Multi-column documents typically fail on the Web because they require a great
ning the information across the columns before scrolling down to the next screen.
Lack of hyphenation
The Web's lack of hyphenation also works against columns of narrow text. All too often, lines containing a few long words will be deeply indented at the right-hand margin, while lines containing several short words will be significantly longer.
This creates an unsightly rag-or
Placing subheads in web documents
Subheads should appear in two locations on a web page.
The subheads should be summarized at the start of the document, so that, in the first screen, readers can see what subjects are covered in the text that follows.
The subheads should then be repeated within the body copy of the Web page as necessary

Figure 4-3: Multicolumn documents, with text snaking from the bottom of one column to the top of the next, are hard to read on the Web.

Page, or front cover, of a Web document is likely to consist mainly of short teasers that point the way to longer, more detailed treatments of the topic on the following pages, as shown in Figure 4-4.

Links indicated by underlined and/or different colored text make it easy for the reader to find the linked material simply by clicking on the link.

Because of the different way Web documents are seen (as well as technical limitations described in Chapter 17), designing for the Web usually involves going back to your source files and re-importing them into a new publication rather than shoehorning a finished print publication into a Web site. Using a print document to make a Web site is easy if you keep every file associated with a project together in the project's folder on your computer's hard disk.

I need to address two points here:

- I disagree with the concept/belief/rumor that "Web readers won't read long articles." Look at the length of the articles on Microsoft's Salon site or some of the online investment newsletters. Especially when money is concerned, length isn't as important as content! If people are learning how to get rich and enjoy a better life, article length doesn't matter — in print or on the Web. So the idea that the Web requires short articles doesn't hold water with me.

  However, you need to group together subheads as links to bookmarks, or other subheads, within an article so that visitors can glimpse an article's contents at the start, instead of scrolling through it to locate the subheads.

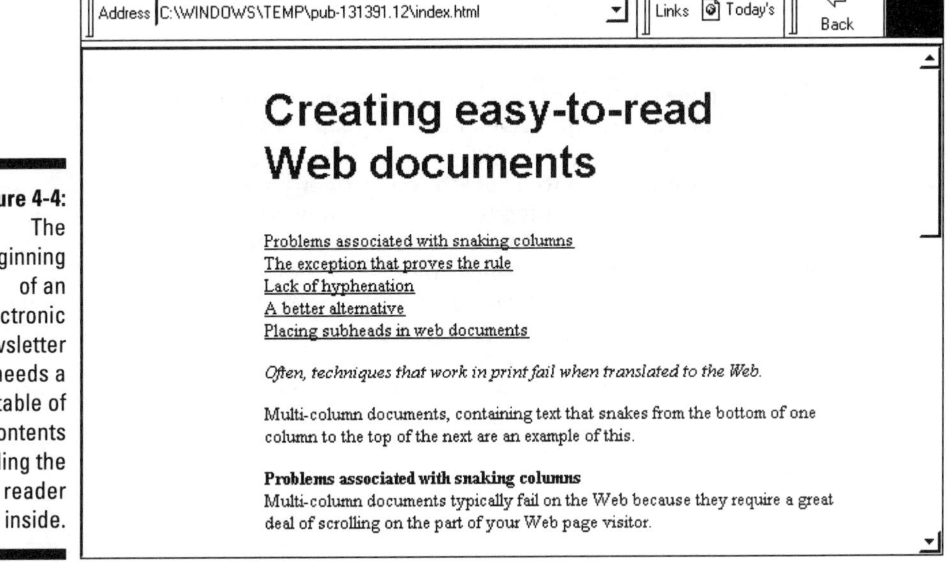

Figure 4-4: The beginning of an electronic newsletter needs a table of contents leading the reader inside.

- It is far easier to import "fresh" text and word-processed files into a Web site than try to copy and paste — or reformat them — from a page layout program into a Web authoring program or to create a differently shaped document and save it as a Web document.

Many people make the mistake of doing too much writing in their page layout or Web authoring program, which makes it difficult to repurpose, or change the media, of their message.

Mastering file management

To efficiently create messages that you can use both online and in print, you must master the essential skill of file management. This often-overlooked file management stage can make it easy to quickly locate and import standard paragraphs (called boilerplate) and visuals that accurately convey the image you want. The typical print or Web document should include files that you create with several software programs:

- Text files that you write with a word processor, such as Corel WordPerfect or Microsoft Word
- Scanned images you create with the software that came with your scanner (I talk more about scanning in Chapter 18)
- Scanned images after you have resized and manipulated them with an image editing program, such as Adobe PhotoShop
- Business graphics you create with programs such as Shapeware's Visio
- Charts and graphs you create with a spreadsheet program, such as Excel
- Logos and department heads you create with illustration programs, such as Adobe Illustrator

For Web pages, you may also have animation files created with a program such as Shockwave and even audio files using SoundBlaster.

If you allow these files to be scattered all over your hard disk, you're likely to have a hard time locating them when you need them. A better alternative is to keep every file associated with a project — no matter which program you use to create it — in a single folder on your hard disk. By keeping project files together, you make it easy to quickly locate and reuse the original files when you create Web versions of print documents and vice versa.

Developing a system of file management that enables you to quickly and easily find the correct files helps immensely when you need to repurpose material. And you *will* need to repurpose material at some point in your design career.

Part II
Web Marketing and Design

The 5th Wave
By Rich Tennant
©RICHTENNANT
Well, there's your Web page, Crypto. Designed like you asked. But personally, I think it has too many spinning spirals and blinking lights. It makes...hard reading. Make...tired... look...at... lose...all... con...cen...tra...tion...
Perfect!
CRYPTO THE HYPNOTIST

In this part . . .

Seemingly everyone's on the Web these days. This part helps you take your place on the Web with marketing savvy and design tips that deliver your message quickly and clearly. What can the Web do for you? What do you want to do with the Web? These chapters give you more than a few good ideas for weaving a little Web magic at your site.

Chapter 5

Web Site Realities

In This Chapter

- What can the Web do for you?
- How does the Web operate?
- What steps are involved in creating a Web page?
- Do you need to be a programmer to create a Web page?
- How do you select software programs?
- What are the strengths and limits of Web marketing?

Although you can spend a lifetime mastering the ins-and-outs of the World Wide Web, all you really need to know is that the Web is a worldwide network of computers that you, your friends, your customers, your prospects, and your employees can access by using personal computers at home or at work that are connected through telephone lines by devices called modems.

In many ways, the Web has been oversold on its ability to develop nationwide, or global, markets and to attract large audiences (as a proportion of the population). This overselling has caused a lot of confusion because, in many cases, businesses don't have products or services that lend themselves to international sales and, therefore, don't use the Web to its true advantage or see themselves reaping far fewer benefits because of unrealistic expectations.

In this chapter, I present just enough information to help you decide whether setting up and maintaining a Web site is something that you want to do. If you want more information about the Web and its older brother, the Internet, check out *The Internet For Dummies* and *Creating Web Pages For Dummies,* both published by IDG Books Worldwide, Inc.

Establishing "Web-Spectations"

Establishing realistic expectations for your Web site is important. The Web will not make you an overnight international success. What the Web will do, however, is offer a way of communicating a great deal of information to past, present, and future customers and colleagues at a remarkably low cost.

Although some products and services do lend themselves to actual sales over the Web, for most businesses, the Web offers an ideal medium for

- **Preselling new customers:** The Web enables you to *presell* yourself to new customers and prospects before you meet them. A good Web site establishes your credibility and professionalism as you tell your story and explain the products, services, and benefits you offer customers that make you stand out from the competition.
- **Establishing customer relations:** Good customer relations pays off in repeat sales and word-of-mouth referrals to friends. Research has repeatedly shown that reaching a new customer costs six times as much as reselling to a previous customer. You can easily build close relationships with past customers by using the Web to alert them to new products and services, conduct user surveys, provide news and information about your business or industry — you're limited only by your imagination.
- **Maintaining visibility:** Using the Web, especially in conjunction with e-mail, you can offer past and present customers special sales and promotions as well as information that they can't obtain elsewhere, which further develops customer relationships and keeps your business in their thoughts.
- **Eliciting customer response:** The Web's e-mail function also lets your Web visitors easily communicate with YOU, expressing satisfaction or dissatisfaction with your products or services and even suggesting new lines of endeavor.

Although you may believe that many fortunes are being made by people in Montana selling products to Europe and the Far East, don't let this idea blind you to the success you can enjoy by putting the Web to work for you on a basis more realistic for your situation. Following are some of the reasons why Web marketing can be so powerful:

- **Economy:** You gain freedom from the production, printing, and distribution costs incurred by print media.
- **Immediacy:** After you create or modify your Web site, you can immediately post or update it — no matter what time of day or night it is — without delays. Within minutes of introducing a new service or a

special price promotion, your message can be read by your customers and prospects. (Assuming, of course, that Web itself has not been struck by any of the many ills that computers can be heir to.)

- **High-impact:** Marketing on the Web succeeds because you can use color, one of the most powerful communications tools available. Printed color can be expensive and time-consuming, especially if you want to show four-color photographs of your products or your staff. Because of high preproduction and printing costs, color was once available only to large advertisers printing tens of thousands of brochures or catalogs. But now, on the Web, color is available to all at no cost.
- **Information depth:** The amount of information you can communicate in a brochure or newsletter is limited by size considerations as well as printing and mailing costs. In general, the more information you include, the more pages you need to print and mail. On your Web site, unless your Internet Service Provider charges by the number of pages or the size of your files, you can (without adding costs) include as much information as you need in order to tell your story and motivate your prospects to act.
- **Environmentally friendly:** Information posted on the Web doesn't require trees to be cut or landfills to be filled with out-of-date brochures and newsletters. In comparison, most print marketing is wasteful in that, often, your brochures and newsletters are discarded soon after distribution.

Case study in Web marketing

The model railroading field offers an excellent example of the advantages of Web marketing.

Several retailers around the country sell custom-painted brass locomotives. These trains are imported in very limited quantities and can cost several hundred dollars.

Traditional print advertising techniques do not serve the model railroad market very well because of high costs and the long delays involved in preparing, printing, and mailing catalogs. By the time the catalogs arrive, the inventory list is outdated, and many models have already been sold.

The Web offers a practical, low-cost way to advertise these limited-availability products to model railroaders around the corner and around the world. Retailers can place their inventory on the Web and easily keep their inventory list updated. When visitors see a particular model available at the right price, they can order it, knowing that it is likely to be in stock. (See Chapter 17 for an even more sophisticated approach to marketing limited-quantity products.)

Although most products and services are not as exclusive in terms of limited availability, the example shows how the low costs and immediacy of the Web offer significant advantages over traditional print media, which can never keep up-to-date.

Although the Web can become one of your most potent marketing tools, it shouldn't become your only marketing tool. Following are some of the reasons why:

- **Accessibility:** Although interest in the Web has reached such proportions that it is adversely affecting television viewership, everyone is still not connected. Not all of your prospects are likely to own the computer, modem, and software necessary to access your Web site. (Offsetting this is the growing number of homes able to access the Web by using the latest consumer electronics toy — under-$200 appliances that eliminate the need for a computer by displaying your Web site on a television.)
- **Privacy:** Your competitors may check out your Web site, which is a lot easier than getting added to your mailing list. This allows them to monitor your advertising and promotion. (Of course, you're doing the same thing to them — just don't give away the store.)
- **Tangibility:** Print publications have a long life. Brochures and newsletters stick around until no longer needed. They can be filed and reread at leisure, as well as shared with others. Your Web site is visible only as long as the visitor is logged on. (Offsetting this is the fact that visitors can print out relevant pages of your Web site, transferring the printing costs from you to them.)
- **Portability:** Because visitors to your Web site need a computer, they won't be able to read your message in bed, the bathtub, or while driving, unless they print a copy of your message for themselves.
- **Control:** Although you can completely control the appearance of print publications by specifying the typeface, type size, line spacing, letter spacing, and colors used to communicate your message, Web-based messages are likely to appear significantly different to each visitor depending on the Web browser and the monitor they are using. Users can also choose the typeface and type size used to display a message.

All things considered, however, the advantages of the Web far outweigh the disadvantages. The Web offers you a unique way to communicate a lot of information to past, present, and future customers without spending a lot of money. Already one out of ten small businesses has a Web presence, and this number is expected to triple by 1998.

Weaving Your Way onto the Web

A *Web site* is a collection of files located on a server. Each page of your Web site occupies a different file. Visitors to your Web site *navigate,* or move, from place to place within your Web site by clicking on links. *Links* can be either highlighted text or graphic images.

Few Web sites are maintained in-house by the people who create them. Instead, most Web marketers rent hard disk space time on computers maintained at ISPs, or Internet Service Providers. These firms have the multiple, high-capacity computers and numerous telephone lines and modems needed to provide simultaneous connection to the files that make up your Web site.

Most Web sites are identified by their domain name, or *URL* — which stands for Uniform Resource Locator. The advantage of obtaining your own URL is that your Web site address will be shorter and appear more professional than if you can only be located through another name. More importantly, after you obtain your URL, it will remain the same, regardless of whether you change Internet Service Providers or move across the country. A search is required to see if a desired Web site address has already been taken. A typical address is `http://www.rcparker.com`.

The alternative to obtaining a domain name is to place your Web site on a national network, such as The Microsoft Network or America Online or a local network such as Buzz.net. If you place your files on a network, the network name becomes part of your address, for example, `http://www.buzzybee.net/~rcparker/` (a made up example — don't waste your time trying it). You can see that the latter address is more cumbersome and implies that you don't want to make enough of a commitment to Web marketing to invest in obtaining your own permanent address.

Visitors access your Web site by using their modems; browser software, which acts as an interpreter, to convert the data contained in your Web site into text and images that are displayed on the visitors' computer monitors; and online networks and Internet Service Providers (ISPs). Browser software is not expensive; it is often distributed for free by networks such as America Online, CompuServe, and The Microsoft Network. Or, visitors can choose a local Internet Service Provider and download browser software, such as the Microsoft Internet Explorer or Netscape Navigator.

Choosing Web Publishing Software

The good news is that Web publishing doesn't require expensive, specialized software. In fact, you can create Web pages by using even the most rudimentary text editing software, such as the Windows 95 Notepad. This isn't to say that you'll want to use a text editor, but it's nice to know that you don't have to spend several hundred dollars to create a Web page.

The bad news, of course, is that — as always — you get what you pay for, and definite advantages come with dedicated Web-authoring software programs. So, although you may get started by using your existing software, at some point you're likely to want to step up to a software program like Microsoft FrontPage 97 or Adobe SiteMill.

HTML (or not)

The Web is based on files created according to HTML codes. *HTML* stands for HyperText Markup Language. Coding is the act of formatting text into headlines, subheads, body copy, and lists. Coding is done by inserting formatting codes, or symbols, into the text before and after the text you want to format.* Backgrounds and graphic images are imported when you insert codes that point to the graphic file that you want to include.

You no longer have to know HTML programming to create an effective Web site. You do, however, have to identify your audience, your message, and your goals, and you have to commit to keeping your Web site up-to-date.

All of the above is done in a non-WYSIWYG environment. WYSIWYG refers to a What-You-See-Is-What-You-Get environment. If you specify 24-point Bold Italic Times New Roman font for your text, you see the text in 24-point Bold Italic Times New Roman font on the screen of your computer. If you insert a graphic image containing a picture of a flower to your Web page, you see the flower displayed on your computer's monitor.

Code Shy versus Code Savvy

Although knowledge of HTML may someday be invaluable to you, to create a great-looking Web site without knowing anything about HTML is entirely possible. This is because many, if not most, of today's software programs are Code Shy.

Code Shy means that the HTML is hidden in the background. You do your

*If you're an old-timer from WordStar days, you probably remember placing a "b" before and after words that you wanted to appear in bold, and so on.

thing in the foreground, choose a background, format text, add graphics, and create links between pages (and other Web sites) working in a WYSIWYG environment. When you're through, the software creates the HTML coding for you based on the layout you have created. Examples of Code Shy programs include Microsoft Word 97 and Microsoft Publisher 97. These programs isolate you from the HTML code.

Code Savvy programs, on the other hand, provide you with access to the actual HTML codes. These programs offer you more flexibility in terms of your ability to add advanced special effects to your Web site.

Code Shy programs hide the HTML codes in the background, enabling you to concentrate on the appearance of your Web page. Code Savvy programs give you access to the HTML code that formats your pages, providing you with more creative power.

Word processing programs

Today's word processing programs like Microsoft Word 97 offer a lot of Web publishing power. Not only do you work in a WYSIWYG environment, but a number of features have been added specifically for Web publishing applications. For example, Microsoft Word 97 includes Format⇨Background and Insert⇨Hyperlink commands that greatly simplify the creation of your Web site by making it easy to create backgrounds and links. Programs like Word 97 also include several ready-to-finish Web templates that give you a head-start on creating your Web site.

The primary disadvantages of working with word processing programs are that

- You must save your work and launch your browser to preview what the finished page will look like.
- Precisely positioning text and graphics on the page is more difficult with word processors. For example, unlike Publisher 97 (which is a Web authoring program), Word 97 doesn't allow you to work with a multi-column grid that helps you maintain consistent spacing and line lengths. (Offsetting this is the powerful table editor of Word which can perform many of the functions of a background grid — I discuss these issues further in Chapter 9.)
- The most serious failing is that word processors typically do not include built-in, fail-safe checkers that enable you to make sure that your links work and that every page is linked to your home page.

Word processors are ideal for creating text-heavy *intranets* — Web sites designed to be used internally by employees and vendors. Instead of printing an employee benefits brochure (which is likely to go out of date the minute its delivered), health and vacation benefits can be posted on a Web site accessible only to employees.

Entry-level Web layout packages

Web layout packages range from the simple to the extremely complex. Most people new to Web design want a package that's simple to use and easy to understand. Entry-level Web layout packages include Adobe PageMill, Claris Home Page and Microsoft Publisher 97. Programs such as Adobe PageMill and Claris Home Page are limited to creating Web sites, while you can use others — such as Microsoft Publisher 97 — to create printed ads, brochures, and newsletters, as well.

The primary advantage of these entry-level programs is their ease of use. They were designed to simplify Web page creation. Often, they include detailed step-by-step online assistance to guide you through the creation of your Web site. Table 5-1 compares the most popular entry level packages.

Table 5-1 Web Layout Packages to Get You Started

Product Category	*Examples*	*Advantages*	*Disadvantages*
Text editors	Windows NotePad	Free Code Savvy: You can do anything (if you have the patience)	Requires knowledge of HTML code and a lot of patience No spell checker Pages must be saved before previewing by using Web browser
Word processing programs	Microsoft Word 97, Corel WordPerfect, Lotus WordPower	You can see what you're doing as you do it No additional acquisition or training expense Includes templates and Web commands to add backgrounds and Hyperlinks	No way of checking completed Web site links Limited ability to edit graphic images Pages must be saved before previewing by using Web browser

Product Category	Examples	Advantages	Disadvantages
Code Shy Web programs	Microsoft Publisher 97, Adobe PageMill, Claris Home Page	Easy to use WYSIWYG environment, includes templates and (often) step-by-step guidance Often, built-in link checker. (Publisher 97 Design Checker watches out for overlapping graphics and graphic that will take too long to download.)	Often, no way to access HTML code in order to insert ALT attribute (description of graphic images which load before the images load) Limited ability to check links Can only be used to create Web pages
Code Savvy Web site management programs	Microsoft FrontPage 97, Adobe SiteMill	Designed to manage Web links as well as format good-looking Web pages Perfect for controlling large sites with multiple pages Access to HTML for fine-tuning Web pages Acquisition and training expense	Limited to creating Web documents
Professional page layout programs	Adobe PageMaker 6.5, Quark XPress	Multi-purpose; can be used to produce sophisticated print communications as well as Web communications Numerous typographic formatting options, sophisticated ability to manipulate graphic images	Limited ability to check links Larger up-front acquisition and training costs

Web site management packages

Web management packages like Adobe SiteMill and Microsoft FrontPage 97 pay as much attention to creating and maintaining links as they do to formatting Web pages (see Figure 5-1). These programs often offer a visual display of your Web site, permitting you to visually add (modify and delete) links by using your mouse and dragging and dropping. Microsoft FrontPage 97 even includes a to-do list that helps you track the various steps involved in creating a Web site and monitor your progress.

Page layout programs

Dedicated, high-end page layout programs such as Adobe PageMaker 6.5 and QuarkXPress enable you to easily format your documents and add links between pages. Their strength is their ability to control the nuances of typographic design and produce four-color separations. Designed for producing professional publications, newspapers, and magazines, these programs enable you to control letter spacing to the .001 decimal place. Dedicated page layout programs also enable you to edit images and produce four-color process separations (see Chapter 18).

In many cases, however, dedicated page layout programs offer more control than is needed by average users (such as entrepreneurs and managers who don't produce four-color magazines or annual reports printed on glossy paper).

On the other hand, investing time in acquiring and mastering sophisticated programs gives you a head start on the future, providing room to grow as your communications become more complex and Web technology incorporates the ability to transmit improved typography and layout. As always, a few hours spent in planning your future businesses needs and your career path should precede the purchase of any software.

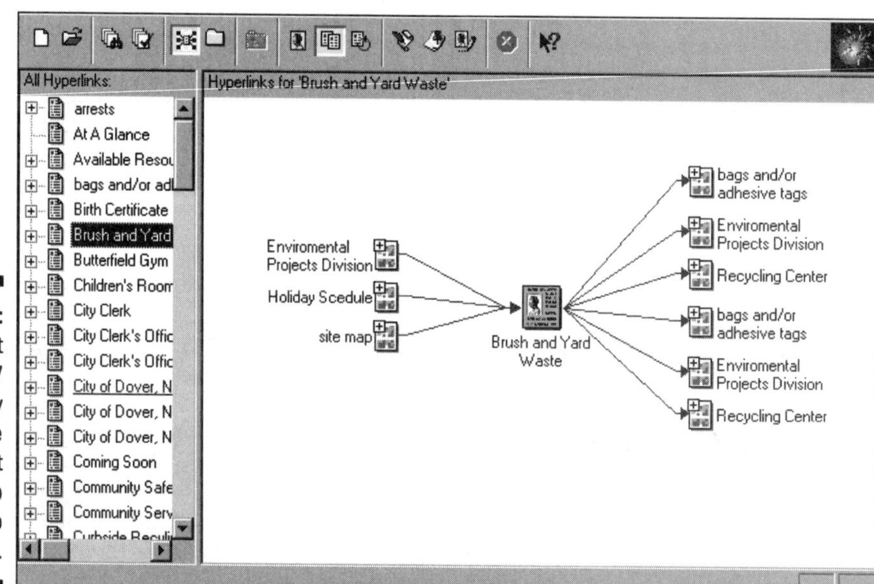

Figure 5-1: Microsoft FrontPage 97 visually displays the links that make up your Web site.

Start now: upgrade later

Rather than delay establishing a Web presence until you can master the most advanced software, consider using either your current word processor, assuming it has Web capabilities as does WordPerfect 8 or Word 97, or one of the simple programs like Claris Home Page or Microsoft Publisher 97 to get started.

Then, after you get your feet wet and are thrilled to see your Web page up and running — and you begin enjoying results — migrate upward.

Pages created with Microsoft Publisher 97 and Word 97 can be incorporated into Web sites managed by Microsoft FrontPage 97, just as Web sites created by using Adobe PageMill can be incorporated into sites managed by Adobe SiteMill.

Improvement can only take place after that first step has been taken!

Art programs

Many of today's word processing programs and page layout programs contain art programs, such as WordArt or MacPaint, that enable you to place words into graphic images, creating special text effects by stretching, compressing, or squeezing words into irregular shapes or by setting type into circles.

By setting text in an art program and creating graphic files that are downloaded as your Web site displays, you can enjoy almost absolute control over the typeface, type size, and letter spacing your visitors will see on their computer screen. (The downside, of course, is that downloading time can be significantly increased.)

Programs such as Adobe Illustrator, Adobe PhotoShop, Fractal Design Painter, CorelDRAW!, Painter, and Corel Xara! offer you even more creative control. You can add a variety of creative effects, such as blurs, embossing, and shadows. These programs also enable you to easily combine text with scanned images. You may also want to use business graphics programs like Visio from Shapewear. Visio enables you to easily create diagrams like flow charts that display sequences.

Other programs

Today, just about every new software program can be used to create Web documents. You can create Web sites with presentation programs like Microsoft PowerPoint 97, and Freelance Graphics. You can even use spreadsheet programs such as Microsoft Excel 97 and database programs such as Access 97 to post spreadsheets and databases on the Web. However, these applications are generally only used in special circumstances, such as when you want to include your entire product line so that anyone can access it by name of product or product category.

MacroMedia FreeHand is especially popular with Web designers because it can compress files as they are saved and has cross-platform compatibility; that is, its files can easily be exchanged between computers using the Apple Macintosh and Microsoft Windows operating systems.

Successful Web marketing is software-independent. Your ability to plan and craft your message and choose an appropriate image is more important than the software program you use to create your Web site. Just as you can create nonproductive Web sites with expensive programs, you can create high-performance Web sites by using the simplest tools available if you're willing to put forth the effort into planning, creating, testing, maintaining, following-up, and promoting.

Six Steps to a Winning Web Site

Setting up a winning Web site involves six basic steps. Your Web site and marketing efforts can succeed only to the extent that you commit to all six steps. Although today's Web authoring programs make Internet sites easy to create physically, any successful Web site requires a marketing strategy, as described in the next section, involving more than mastering your software. This strategy includes:

- Planning
- Creating
- Testing
- Maintaining
- Following-up
- Promoting

All six steps must be completed in order for your Web marketing efforts to succeed.

Planning your site

Planning involves turning off your computer and spending some time answering a series of questions that focus on specific planning issues. These issues and questions include:

- **Market:** Who is your target audience? Whom do you want as visitors to your Web site? What are their needs? What are their concerns and questions? What are their expectations?

  The starting point for answering these questions often involves identifying *prototype customers* — those who you believe are the easiest and most profitable to serve — and thinking about your sales interactions with them and the questions these customers bring up. You may even prepare a survey and send it to a handful of customers, seeking their opinions.

- **Goals:** What action do you want visitors to your Web site to take? Do you want them to contact you for further information, place an order, lobby a Congresswoman, or visit your place of business? This involves determining where visitors to your Web site are likely to be in the decision-making or purchase cycle.

- **Proof:** What evidence can you provide to presell your competence and ability to satisfy audience needs? Can you point to case studies, articles you have written, testimonials from previous customers, or other third-party evidence of your excellence? Are you comfortable establishing yourself as an expert by discussing the issues and trends of the day and how they affect your present and future customers and clients?

- **Immediacy:** What can you do to keep your Web site fresh and up-to-date to encourage repeat visits? What kinds of information are you likely to be aware of that your site visitors may also want to know? What features can be cycled in-and-out of your Web site that visitors will miss if they don't frequently return?

- **Competition:** What is your competition doing? Check out their Web sites. Can you identify their goals and target market? Are they the same as yours? What about you and your product or service sets you apart?

  TIP: When you create your Web site, make sure that you emphasize the ways you differ from your competitors and the unique benefits customers enjoy when they buy from you.

Use the Planning Worksheet in Table 5-2 as an aid in planning your Web site.

Table 5-2 Roger C. Parker's Web Site Planning Worksheet

Target Market	***Characteristics of People You Want Visiting Your Web Site***
Who are they?	
How old are they?	
What sort of image are they likely to be attracted to?	
Where in the purchase cycle are they?	
How much do they know about your product or service?	
What kinds of information do they desire?	
Goals	***What you want to happen***
What action do you want Web site visitors to take?	
Competition	***Differentiating Yourself from Your Competitors***
Who are your competitors?	
What sets you apart from them?	
What do their Web sites look like?	
Proof	***Preselling Prospects on Your Competence***
What evidence can you provide to back up your arguments?	
Immediacy	***Ways to Generate Excitement***
What can you do to keep your Web site fresh?	
Do you offer new products or services — or can you discuss new ways to take advantage of existing products and services?	
What types of time-sensitive information, such as upcoming conferences and conventions, is your market likely to want to know about?	

Immediacy	*Ways to generate excitement*
What can you do to keep your Web site fresh?	
How can you encourage the Web Site visitor to immediately respond?	

Creating your site

Your Web site can be as simple or as complex as you want. To create a Web site, you must assemble the text and graphic files that fulfill the goals identified in your Web Site Planning Worksheet. Keep these files together in one location on your hard drive, using folders and subfolders. If this stuff about your hard drive confuses you, take a look at Chapter 6.

To create a Web site, begin by choosing an image, or *look,* as discussed in Chapter 4. You have several options:

- Most software programs include a number of ready-to-finish *templates,* predesigned (by the software maker) combinations of foreground and background colors and boilerplate text and graphics that you replace with the words and images appropriate to your Web marketing goals.

  Microsoft Publisher 97 goes further than most programs by including Wizards, which ask you questions and format the template based on your response to the questions (see Figure 5-2). On the Mac, programs like ClarisWorks offer Assistants that serve the same purpose.
- Many independent graphic designers sell templates, and some templates are available for downloading from the Web.
- You can also work on your own from scratch, choosing a background, layout, and colors appropriate for the image you want to project. Web authoring programs like NetObjects Fusion and Microsoft FrontPage, give you great flexibility in creating your own designs.

Regardless of the Web authoring software you choose and whether you work with a template or from scratch, creating a Web site involves importing text and graphic files created with your word processor, page layout, and graphics programs such as Adobe Illustrator or image-editing programs such as PhotoShop into the Web-authoring software to create the site.

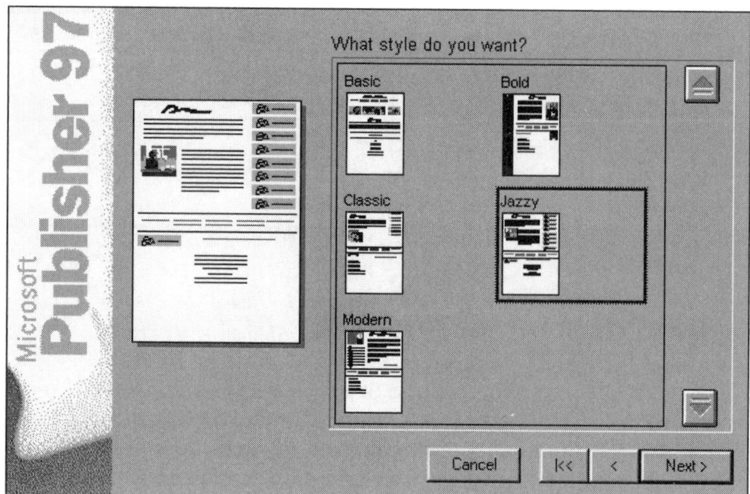

Figure 5-2: The Microsoft Publisher 97 Wizards pick a template and organize your Web site based on your answers to a series of questions.

You assemble your Web site on your personal computer. After you create the files and test the links to make sure that everything works properly, upload your Web site to the network or Internet Service Provider using software that either comes with your program or is given to you by your service provider.

Testing the links

Testing is an essential part of creating a Web site. When you link the various pages of your Web site together, you have to make sure that every page is linked and that all of the links work properly. In addition, you have to make double sure that links to other Web site addresses have been entered properly. One omitted letter or transposed letter-pair is enough to cause a great deal of frustration among Web site visitors. Instead of making a positive impression, you do more harm to your image than good.

Testing is one of the most important stages in creating a Web site. Don't neglect it. You want to make sure that visitors will be taken to the appropriate page of your Web site when they click on a link. Frustrate your audience, and you'll soon have none.

Maintaining immediacy

Although consistency is a hallmark of a good Web site, don't interpret that advice as meaning your site should always stay the same. To be successful, your Web site must never remain static. Good Web sites are in a constant state of change.

Give visitors to your Web site a reason to frequently return. Frequently add new material and replace old material, archiving materials that are still useful — such as back issues of a magazine. Place archived material at a different location (a different page) on your Web site and include a link to it.

Frequently maintaining your Web site adds the element of immediacy. You can keep your Web site up-to-date by

- Describing new products and services that you're offering or new ways to take advantage of existing products and services
- Listing upcoming events, such as conferences and conventions of interest to your market
- Addressing the challenges and issues that affect your field and your market; if well done, these *editorials* can position you as a credible expert or, at the least, a responsible individual trying to meet current industry challenges

Everybody loves a bargain. So another way to build immediacy into your Web site is to offer something for free or offer limited-time savings on selected products and services. Procrastination is the enemy of successful marketing. If you don't give prospects a reason to act now, they're not likely to act later. Special limited-time savings available only to Web site visitors can turn prospects into customers.

Most software allows you to upload just one page of your Web site at a time. This greatly reduces the amount of time necessary to keep your Web site fresh and up-to-date. It also reduces the amount of time that customers and prospects cannot reach your Web site.

Following up

Following up with your site visitors lets you take full advantage of the contacts your Web site creates. It involves getting back to your site visitor by e-mail, telephone, conventional mail, or in-person.

If you ask Web visitors to register by using their e-mail addresses, you can easily send them e-mail that informs them of upcoming sales and promotions. You can also maintain their enthusiasm if you e-mail them whenever you update your Web site. Always be sure to send requested information or answer questions as quickly as possible.

Promoting your site

The final step involves promoting your Web site — letting your audience know where the site is and what it can do. You need to include your Web site address in all of your business communications. Have it appear on your business card and letterhead as well as your ads, brochures, and newsletters. (Notice how many TV ads now include a Web site address!)

After you create your Web site, inform the companies that run the various Web search engines of your Web site's presence. By notifying search firms, such as Yahoo! and Digital AltaVista, of your Web site address and the type of content it includes, your Web address will appear on the suggested list of sites when newcomers search for sites on the Web by name or by topic.

Finally, look for synergistic marketing opportunities that enable your Web site to be linked to others. For example:

- If you're a retailer, most Web sites maintained by the manufacturers whose products you sell list the Web addresses of stores selling their products. Link to their sites.
- You can also look for co-marketing opportunities with Web sites that attract the same types of buyers. For example, if your market involves selling ski equipment, link your site to the Web sites maintained by ski slopes in your area as well as manufacturers of ski equipment.

After you have established a Web presence, don't hide your Web address under an umbrella! Publish it in the phone book, on your business cards, your stationery, brochures, and newspaper ads — anywhere your name appears, your Web address should be there also.

Chapter 6

The Architecture of Web Design

In This Chapter

- Defining the elements of Web page architecture
- Determining what you can and can't control
- Enabling visitors to navigate from page to page
- Differentiating between graphic text and live text

The starting point for effective Web page design is identifying the materials and tools that you have to work with. The materials include the various elements that, together, present your message to your audience. The tools include the techniques you can use to control the appearance and placement of the elements.

Getting Your Blocks in Order

Web sites, regardless of their size or sophistication, are based on the same building blocks, or content elements. All Web sites contain the following six elements of page architecture:

- Background
- Words (text)
- Visuals
- Links and navigation tools
- Logos
- Feedback and response vehicles

The following sections look at each element in turn and analyze ways of optimizing these elements. This is an artificial breakdown, of course, because in reality the design of each element affects the others, and you want to design your Web site so that it eventually becomes a totality.

Background

Background refers to the layer behind your words and visuals. You can choose solid, textured, or patterned backgrounds. If you have a digital file of your firm's logo, or access to an image scanner, you can use your firm's logo as a background (providing your logo is relatively simple and won't interfere with the foreground text).

The most frequently encountered problems with most Web backgrounds is that they are usually:

- **Too bright** and overwhelm the message
- **Too dark** so you can't see the message (and feel gloom-and-doom at the same time)
- **Too uniform** so nothing stands out
- **Too busy** so everything fights everything else for attention

Here are some background issues to look out for:

- **Default gray:** Always specify a background color rather than accepting the default gray background most web browsers provide, unless an alternative is presented. Gray backgrounds typically create a very dull, somber appearance (see Figure 6-1). Gray backgrounds also make black text (the standard default color for text) hard to read by reducing the foreground/background contrast necessary for easy recognition of the letters making up each word. The Web is too graphically competitive to attract today's visitors while using yesterday's acceptable standards.
- **Bright and dark colors:** Avoid choosing overly bright or overly dark background colors, which limit your choice of typeface colors. Bright background colors, although initially dramatic or exciting, are very stressful and hard to read for long periods of time. Dark colors can also be dramatic, but are more likely to be somber and depressing. Although bright and dark backgrounds can sometimes be appropriate, they usually make comfortable reading of more than a few paragraphs difficult. For this reason, they should be reserved for accenting areas with relatively small blocks of large or very bold text, which can more easily be read against the vibrant backgrounds (see Figure 6-2). Remember that white is a color and that a white background can visually blast the reader's eyes. The best backgrounds tend to be light shades of white or yellow, which don't interfere with reading because they don't shine too brightly in the reader's face.
- **Uniform backgrounds:** In most cases, you want to use some left-to-right variation in the background of your Web site. Boredom results when absolutely no variation from left to right emerges in the background of your Web site. Figure 6-3 demonstrates one technique that works well — running a light or dark panel down the left edge of the screen (as described later in this chapter in the section "Think horizontally").

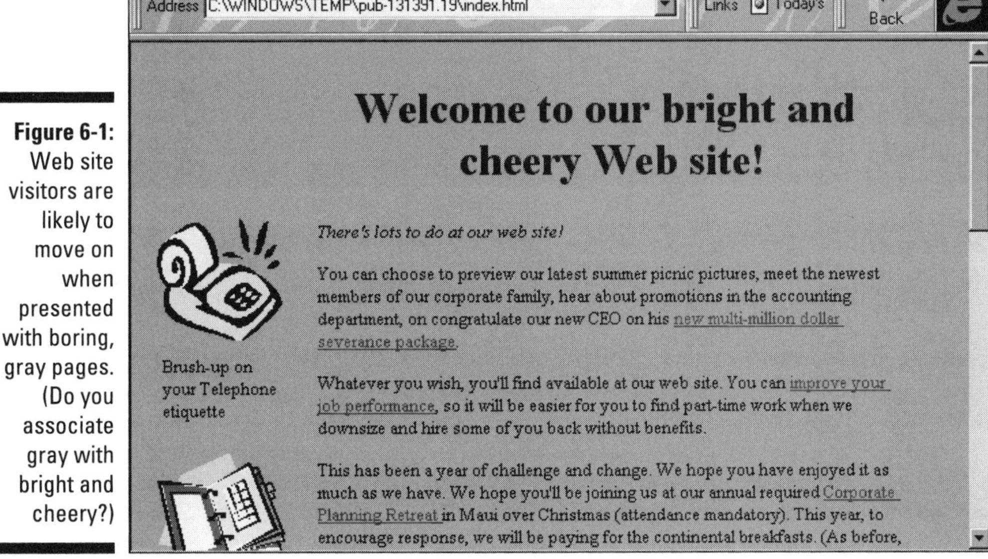

Figure 6-1: Web site visitors are likely to move on when presented with boring, gray pages. (Do you associate gray with bright and cheery?)

Figure 6-2: Limit bright or dark backgrounds to pages that contain just a few words in a large size, as in this Web banner.

Figure 6-3: Instead of a uniform background, try using a vertical panel arranged along one edge to organize the page.

- **Busy backgrounds:** Avoid backgrounds with large illustrations and strong colors. These backgrounds inevitably interfere with easy reading by cutting the foreground/background contrast and by obscuring the text that runs over them (see Figure 6-4). Most of the backgrounds that ship with Web creation software are far too bright and noticeable to be used safely.

  If you otherwise like a template, you can always change the background and resave it as a template under a different filename. You can create your own backgrounds using programs like Adobe Photoshop.

- **Textured backgrounds:** As with backgrounds that contain prominent illustrations, use the textured backgrounds that come with many software programs with care — or not at all. Usually, the textures are so strong that they either compete with the text or blend into it, interfering with easy recognition of letter and word shapes (see Figure 6-5).

Clearly, the best advice for backgrounds is to remember that they are just that — backgrounds. A background that overwhelms the message or makes it tiresome or painful to absorb conveys its own message about your competence and consideration. Keep your backgrounds both subtle and distinctive — but most of all, keep them back.

Words (text)

Words are the essential building blocks of Web sites; *successful* Web sites are characterized by words that are *easy to read* and understand. Understandability is the writer's and editor's task. Making words easy to read is the designer's. Making words easy to read is a function of line length, variations in typeface, type size, type style, and — when appropriate — alignment and text color.

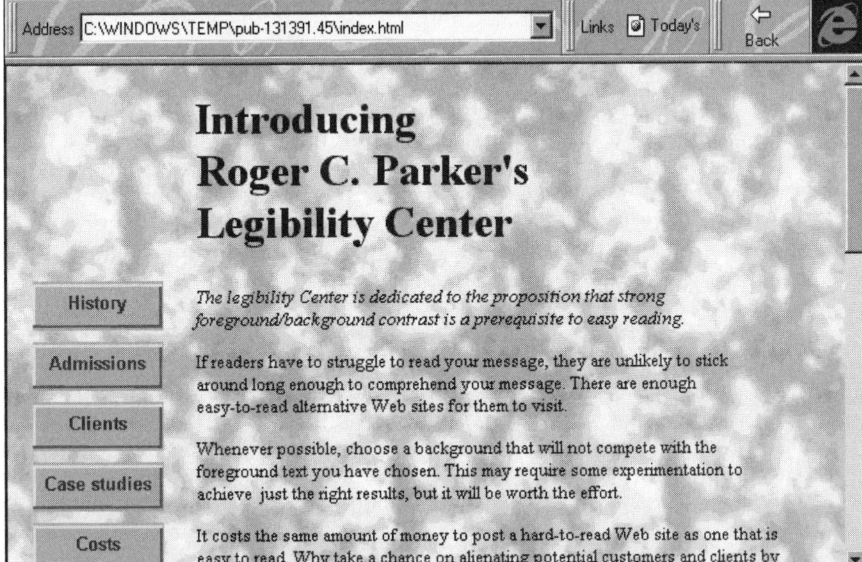

Figure 6-4: A busy background usually makes it a struggle to read the foreground text. Can you read this text easily?

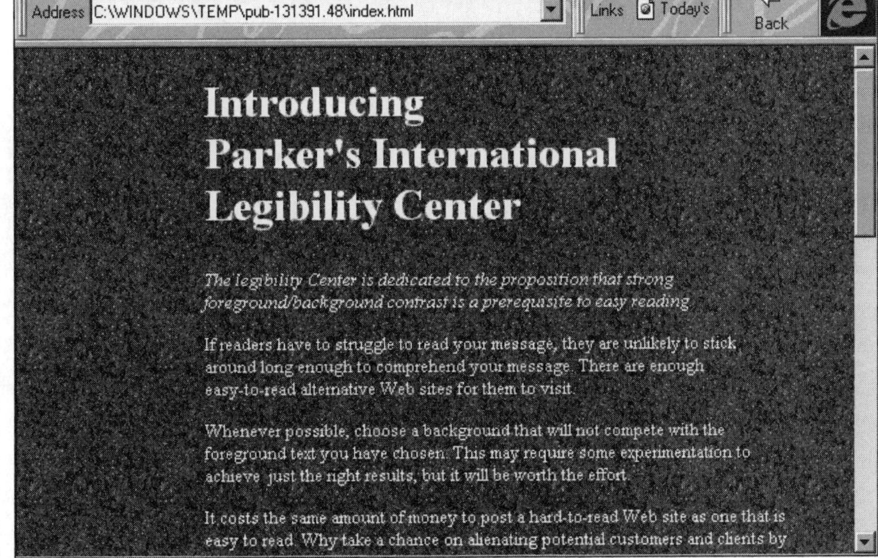

Figure 6-5: Textured backgrounds can interfere with text legibility, as this Web page shows.

Avoid centered headlines

One trap to avoid is the use of large, centered type for headlines. Just because type is easily centered doesn't mean it *should* be! Centered text divides the white space on either side, rather than allowing the space to dramatically concentrate to the left or right of the text, where the white space gains impact and does a better job of forcing the reader's eyes to the adjacent headline. Compare the examples shown in Figures 6-6 and 6-7.

Creating the HTML code necessary to create headlines such as those in Figure 6-7 used to be extremely difficult (see Chapter 5 for more about HTML). But today, both the improvement of the standards that define how text is coded plus a new generation of Web authoring software that can interpret your Web page layouts have made such coding relatively easy to do. And, given the way of computer software, such coding is likely to become even easier in the future.

Avoid ALL-UPPER-CASE heads

Just as you want to use centered text with care — if at all — avoid words or phrases set exclusively in uppercase (all capital letters) type. Words set exclusively in uppercase type occupy significantly more space than the same words set in a combination of uppercase and lowercase text. (You're going to see this more than once if you read through this book!)

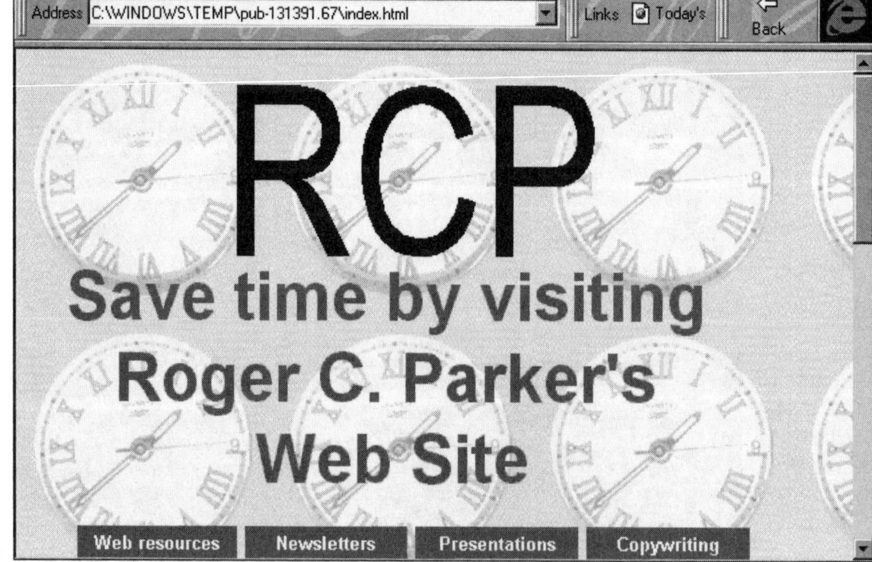

Figure 6-6: Just a few words set too large occupy almost the entire screen, leaving little space for visual contrast or elaboration.

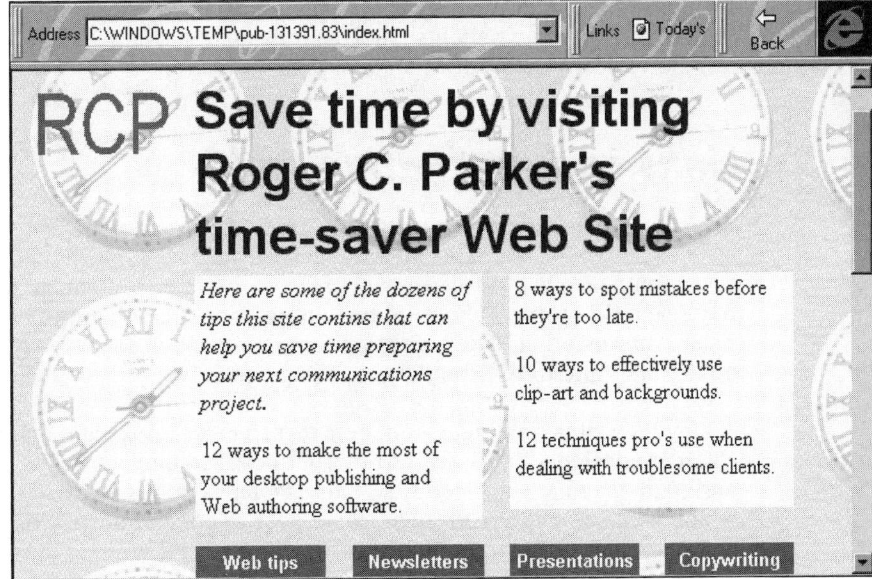

Figure 6-6: Using a smaller type size, set flush-left presents a more effective alternative.

Visuals

Few Web sites consist entirely of words. Most contain visuals — photographs, illustrations, charts, and tables. In fact, the real difference between the Internet and the World Wide Web is the Web's ability to easily process graphics, and many Web sites have taken good advantage of this capability.

Visuals are different than text in that they are separate graphic files, which are downloaded as needed. Because visuals are downloaded independently of the text, you want to use them with discretion because of the time involved in downloading them. The larger and more complex the visual, or the more colors it contains, the longer it takes to download.

As Web site designers become more sophisticated, they tend to use smaller, faster-loading visuals . . . and to make sure that visuals are used only when they communicate information better or faster than text.

When you add visuals to your Web site, or evaluate your present Web site, ask yourself the following questions:

- Is this visual really needed? Does it provide information or create an image that can't be accomplished by using text?
- Is this visual as small as it can be in order to effectively communicate the information?

A large, slow-loading logo, for example, is a characteristic design error made by newcomers to Web site design.

Remember that your logo, by itself, only satisfies your ego and doesn't offer Web site visitors any benefits, such as information or advice. Making it large only slows down the performance of your Web site.

Links and navigation tools

Web sites are designed for jumping around. Visitors to your Web site are likely to not visit each page, at least on their first visit. More than likely, they'll jump directly to the topic of greatest interest to them, and — when they reach that topic — jump to the subhead or subdivision of the topic they're interested in. Therefore, visitors to your Web site have to be able to move from topic to topic and page to page quickly.

Making Web sites nonlinear — in contrast to most books and magazines, which are designed to be read from front cover to back cover — is important. (You may have noticed that *...For Dummies* books are also designed to be nonlinear. You can read them from cover to cover, but they're designed to let you look up just what you need when you need it with no muss or fuss.)

Links — highlighted bits of text or graphics that people can click to get to new pages or areas of your site — are the key to directing users through your Web site to find the information that interests them. Links can be either simple or elaborate. On the better Web sites, links become a part of the overall design. On Web sites characterized by less sophisticated design, the links can detract from the site's overall design and image. Often, you see links that are larger than needed to be effective. When links are too large, they become distractions rather than signposts.

Another frequent mistake is to center the links on a page, instead of tucking them away along the right, left, or top edges of the screen. ***Remember:*** You want visitors to pay attention to the content of your Web site, not the links that direct visitors to the content.

Links can consist of text, icons, or buttons. Links also can consist of graphics that, when clicked, take the Web site visitor to another location. Most software programs come with a variety of buttons and *clip art* (simple drawings you can use in your programs without violating copyright laws).

Because buttons and icons take time to download, a good idea is to always include a text link next to them (see Figure 6-8). That way, Web site visitors can link to a new page by reading the link's description, which immediately downloads, rather than waiting for the graphics to download.

Remember that visited links change colors after the text has been clicked. This means that the basic Web page consists of three text colors — even if you don't change any of your software's defaults:

- Default text
- Text links to different parts of the page, different pages, different Web site addresses, or e-mail links
- Visited text links

As a rule, use the fewest possible words when you create text links within paragraphs. Don't highlight an entire phrase, simply highlight the most important words. And avoid introducing text links with "Click here." Today, most Web users understand that colored text indicates a text link.

Adding "Click here" before text links is the equivalent of printing "Go on to the next page" at the bottom of each page in a book! Don't do it.

Logos

Logos usually consist of a unique text treatment or an illustration accompanying your firm's name. Your logo, in combination with the colors of the text and background, can go a long way towards creating a unique visual identity for your Web site.

Examples of logos that you may know include the golden arches and unique typeface of McDonald's restaurants, the CBS eye, and the NBC peacock in its various permutations. Store your logo as a downloadable graphic file giving you total control over your logo's appearance and placement on the page. And remember to keep it small to save downloading time.

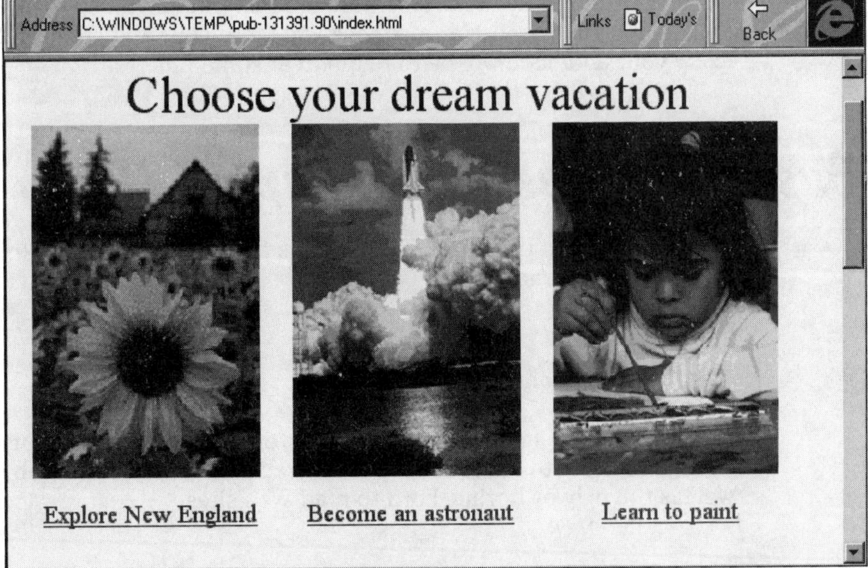

Figure 6-8: Always include a fast-loading text link next to an icon or button used as a link.

Feedback and response

The Internet is an interactive medium. Whereas few who receive your brochure or newsletter are likely to correspond with you, one of the major purposes of the Web is to establish communications with Web site visitors.

Most Web site authoring programs make creating e-mail links back to you easy. In some programs, you simply highlight the text you want to use as a link to the Web site visitor's e-mail program. Other, advanced programs contain electronic forms for Web site visitors to use when registering, or identifying themselves to you. This interaction is a powerful tool for customer relations as well as product and message modification in response to stated and measured audience needs.

Any program capable of creating a Web page allows you to add an e-mail link to your business. All you have to do is say `Click here to contact me`, highlight the text, and create a hypertext link to your e-mail address.

Programs such as FrontPage 97, however, allow you to create *forms,* which are structured pages that contain check boxes, radio buttons, and pull-down menus, as well as space for adding open-ended comments.

Look at it this way: An e-mail link simply makes it possible for the visitor to send a message to an e-mail address without needing to type in the e-mail address. A form, however, asks a series of questions and is transmitted as a file.

In addition to providing e-mail links back to you, always include your phone, fax, and postal address so that readers can contact you via more conventional means, if they wish. The more contact points you present, the more convincing your desire for feedback will be to your audience, and the more likely your audience will be to respond at some time.

Basic Web Design Principles

Two simple ideas provide the framework for creating good-looking, easy-to-read, fast-downloading Web pages:

- Think small
- Think horizontally

Keep these ideas in mind as you create your own Web site and use them as you surf the net to analyze both the attractive, easy-to-read Web sites as well as the ugly or boring, hard-to-read Web sites.

Think small

Many Web designers create their Web sites as if the site consists of a number of vertical $8^1/_2$-x-11-inch pages. This is vertical thinking, treating your Web page like a print page, and often results in text that is too long and graphics that are too large. The problem with vertical thinking is that it encourages scrolling, which is counter to the goal of discouraging scrolling whenever possible. (I discuss horizontal thinking in the next section.)

You want visitors to your Web site to be able to experience as much as possible in a single glance, without scrolling. You want them absorb your image, be presented with information, and have opportunities to visit other pages without having to reach for the mouse and drag the vertical elevator box down. Why? Because the quicker visitors can get your point, the more likely they are to stick with your site. If they have to continually scroll down to figure out what you're doing, they may surf to another site instead.

Large graphics are especially vexing when they do not contain valuable information. All too often, visitors wait several minutes for a large image to download, only to be greeted by the firm's logo, which is only of interest to the firm, not the Web site visitor! Then the visitor must click on something and maybe wait for another download before any meaty images are presented.

This problem can be cured by thinking small and reducing the size of your logo or other graphic files. This method creates space that can be used to bring up important selling information that otherwise would only be revealed if the Web site visitor scrolled down to the lower part of the page (which many visitors may not do).

Avoid overusing large graphic files because of their slower downloading speed. Strive to strike a balance between appearance and speed. Remember that you may be creating your Web site on a far faster computer than the one your Web site visitors may be using. You're always safest preparing your Web site for the worst possible scenario (such as a 486 computer connected to a 14.4 Kbps modem).

Many software programs, such as Microsoft Publisher 97, contain a Design Checker that goes through your Web site and identifies graphics that may take too long to download.

Think horizontally

The key to Web success is to break up the horizontal rectangle on your Web site into discrete left-to-right zones. These zones can be empty, in the sense that they're there simply to provide breathing room to highlight the text on the page, or you can use the zones to group the navigation elements or miscellaneous text and visual elements, such as subheads, pull-quotes, or photographs.

Until recently, controlling the horizontal placement of text and visuals on a page was painfully difficult. Various, clunky workarounds had to be devised that represented knowledge available only to full-time graphic designers or computer programmers willing to finesse their pages into shape. Today's Web authoring software makes controlling the horizontal placement of text and graphics far easier. You can simply place elements where you want them and, automatically in the background, the design software creates the code that replicates your desired placement on the Web site visitor's screen.

Programs such as Microsoft Publisher 97 and Adobe PageMaker 6.5 enable you to create column grids that encourage you to think horizontally and define the horizontal placement of columns of text (see Figure 6-9). I talk more about grids in Chapter 8.

Using the table format is another way to easily implement horizontal thinking and organize text and visual elements on the page (see Chapter 19 for more about tables). Remember, tables don't need to contain lines between the cells when the Web site is viewed: These row-and-column dividers only serve as guides while creating your Web site, not while displaying it.

A table can provide a background for good-looking pages created with word processors, such as Microsoft Word 97. Notice how the page in Figure 6-10 is based on a one-row table containing three cells of different widths.

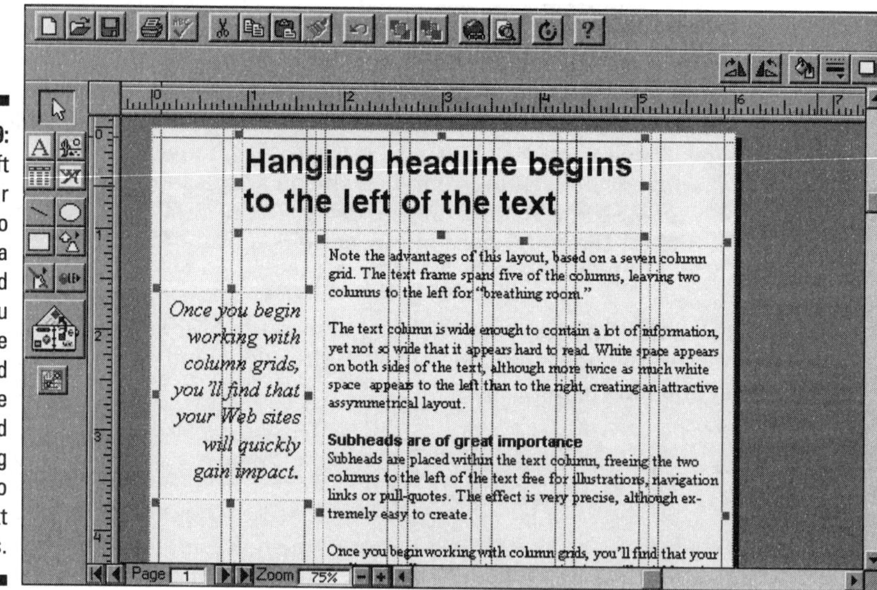

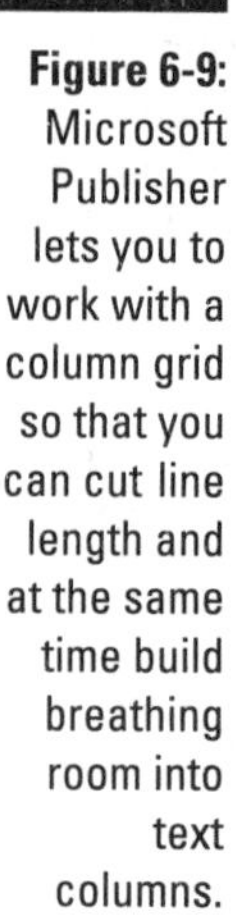
Figure 6-9: Microsoft Publisher lets you to work with a column grid so that you can cut line length and at the same time build breathing room into text columns.

Navigation icons are grouped together in the first cell. Text is placed in the middle cell, which expands vertically to accommodate the text. The right cell is empty and is included simply to build space into the page.

When viewed using a browser that reads tables (most do, these days), the result is a Web page divided into zones from left to right, with a text column of appropriate width surrounded by white space to the left and right (see Figure 6-11).

Avoid snaking columns

Although thinking horizontally in terms of tables and columns is useful, do not include snaking columns in your Web site. *Snaking* refers to two or three parallel columns containing text that begins at the top of the left-hand column, extends to the bottom of the page, and then requires the reader to scroll to the top of the page to continue reading the next column.

Web site readers are unlikely to continue reading text set this way! Continually scrolling up and down each page simply takes too much effort. It's too easy for Web site visitors to get lost and forget what they've just read as they reach for the mouse to reposition the page.

Snaking columns work in print communications because readers don't have to reach for the mouse and scroll! They can simply and instantaneously shift their eyes from the bottom of one column to the top of the next.

The only exception to avoiding snaking text columns is on pages of your Web site that contain short, non-ordered directories or resource listings that can be read in any order. When the items in the directory appear in random order, as opposed to alphabetical order or order of importance, readers can scan from left to right.

In Control versus Out of Control

A major issue in Web design involves who controls the look of the site — the designer or the Web site visitor. Because of the current nature of the Web, you can design a Web site to look one way, but you can't guarantee that your visitors will see it the way you designed it. Unlike print pieces, over which the recipient has little control except to add mustaches to the photographs, you do not enjoy the control over the appearance of your Web site that you as the designer should, although the degree of control you do have is constantly changing.

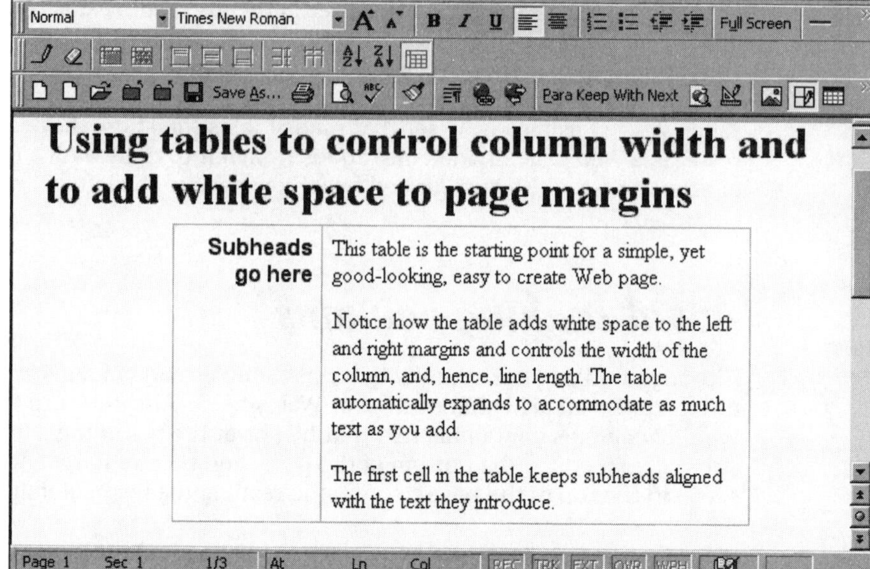

Figure 6-10: The structure for this Web page is provided by a table that consists of just one row of cells.

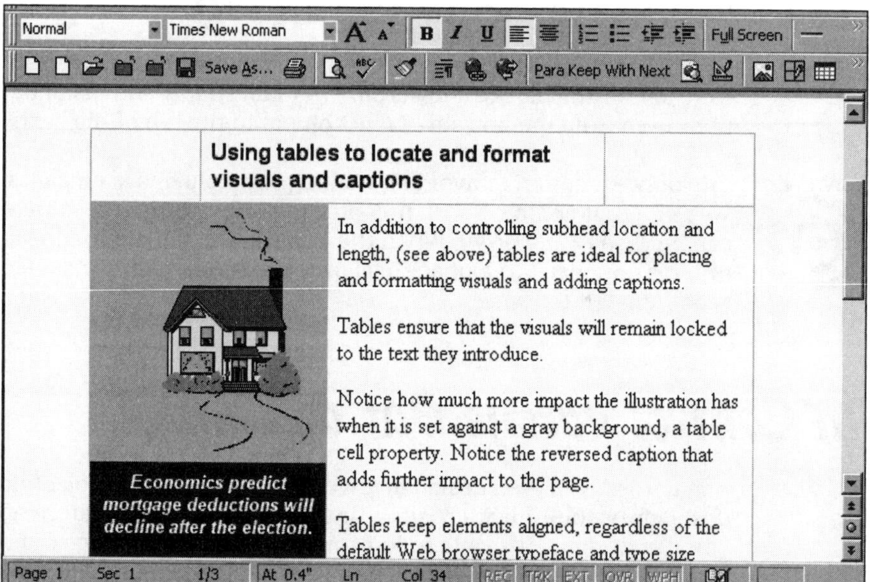

Figure 6-11: Assembling a Web site based on a table.

It all depends on your point of view

Following are factors that you can't control, but that affect the way your Web site appears to your audience:

- **Monitor:** You never know what size of a monitor that your visitor is using or its settings. These factors influence the size of the graphics that the monitor can display, the sharpness of the text, and the number of colors that can be accurately and attractively displayed.
- **Text:** Typically, you are not able to control the typeface design, the type size, nor the color of the text used to display your message. Although this is an area of constant progress, and ways exist that enable you to work around this lack of control, progress and workarounds come with the disadvantages of a loss of universality and a slower downloading speed.

As a result, the Web site that looks so great on your 20-inch monitor looks cluttered and hard to read when viewed on the typical Web surfer's 14- or 15-inch monitor. And, without choosing universally accepted colors, your Web site may display very unattractive, grainy colors.

The following sections discuss some of the ways you can work around these problems.

Text in graphic form gives more control

A successful workaround to controlling the appearance of your text involves an understanding of the differences between graphic text and live text and knowing when the use of each is most appropriate:

- **Graphic text** is text that has been created as a graphic image (a picture) and that is downloaded as a graphic image. Graphic text offers you total control over the typeface, type size, text color, line spacing, and line breaks (see Figure 6-12).

  Graphic text is ideal for the title of your Web site, major headlines, pull-quotes, and the titles of pages beginning new sections of your Web site. Use graphic text when you want to control the image your Web site projects.

  Graphic text permits creative options that are limited only by the Web site creator's software and design talents. Programs such as Microsoft WordArt, Adobe PhotoShop, and Corel PHOTO-PAINT are often used to create graphic text because they permit a virtually unlimited variety of creative effects, such as overlapping letters, filled characters, fades, shadows, outlines, and text that is angled or curved. You can set the type against illustrations, photos, or colors different from the background of the remainder of the page. Of course, the price of this power is increased downloading time for your text blocks.

  Consider a page with a blue background. You want to add impact to the title set in yellow. You want it to appear against an ivory background. You create the title in Photoshop against an ivory background. When the title downloads, the title will appear against an ivory background, even though the remainder of the page is blue.

Graphic text is ideal for logos, Web site titles, major subheads, as well as the category dividers that introduce new topics. Use graphic text to establish an image and maintain unity throughout your Web site.

- **Live text** is downloaded and formatted into headlines, subheads, and body copy as it is downloaded. Live text instantly downloads, but at the sacrifice of control. Your Web site may look completely different from one computer to another, and you do not have any control over the appearance of the text or *line breaks* (where lines split).

  Because live text is immediately downloaded and formatted into headlines and body copy when it arrives at your computer, live text loads quickly. Line breaks are likely to change depending on the typeface and type size chosen by the Web site visitor.

  The biggest problem with live text is that it usually creates long, boring, hard-to-read lines of text that span the visitor's monitor from margin to margin (see Figure 6-12). However, you can control this problem by thinking horizontally as described in the previous section.

In Chapter 19, you can look at some of the other options that are available now, and some that are coming down the road, that can help you take more control over the appearance of your text.

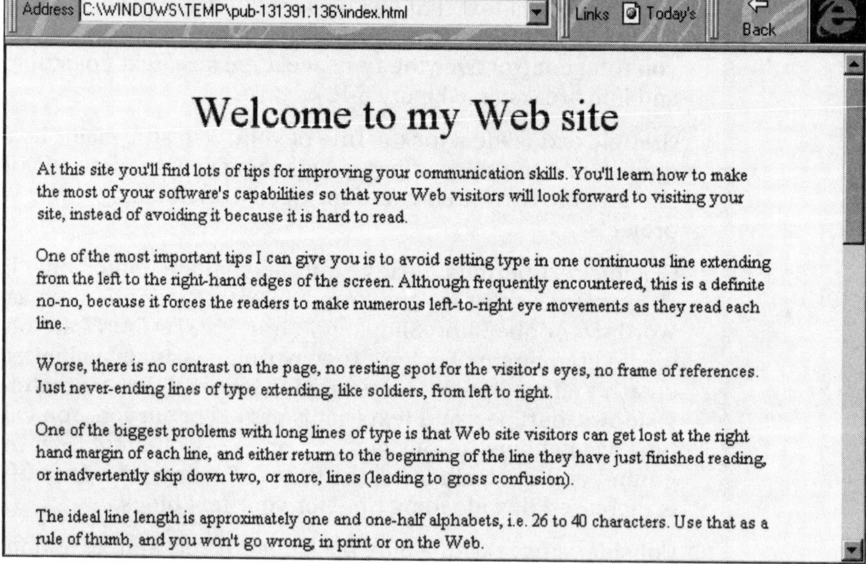

Address C:\WINDOWS\TEMP\pub-131391.136\index.html
Links
Today's
Back
Welcome to my Web site
At this site you'll find lots of tips for improving your communication skills. You'll learn how to make the most of your software's capabilities so that your Web visitors will look forward to visiting your site, instead of avoiding it because it is hard to read.
One of the most important tips I can give you is to avoid setting type in one continuous line extending from the left to the right-hand edges of the screen. Although frequently encountered, this is a definite no-no, because it forces the readers to make numerous left-to-right eye movements as they read each line.
Worse, there is no contrast on the page, no resting spot for the visitor's eyes, no frame of references. Just never-ending lines of type extending, like soldiers, from left to right.
One of the biggest problems with long lines of type is that Web site visitors can get lost at the right hand margin of each line, and either return to the beginning of the line they have just finished reading, or inadvertently skip down two, or more, lines (leading to gross confusion).
The ideal line length is approximately one and one-half alphabets, i.e. 26 to 40 characters. Use that as a rule of thumb, and you won't go wrong, in print or on the Web.

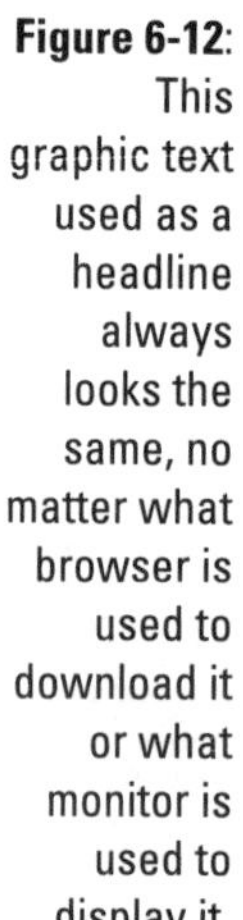
Figure 6-12: This graphic text used as a headline always looks the same, no matter what browser is used to download it or what monitor is used to display it.

Chapter 7

Making a Splash with Your Home Page

In This Chapter

- Including the right stuff on your Home page
- Understanding the difference between a Splash page and a Home page
- Determining the elements of a successful Home or Splash page

As the first page that visitors encounter at your Web site, your Home page is the springboard for the success of your Web marketing efforts. The first page visitors encounter at your Web site is your Home page. It sets the stage for what follows. A Home page is similar to the front cover of a book or brochure. A good Home page

- Makes a favorable impression
- Projects an appropriate image
- Provides benefits that tease or entice the Web visitor into exploring further

In other words, a good Home page introduces yourself or your business to the visitor, establishes a mood (based on color, text, and graphics) that your visitor finds attractive, and displays links describing the categories of information that your Web site contains.

What to Include on Your Home Page

Following are some of the elements that your Home page needs to contain. Use this list to evaluate your current Home page as well as the Home pages of Web sites that you visit. Photocopy the Home Page Planner and Checklist and use it as a guide whether you're starting your own site from scratch or evaluating the efforts of others. Try to keep these elements visible on the screen without requiring the visitor to scroll down (to read more about the advantages of scroll-free viewing, look at the "Think small" section in Chapter 6):

- Theme
- Logo (or other identification)
- Position statement
- Links
- News
- Contact information
- Housekeeping information

In the following sections, I take a look at each of these elements.

Theme

As noted in Chapter 2, successful designs of any kind are based on a theme that offers an easily-understood benefit to your audience. Your text, your graphics, and your general layout should all reflect and support that theme.

For your Web site, carrying out that theme should be the most important element of your Home page, possibly even its title. Developing a theme for your Web site provides you an opportunity to begin focusing your thinking on what you really want to appeal to your Web site visitors. Here are some ideas:

- Suppose that you're a manufacturer of color printers for computers: Consider titling your Web site "Making the Most of Color," which tells your audience more about what you and your product can do for them than a title like, "Welcome to Hyperbole Technology's Home page." Note the promise of non-selling, educational knowledge: "Making the Most of Color" implies that Web site visitors will find out something they don't already know about color, which can be applied to future decisions about using color. This title promises your audience more than pages of printer specifications and reprints of favorable product reviews — information that is useful but not likely to attract a large audience.
- If you sell imported luxury cars, instead of concentrating on your name and telling how good you are (which is simply brag-and-boast advertising), the theme of your Web site may be "Affordable Excellence." "Affordable Excellence" promises that visitors who use your Web site can make better-informed buying decisions and possibly afford a better car than they may otherwise have thought. Make sure that everything about your site consistently and completely reinforces your theme.

- A firm that sells fresh fruit juices without artificial flavoring or preservatives may choose a theme like "Recipes for Natural Living," rather than naming its site "Hyperbole Juices." The key word is "Recipes," which implies that useful, free information can be found as well as sales material.

In the case of my own Web site, I know the world is full of writers and designers. Few people know or care enough about Roger C. Parker to want to visit a Roger C. Parker site (though I'm a nice guy when you get to know me). So, instead, I chose "Meaningful Content" as the theme for my Web site. That way, the audience who appreciates the information on my Web site will come to associate "Meaningful Content" with Roger C. Parker — and we all benefit. And because my theme emphasizes content, I'm free to concentrate on creating meaningful text for my site — that's what people expect — without the need to dress my site with snazzy colors or cutting-edge graphics.

Identification

Your *identification* — who and what you are as sponsor of this Web site — needs to be visually subordinate to the theme. Web site visitors certainly need to know whose Web site they're visiting, but the who needs to be of less importance than the why, which is your theme.

Always make sure that your Home page contains your firm's logo, displayed in the same manner — using the same typefaces, relative type sizes, and colors — as when encountered on a brochure or newsletter. I find it amazing that a number of businesses use several, slightly different logos. Varying your logo dilutes its impact as your audience wants to know "the real you." Small differences in logos confuse your image and can be more easily "stolen" by competitors hoping to trade in on your reputation. If you don't keep your logo the same, how will your audience always identify it as belonging to you?

You don't have to run your logo in a large size to use it successfully on your Web site. Face it: Logos have little or no informational value to your audience, other than to identify the owner of the site they're visiting. Making your logo too large slows down your Web site and limits the presentation of other, more reader-oriented, information.

Position statement

In addition to identifying your association or firm, your Home page needs to identify the firm's field of activity. Strive to answer the question: "What do you do?" using as few words or visuals as possible. You want your *position statement* — which can be as short as a motto — to also begin the process of differentiating you from your competition.

Your position statement should summarize your business or other philosophy, for example "imported cars and only imported cars" (to differentiate yourself from auto dealerships that sell domestic cars, too). Other examples include: "Maine's source of all-natural gardening supplies" or "100% employee owned." Your position statement should be the source of your theme, and your theme should reinforce your position statement.

Avoid abstract, pious, self-important "Mission Statements" that appeal to egos and stockholders but don't offer Web site visitors any benefit. "Our mission is to help people communicate better and handle the challenges of the millennium" isn't as focused as saying "We publish a weekly newspaper that keeps people in the Upper Connecticut River Valley informed of challenges to the economy and the environment."

Web site visitors don't really care what you do; they're more interested in *what you can do for them*. Try to frame your position statement in a way that offers a benefit and differentiates your association or firm from others in the same field.

Links

After identifying yourself, identify the categories of information contained on your Web site — categories that visitors can access by clicking on highlighted text or graphics (the equivalent of "turning the page" in a print piece). You want your links to be as large and self-explanatory as possible, enabling Web site visitors to locate desired information easily.

Again, think in terms of your Web site visitor. Instead of providing links like "Who we are," "What we sell," and "Our history," rephrase the same information in ways that tease the Web site visitor into visiting the links. For example, if you run the natural foods site, consider these options:

- Replace "Who we are," with "Shopping information" or "Why natural is best."
- Replace "What we sell" with: "Preview the finest" or "We have your favorite flavors."
- Replace "Our history" with "Our tradition of quality" or "Our rave reviews."

Links can be freestanding, such as buttons, or they can be words appearing within a line of text. Avoid including too many links within a paragraph, as the changing colors of the linked words distract the reader. Avoid unnecessary words as well, such as. "Click here"; by now, most Web site visitors recognize that words set in a different color are links.

The templates that accompany most software programs include predefined color choices for links. In addition, most software programs will suggest colors for links based on the background colors you have chosen. In most cases, you're best off using the background and link color choices provided with these templates than developing your own color combinations.

Avoid making your "visited links" more noticeable than "current links" or "unvisited" links. Your visitor's eyes should be attracted to links that promise them new information, not to links that remind them of where they have been!

Links are not only used internally within your Web site. Your Web site should also contain links to other resources that your visitors may find useful, such as vendors, government agencies, or media that may be of interest to your Web site visitors. For example, if you're a model railroad dealer, you may want to include links to the various model railroading magazines, as well as links to the National Model Railroading Association and railroad museums throughout the country. You could even include links to the Web sites of railroads.

News

You never want your Home page to be static. Your Home page needs to change regularly. In addition to teasing visitors and providing links, make your page begin to tell a story, using product news and up-to-date information. You can start by discussing your latest product or client success story:

- In the case of the color printer manufacturer, consider showing your latest model and including a few key phrases, or callouts, describing why it's better than previous models ("The Color 240: sharper colors, higher speed") or quote a sentence or two from a favorable review.
- If you're a writer or consultant, describe a new book or upcoming seminar.

You don't have to tell the entire story, just enough of the story to get the Web site visitor involved. Include a text link to the page where the news story is continued, and you're on your way to Web success!

Contact information

Always make it easy for Web site visitors to contact you. Always provide e-mail, phone, fax, and mailing address information. If you want people to visit your place of business, include a link to a page containing a map showing how to get to your location (as well as a picture showing visitors what to look for when they arrive).

One sure-fire way of building your prospect mailing list for later follow-up is to offer something free in exchange for the Web site visitor registering, or sending you their address and contact information. For example, I offer free article reprints and back issues of a newsletter.

You can overcome the natural resistance of many Web site visitors to give you their name and mailing address by promising not to share their names with others. Just be sure that you live up to the promise.

Housekeeping information

Always include notice of copyright protection (for example, © 1997 Roger C. Parker). This protects the information on your site by discouraging rampant unauthorized copying of the contents of your site. A copyright also serves legal notice of your ownership of the contents. Although this can't prevent unauthorized use of your text and graphics, it does offer you a legal leg to stand on in the case of flagrant misuse.

If you *do* invite others to copy and distribute the ideas contained on your Web pages, spell out the details. For example, I allow teachers and seminar leaders to print out my "how to" ideas and use them as handouts or teaching aids, as long as they ask for permission in advance, include my name and Web site address on the handouts, and let me know that they're doing it. This makes friends, builds my mailing list, and promotes my name and Web site address to new audiences.

Table 7-1 provides a handy checklist that you can use when planning your Home page. This table includes far more elements than found on many Home pages, but including all of them in some way will increase the usefulness of your Home page as a springboard to further interaction with your Web site. Figures 7-1 and 7-2 illustrate *before* and *after* examples of applying the principles itemized in Table 7-1. Which Web site would you rather visit?

Counters and "last updated" information

Many Home pages contain a counter that shows how many times the site has been visited since a given date. Counters can be a double-edged sword. If your page has not received significant traffic, the low numbers add an image of disinterest and inactivity to visitors. After all, how good a Web site can it be if only 133 people have visited it since June 1996?

Table 7-1 Home Page Planner and Checklist

Element	*Description/Purpose*	*How Well Evaluated Web Site Meets Goal*
Theme	Why Web site visitors have a reason to continue exploring your Web site	
Identification	Your logo	
Positioning	The benefits you offer and/or how you differ from others in the field	
Links	Visual and text representations designed to organize your Web site and induce visitors deeper	
News	Changing element describing something new and different, such as a new product or service	
Contact information	E-mail links plus address, phone, and fax information	
Housekeeping	Copyright and reprint information	

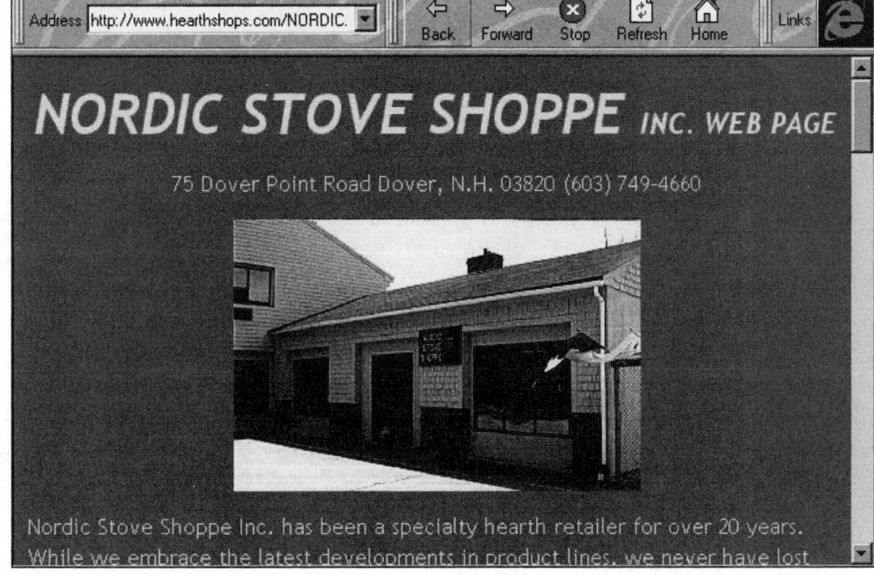

Address http://www.hearthshops.com/NORDIC.
Back
Forward
Stop
Refresh
Home
Links
NORDIC STOVE SHOPPE INC. WEB PAGE
75 Dover Point Road Dover, N.H. 03820 (603) 749-4660
Nordic Stove Shoppe Inc. has been a specialty hearth retailer for over 20 years.

Figure 7-1: A slow-loading, inward-looking Web site that doesn't tell visitors why it matters.

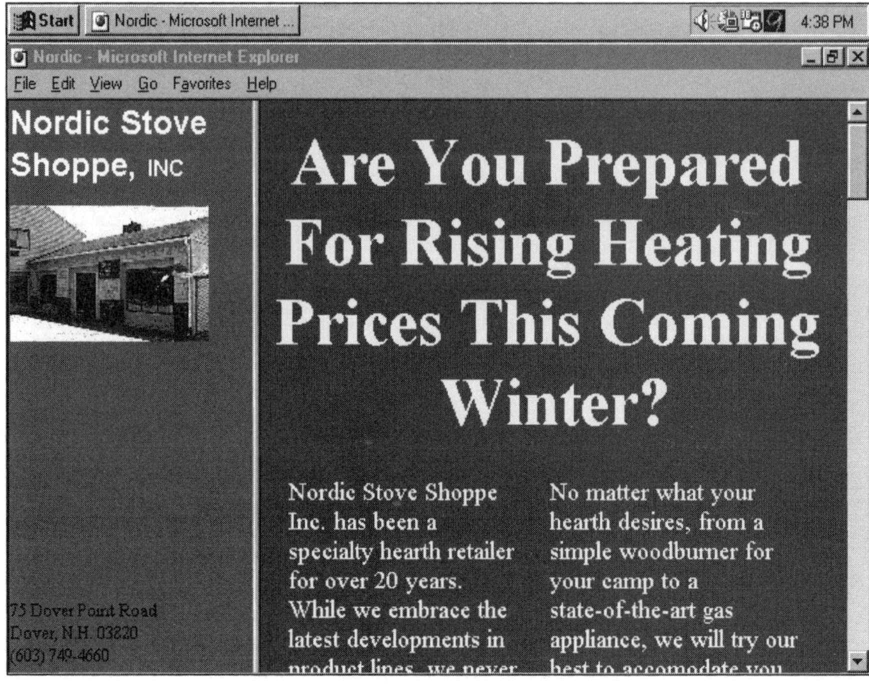

Start
Nordic - Microsoft Internet ...
4:38 PM
Nordic - Microsoft Internet Explorer
File Edit View Go Favorites Help
Nordic Stove Shoppe, INC
Are You Prepared For Rising Heating Prices This Coming Winter?
Nordic Stove Shoppe Inc. has been a specialty hearth retailer for over 20 years. While we embrace the latest developments in
No matter what your hearth desires, from a simple woodburner for your camp to a state-of-the-art gas appliance, we will try our
75 Dover Point Road
Dover, N.H. 03820
(603) 749-4660

Figure 7-2: A revised Web site containing the same information packaged in a different, more visitor-oriented way.

In addition: What value does a counter offer visitors? A counter may be of interest to you, but how does it help the visitor save money or make a better buying decision? Plus, counters are rarely accurate; every time you check your own Web site, you're artificially inflating the count. (Of course, you can increase your numbers significantly this way, but why?)

Many Home pages include "last updated" information. Unless you frequently update your site, you're probably better off omitting this information as time quickly flies by and an old date implies that the information is out of date — even when it isn't. All your information is new to first-time visitors; unless some information has changed, you revise your site for repeat visitors — so they don't give up on you as never having anything new.

Always keep your Web site visitor's needs uppermost in your mind. From this perspective, including "best viewed with (browser)" or "created with (name-of-software)" information is less important. Likewise, you ought to reconsider having a Home page link directly to sites that don't relate to your site's content, such as your Web site designer's site. Instead, consider grouping this type of information under a "Resources" page.

The pros and cons of image maps

Instead of including individual buttons, icons, and text links to the remaining pages of a Web site, many Home pages use an image map (see Figure 7-3).

An *image map* is a single large graphic image that functions like a road map. Typically, it is an illustration that visually represents the contents of your Web site. The image map contains *hot spots,* areas that contain links to individual pages. You can identify hot spots in an image map by the way the pointer of your browser changes to a hand as it passes over them and the way that the status line at the bottom of the browser indicates the address the hot spot links to.

If your visitor has the Show Status Bar option activated, a description of the destination or the description of the page to which the hot spot on the image map relates will appear in the status bar. For example, if your visitor moves the mouse pointer over a telephone, the status bar could read `telephone numbers`. If the pointer is over the picture of a clock, `departure times` might appear in the status bar.

Advantages of image maps

Image maps can provide several advantages:

- **Looks impressive:** Image maps represent a level of graphic sophistication that indicates the presence of a trained, professional hand. This professionalism reflects well on your entire organization.

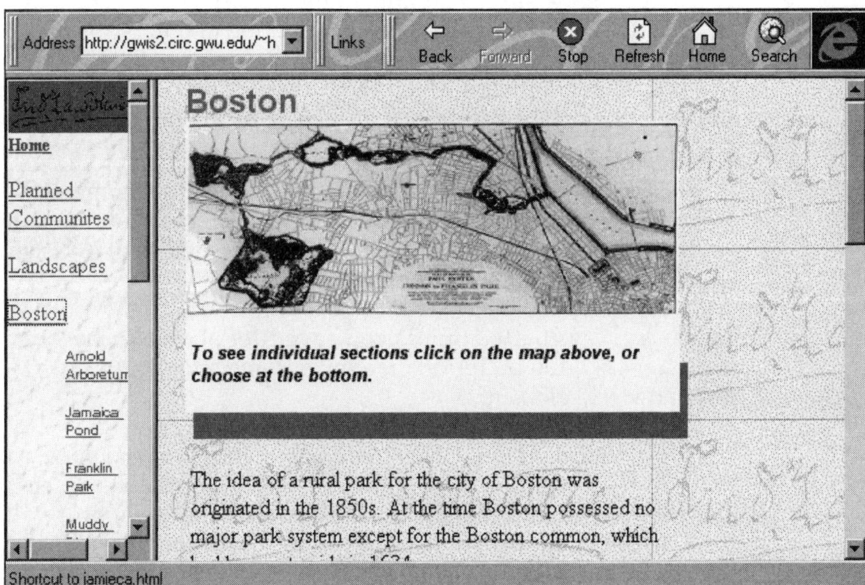

Figure 7-3: An image map.

- **Provides visual orientation:** Image maps communicate at a glance and appeal to Web site visitors who would rather watch than read.
- **Saves space:** A single image map can contain links to numerous sites.
- **Saves time:** A single large image map usually downloads faster than several individual graphic images that serve as links.

Image maps, when they are obvious and intuitive, appeal to visitors who appreciate visual treats. They communicate a contemporary, techno-savvy image that's more appropriate for high-tech firms than antique stores.

Disadvantages of image maps

Image maps are not without fault, however. Following are some problems of image maps that you need to be aware of:

- **Lack of flexibility:** After you create an image map, adding new links is difficult. You usually must completely redraw the image map when you add new pages to your Web site.
- **Space hogging:** Large image maps reduce the space available for your logo and the statement of the your Web site theme. Often, image maps don't leave space to include timely information of news value.
- **Cost:** You may need to hire a professional designer to draw an image map that projects a first-class appearance. Employing a professional Web site designer can make site development costs quickly rise.
- **Quality:** When image maps are created on one platform, such as the Apple Macintosh, but the Web site is viewed on another platform, such as a Windows-based computer, the quality of an image map can be jeopardized. The color palette (selection of colors) used on the Apple Macintosh is slightly different from the color palette used on the typical Windows computer, which tends to be darker. Results can be disappointing unless care is taken when selecting image map colors.
- **Downloading time:** Although a single image map often downloads faster than separate images, image maps still take time to download. Each second of delay increases the chance that your impatient Web site visitor may move to another site. And the delays may discourage Web site visitors from revisiting your site.

Simple is always better. Unless you have a lot of time to invest in an image map, you are often better off creating a Home page using several smaller text and visual elements.

If you're in a design-intensive environment and want to appeal to design-savvy visitors — and can take the time to develop a 100-percent intuitive image map — then investing in an image map may be appropriate. Remember, however, that many folks surf the Web with their graphics option turned off, and image maps take a lot of time to download.

Splash Page versus Home Page

Splash pages are simpler than Home pages and contain fewer elements, as you can see in Figure 7-4. The typical Splash page is very image-oriented and contains only one link — to a Table of Contents page that follows. At most, Splash pages often contain just a logo and a brief statement describing the Web site's goals and/or the benefits the visitor can enjoy while exploring the site.

The difference between a Splash page and a Home page is similar to the difference between the front cover of a novel and the front page of a direct-mail catalog. The front cover of a novel usually just contains a title, the author's name, and a graphic image that suggests the contents of the book (the Splash page). The front cover of a direct-mail catalog, however — where results are measured by orders received — usually contains a variety of elements, such as a theme, positioning elements, specific products (usually the best deal in the catalog), and ordering information (the Home page).

In general, because the image on a Splash page must attract the interest of your visitors without a lot a supporting elements to help, you probably need a professional designer to create one. You can more surely and easily create a Home page that has numerous elements than you can take chances with an inadequate Splash page that may entice fewer of your Web site visitors into linking deeper into your Web site.

Figure 7-4: With a minimum of words and graphic images, this Splash page establishes a mood and invites you to go on.

Thoughts on choosing a domain name

You have two ways of obtaining a domain name for your Web site: You can get your own by registering it and paying a fee to the keeper-of-domain-names, InterNIC (check out www.internic.net to find out how), or you can get one from a network you choose for your site, which will give it one of the names it has available.

Whenever possible (translated: whenever there's enough money), get your own domain name instead of placing your Web site on someone else's network and receiving an electronic address that's related to a specific server.

When you see Web addresses like www.banana.net, it means that the firm's or individual's files are located on a specific network server; in this case an ISP — run by a large guy with a hairy chest. *(Don't tangle with him!)*

When you see Web addresses like www.rcparker.com, however, it means the firm has invested $50 to $100 to obtain a domain name, which will remain the same, regardless whether the firm moves from www.gorilla.net to www.snake.net (which has a much lower profile). The domain name (sometimes referred to as URL, or Uniform Resource Locator, which represents the specific elements of your Web address) will remain the same whether the firm moves across the street, across the country, or around the world.

Characteristics of a good domain name

A good domain name is short and obvious — like idgbooks.com. Short is better because short names reduce the number of characters the Web site visitor has to type, eliminating possibilities for error and making access to the site faster and easier.

Obvious is better because Web site visitors are more likely to remember the address and relate it to you or your business — in this case, IDG Books Worldwide, Inc., even if they encounter it only briefly as part of an ad, a newsletter, or a directory listing.

As a starting point, acronyms work well. A Web address like idgbooks.com obviously can refer only to IDG Books Worldwide, Inc. Of course, it helps if the name of your association or firm is already well known.

Sometimes, you can use your entire name, for example, www.rcparker.com, but this works only if another Roger C. Parker hasn't already registered the name. Many business names also have already been registered, making it more difficult to make yours short and obvious if your company's name is similar to some others' names.

Descriptive domains

Instead of attempting to shoehorn your name into a URL, consider choosing a domain name that describes the activity that your firm is engaged in or one that offers an obvious benefit for visiting.

One of my favorite names belongs to a firm called American Transport Services. Now, that long name doesn't lend itself to an acronym because probably no one knows what ATS represents. Luckily, having access to qualified help, the company chose a name that describes the nature of its business. The result is the URL www.carship.com that concisely describes the firm's business in a way that lends itself to radio broadcasting.

Another example of a descriptive URL comes from an automobile dealer that sold only Mercedes-Benz. The dealer's original Web address was www.smithmotors.com, which didn't communicate anything about the firm. At my suggestion, the dealer changed its URL to www.onlymercedes.com, which offers a distinct benefit.

Chapter 8

Building Continuity and Change into Your Web Site

In This Chapter

- Maintaining consistency
- Building unity into your Web site
- Choosing a background
- Placing navigation links
- Controlling line length and text placement
- Using graphic accents, department heads, and pullquotes
- Determining the need for change

Consistency is one of the primary characteristics of easy-to-read, well-constructed sites. Consistency implies that you don't unnecessarily surprise your Web site visitor or change the rules on them. Consistency creates comfort and reinforces the uniqueness of your Web site, so it stands apart instead of being confused with other Web sites visited during a surfing session.

The inside, or linked, pages of your Web site need to maintain the look and image established on your Home page (they do not need to be exact duplicates of your Home page). Inconsistency not only implies a haphazard, as contrasted to professional, way of doing business, but it may also lead Web site visitors to think that they've left your site and are visiting another.

Consistency doesn't mean boredom, however. If you establish consistent ways of handling the basic building blocks of your Web page from the start, you can allow the *content* — the necessary text and graphic images — of your Web site to introduce variety rather than relying on changing decorative design elements. In this chapter, I discuss some of the ways that you can build visual variety into your Web site without destroying the underlying unity of your site.

Elements of Consistency

The elements that must maintain consistency include the background color and texture, typeface of text, treatment of links, and the size and placement of visuals.

Background

The background of your Web site needs to remain consistent from page to page. This means that you should use the same color (or colors) on the background of all of your pages, including the same texture or pattern. If you use a light scan of your logo on one page, you might want to use it on every page.

One of the biggest mistakes newcomers to Web design make is to use different background colors for each page. This destroys page-to-page unity and often leads to the inadvertent creation of hard-to-read pages when the text lacks sufficient contrast with the background for easy reading. (There simply aren't enough colors with sufficient contrast to work in a changing-background, changing-text-color scenario, especially when you add the color changes necessary for links.)

The starting point for creating a Web site background that you can live with is to think horizontally and use columns or tables (as described in Chapter 6) to divide your background into zones, as shown in Figure 8-1. These zones also make the process of grouping navigation elements together along one side of your Web site easy. You can also think vertically and create zones along the top of your page in order to group repeating elements such as navigation elements.

One of the easiest ways to create zones is to choose a single color for the background of your Web site, using the color at full strength (also known as 100 percent saturation) along the left-hand margin and applying a 10 percent or 20 percent tint, or screen, to the remainder of the background (see Chapter 15 for more about using color on the Web). You want to test your color choices with a variety of monitors, perhaps on a friend's or coworker's computer, to see which tints work better than others. This effect of using tints can be extremely effective and simple to maintain.

Later in this chapter, you can find out about some of the ways to code the sections of your Web site to create a unique look for your various topics.

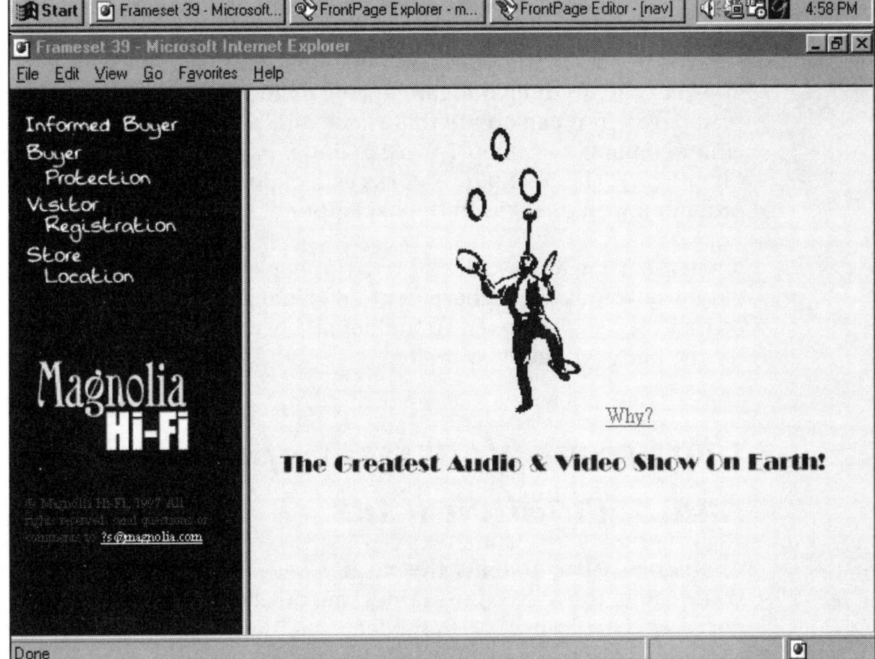

Figure 8-1: Divide a background into zones by using the same color full-strength and tinted.

Text

Text is the second most noticeable element of Web site consistency. Always use the same typeface, type size, type style, type color, alignment, and column width for identical elements of your Web page.

Yes, I have said that you don't have total control over the typeface, type size, and type style used to display your words. But, that's true in an absolute, not a relative, sense! Although you may not yet be able to specify the specific typeface or type size that is to be displayed in your Web site visitor's browser, you *can* define their relative relationships. For example, as long as you always use Heading One fonts for page titles, Heading Two fonts for primary headings, and body fonts for text, you can maintain a consistent relationship between these elements because no matter how other browsers represent Heading One fonts, they are still Heading One fonts that will maintain the same relationship between Heading Two and body text fonts across browsers.

Unifying the various pages of your Web site and making text columns easier to read can be as simple as using the same amount of white space to separate the text from the right and left edges of the screen. This technique doesn't cost anything but can pay big dividends in terms of creating easy-to-read pages. You can create this effect with software programs that support either columns or tables. (You can find more about columns and tables in Chapter 7.) This technique works especially well when the text is coordinated with changes in the background, as shown in Figure 8-2.

If you are using a two-color or two-tint background for your Web site, one easy way you can add character and visual interest is to place the subheads so that they slightly overlap the boundary that lies between the colors used for the background of your site.

Consistent placement of logo and navigation links

Another easy way to unify the various pages of your Web site is to place your logo in the same size in the same position on each page. The size of your logo isn't as crucial as the fact that it always appears in the same location at the top, bottom, or sides of your pages.

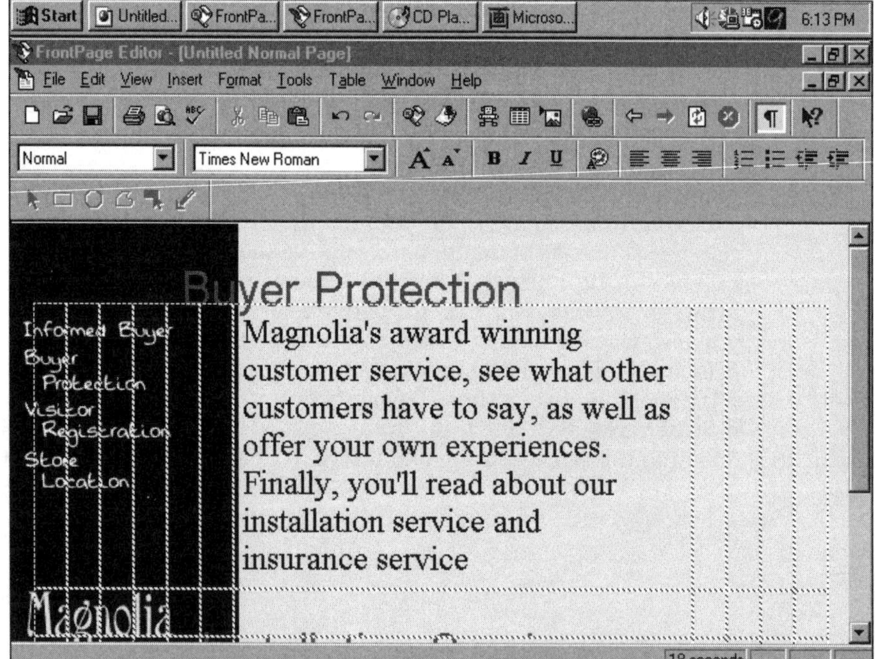

Figure 8-2: Add impact to narrower columns of text by aligning the left margin of the text column with changes in the background.

Likewise, you can unify your Web site as well as make it easy to navigate by placing buttons and icons used for navigation links in the same position on each page. You can group these links along the top or bottom or along the upper left or right of each page. The goal is to make each page of your Web site familiar to your visitors so that they don't have to hunt for navigation icons.

When using a two-tone background, one of the best ways you can organize and unify your pages is by always placing the navigation buttons or icons against the background (see Figure 8-3), rather than against a border or some other place.

Theme, title, and department heads

One of the easiest ways to unify your Web site without slowing it down is to use graphic text (see Chapter 6) for repeating elements such as titles, section dividers, headlines, and subheads, as well as pull-quotes. (*Pull-quotes* are short text passages summarizing, or pulled from, adjacent material.) You want the typeface, colors, background, and shadows of these elements to be the same as the typeface, colors, background, and shadows used to communicate the theme of your Web site on your Home page.

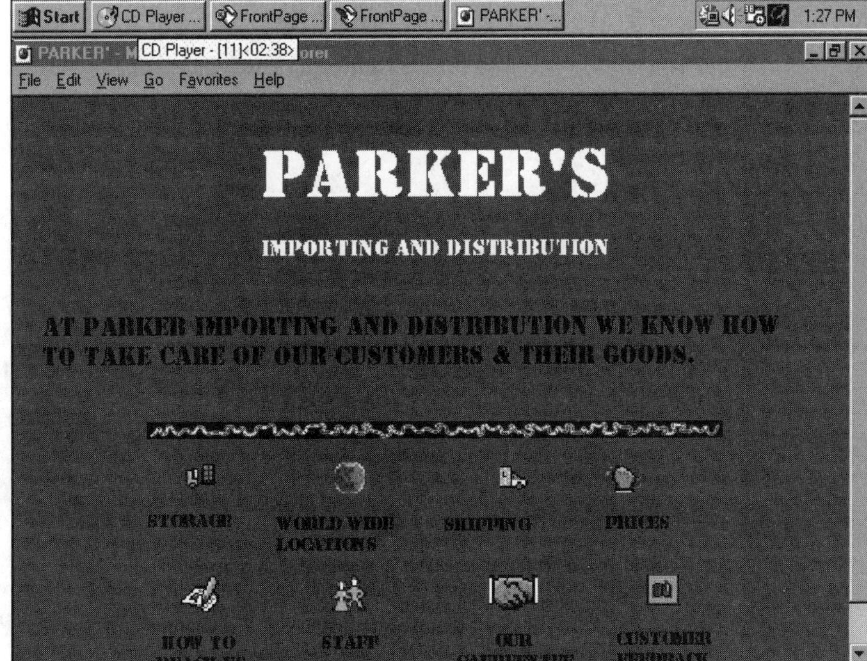

Figure 8-3: Organizing navigation tools makes them easy to locate.

The advantage of using graphic text as a unifying element is that, on the inside pages, these text elements can be relatively small — so that they download quickly — yet even when small they will inevitably form a strong contrast with whatever typeface and type size your Web site visitor has specified for their browser. In addition, you exercise more control over the appearance of the type. Although the individual browser may change the typeface of live text from Times New Roman to Trebuchet, yet each page is introduced by the same title and reinforced by the same pull-quotes.

Even just one or two words set in a distinctive, non-changing, typeface will be enough to establish and maintain a unique look.

Visuals

One final way to build unity into your Web site is to always place photographs or illustrations in the same relative position on each page and always treat them the same way.

For example, one very strong alternative to placing them in the same position is to always place photographs against a different colored background to the left or right of the text columns, as shown in Figure 8-4.

You can also create unity in the way you handle scanned photographs by always placing the same colored borders, image-edited borders, or shadow effects around your photographs. Just be sure that you don't inadvertently insert a photograph and forget to modify the border or background.

After you have established a standard, make sure that you stick with it!

Building in Variety

You can build visual variety into your Web site by using one of several different methods. You can color-code the various pages of your Web site by using small graphic elements, and you can vary the placement of text from page to page, as long as the purpose is easily identified.

Color coding your Web site

The easiest way to color code your Web site is to use a consistent background color but vary the accent colors for different sections of your Web site. This works best when the colors used to identify the inside, or linked, pages of your Web site are identical to the colors used on the corresponding navigation links of your Home page.

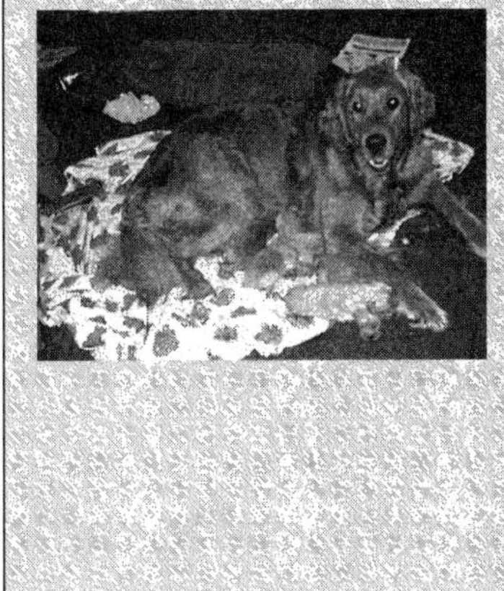

This is a tale about Murphy and her puppies. These Golden Retriever puppies were born on June 16 at 3 am. it was a long night of going to and from the hospital in the car. In fact, Murphy had three of the puppies in the car (any one want a good deal on a Ford Explorer?). This is a picture of the puppies two days after they were born.
There are five puppies of which four are female. Since we already have 2 dogs, Murphy and a Yellow Lab named Dixie, we decided not to keep the puppies and are selling them. To date we have been able to sell four out of the five.
Click here to see a picture of the puppies a month later.
Or here to see a picutre of Bailey, the cutest

Here is a picture of the puppies on August 16. See how much they have grown. It is amazing. In such a short time they have grown a lot and they are even eating real puppy food.
The puppies soon grew out of their small pen and now take up a third of the kitchen.
They are quite active. We take them outside and they play around in the grass, dirt and like to play hide and seek in the shrubbery.
Murphy is pretty good about letting people touch her babies. She just has to smell them first and get a scent to know who you are. Overall, she is a good mother.
Click here,.to see a picture of them a month earlier.

Figure 8-4: Consistent photo placement unifies the various pages of a Web site.

Be careful to make your color coding noticeable, but not distracting. Colors should draw attention without being the focal point of the page.

Here's how this idea works at a glance: On your Home page, use different colors for the buttons linking to the inside pages. Then, on each of the linked pages, use the same color as its button for the backgrounds or the title of the page or the headlines (or subheads) used on that page or in that section.

Visitors to your Web site quickly pick up on the relationship between button color and accent color. The resulting Web site is unified, yet maintains enough differences from section to section to keep visitors interested. This technique is surprisingly simple, yet offers tremendous creative options, especially if you are careful to choose the linked colors from a common palette.

When you choose colors for buttons and graphic accents, you should choose them from a common palette instead of randomly to ensure that the colors will relate well to each other, maintaining your Web site's image while unifying it.

Another way you can code the various sections or pages of your Web site is by changing the color of the borders placed around photographs or illustrations. You'll be surprised by the difference that simply mimicking the colored graphic accents used on various sections of your Web site can make.

Varying column width and placement

You can also build variety into your Web site without destroying continuity by varying column placement and column width depending on page content.

My Web site, for example, is based on a five-column grid. (You can find it at `www.rcparker. com.`) Never are more than four of the five columns used (see Figure 8-5). The fifth column is usually empty, which provides breathing room for the remainder of the page and a place to locate links back to the top of the page and back to the home page (or, when appropriate, the next page). Page layout programs such as Microsoft Publisher 97 and PageMaker 6.5 make creating Web pages based on grids this easy.

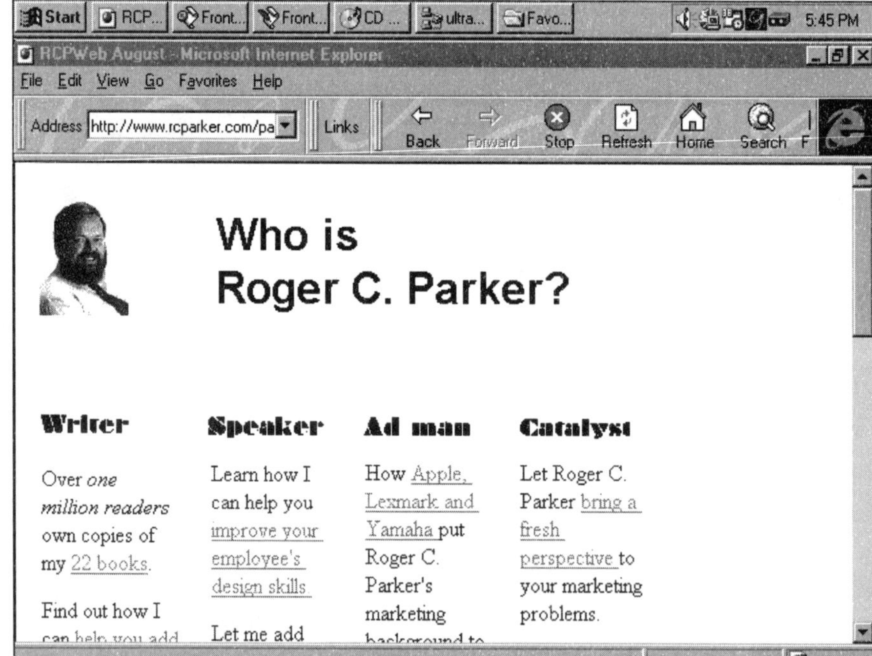

Figure 8-5: The directory page of my Web site demonstrates a five-column grid.

Parallel single columns spanning four of the five columns are used on pages where new topics are introduced. Parallel columns are permissible in this instance because each column is likely to be independently read rather than in sequence from left-to-right.

More importantly, the text on pages linked to this mini-table of contents page is placed in the same relative location as the text columns on the mini-table of contents page. For example:

- The left margin of the text on the "Writer" linked page corresponds to the location of the "Writer" link on the directory, or table of contents page (see Figure 8-6).
- The left margin of text on the "Speaker" page is in the same position as the "Speaker" link on the directory page.
- The left margin of the text on the "Ad Man" page corresponds to the placement of the "Ad man" link on the directory page (see Figure 8-7).
- The left margin of the text on the "Catalyst" page corresponds to the placement of the "Catalyst" link on the directory page.

Notice, also, that the same typeface, type size, and type style are used throughout each of the pages. Alignment is always the same — in this example, flush-left. If centered headlines and subheads were used on one of the pages, the Web site's unity would be seriously compromised.

Notice that the same typeface, type size, type style, and color are always used for headlines, subheads, body copy, and sidebars (that is, client testimonials) throughout the Web site. The headlines and subheads are always set in a bold sans serif type, while a serif typeface is used for body copy and sidebars.

Writer
Put Roger C. Parker's writing ability to work for you!
Over one million readers around the world own copies of the over twenty books I've written.
Your understanding of electronics and computers goes beyond mere comprehension

Figure 8-6: Text on the "Writer" page is placed in the same position as the "Writer" header introducing the linked page.

Ad man
Applying the tenets of your Promoting Specialist concept has resulted in a history of
Roger C. Parker has helped firms like Apple Computer, Bang & Olufsen of America, Bose, Hewlett-Packard, Lexmark and Yamaha help their retailers advertise and sell more effectively.

Figure 8-7: Text placement on the "Ad Man" page corresponds to the "Ad Man" link.

On the linked pages, notice that a testimonial letter placed in a single column is separated from the double-column of text by white space. Sidebar text is always set smaller than the main body copy to set it apart from the body copy.

Repeating the Standard

Well-thought-out simplicity easily and simultaneously unifies the various pages of your Web site, subdivides your Web site into various topics, and gives each page a unique look.

By minimizing changes in the background, text, and visuals of your Web pages, you set up a *repeating standard* that unifies your Web site. This ground zero makes it easy to subdivide and color code the various sections of your Web site by making relatively minor changes on the various pages. The result will be a unique, yet memorable Web site that visitors will respect and remember.

Part III

Print Design for the Millennium

"I APPRECIATE YOUR COMPUTER HAS 256 COLORS; I JUST DON'T THINK THEY ALL HAD TO BE USED IN ONE BOOK REPORT."

In this part . . .

In the beginning, there were words, and this part helps make them shine by their placement on the page in a variety of documents. Using a marketing approach to design, you can see how to analyze your product (your printed piece), your market (your readers), and your competition (other publications competing for your readers' time and attention) so you can quickly reject inappropriate designs and identify possible solutions. Then I give you tricks to keep your readers interested once you have their attention.

Chapter 9

The Basics of Effective Print Design

In This Chapter

- Finding out the basic elements of page architecture
- Understanding importance of white space
- Understanding the importance of a grid
- Choosing the right number of columns
- Choosing and using type

As I mention in Chapter 2, the design of print communication uses many of the same tools that you use in the design of Web communication. Print offers you much greater control over your design, especially regarding color and the use of type.

With print communication you enjoy total control over typeface, type size, and the subtlest nuances of letter, line, and paragraph spacing. You also have more control over color and texture. Your choice of paper and ink, which I describe in Chapter 13, allows you to control the way your printed document looks and, most important, *feels* in the reader's hands. In addition, you can make sure that all of your readers enjoy the same-size document.

Because they're tangible — readers can touch and carry them — print documents are to easier to navigate (go from page to page) than Web pages. Readers can have the entire publication before their eyes at one time so they can easily thumb through it and find what attracts them with ease. Clicking and scrolling through your Web site takes far more time. In addition, readers can view two-page spreads (left- and right-hand pages that face each other), as well as the top and bottom halves of a page at the same time. This tangibility offers more creative flexibility because you have more options in relating the design elements, but it also creates design challenges not faced on your Web page.

Elements of Print Page Architecture

Ten basic elements of page architecture provide the basis for most print documents, regardless of whether you're producing brochures, newsletters, or long documents like proposals or instructional manuals. The purpose of this section is to help you identify the basic elements and important attributes you must work with, regardless of the specific type of document you're creating.

I cover specific types of print documents in later chapters and give you a closer look at these elements and how to manipulate them for various effects. But to get the broad picture of what those other chapters deal with, take a few moments to get an overview of these elements of page architecture, from the top to bottom (see Figure 9-1).

Headers (and footers)

Headers and footers refer to text and graphics at the top and bottom, respectively, of each page. Headers typically repeat the title of the publication and/or the chapter or section title for longer documents. (If you look at the top of the page in this book, you see the header, or running head, that IDG uses in its books; it repeats the part number and title on left-hand pages, and the chapter number and title on right-hand pages. It also includes the page number.) In newsletters, the firm or association logo and/or the newsletter's title often appear at the top of each page. Headers are especially useful in larger documents to help the reader retain their place in a document or locate where in a document certain information can be found

Headers frequently contain *rules,* or horizontal lines, that help define and visually reinforce the text area of each page.

The typeface you use in headers needs to be visually compatible with those that you use elsewhere on the page, but it must not be so prominent that the headers blend in with the body copy or so strong that the headers distract from the information on the page.

Page numbers and other information, like volume number or date, often appear in *footers* at the bottom of the page. Like headers, footers need to be noticeable enough to provide guidance without distraction. Rules along the bottom of the page that match the header rules often provide a needed touch of symmetry.

Usually, you omit headers and footers from the front pages of documents like correspondence, proposals, and training manuals to avoid a cluttered look. You also want to omit headers and footers from pages that introduce new sections of a document.

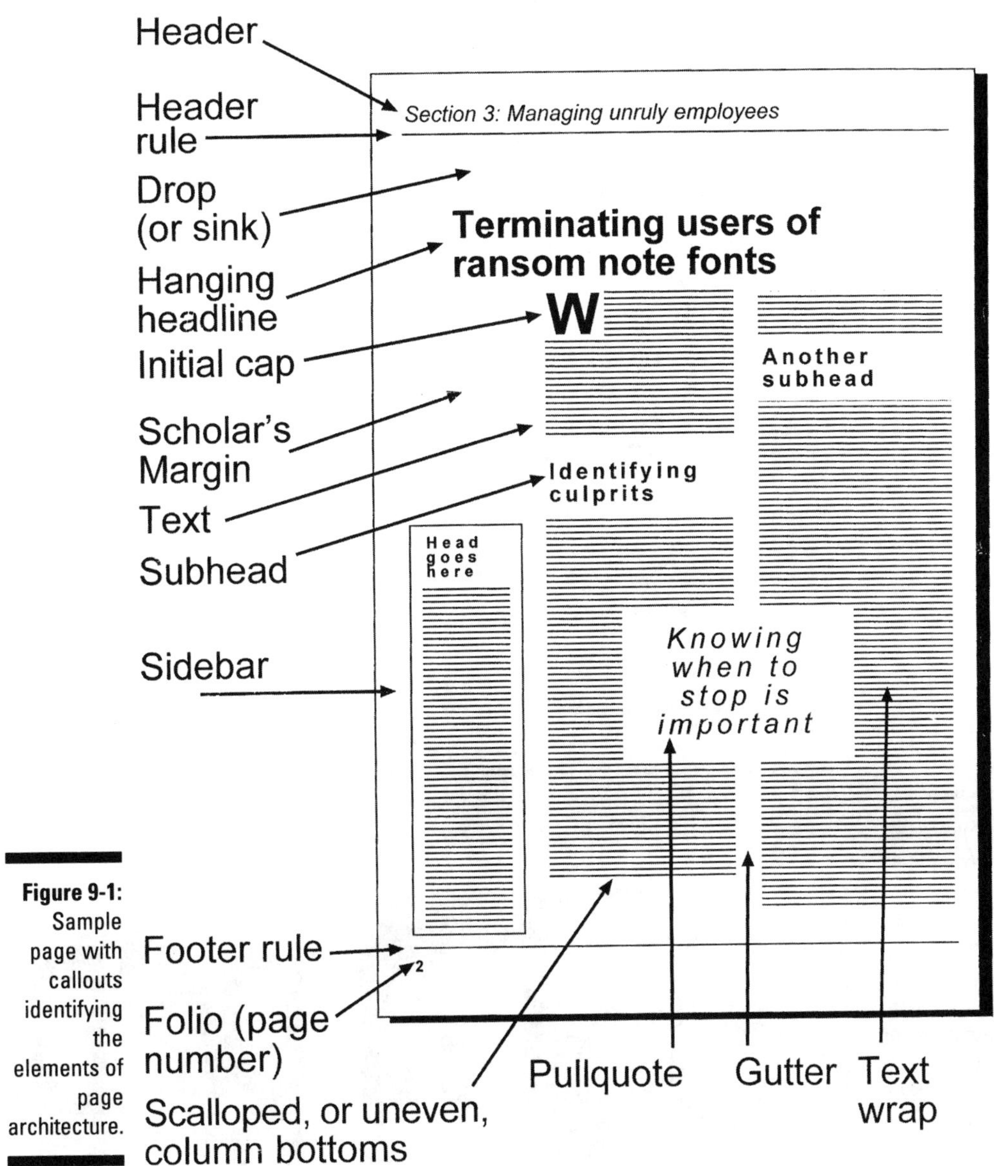

Figure 9-1: Sample page with callouts identifying the elements of page architecture.

Logos and titles

Logos and titles are similar in that you use them more to be "recognized" than to be deciphered or read. Because you don't have to worry about your logo or title actually being read, you can be more creative in your choice of typeface. You can use typefaces for logos and titles that are totally inappropriate for extended text passages like paragraphs of body copy. Take liberties with logos and titles by stretching or distorting the letters or by overlapping certain letter pairs. You can also fill letters with patterns or place them against unique textures (see Figure 9-2).

Logos differ from titles in that the designer usually includes graphic elements representing the firm's business or philosophy as part of the association's or firm's name.

You can create logos and titles, such as the newsletter name, with programs, like Adobe Illustrator or CorelDRAW!, and then save them as separate graphic files, which you can later import.

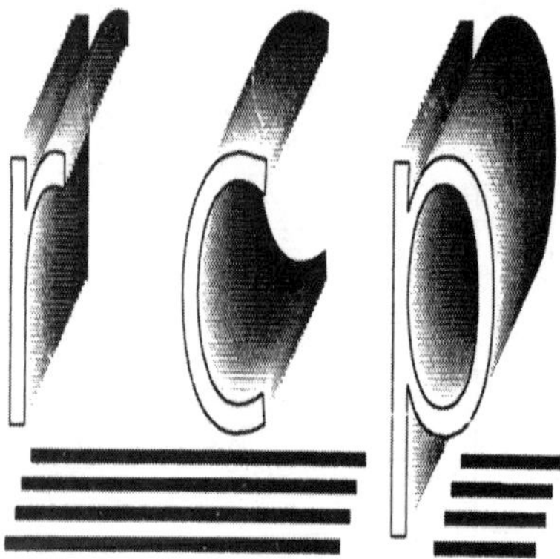

Figure 9-2: With logos and titles, you can manipulate text by stretching, distorting, or overlapping letters, filling them with unique textures or placing them against backgrounds.

By saving them as separate graphic files, you ensure that the title always appears the same for each issue. In formal documents, such as proposals or reports, the publication title and section titles need to be set in the same typeface but at a significantly larger type size as the type you use for headlines or subheads.

Headlines

Headlines differ from titles in that you design headlines to be read; therefore, headlines must offer the readers a benefit rather than just providing a memorable name. And the typeface you choose should be easily read and reflect the weight you give to the information they signal and the density and layout of the text they introduce. In other words, don't use a small headline in a 14-point light italic typeface to signal a major development in your company that requires a full-page article. Such a headline performs no useful function in this case, because readers are likely to overlook it or decide that the article it heads is not very important.

Give the writing of headlines and the selection of headline type a great deal of attention when creating advertisements and brochures, because the headline almost single-handedly determines whether or not a person reads the material.

Easy-to-read headlines that offer a benefit encourage readers to pay attention to the text that follows; light-weight or hard-to-read headlines that don't tell the reader anything he or she cares to know encourage readers to turn the page.

To a great degree, how well you handle the typeface, typesize, and placement of headlines (not to mention what they say) determines your success as a desktop publisher. Easy-to-read headlines encourage readers to continue; hard-to-read headlines usually don't get read at all.

Headlines must form a strong visual contrast with the body copy they introduce. You can create this contrast by choosing a different but compatible typeface for the head than for the body copy (as in a Univers headline over Times Roman body copy), by setting the headline significantly larger than the body copy (for instance, an 18- or 24-point headline over 10- or 12-point text), or by setting the headline in a bolder, or heavier, typeface. Often you obtain best results by using a combination of the above techniques (a 24-point Univers Bold headline over 12-point Times Roman body text), depending on the amount of text the headline introduces and the role of the text in the information hierarchy.

Three things to avoid:

- **Never set headlines in all uppercase type.** Although newcomers to desktop publishing often set headlines in uppercase type to make them easier to read, the exact opposite usually happens. Headlines set entirely in uppercase type are harder to read because the words lack the unique shapes that readers rely on to identify the letters (see Figure 9-3).

Figure 9-3: Readers rely on word shapes to recognize individual words.

- **Never underline headlines.** Underlined headlines are a surefire indication of newcomer status to the world of desktop publishing. Underlining obscures the descenders, the portions of letters that extend below the baseline (the invisible line the words rest on) and makes the words harder to read.
- **Never center headlines out of habit.** Just because desktop publishing software makes a technique easy to use, doesn't mean it's effective! Often flush-left headlines stand out better because the white space is concentrated to the right of the headline.

Subheads

Subheads are one of the most overlooked elements in effective publication design. Use subheads to break up long text passages into manageable, bite-sized chunks.

Subheads advertise the text they introduce. Each subhead provides a glimpse into the content of the text and invites skimmers to become readers.

To succeed, subheads, like headlines, need to form a strong contrast with adjacent text; readers may overlook subheads that blend into adjacent text. Often subheads fail in their mission because the designer simply set them in the bold or italic (or bold-italic) version of the same size and typeface chosen for the body copy, which does not form a strong enough contrast with the adjacent body copy.

Here are a few rules to guide you:

- **Use contrasting typeface.** Subheads work best when set in a contrasting typeface. Try to use the same typeface that you use for your headlines, rather than simply using the bold version of body copy typeface.
- **Use extra space to emphasize subheads.** Place extra space above the subheads. The extra space helps emphasize a definite break with the preceding text and keeps the subhead connected to the text it introduces.
- **Use graphic accents to emphasize subheads.** Place horizontal rules, or lines, above them to further emphasize the subheads.
- **Use hanging subheads.** Hanging subheads begin to the left of the left margin of the text they introduce. A hanging subhead is especially effective in single-column documents, like proposals or reports.

- **Use color with care.** Contrary to what you may expect, text set in color is often less noticeable than text set in black. When you use color for your text, add extra size or weight to the typeface to make sure your subheads stand out.
- **Don't center subheads out of habit.** Subheads set flush-left often stand out better than centered subheads.

Body text

The paragraphs of your body copy most likely contain the bulk of your message in a print piece. Therefore, for successful desktop publishing, your body copy has to look easy to read. Here are some of the things to look for when selecting easy-to-read body copy.

- **Choose the correct text alignment.** The two most popular options are flush-left/ragged-right and justified. In a ragged-right text arrangement, the right-hand margin does not align exactly. Each line has its own length and words seldom need to be hyphenated because you don't need to fill out the line. The key to a good ragged-right layout is to watch the variation in line length along the right margin so that no line is too long or too short in relation to the lines above and below it and the text block as a whole. You want a graceful rag that gently leads the reader from one line to the next. Avoid a staggered look that interweaves very short and very long lines, which is tiring to the reader. The body text of this book is set ragged right.

Justified alignment occurs when each line must be the exact same length. The sidebars of this book use a justified alignment. Your word processing or page layout software assures the alignment of the first and last letters in each line by incrementally expanding or contracting the letter spacing. Justified text usually has a number of words that need to be hyphenated in order to avoid awkward spacing within the line. Justified type is used to give a traditional, precise, more formal appearance. Newspapers use justified text because it can fit more words on a line, maximizing the space available for text.

- **Choose the right typeface.** Typefaces differ in their shape as well as their *density,* which is the number of words that fit in a given line of type. Some typefaces work best for headlines, and others work best for body copy. Success comes from choosing the right typeface at the right time as well as avoiding overly stylized typefaces that call too much attention to themselves.
- **Choose the right type size and line spacing (leading).** Avoid long lines of small text because they are a certain readership killer. Your success in creating easy-to-read text depends on choosing the right type size and line spacing.
- **Hyphenate always**. Hyphenation refers to splitting words that are too long to fit on one line over two lines. Hyphenation is as necessary with flush-left/ragged-right text as it is with justified text, although you are not likely to use it as often. (Remember, a hyphen stack of more than two is a no-no anywhere.)
- **Use bulleted and numbered lists to break up long passages of type.** Use bullets when the order of the listed items is not important; use numbers when priority and sequence are necessary.

End-of-story symbols

Small end-of-story symbols add character to publications such as newsletters. Symbols signal readers that they have come to the end of a story. The best symbols reflect the nature of the communication. Instead of letters and numbers, many typeface designs consist of symbols or small illustrations, called picture fonts, with more becoming available each day. Figure 9-4 gives an example of such fonts.

Initial caps

Initial caps are oversized capital letters that designers use to indicate the beginning of an important article or all articles. (Choose either method, but be consistent.) Sometimes, smaller versions of the initial cap are used to

Figure 9-4: Many typefaces consist of small icons or drawings rather than letters. These are perfect for end-of-story symbols.

separate sections of articles. Initial caps work as magnets drawing the reader's eyes from the headline to the beginning of an article. You can also use initial caps within articles to provide visual relief and break up long passages as well as introduce new topics.

You have several types of initial caps from which to choose:

- **Raised caps:** extend above the first line of type. Raised caps force space above the first line of type and open up text columns.
- **Drop caps:** extend into the paragraph of text. Drop caps need to be at least as tall as three lines of text, and the drop cap's baseline must align with one of the lines of text.
- **Adjacent caps:** appear in the margin before the text. These work best with one- and two-column documents where you have the space to place the initial cap to the left of the text. The baseline needs to align with one of the lines of text.

You can find many typefaces designed specifically for use as initial caps, which can project an artistic or classical image. When choosing a typeface for initial caps, several options are available:

- The simplest option is to choose a larger size of the same typeface you use for the body copy, which is often the *default* choice. But, like most defaults, its use can lead to a uniform look that may appear too conservative or boring.

- You can also choose the same typeface that you use for headlines and subheads. This builds more visual interest into your documents and projects a more contemporary image while maintaining continuity of design.
- You can find many typefaces designed specifically for use as initial caps. These often project a classic image, approaching the first use of initial caps in Medieval manuscripts when people drew initial caps with painstaking care.

Visuals and captions

Visuals include information-communicating graphics, such as pie charts, flow charts, graphs, illustrations, organizational charts, tables, and scanned photographs.

Whenever possible, strive to replace text with visuals. Visuals permit you to communicate information and relationships at a glance. Often information and relationships that get lost in a text format become easy to understand when you use graphics instead. Chapter 14 gives you all the details about business graphics like charts and graphs. Chapter 18 looks at photographs and illustrations.

Illustrations and photographs need captions that describe the contents and importance of the visual. Captions work best when you set them in a small typeface that clearly stands apart from nearby body copy. A few tips concerning captions:

- **Do not set captions in italics out of habit.** Try to use a contrasting typeface rather than the italicized version of the typeface you use for the body copy.
- **Avoid long lines of small type.** Don't use captions that are so long that they require several left-to-right horizontal movements of the reader's eyes.
- **Don't hyphenate captions.** Frequently captions contain proper nouns, which aren't hyphenated. To avoid hyphenating captions, use flush-left/ragged-right text alignment.
- **Don't set captions in color.** You usually set captions in a smaller type size than body copy, so captions set in a color other than black are hard to read.

Sidebars

Sidebars are just what you think they'd be — blocks of text dealing with secondary, or side, issues that are placed to the side of the main articles and clearly separated from them in some way. Sidebars can further help break long articles into manageable, bite-sized chunks. Use sidebars for visual interest and when you want to focus the reader's attention on a topic that would break the continuity if you covered it in the longer adjacent article.

You can set sidebars apart from the main article in several ways:

- **Place sidebars inside a box.** Although this technique is popular (you see it in the sidebars of this book), it is so popular that it's almost a cliché. Strive for more creative approaches when you can, but this one is always safe.
- **Screen the background behind the sidebar text.** Screening the background is another popular technique (again, you see the sidebars screened in this book), so use it with care. Screening (using a shade of black or some other color) can make the text harder to read by weakening the foreground-background contrast readers rely on to recognize words.
- **Use a contrasting typeface.** A more creative approach is to set the sidebar in a contrasting typeface. This avoids the familiar boxed look and projects a more contemporary image. (The sidebars in this book also use a contrasting typeface.)

Footnotes and endnotes

Footnotes and endnotes are primarily used in reports and proposals, though you may occasionally see them in a brochure. You use them to reference source material, add information relevant to the text but out of place in it, or note humorous asides. Set references to specific sources in a significantly smaller typeface than what you use for body copy. Footnotes appear on the same page as the text to which they refer; endnotes appear all together at the end of the document.

Elements of Page Layout

After you understand the individual elements of print page architecture, you need to look at the tools you can use to assemble those elements into finished pages.

White space: Your secret weapon

White space is the most important design tool at your disposal, although it is merely the absence of text and graphics. Beginning designers often make the mistake of trying to cram too much into a page, seeing white space as wasted space. White space performs several useful functions, depending on where you place it on the page. The following describe standard areas of white space:

- **Margins:** White space at the top, bottom, and sides of a page or surrounding an advertisement provides a visual buffer that emphasizes the contents of the page. Practically, white space provides a place for your readers to hold your publication without their thumbs obscuring the contents of the page.
- **Bleeds:** The absence of white space surrounding a page is a bleed. Bleeds occur when text or a graphic element, such as a photograph, extends to the physical edges of a page. When used with restraint, bleeds add drama and emphasis. They expand the area of the page that you can use for text or graphics, and they darken the side of your publication to "advertise" a special treatment. Bleeds can add to the cost of your publication because they require a larger paper size, which is then trimmed to provide an even color through to the edge of the page.
- **Frames:** White space draws the reader's eyes like a magnet. By surrounding the headlines with sufficient white space, or "breathing room," you can greatly increase the impact of your headlines and visuals.
- **Gutters:** Gutters are the narrow space between text columns. Gutters prevent readers from jumping across two columns of type rather than continuing to read in the same column.
- **Drop:** The significant amount of white space between the top of a page and the first line of type in a text column is a drop, or a sink. By using a consistent and significant amount of white space to separate text columns from the top of each page, you help emphasize headlines as well as build page-to-page continuity.

The one thing to remember about white space is that the reader shouldn't notice it. Your page should look open and easy-to-read, not empty or disjointed.

Columns

Text in newsletters and brochures rarely extends completely from the left margin of a page to the right margin. Instead, you usually place text in two or more parallel columns. There are several reasons for this.

- **Long lines of text are difficult to read.** Because your readers' eyes have to make numerous left-to-right movements as they read each line, scanning groups of two or three words can be tough. (Readers don't read, or decode, individual letters and words; they scan groups of words and recognize them by their shape.) Long lines are tiring because they require several left-to-right movements. In addition, it is easy for readers to get lost at the end of long line of text and inadvertently return to the beginning of the line (called *doubling*) or jump down two lines.
- **Columns increase word density per page.** Because type size and line length are related, you can get more words on each page of your documents by using columns, which enable you to use a smaller type size.

A page containing a single column of type contains fewer words than the same page containing two columns of type set in a slightly smaller type size.

Grid

Grids form the basis for handling white space and columns. Grids consist of a non-printing framework of horizontal and vertical lines, sort of like graph paper, which define the placement of margins, gutters, and text columns on a page. Grids provide a flexible framework for placing text columns and other page elements.

- Grids are important to maintaining page-to-page consistency. You use grids to keep consistent margins on all your pages and surround your headlines and other page elements with consistent amounts of white space. Grids also enable you to align page elements correctly and consistently, such as aligning photographs with the top line of your text if you prefer.
- Although you may think grids are restricting, in fact, grids add to your creative options because you don't need to have a one-to-one relationship between the number of column grids and the number of text columns. You can vary the way you place the text columns and visuals on the underlying grid. For example, you can have a six-column grid for purposes of alignment, but your page will only show three columns to the reader if you choose to place text across two columns of the grid.

One of the most flexible formats is the five-column format. Here are some of the ways you can employ it:

- You can have a single column of text extending the width of all five columns. (But doing this is likely to create hard-to-read text columns.) One reason for doing this rather than simply starting off with a one-column grid is that it enables you to consistently align any charts or other graphics you may have.
- You can use four of the five columns for a wide column of text and leave the fifth column empty or place small text and visual elements in it. The difference the white space adds to the page may surprise you. On one-sided documents, you can place the white space always to the left of the text. On right-hand pages of two-sided documents, the empty column can appear to the right so that the white space pushes the reader's attention to the center of the two-page spread.
- You can use two double-columns of text and reserve the fifth column for small text or visual elements (see Figure 9-5).

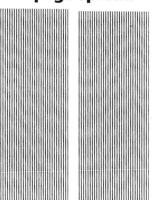

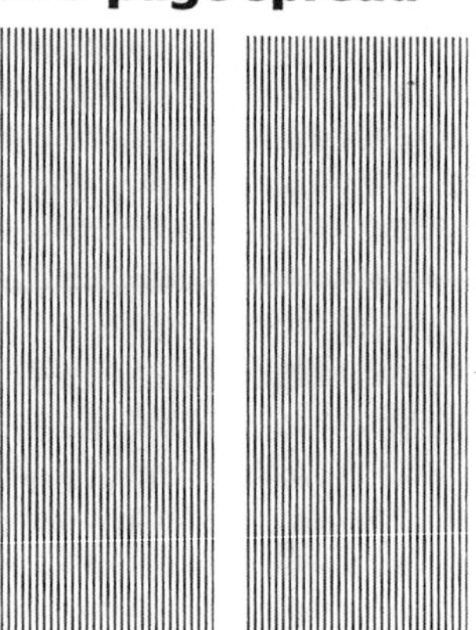

Figure 9-5: A two-page spread with double columns of text on each page and white space at the page edges.

- You can combine a three-column wide visual or text element with a double-column of text.
- For pages containing numerous bits of short text or visual elements, you can use either four or five single columns of text.

For more about using grids and white space, see Chapter 10 on newsletters.

Graphic accents

You can use several types of graphic accents as visual design elements and to add selective emphasis to your pages. These include:

- **Borders:** These consist of lines at the top, bottom, and/or sides of your pages. You can box pages, surrounding the page on all four sides with lines of equal thickness. Or you can omit the side borders and use lines of different thickness at the top and bottom of each page, with the heavier line at the bottom to *weight* the page.
- **Rules:** These are lines that appear above or below subheads in order to emphasize a definite break in the text. You can place dashed lines, for instance, to emphasize coupons.
- **Reverses and screens:** Reverse type is white type that appears against a black background. Screens occur when type appears against a gray background. You can vary the degree of grayness (it's actually a percentage of black or whatever color ink you're using). The sidebars in this book are screened.

  Reverses and screens can be extremely powerful design tools, but use them with restraint. In general, avoid reverses of small, serif typefaces. Large, bold sans serif type works much better when you reverse it. And keep your screens light, not more than 20 percent behind text, or you won't be able to see the type clearly enough to read it.
- **Drop shadows:** These can add an illusion of depth to illustrations and photographs by adding a thicker border to the right and bottom edges of photographs.

Type: The Medium for Your Message

Next to white space, type is your most important design tool. The choice and use of the right typeface is part art and part science. Typesetting was once an apprenticeship occupation requiring specialized training that took a person years of study and work to master. Now, of course, everyone has access to numerous typefaces, and people expect designers to use them as effectively as those who spent 20 years mastering the topic.

Here is a brief overview of what you need to know to use type effectively, as well as an introduction to the terminology you use when working with type. (Check out Chapter 19 to get more details about type.)

Design

Typeface refers to the shape of the characters. You need to be aware of two key terms when considering type.

Readability refers to the ease with which readers can read extended text passages. It is a measure of speed and efficiency and determines how easy it is for readers to understand long passages of text.

Legibility refers to the ease with which individual letters stand out. Legibility is a measure of how effective your titles and headlines are. Legibility measures how far away a reader can be and still read the letters as well as decipher the individual words.

Although thousands of typeface designs are available, there are basically four major categories of type, shown in Figure 9-6: serif, sans serif, script, and decorative.

Serif (Minion)	Sans serif (Frutiger)
PANOSE Abcdefghijklmnopqrs tuvwxyz	PANOSE Abcdefghijklmnop qrstuvwxyz
Script (Brush Script)	Decorative (Stencil)
PANOSE Abcdefghijklmnopqrstuv wxyz	PANOSE ABCDEFGHIJKLMN OPQRSTUVWXYZ

Figure 9-6: Examples of each of the four typeface categories.

- **Serif typefaces** consist of tiny horizontal strokes at the edges of each letter. These strokes reinforce each letter's unique shape as well as aid reading by leading the reader's eyes from letter to letter. Serif typefaces usually differ in thickness; their vertical strokes are usually thicker than horizontal elements. Serifs can be thick or thin, of equal thickness, tapered, or rounded. Times Roman and Century Old Style are popular serif designs. Serif type is usually the best choice for body copy.
- **Sans serif typefaces** are simpler and lack the finishing strokes of serif typefaces. Sans serif typefaces are usually, but not always, composed of strokes of equal weight. Arial, Helvetica, and Univers are popular sans serif typefaces that designers frequently use for headlines and subheads. Sans serif typefaces more nearly resemble the way you were taught to print as a child.
- **Script typefaces** resemble handwriting and project an informal image. Sometimes the letters join together, other times the letters don't touch each other. Script typefaces are ideal for informal purposes, such as invitations, which contain relatively small amounts of text.
- **Decorative typefaces** are designed to project a specific image. Some may remind you of Art Deco movie theaters from the 1920s, and others resemble stenciled lettering on packing cases. Still others can look like instrument panels or the screens of early computers. Decorative typefaces generally are not meant to be read in large text blocks, but are used for headlines or accent type.

In general, serif designs excel at readability while sans serif designs sacrifice readability for legibility. (That's why so many billboards are in sans serif type; the amount of type is limited but you need to read it quickly and easily at a distance.)

Contrast refers to the amount of difference between the thick and thin strokes of a typeface design. Contrast aids readability by providing visual interest and by emphasizing each character's unique shape.

Style

Style refers to modifications to a typeface design to provide selective emphasis.

Bold text consists of thicker strokes than regular, or Roman, text. Avoid setting too much type in bold because the thicker strokes contain less white space within the character, making it more difficult for readers to recognize each character. Reserve the use of bold type for headlines, subheads, and occasionally captions.

A true *italic* typeface has been redesigned and angled to closely resemble handwriting. A close analysis shows that many of the letters are completely different from the normal type in the same typeface. Like any spice you use for seasoning, use italics with restraint. Long passages of italics are hard to read because the characters are narrower, and the reader has to adapt to the angle.

Oblique typeface, however, is simply Roman type that a computer slants.

People often overuse *bold-italic*. Bold-italic is difficult to read because the slanted letters and the thicker characters reduce readability. Use it in small doses, such as for subheads and the occasional sidebar.

Although you can use underline as a style attribute, it's best if you don't use it at all. Underlines interfere, or bump into, the descenders of letters, like *g*, *p*, and *y*, which extend below the type's baseline.

Weight

Many typefaces are available in more than Roman and bold. Most sans serif designs offer *light* and *black* (or *heavy*) alternatives. These designs have been redrawn for added impact. Although not suitable for body copy (in most cases), light and heavy options allow you to "voice" your titles and headlines, depending on the number of words they contain, and enable you to get the emphasis you desire (see Figure 9-7).

Fewer serif typefaces offer weight options. Some, like Times Roman, offer semi-bold and extra-bold, which permit you to add slight emphasis within paragraphs and create extra-strong subheads.

Width

Most sans serif typefaces are available in specially redrawn, or condensed, designs. Condensed designs permit you to add emphasis to headlines and subheads without taking up too much space.

Condensed does not mean that it is distorted or squished; rather, these typefaces have been specially redrawn for maximum impact. Their *x-height* is raised to increase the amount of white space within each character, which helps maintain legibility.

Frutiger Light
Frutiger Regular
Frutiger Bold
Frutiger Ultra Black

For impact,
Contrast Light with Ultra Black

Figure 9-7: Typefaces with different weights offer extra options for designing visually pleasing, highly communi-cative pages.

X-height: Typeface design for Generation X

Each typeface has its own distinct x-height. X-height is a fundamental design characteristic and refers to the height of lowercase vowels like a, e, i, o, and u.

When set the same size, typefaces with a low x-height usually appear smaller on the page than typefaces with a high x-height. Low x-height typefaces increase the word density of your documents by permitting more words per line and, hence, more words per page.

Low x-height serif typefaces include Garamond and Minion. Times Roman has an average x-height. Bookman and Sabon are examples of serif typefaces that have a high x-height.

Most sans serif typefaces have a significantly higher x-height than serif typefaces — a 12-point Times Roman (with serifs) and a 9-point Arial (without serifs) look the same size.

Letter, line, and paragraph spacing

One of the major tools that separates the experienced from inexperienced (or uncaring) desktop publishers is the amount of attention and care a designer places on letter, line, and paragraph spacing. Here are some things to be aware of when dealing with type:

- Letter spacing affects both readability and legibility. You can make major improvements in the appearance of your print documents by adjusting the letter spacing of both headlines and body copy.
- Tracking and kerning are two terms you need to be familiar with. *Tracking* refers to increasing or reducing letter spacing throughout a document by the same amount (or percentage). Most software programs permit you to adjust tracking by using terms like tight and loose. *Kerning* refers to adjusting the letter spacing of selected letter pairs in headlines set at a large size.

Letter spacing greatly impacts the appearance of your print documents (but not yet the appearance of your Web pages).

Special characters

The previous section just touches on some of the many ways you can fine-tune the appearance of the words in your print publications. Figure 9-8 shows just a few of the ways to use type as a design and communication tool:

- **Ligatures** improve the appearance of body copy by eliminating bumping letter pairs, like lowercase f i and f f combinations. Ligatures combine two or more characters into a single, better-looking character by omitting or by repositioning elements that interfere with each other.
- **Display or titling fonts** are for use with large size type. These fonts preserve the integrity of the typeface design that can be lost when typefaces designed for setting at 12 points are set to a large size.
- **Swash characters** add emphasis to the first or last letters in a word and provide a distinctive note to your publications.

Your Image in Print

Because traditional print media offer you so much control over type, color, size, paper, and special printing and folding effects (see Chapter 13), you have great power over the image your message projects. You can define image in subjective terms like youthful, informal, conservative, classic, cutting edge, or trendy. Characteristics like these define your image in print:

Without ligatures	With ligatures	Swash letters
ff offense	ﬀ oﬀense	ABCDEF
fi final	ﬁ ﬁnal	GH IJKL
fl flush	ﬂ ﬂush	MNOPQ
ffi official	ﬃ oﬃcial	RSTUV
ffl affluent	ﬄ aﬄuent	WXYZ

Figure 9-8: Ligatures avoid the problems caused by bumping letters; swash characters add flair to titles or body copy used in poetry or formal invitations.

- **Typeface:** Serif typefaces project a more conservative image than sans serif designs.
- **Type size:** Documents with significant differences in type size project a more contemporary or informal image than those with fewer type size variations.

- **X-height:** Typefaces with low x-heights project a more conservative or classic image than those with high x-heights.
- **Alignment:** Most consider flush-left/ragged-right body copy text more informal than justified text.
- **Balance:** Asymmetrical pages project a more informal image than balanced pages or two-page spreads.
- **Colors:** Bright colors, like reds and greens, project a more youthful appearance than deep rich colors, like blues and purples.

Because you have so many page layout and typographic tools at your disposal, the process of creating an image may seem overwhelming. Success, however, is not as difficult to attain as it may seem if you have a good smattering of plain old common sense.

Here are two common-sense considerations to guide your efforts:

- **Strive for balance.** Balance is a term that may sound artsy and conceptual, but is basically easy to deal with if you can identify the image you want to project. To start with, there are two types of balance: symmetrical and asymmetrical.
    - *Symmetry* refers to balanced elements or balanced pages and means roughly equal top/bottom and/or left/right balance.
    - *Asymmetry* refers to unbalanced pages where large text or visual elements "outweigh" or overpower small elements, yet the page as a whole appears unified, not cluttered or disjointed.

  Symmetry and asymmetry can work for you or against you. Choose symmetrical layouts if you want to project a quiet, conservative image. Choose asymmetrical layouts if you want to communicate a contemporary or youthful image.

- **Pay attention to hierarchy.** The degree of emphasis you place on a text or visual element needs to be directly proportional to the importance of the message it communicates. You denote important elements by making them larger, bolder, or more distinctive. Items of less importance need to be relatively smaller, lighter, and less noticeable.

What this means, of course, is that design is not art as much as it is logic. Your design image becomes easier to define to the extent you understand the message you want to convey and can identify the importance of the various text and visual elements that comprise it.

Chapter 10

Newsletters: Up Close and Personal

In This Chapter

- Why newsletters?
- What's in a newsletter?
- Nameplates, mastheads, headlines, and more
- What can a grid do for you?
- A primer on Editing Newsletters For Dummies

For many associations and businesses, a newsletter can be the single most effective form of print marketing because it builds your credibility over time with your various audiences. Newsletters offer tremendous creative and marketing potential, providing a forum for you to tell your story and reinforce it — updating it at frequent intervals. In contrast to the limited real estate available in 30- and 60-second radio spots and small newspaper ads, newsletters offer the space to provide numerous details.

A quick primer on newsletters with before-and-after samples of design is at the end of this chapter.

Why Newsletters?

Newsletters enable you to couch your advertising message in editorial terms. Marketing messages that people may dismiss as "advertising" become credible when you communicate those messages as newsworthy articles. With newsletters, you can personalize your firm by introducing your employees to your customers and stressing their competence and zeal. Finally, newsletters permit you to communicate information about your firm that just doesn't comfortably lend itself to advertisements or brochures.

Newsletters are also cost-effective. With newsletters, you can save money by targeting distribution to only serious prospects, who previously expressed an interest in your product or service, and your customers, who have already voted with their wallets, and thus are more likely than strangers to buy from you again — or recommend you to their friends. Newsletters are personal in that there is a certain "down home" friendliness to them that glossy four-color brochures and direct-mail pieces lack. Newsletters provide inside information about your company, your philosophy, and the people who work for you and with you. Newsletters can offer a personal touch in an impersonal world.

Newsletters are far more difficult than they may seem at first glance, however. The typical newsletter contains numerous text and graphic elements that you must assemble carefully, often under last-minute deadline conditions and with insufficient budget and time resources.

The fastest, easiest, and lease expensive way to consistently produce a quality newsletter is to plan your newsletters to be as simple and practical as possible so you don't let your customers, prospects — and yourself — down. If you can't guarantee the timeliness of your newsletter, you're better off not producing it at all. If you're pressed for time or ideas, stick to your basic message instead of getting too creative and overly ambitious. Don't undertake more of a challenge than you can live up to.

It's All a Matter of Timing

When you consider the characteristics of a successful newsletter program, on-time performance and consistency are far more important than page count and number of colors.

Assuming that your newsletter is well thought out so that its content is something your audience actually wants to receive, a newsletter printed on two sides of a single sheet of paper that arrives every month is better than a four-page newsletter that arrives every other month or an eight-page newsletter that arrives every quarter. The goal of a successful newsletter program is to keep your name in front of your customers and prospects while associating that name with an image of professionalism, competence, caring, and customer service. The more often your marketing message shows up and is welcome in their mailbox, the more successful you are going to be.

Consistency and quality are the essence of newsletter success. A single-page, two-sided newsletter that arrives every month filled with information the reader wants to know is far better than an eight-page newsletter that comes out sporadically with "filler" material or sales hype that is easily discarded. If you have no real news for your audience, don't have a newsletter.

The search for perfection torpedoes more newsletter marketing programs than any other single factor. Remember that your goal is not to win awards, but to write a "letter containing news" to your various publics — customers, prospective customers, supporters, colleagues, constituents, or friends. If you attempt too much and don't keep on schedule, the contents of your newsletter may be old news by the time your newsletter arrives.

The Parts of a Newsletter

Newsletters are surprisingly complicated. Each newsletter must accommodate a constantly changing mix of text and graphic elements. Despite this variety, you find similar elements in most successful newsletters.

Successful newsletters reflect a great deal of page-to-page consistency, which helps the reader know where to go and what to look for as he or she reads through your newsletter. To maintain this consistency, you base the inside pages on the same column grid and typographic choices that you choose for the front page. Figures 10-1 and 10-2 demonstrate the internal carryover of the tone set by the front page.

Nameplate

The nameplate, or newsletter title, is the most prominent element on the front page of your newsletter. Like your firm's or association's logo, the nameplate is there to be recognized rather than read. It is like a familiar face that your reader encounters in a sea of faces at a concert or sporting event.

Nameplates should not occupy more than 20 percent of the space on the front page of your newsletter. Nameplates are normally along the top of your newsletters, but can also be run vertically along the left-hand side of the front page.

One of the biggest challenges with your newsletter is coming up with a name. Here are a few keys to successful newsletter titles:

- Newsletter nameplates need to offer a benefit. Which would you rather read: *The Roger C. Parker Newsletter* or *The Desktop Publisher's TimeSaver*? The former is a brag-and-boast title that doesn't offer readers a benefit or explain what type of contents they are likely to encounter inside. *The Desktop Publisher's TimeSaver,* on the other hand, targets its market and identifies a clear benefit for reading.

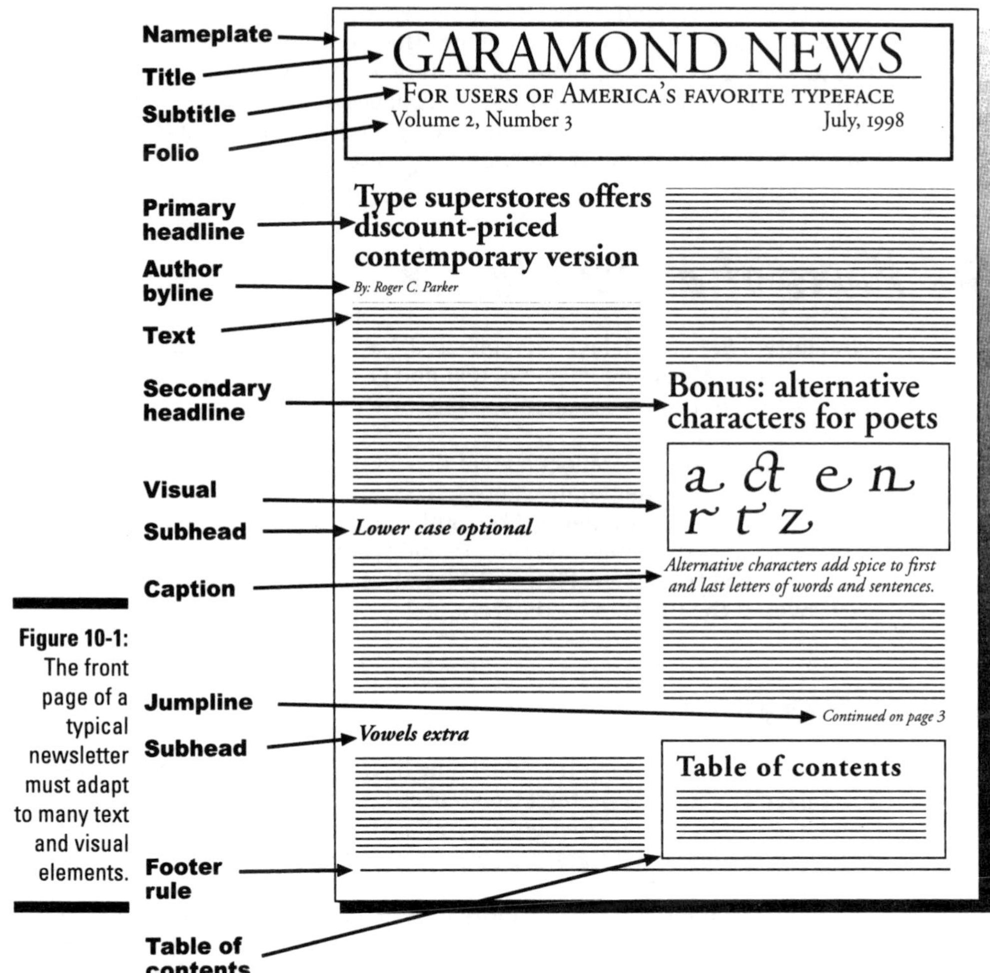

Figure 10-1: The front page of a typical newsletter must adapt to many text and visual elements.

- Shorter is always better. The best newsletter titles are the shortest; they telegraph rather than explain their contents and their intended market. Most important, you can set shorter titles in larger type sizes, helping the nameplate to stand out better by making it easier to recognize.
- Newsletters need typographic contrast. Instead of setting each word in the title in the same typeface and type size, consider emphasizing the most important word and de-emphasizing longer, or merely supportive, words.
- Avoid unnecessary graphic elements. Often, you see newsletter nameplates boxed or placed against screened backgrounds. Always ask yourself: "Does this graphic element support, or detract, from my message?"

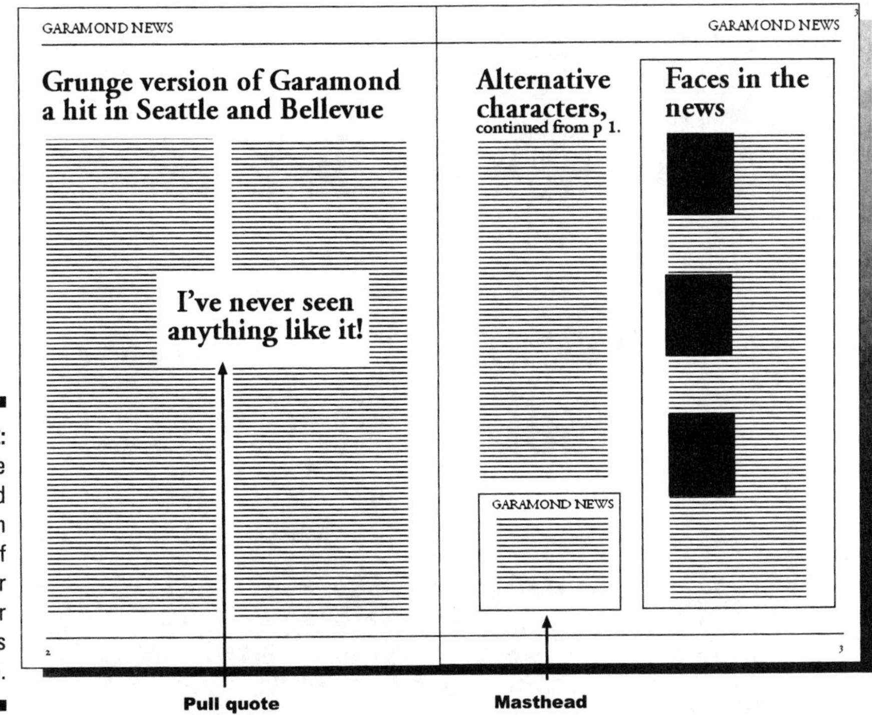

Figure 10-2: The page layout and typeface on the front of your newsletter continues inside.

A hierarchical approach to newsletter nameplates stresses the most important word, the key word that identifies the editorial focus of the newsletter or its intended audience. This word, or phrase, should be set significantly larger than supportive words, such as the name of the firm or association publishing or sponsoring the newsletter or amplifying the editorial or audience focus (see Figure 10-3).

You also commonly see newsletter nameplates centered, primarily out of a habit that dates back to grammar school homework assignments. Often, you can obtain a better appearance if you set the nameplate flush-left or flush-right and align it with the grid that forms the framework for the newsletter. By using this method, you anchor your nameplate to one side or the other rather than letting it float in the middle where it can get lost. This method also creates breathing space to the left or right of the title, helping it stand out.

In Figure 10-4, you can see the cumulative effect of introducing typographic contrast into a newsletter while aligning the various title elements flush-left and flush-right with the second column of the underlying grid.

Nowhere School
Administrative District
Parent-Teacher
News

Figure 10-3: Emphasize the shortest and most important word.

Western Montana
CelebrityVisitor
Watch the stars gather to see the stars!

Western Montana
CelebrityVisitor
Watch the stars gather to see the stars!

Figure 10-4: A series of relatively minor changes to the boring nameplate above creates a nameplate that's more appropriate for its intended market.

Folio information

Folio information refers to the issue date, and, if appropriate, the volume and issue number that needs to accompany your newsletter's nameplate. (Folio is a printer's prose for a page in a book and its page number.) Folio information is reference information, which doesn't really offer information-hungry or savings-starved readers a benefit except to know how current the publication is, how regularly it's produced, and, in the case of a volume number, its longevity.

Make the issue date noticeable, yet not excessively prominent. Don't make folio text too large. On too many newsletters, the issue date is so prominent that it competes with the headlines for attention.

Likewise, avoid cluttering the nameplate area with association seals and business logos. These work better at the bottom of the page so that the title can emerge with clarity. If you want the logo to be part of your nameplate,

Ten ways to create a newsletter nameplate

1. Emphasize the most important word.

In most cases, some words are more important than others. Emphasize the most important words by making them larger or heavier than lesser words. For example, set the important word or words in a Heavy typeface and lesser words in a Light version of the same typeface. You can also experiment with serif/sans serif contrast as well as style contrast — try using italics in one of the words.

2. Add borders.

By themselves, large words often appear to "float" on the page. Use one or more horizontal rules to frame the words and/or anchor the nameplate to the page. Be careful with four-sided boxes, however, as they may appear trite.

3. Add a background.

Reverse one or more words out of a black or colored background, but don't feel that all the words have to be reversed. Try reversing the most important word, or the shortest or longest. Be creative. Also experiment with placing one or more words against shaded or colored backgrounds.

4. Avoid long titles.

Because it's often easier to add impact to short words set in large type, try to break cumbersome long titles into a short title with a longer subtitle that amplifies its meaning.

5. Allow selected letters to touch or overlap.

To create a distinct icon out of a series of individual letters, use a drawing program to modify letter spacing and allow selected letters to touch or overlap. If you have access to a font editor, try adding or removing serifs or making other alterations that change "off-the-shelf" letters into eye-catching graphics.

6. Bleed backgrounds and graphic accents.

To make your nameplate look larger than it is, bleed the background or one of the text or border elements to extend to the physical edge of the page. Doing this avoids an inadvertent "white frame" that makes the nameplate appear smaller.

7. Align the nameplate with one of the text columns.

A centered nameplate often appears to "float" above the accompanying text and graphics rather than being solidly anchored to them. Unless you have a specific design reason for centering the text on your nameplate, try left-aligning it with the underlying grid.

8. Add equal spacing between letters.

Many page layout and word processing programs offer a Force Justification option that can automatically space letters equally across a column or a page to create an interesting visual contrast between a short word set large across the top of a long word set smaller. Just make sure that the letters aren't spaced so far apart as to make the words too difficult to read.

9. Use right alignment.

Experiment with right alignment, especially if the first line of the title is shorter than the second. This little-used technique builds white space to the left of the nameplate for an interesting effect.

10. Eliminate unnecessary words, symbols, and graphic elements.

You don't need to put "newsletter" in your title. Readers will usually recognize that your publication is a newsletter and not confuse it with an advertisement, brochure, or bill from the phone company. Let the obvious speak for itself.

run it in a smaller size than the text of your title and position it carefully so the logo does not become your message. The point is to let your nameplate be a nameplate and not a billboard for your logo.

Table of contents

Following the nameplate, the table of contents needs to be the next noticeable element because it permits readers to locate articles of interest easily.

Avoid clichés when creating your newsletter's table of contents. Clichés are old-standbys that you see so often you think they're engraved in stone. Cliché treatments of tables of contents that you typically encounter include

- **Unnecessary boxes:** You don't need to place your table of contents in a box. Alternatives include just placing horizontal rules above and below the newsletter contents, or you can omit the border completely and use a contrasting typeface to emphasize the table of contents. Just make sure you include sufficient white space (at least 12 points — I explain about points in Chapter 9) so readers recognize it as a separate element.
- **Dot leaders:** All too often the title of an article on an inside page connects to the page number by a row of dots. These dots are visually distracting. One good alternative is to set the page number in a large type size before the title. Another alternative is to place the page number in the margin of your pages so it doesn't abut any text.
- **Screened backgrounds:** Screened backgrounds often make the table of contents harder to read instead of more noticeable, so avoid them.
- **Hidden table of contents:** Often the table of contents appears in the lower-right portion of the front page. A better choice is to place it in the narrow text column to the left of the two-text columns if you use a five-column grid, as shown in the illustration introducing this chapter.
- **Overuse of page numbers:** You see it all the time: a listing of page numbers for articles that appears next to the table of contents on the front page of your newsletter. Ask yourself if you really need page number references for articles on the inside spread of a four-page newsletter?

Following are some other ways you can dress up an otherwise boring table of contents:

1. **"Sell" article content.**

   Replace article titles with a short description of the content and importance of the articles on the inside of your newsletter. Or place the article titles in bold and add a sentence below to describe the article.

2. **Include photographs.**

   If you're preparing a lengthy newsletter and the inside articles contain photographs, reproduce the photographs at a small size as part of the table of contents on the front cover of your newsletter.

3. **Use tables to maintain consistent spacing.**

   A borderless (or gridless) table provides an ideal structure for a good-looking table of contents. A table makes it easy to use a larger type size for the numbers than the article titles, and maintains precise vertical alignment and horizontal spacing regardless of the number of lines in the title.

Regular columns or department heads

One way to organize the contents of your newsletter is to have a number of standard departments, each having its own signature head. For example, consider a "People in the News" department that would appear in every issue under the same headline and would feature clients or staff or others who have made a difference. Readers would recognize that department in each issue because of the consistent treatment of its name and headline.

Department heads succeed most when they reflect the typeface and backgrounds you use for the nameplate, creating a unity between the front cover of your newsletter and the inside pages.

Headlines

Whether people read your newsletter depends in great measure on how successfully you handle the headlines. Here are ten characteristics of effective newsletter headlines:

- **Make headlines short and to the point.** Avoid excess words. State the point of the article in subject, verb, noun format but avoid unnecessary qualifiers (adjectives or adverbs). Compare the impact of "Man bites dog" to the impact of "Large man bites scruffy brown dog." The extra words actually subtract impact.
- **Use a contrasting typeface.** Not only does your headline need to be easy for readers to notice, but the headline must form a pleasing contrast with the body copy text. The standard safe bet is to combine headlines set in a sans serif typeface with body copy set in a serif typeface.
- **Use a condensed typeface.** Headlines set in condensed bold or condensed heavy type take up less space — meaning more white space surrounds them — and the thicker strokes of heavy typeface form a

stronger contrast with the remaining text on the page than headlines set in bold alone (see Figure 10-5), making them stand out more while giving you more characters to work with in writing the headline.

Bold headlines lack impact	**Bold headlines lack impact**
Visual impact plays a major role in the success of a headline. The stronger the weight contrast between a headline and the text it introduces, the more effectively it performs its role as "advertiser" of the text that follows. Often, bold type doesn't perform as well as Heavy type. Compare the headline set in Frutiger bold at left with the same headline set in Frutiger UltraBlack at right.	Visual impact plays a major role in the success of a headline. The stronger the weight contrast between a headline and the text it introduces, the more effectively it performs its role as "advertiser" of the text that follows. Often, bold type doesn't perform as well as Heavy type. Compare the headline set in Frutiger bold at left with the same headline set in Frutiger UltraBlack at right.

Figure 10-5: Notice the added impact of the headline at right, set in a condensed heavy typeface.

- **Don't set headlines in all uppercase type.** Because headlines set entirely in uppercase type take up to 30 percent more space, they are harder to read than headlines set in a combination of uppercase and lowercase type.
- **Use uppercase letters sparingly.** Avoid the temptation to capitalize the first letter of each word. This makes it difficult for readers to differentiate between words that you use as nouns and adjectives. A better alternative is to capitalize only the first letter of the first word as well as the first letter of proper nouns. This method of headline capitalization is referred to as *downstyle.*
- **Don't underline headlines.** Underlined headlines are hard to read because the horizontal line distracts the reader. Also the underlines interfere with the descenders of lowercase letters like *g, y,* and *p*. You have already indicated the importance of the headline by your choice of typeface and typesize. You shouldn't need anything else.
- **Reduce headline letter spacing.** Use your software program's tracking control to adjust headline letter spacing. Experiment with the normal and tight settings and check out how the reduced letter spacing creates more white space around the headline.
- **Decrease headline line spacing.** You can reduce your headline's leading, or line spacing, by going to the Paragraph dialog box that you usually find in your software's Format menu. The auto or default setting of your software is likely to create more line spacing than necessary for good readability and appearance of headlines.
- **Avoid centering headlines out of habit.** Although centered headlines are sometimes effective, in many cases flush-left headlines are more attractive because they are set off by the area of white space to their

right. White space is less noticeable with centered headlines because the white space is divided equally to the left and right of the headline.

Never end headlines with a period. Studies show that ending headlines with a period reduces readership of the text that follows because it implies completion. Your headline is the beginning of your message, not the end, so leave it open.

Use styles to speed setting headlines. Styles save time by permitting you to apply multiple formatting options with a single click of the mouse.

Hint: Establish two headline styles, one style for the most important headline on a page and another style for secondary headlines. Having two different headline styles helps the reader scanning your page to separate the most important article from secondary articles.

Kickers and blurbs

A *kicker* is a short phrase above a headline often set in a smaller, italicized typeface. Kickers introduce the headline, amplify its importance, and relate it to the reader's self-interest.

A *blurb* is similar to a kicker in that it further explains the importance of the headline, but blurbs appear after the headline.

Consistency is important. If you use kickers and/or blurbs for one headline, use them for all headlines. Make them one of the distinguishing features that sets your newsletter apart.

You may sometimes see kickers or blurbs used in isolation on a page to highlight an individual article. I find this treatment distracting, as it breaks the cohesive look of the page. Avoid any treatment that can confuse readers about your image and your message.

Bylines

Bylines are just what they sound like — lines of type that identify the author by whom the article is written. Bylines are often the author's only reward for writing an article. In addition, bylines that identify the author and explain the author's qualifications can further enhance the credibility of the article's contents. As with other regular elements of your newsletter, you should handle all bylines the same.

Many people set bylines in a bold-face version of the body text. They can be centered above the start of the text, set flush left, or printed after a dash or below the last line of the text. The important thing is to make sure the byline is not so large that it detracts from the headline or body copy. Some publications set the bylines in smaller type than the body copy; you know your relationship with your writers. This is another case where using both capital and lower-case letters works best for readability, though you may see some bylines done in all caps. (Only the poet e.e. cummings preferred all lowercase that I know of.)

Subheads

Always break long articles into short segments with subheads. Introduce a subhead every time you introduce a new idea in the article. Here are six things to consider when formatting subheads:

- **Choose a contrasting typeface:** Don't just place the subheads in the bold or italic version of the body copy. A better alternative is to use a smaller size of the typeface and type style that you use for headlines.
- **Use the appropriate subhead alignment:** If you use flush-left headlines and set body copy flush-left/ragged-right, then use flush-left subheads. The white space to the right of the subhead helps emphasize it, and the consistency between headlines and subheads projects a unified, professional, detail-conscious image. Reserve centered subheads for use with centered headlines and justified body copy, where they add to the measured formality.
- **Don't hyphenate subheads:** When you set up your style definitions for subheads, make sure that you turn hyphenation off.
- **Use short subheads:** Remember, shorter is better. Subheads need to consist of significant words and key phrases, but they don't have to be full sentences. Strive for subheads that fit on one line because they look significantly better than two-line subheads without taking too much space from your main message.
- **Place extra space above the subheads:** The extra space emphasizes that the subhead introduces a new topic while keeping the subhead itself closer to the topic it introduces.
- **Use color with care:** Subheads set in color are often harder to read than subheads set in black, and they tend to get lost in the white space. If you must use color in your subheads, set the text slightly larger and bolder than the body text so it looks "equal."

Body text

Most of your newsletter likely consists of text, so your choice of type for your body text can determine how much of your newsletter will actually be read. Here are ten important tips:

- **Choose an unobtrusive typeface:** The image you want to project and the quality of the paper on which you print your newsletter should influence your choice of typeface. (See Chapter 13 for the way paper affects your choice of typeface.)

  Basically, for text that you want people to read, you want to select a typeface that can be read easily. Avoid typefaces that draw too much attention to themselves, like Souvenir or Korinna. All that attention can be tiring to the eye. Instead, choose a simple serif typeface that's easy to read (remember, sans serif typefaces are harder to read because they lack the stroke variation that helps readers recognize individual letters).

  Try to avoid overused typefaces like Times Roman, however; it's harder to make a unique statement with a typeface that's a cliché. Investigate alternatives like Bookman, Century New Style, Garamond, Minion, and Sabon.

- **Choose the right type size:** It's as important to avoid short lines of large type as it is to avoid long lines of small type. Short lines of large type appear bloated and slow the reader down; the eyes can't scan enough words on each line for comfortable reading. Long lines of small type strain the eyes and make it easy for the reader to get lost at the end of each line.

  Depending on the width of your columns, type that measures from 9 to 12 points is acceptable. The wider your column, the larger the point size you can use. If you need to use a small type size, make sure you have sufficiently narrow columns.

- **Adjust line spacing on the basis of typeface and type size:** Avoid the use of your software program's default, or auto, setting. Instead, experiment with different leading or line spacing settings to find a measurement that separates lines enough to make each line easy to read but that doesn't waste space between the lines. Increase line spacing if you use a sans serif typeface; decrease leading if you use a typeface with a low x-height like Adobe Garamond.

- **Choose the right text alignment:** Your choice of text alignment contributes to an appropriate image and can make your message easier to read. Your options include flush-left/ragged-right or justified.

  - Flush-left/ragged-right projects an informal, easy-to-read image because both word and letter spacing remain consistent, and white space appears at the end of each line.

  - Choose justified text if you want to project a conservative or classic image — the result of centuries of setting type in rigid blocks of lead.

  (In case you're wondering, setting text flush right creates a nightmare for the eyes; they don't know where to go to find the start of the next line and soon tire of the attempt. You may occasionally see text set flush right, but it's likely to be a very small block set that way to achieve a specific design effect. Text that's meant to be read should never be set flush right.)

- **Use one, and only one, way to introduce new paragraphs:** Some people want to make sure the reader knows there is a new paragraph by using every way they can think of to introduce it. All this does is waste space. Don't both indent the first line of each paragraph and *also* add extra space between paragraphs. Choose one alternative or the other. As a rule, indent the first line of justified paragraphs, but add extra space between text set flush-left/ragged-right.
- **Don't insert two lines between paragraphs:** Instead of pressing the Enter key twice after each paragraph, use your software program's Space After command, (you can find it in the Paragraph dialog box under the Format menu), to insert approximately a line and a half of space between paragraphs. This is enough to visually indicate a new paragraph but not enough to create holes in the text.
- **Don't press the space bar twice after periods:** By pressing the space bar twice after periods you create noticeably large gaps between sentences, especially when you use justified text because each space expands. If you work with files that other people create, use your software program's Replace feature to search for every occurrence of two spaces in a row and replace them with a single space.
- **Hyphenate with care:** Hyphenation is as important with text set flush-left/ragged-right as it is with justified text. Without hyphenation, line endings range from too short to too long with flush-left/ragged-right text.

  Without hyphenation in justified text, word spacing is exaggerated; words cramp together in lines containing several short words while big holes appear between words in lines containing a few long words (see Figure 10-6). Nevertheless, the reader prefers words that don't break across lines, and three or more hyphens in a row is a definite no-no. Use your own eyes to make sure that letters and words are pleasantly spaced without unnatural gaps or ladder-like hyphen stacks.
- **Adjust tracking:** Make sure that you set your program's tracking to normal. (The default for some programs is none.) For the most part, tight tracking is best. Experiment with how your particular program handles the tracking issue.
- **Use text wraps with care:** Text wraps occur when illustrations or photographs from adjacent lines break into a text column (in other words, photos and text share the same lines), reducing line length. By changing line lengths, text wraps interfere with the reader's rhythmic eye movement across each line. Text wraps are especially difficult to use with justified text because the word spacing is likely to be noticeably different in each line.

If you use first line indents with flush-left/ragged-right text, don't indent the first line after a headline or subhead. The purpose of a first-line indent is to indicate a new paragraph, and if the paragraph follows a headline or subhead, it's *obviously* a new paragraph!

Justified text, no hyphens	**Justified text, hyphenated**
Always hyphenate body copy, especially when employing justified text. Hyphenation reduces distracting variations in word spacing within each line. Without hyphenation, word spacing in lines of text containing a relatively small number of extremely long words is inevitably exaggerated whereas word spacing in lines with lots of short words is noticeably reduced.	Always hyphenate body copy, especially when employing justified text. Hyphen-ation reduces distracting variations in word spacing within each line. Without hyphenation, word spacing in lines of text containing a relatively small number of extremely long words is in-evitably exaggerated whereas word spacing in lines with lots of short words is no-ticeably reduced.

Figure 10-6: Non-hyphenated justified text often creates awkward word spacing.

Jump lines and article jumps

When an article begins on one page and finishes on another, it is said to *jump,* and the continuation of that article on the other page requires a *jump head* so people can find it. Use article jumps with care. Balance the need to offer your reader two or more topics on the front cover (which increases the likelihood that at least one article interests the reader) with the need to continue articles on inside pages (or the back page).

Jumps cause problems for the following reasons:

- You're apt to lose readers each time you include a jump.
- Studies show that readers who leave the front page to continue reading inside often don't come back to read the other articles on the front page.
- Readers are less likely to return to the pages that separate the article to see what's on them.

If you decide that jumping an article is worth the risks, be sure to include a jump line, also called a continued line, to indicate the page where you continue the article. This line should align with the bottom line of your grid. Some set the jump line in italics, flush right, or in parentheses to set it off from the main text. Use a "continued from" kicker to introduce the headline on the jump page and repeat as many words of the original headline in the continued article headline. To avoid confusion, make continuation headlines smaller than the headlines that introduce new articles.

Article jumps can present some layout problems. How do you prioritize jump text on a page that contains both new and continued material? Should all jumped text go on one page? Should the back page be used as a standard jump page because it's easy to find? How important is the back page anyway? Once again, consistency is your friend. Determining how you want to handle continuations and treating them the same way issue after issue trains your reader for what to expect. Handling jumps differently each time you have one is likely to leave your reader jumping to another publication.

Visuals

Illustrations and photographs communicate information at a glance. They can also clarify information difficult to convey in mere words. Here are six important ideas to bear in mind when adding photographs and other visuals to your newsletter:

- **Make the size of the illustration or photograph proportional to its importance:** Important photographs need to be significantly larger than secondary photographs. Avoid the use of two photographs of approximately equal size because they can cancel each other out. Rather, make one significantly larger so it provides a dominant focal point for the page. (See Chapter 18 for more on using visuals.)
- **Always place photographs within columns to avoid floating photographs:** Alignment with the edges of adjacent text columns prevents unnecessary text wraps and projects a professional image. Alignment with column margins also eliminates unnecessary text wraps, where you have to shorten the lines of text to avoid bumping into adjacent photographs.
- **Eliminate unimportant information from photographs:** Crop your photographs to eliminate unimportant details at the top, bottom, or sides. By cropping your photos, you focus the reader's eyes on the most important story-telling elements of your photographs.
- **Provide a border when a photograph or illustration needs one:** Add a hairline border around photographs with white backgrounds, such as clouds or skies. If the background of a photograph just fades into the background of your newsletter, it can project an unfinished image.
- **Avoid running text on top of photographs:** If you run text on top of photos, usually both the text and the photographs lose. Text on top of photographs reduces the foreground/background contrast necessary for easy reading. The lines of the photo also interfere with the eye's ability to pick out text.
- **Don't use unnecessary borders:** Thick, black borders project a dark, "death-announcement" image. Avoid drop shadows unless you use them consistently as a design element — even then, they usually cost you more in space than they add in attraction.

Captions

Always include captions (also called cutlines or legends) to explain the relevance and content of photographs, charts, and tables. Here are four important caption considerations:

- **Typeface:** You often see captions set in the same typeface as the adjacent body copy, but this may not be a good choice, as it may blend into your text. The best solution for captions is to set them in a sans serif typeface with extra line spacing so that they stand on their own.
- **Type size:** Set captions in a smaller type size than adjacent body copy and separate the captions with enough space so that the captions are clearly distinct from the text.
- **Type style:** Often people set captions in italic text, but this isn't necessarily the best solution. Most readers find it easier to read Roman text rather than italic text. This is particularly true at small sizes.
- **Alignment:** You don't want to hyphenate captions because they frequently contain proper nouns (which aren't to be hyphenated). For this reason, flush-left/ragged-right captions are often preferable to justified captions.

Pullquotes

A *pullquote* is a short phrase that advertises the contents of adjacent paragraphs or reinforces adjacent content by repeating the most important words or idea. Because they are short and set in larger type, many people read pullquotes and then decide whether to read the article. If the quote is good enough, it "pulls" the reader into the rest of the story. Four things to bear in mind with pullquotes:

- **Location, location, location:** Place pullquotes in the middle of paragraphs rather than between paragraphs so they can't be confused with headlines or subheads.
- **Size matters:** Shorter is better. Pullquotes need to be telegrams. Avoid pullquotes longer than three lines because long pullquotes are as difficult to read as the adjacent paragraphs of text.
- **Pullquote placement:** Avoid placing pullquotes too near the top or bottom margins of a page. Pullquotes work best when text surrounds them in the middle two-thirds of a page.
- **Hyphenation:** Do not, I repeat, do not hyphenate pullquotes. There is nothing like a hyphen to ruin the impact of an important quote.

Logo

Place the logo of the organization or firm sending the newsletter discretely on your newsletter. It isn't necessary to put the logo on the front cover of the newsletter. If you do put it on the front cover, you want the logo to appear near the bottom of the page rather than the top where it can clutter the nameplate area.

Another alternative is to add your logo as part of the masthead listing your publication's staff (see the next section) and subscription information. Or you can also make the logo part of your newsletter's table of contents, as a "brought to you by" type of statement.

Masthead

The masthead provides contact information for the newsletter, such as your address, phone, fax, e-mail information, and the names and positions of everyone involved with producing the newsletter.

Although masthead information often appears on the front page of a newsletter, that's really not the appropriate place for it. The front page of your newsletter needs to contain information that is of more importance to readers, so the consistent placement of the masthead on page two of your newsletter is usually sufficient. Sometimes the masthead is placed on the last page of the newsletter, next to the mailing area.

Address label area

One of the earliest decisions you have to make when publishing a newsletter is whether you want to make your newsletter a self-mailer or distribute it in envelopes. Each approach has pros and cons.

Check with the post office for its regulations regarding self-mailers, but in many cases, using a self-mailer has the following advantages:

- **Lower cost:** You don't need to print envelopes and insert the newsletter into them.
- **Easier handling:** Just add the address label to the newsletter and it's ready for mailing.
- **Reduced postage expenses:** You can really cut your expense if you fold your newsletter into thirds so it is equal to the size of a #10 business envelope.

The disadvantages of self-mailers are

- **Vulnerability to damage:** Self-mailers are more vulnerable to damage (ripping, water, and such) while being mailed, which can reduce their perceived value (as well as their actual value if you lose important content to the damage).
- **Reduced space:** The mailing area of a four-page newsletter can occupy up to 20 percent of the total available space, reducing the amount of information you can communicate.
- **Awkward to include separate coupons or other offers:** You can't insert coupons or flyers that describe additional products or services as easily or safely as you can in newsletters that you mail in envelopes. They often fall out and get lost.

Choosing a Grid for Your Newsletter

The grid, or underlying column structure, you choose as well as the typeface you pick plays a big role in determining the image that your newsletter projects. Always try to base your choice of layout and type on your newsletter's content as well as the image you want it to project. This section describes how content and image influence your choices.

It's important to note that the number of columns of text on your newsletter doesn't necessarily equal the number of columns on the underlying grid, or framework. This is because text columns frequently overlap two, or more, of columns of the underlying grid.

Choosing the right column layout

In general, choose a two- or three-column layout if you want to project a safe, conservative image. Two- and three- column layouts are appropriate if your newsletter primarily consists of long text articles as opposed to newsletters that contain a wider variety of photographs and visuals. Typical paragraph length also influences your decision: Two-column layouts are appropriate for relatively long paragraphs (see Figure 10-7); three-column layouts work well with shorter paragraphs.

Your choice of grid and column layout causes a ripple effect through the other decisions you make in your newsletter's design, for example:

- A two-column newsletter generally requires you to use a larger type size than appropriate for a three-column newsletter, because wider columns mean longer lines of type.

Comparative Anatomy for Dummies Newsletter

For Accredited Members Only May 1998

New findings challenge previous research

1998 World Convention update

Figure 10-7: Two-column newsletters are fine for scholarly, conservative newsletters with long paragraphs.

- Two-column and three-column grid newsletters offer fewer opportunities to place headlines, pullquotes, and visuals because no empty white space columns exist for placing short text and visual elements. You also don't have any space for photographs to grow into the white space adjacent to columns. Often to avoid text wraps, you must increase the size of the photograph so much that it dominates the page.
- Two- and three-column layouts make it relatively hard to include a variety of text and visual elements, such as pull quotes and photographs.

The five-column grid and its more sophisticated cousin, the seven-column grid, offer you more opportunities for creative placement of a variety text and graphic elements:

- With these layouts, you can place short text elements, such as a table of contents or a pullquote, in the narrow column adjacent to two double-wide columns of text.
- Five-column newsletters that use two double-wide columns of text are often the most comfortable to read because the white space to the left of the text provides visual contrast with the text.

- Most important, five-column newsletters make it easy to accommodate a variety of different size photographs without creating any annoying text wrap problems.

You can place many photographs of different sizes and shapes in a five-column grid, as shown in Figure 10-8. Check out how nice the caption appears in the narrow column of white space and how a photograph that may get lost in a two-column layout fits comfortably on a five-column layout.

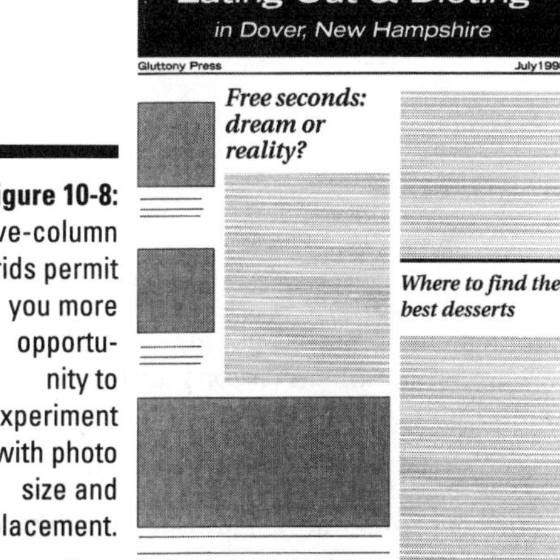

Figure 10-8: Five-column grids permit you more opportunity to experiment with photo size and placement.

The amount of white space on a page plays an important role in determining the image your newsletter communicates. Dense, text-filled newsletters project a conservative, no-frills image. Newsletters with a lot of white space and varied-size photos project a more lively, contemporary image, as shown in Figure 10-9.

Graphic accents such as borders also play a role. Pages with borders on all four sides that have rules of equal thickness project a more conservative image than layouts with a minimum of graphic accents.

Making the right typeface decisions

The typeface, or typefaces, you choose for your newsletter make an immediate impression on your readers.

Remember, typeface decisions are not absolute because typeface alone does not determine your newsletter's image (this does not mean you should change typefaces from issue to issue). You determine image by typeface in

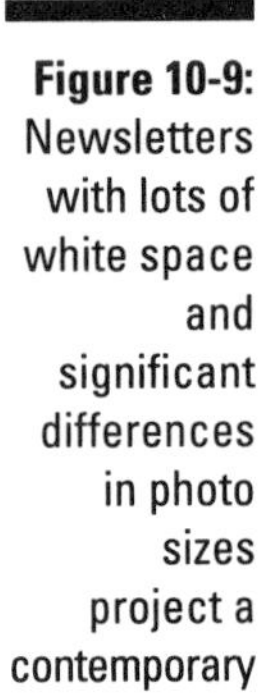

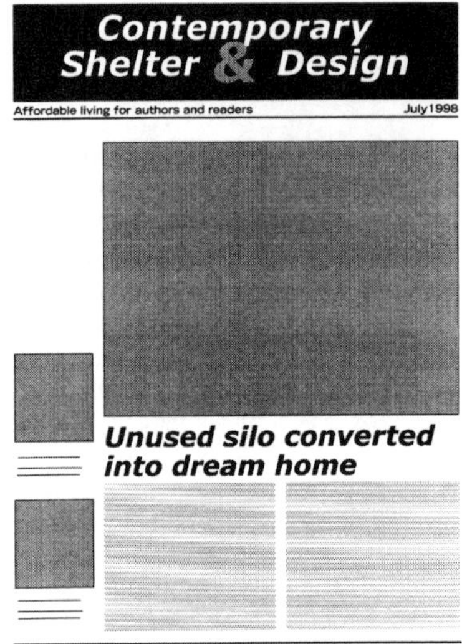

Contemporary
Shelter & Design
Affordable living for authors and readers
July 1998
Unused silo converted into dream home

Figure 10-9: Newsletters with lots of white space and significant differences in photo sizes project a contemporary image.

conjunction with layout and other choices, such as text alignment and the amount of white space on a page. Here are some observations and ideas to start you on a topic that just may occupy you for the rest of your life!

- Modern serif typefaces, like Electra or Photina, with exaggerated contrast (or difference in stroke thickness) project an elegant impression.
- Old-style serif typefaces, like Adobe Garamond or Adobe Caslon, with low x-heights project an antique or classic image.
- Slab serif typefaces, like Monotype Amassis, project a "late-breaking news" or typewritten image.
- Geometric sans serif typefaces, like Avant Garde and Futura, project a modern, trendy image.
- High-character sans serif typefaces, like Maiandra, have varying stroke widths and project a friendly, informal image.
- Distorted typefaces, like Smudge, project a Grunge or Generation X look.

Look at Figures 10-10 and 10-11 to see how different typefaces affect your impressions of the content being delivered.

You don't determine image by type alone, any more than you determine image by layout alone. Rather, image is the cumulative effect of numerous design decisions.

Caslon projects an antique image.
Minion projects a classic image.
Rockwell projects strength.
Photina projects a modern image.
Trump Mediaeval projects trust
Palatino projects readable beauty.
Perpetua projects a quiet, poetic image.
Times Roman projects familiarity.
Goudy projects a scholarly look.
Bodoni projects elegance.
Century Schoolbook is easy to read.

Figure 10-10: Note the different way you react to the image these serif typefaces project.

Akzidenz Grotesque	Quay Sans
Antique Olive	Trade Gothic
Gill Sans	Formata
Frutiger	Eras
Goudy Sans	Folio
Helvetica	Stone Sans
Optima	Futura

Figure 10-11: Sans serif typefaces, too, project different images.

Managing Cost- and Time-Effective Production

The biggest challenges you face when producing a newsletter are cutting costs and keeping it on schedule. Here are some tips on how to keep within your budget and work as efficiently as possible:

- **Use color with care:** A second color can make a major improvement in the appearance of your newsletter, but opting for three- or four color-printing is harder to justify. Consistency is the essence of newsletter success, and if you use up all your money to produce the first issue, you won't have money left for the newsletters scheduled to follow!

- **Use preprinted second color accents:** One way you can save money is by using the second color consistently in the same places in each newsletter.

  For example, you can use the color in the nameplate and along the bottom border of each page. One additional color is usually enough to brighten each page and add character and identity to your newsletter. Simply print "blanks" or "donuts" containing just the second accent color for several issues of your newsletter in advance, as described earlier in this chapter. Then each issue's printing run becomes a single-color job, even though the reader receives a two-color newsletter.

- **Use styles as efficiently as possible:** Styles save time and enforce consistency. Instead of opening the Style menu and selecting a style choice by highlighting it, use keyboard shortcuts to apply styles. In addition, set up your styles so that the body copy style automatically follows your headline or subhead style.

- **Make sure to delegate:** Instead of trying to do the whole job yourself, train yourself to allow others to share in the work.

- **When in doubt, leave it out:** Avoid the temptation to tell too much of a story in your newsletter, unless the point of your newsletter is to communicate the whole story. If your newsletter is designed to tease your reader into calling you or visiting your place of business, give them enough information to whet their desire for more information. Remember, your primary job is usually to perform and sell a service, not to become a publishing mogul. Finally, newsletters containing numerous short-stories or "tips and techniques" are usually more popular than those that focus on just a few ideas. Where there is variety, there is more likelihood that at least one story will deeply appeal to a reader.

- **Don't use odd-sized paper:** Your goal is not to reinvent the wheel but simply to tell a story. Creatively challenging and, hence, creatively satisfying odd sizes may win awards, but they are often counterproductive as far as function and cost are concerned. Small newsletters are easily lost; oversized, tabloid-sized (that is, 11-x-17-inch) newsletters are harder to read and to store. Whenever possible, stick to the standard 8 1/2-x-10-inch sizes. By using standard sizes, you get the maximum choice of paper stocks and the ability to solicit printing bids from a wider variety of commercial printers. See Chapter 13 for more about choosing paper.

- **Prepare a schedule and work from it:** Try to begin on your second, or even third, newsletter before the first newsletter appears. It may be frustrating, but it's an accepted part of life in publishing. Successful newsletter programs are based on a continuing process, not a single event.

Never forget the basic definition of a newsletter: a *letter that* contains *news*. Your newsletter succeeds to the extent that you keep it simple, uncluttered, and consistent; it should appear on time every time and contain news and information of interest or benefit to your readers.

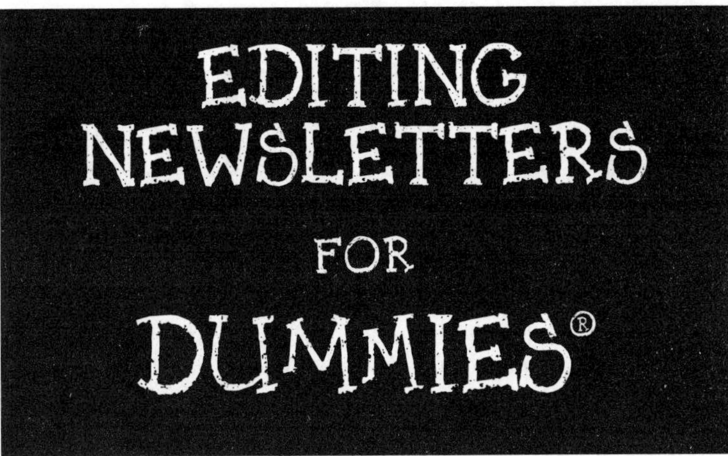

by Roger C. Parker

The first step for an editor in creating a successful newsletter is to answer some fundamental questions. The more thinking you do at this stage, the easier it is to design an appropriate format and prepare the contents for each issue.

Defining Your Newsletter

Start by defining the goal of your newsletter as specifically as possible. The two most common goals are to establish credibility and maintain awareness, You can't buy the respect of prospective customers, but you can *earn* it by proving that you know your subject well enough to write about it. A newsletter is an excellent credibility builder, allowing you to display your expertise in an educational and informative way.

Maintaining awareness is the second most popular reason to do a newsletter. Just as market leaders such as Coca-Cola and McDonald's spend millions of dollars each year on advertising to maintain visibility, you can buy "mindshare" among your target market by sending them a newsletter.

What will be in each issue?

What are you going to include in your newsletter? Are you going to devote each issue to a single, or will your newsletter "tease" readers with several shorter features?

What items are likely to be repeated from issue to issue? Must certain features like a calendar of events, new product introductions, or a barometer of stock performance appear in each issue? Do you have to accommodate ads in your newsletter?

How many visuals will be included? How important are the visuals? Will there be many illustrations, photographs, or charts?

How many pages in each issue?

Remember that in most cases, your primary purpose in producing a newsletter is to establish credibility and maintain visibility and awareness. To succeed in these goals requires consistency, and consistency is based on affordability and practicality.

Producing a two-page newsletter on time and on budget is relatively simple. A four-page newsletter, however, is not twice as hard to produce as a two-page newsletter — it's eight times as hard. An eight-page newsletter is even harder. The more pages you have, the more planning you need to do, the more articles and photos you need to prepare, the more layout issues you need to solve. In short, you make your job harder. And the harder your job is, the more likely you are to fall behind schedule or abandon the program.

In most cases, limit your page count to multiples of four. Six-page newsletters present a challenge. You can insert a single sheet in the middle (which often falls out in the mail or lands in the reader's lap when read), or you can use a six-panel, wide format. The six-panel format costs more to produce because not every printer can accommodate it and not all papers are available that wide. In addition, the six-panel format presents its own unique design challenges. Instead of seeing a two-page spread when they open your newsletter, your readers encounter three parallel pages, making it difficult for the reader to concentrate on a single story. The six-panel format also makes it harder to design pages that work well with each other.

Will the layout be horizontal or vertical?

The content of your newsletter should determine the column layout. A newsletter containing an assortment of short and long articles plus several photographs of different sizes requires a more complex column layout than a newsletter featuring one or two long, analytical stories and few visuals.

If your newsletter contains a variety of article lengths, you need to choose between horizontal or vertical article placement. The tendency is to flow articles vertically, but your readers may appreciate a horizontal placement. A series of short paragraphs side-by-side appear easier to read than long columns of text, which is why newspapers stack articles the way they do.

Planning Precedes Production

Planning involves determining the content of each newsletter — which features to include and how much space to devote to each feature. Planning reduces frustration and helps you work more efficiently, creating the time necessary to fine-tune the details of newsletter typography. You can plan your newsletter in two ways:

- Choose a theme for each issue. After you determine the theme, relate it to each of the regular features or departments you include in your newsletter (choose articles for the various departments that support or contribute to the theme). For example, if your theme is productivity, you might include an interview with a production manager on more efficient procedures, an article on departments that have experienced the greatest productivity growth, a review of products with unique production challenges, and so on.
- List all possible article topics and, one at a time, eliminate articles until the ones that remain are your first-choice selections. You may also prioritize them according to timeliness, creating a list of stories that have immediate interest versus those that can be printed anytime and those that are more suitable for certain times of the year.

The more time you spend planning your newsletter, the less time you'll have to spend later on shoehorning text and visuals into place and the fewer hard feelings you'll create when you discover you don't have room to include everything that you or your co-workers have written.

A good practice is to try and plan the content of your newsletters six months to a year in advance. You can always make adjustments for late-breaking information, and you'll never be caught short, trying to put together a useful newsletter on the fly.

Thumbnails

After you determine the content of each issue, you need to determine how much space to devote to each feature. The best way to do this is to determine article length *before* the articles have been written. Create a reduced-size mock-up of your newsletter, called a thumbnail, as follows:

- If you are creating a four-page newsletter, fold an 8 1/2-x-11-inch sheet of paper in half and trim off the bottom so that the four pages are proportional to the dimensions of an 8 1/2-x-11-inch page.
- If you are creating an eight-page newsletter, fold the paper once more and trim the top edge. This creates eight correctly proportioned pages. Staple the pages together along their left edge.

Create several "blank" newsletters and have a sharp pencil and soft eraser handy. Start by drawing in the borders and page numbers on each page and lightly indicate the location of columns and vertical downrules between columns. Then draw the nameplate and table of contents on the front page, the masthead on page 2, and the mailing label area on the back page. If certain features or departments always appear on the same place in each issue, draw them in at this point.

Indicate the approximate location and length of the articles and photographs you want to include in each issue. Don't worry about being too accurate at this point: work quickly and avoid self-censoring. Use parallel squiggly lines to indicate text, boxes with x's through them to indicate photographs, and just write in headlines as clearly as you can at approximately the size they'll appear.

Don't be afraid if your initial attempts don't allow you to fit everything you want to include — that's the whole point of a thumbnail. The goal is to make as many decisions as possible at the pencil and paper stage rather than after articles have been written, photographs taken, and headlines and body text placed.

Copyfitting

One of the most important ways you can become a more efficient newsletter editor is to write to length and have contributors write to length. Rather than reactively laying out your newsletter on the basis of what's already been written, take a proactive role and assign articles and photographs on the basis of available space. Instead of saying "I want a long article on last week's Planning Board meeting," say: "I need a 600-word article on last week's Planning Board meeting."

Copyfitting is a skill you will quickly acquire on the basis of experience. The easiest approach is to count the number of words per column inch set in the typeface, type size, and line spacing used in your newsletter. Then determine how many words will fit in a column of type that extends half the length of the page. (This takes paragraph spacing into account.)

After you have these figures, you have a rough way of relating our thumbnail layouts to word-processed copy. This saves a lot of time producing your newsletter because you won't have to spend so much time editing or padding previously written copy.

Assigning articles and authors

The production phase of your newsletter involves assigning articles and photographs on the basis of available space. Avoid verbal communications whenever possible. Prepare an *assignment sheet* for each article — even if it's an article that you're writing — that clearly spells out desired article length, submission deadline, and individuals to contact or resources to check.

Assign your articles as early as possible so that writers can write them as far ahead of deadline as possible. This makes it possible to circulate approval copies of articles in word-processed, rather than formatted, form. If others routinely contribute to your newsletter, prepare a written set of *author guidelines* that specify the way manuscripts are to be provided to you.

Tagging copy

If you're in a high-efficiency environment, one of the best ways to increase production efficiency is to investigate how your software program allows you to tag copy.

Tagging involves inserting codes that do not print into the manuscript. These codes automatically apply the appropriate style when the manuscript is placed in your page layout program. Although many styles (or formatting characteristics) successfully carry over from word processor to page layout program, it will be harder to distribute up-to-date copies of your styles than to ask authors to add tagging symbols (such as [PAR1] before the first paragraphs following headlines or subheads).

You'll be surprised at how much time tagging saves you after you've saved styles for each element of page architecture and instructed your authors on how to apply the tags to their word-processed copy. You can also create and distribute style templates for your authors to use.

Fine-Tuning Your Newsletter

Often, words have to be edited or transposed at the page layout stage in order to create attractive, easy-to-read pages. Again, this takes time, which is why you plan ahead and work as efficiently as possible — so you'll have time for the inevitable last-minute revisions and refinements.

Rewriting headlines

No matter how well-written your headlines, it's impossible to know how they will look until they are formatted using your publication's headline style (set in the desired typeface, type size, style, weight, width, and case). With flush-left headlines, one line will often appear noticeably longer than others. With centered headlines, the longer line may appear on the bottom of the stack, or the lines of a multiline headline might create a strange shape.

Rewriting is the best way to cure these problems. Few headlines can stand up to rigorous editing. Empty words can almost always be identified, and long words can usually be replaced with short words.

Managing widows, orphans, and line breaks

Widows (portions of words or phrases less than one-third of the column width appearing by themselves at the bottom of a column or a page) and *orphans* (isolated syllables of less than one-third of a line isolated at the top of a column or page) project a less-than-professional approach to page layout and typesetting. Likewise, occasionally several short lines in a row appear in flush-left/ragged-right text following several long lines. Or the line endings create strange shapes.

Even though some programs offer protection against widows and orphans, they don't protect against strange shapes or text overruns. Trial-and-error editing is often the best way to cure these problems. Try the following techniques:

- Transposing a word earlier in the paragraph often causes the line endings to reflow, eliminating distracting problems.
- Adding a discretionary hyphen earlier in the paragraph forces a word break that can eliminate awkward line endings.

- Inserting a non-breaking hyphen can keep a hyphenated word from being split across two lines.
- Adjusting the tracking of a single line early in the paragraph is often enough to smooth out line endings later in the paragraph. Use this technique with care, however, as a single line with tight tracking can often appear smaller than adjacent lines.

Dealing with too much text

In an ideal world, you'd never have too much text. But sometimes, text happens — and you've got to deal with it. When you have to accommodate too much copy and further editing is neither possible nor permitted, making global adjustments is the key — make consistent adjustments throughout your publication so that you don't inadvertently draw attention to just one story by making it appear "different." Options include the following:

- Reducing the type size of all the stories in the issue by one-quarter point. Most readers won't notice the difference, and you may gain enough space to accommodate the extra text.
- Uniformly reducing the space above and below headlines and subheads, modifying your headline and subhead styles' Space Before and Space After specifications.
- Reducing headline type size one-half point.
- Slightly reducing space above headers and below footers or the space between headers/footers and adjacent text.
- Eliminating one or more photographs, reducing the size of large photographs, and/or reducing the space around photographs.
- Replacing captions under photographs with captions placed in the margins next to photographs.
- Dropping pullquotes.
- Reducing the size of the mailing coupon.
- Slightly reducing paragraph spacing.

All the preceding, of course, are less-than-desirable alternatives. When you use any of the preceding techniques, you take a chance on destroying the careful design of your newsletter.

Dealing with too little text

The exact opposite techniques for too much text can be used when there's not enough text to fill available space — such as adding slight amounts of space above and below headlines and subheads or adding pullquotes), you can try the following:

- Use uneven, scalloped column endings instead of completely filling each column with text.
- Add short features, such as "Where Are They Now?" or "Ten Years Ago."
- Add white space above or below the table of contents, use longer titles in the table of contents, or add more space between lists in the table of contents.
- Add small head-shot photographs of the authors of key editorials or lead articles.

Again, the key is to disguise the extra space by adding it uniformly throughout your newsletter.

The following pages contain before-and-after examples illustrating basic principles of newsletter design.

Simplify and add typographic contrast to nameplates

Desktop Publishing
and Design Newsletter
Volume 3, Number 2 Feb. 1995

NEW TYPEFACE DESIGNS APPEAR

Dolor sit amet, consectetuer adipiscing elit, sed diam nonummy nibh euismod tincidunt ut laoreet dolore magna aliquam erat volutpat. Ut wisi i tation ullamcorper suscipit lobortis nisl ut aliquip ex ea commodo consequat. vel illum dolore eu feugiat nulla facilisis at vero eros et accumsan et iusto omolestie consequat.

ABCabc
ABCabc
ABCabc
ABCabc

New, small foundries

Duis autem vel eum iriure dolor in hendrerit in vulputate velit esse molestie consequat, vel illum dolore eu feugiat nulla facilisis at vero eros et accumsan et iusto odio dignissim qui blandit praesent luptatum zzril delenit augue duis dolore te feugait nulla facilisi.

Lorem ipsum dolor sit amet, consectetuer adipiscing elit, sed diam nonummy nibh euismod tincidunt ut laoreet dolore magna aliquam erat volutpat.

Lorem ipsum dolor sit amet, consectetuer adipiscing elit, sed diam aliquam erat volutpat.

New design trends

Duis autem vel eum iriure dolor in hendrerit in vulputate velit esse molestie consequat, vel illum dolore eu feugiat nulla facilisis at vero eros et accumsan. But et euismod tinciduntlaoreet wollum feugait adipiscing nulla facilisi.

Reduced price for quality

Lorem ipsum dolor sit amet, adipiscing elit, sed diam

Continued page 2

HOW TO CHOOSE A LASER PRINTER

Dolor sit amet, consectetuer adipiscing elit, sed diam nonummy nibh euismod tincidunt ut laoreet dolore magna aliquam erat volutpat. Ut wisi enim ad minim veniam, quis nostrud exerci tation ullamcorper suscipit lobortis nisl ut aliquip ex ea commodo consequat.

Duis autem vel eum iriure dolor in hendrerit in vulputate velit esse molestie consequat, vel illum dolore eu feugiat nulla facilisis at vero eros et accumsan et iusto odio dignissim qui blandit praesent luptatum zzril delenit augue duis dolore te feugait nulla facilisi.

Continued page 3

NEW! LOW CALORIE EDIBLE TONER

Lorem ipsum dolor sit amet, consectetuer adipiscing elit, sed diam nonummy nibh euismod tincidunt ut laoreet dolore magna aliquam erat volutpat.

Ut wisi enim ad minim veniam, quis nostrud exerci tation nibh euismod tincidunt ut laoreet dolorelobortis nisl ut aliquip ex ea commodo consequat.

TABLE OF CONTENTS

Desktop & Publishing
D E S I G N

NEW TYPEFACE DESIGNS APPEAR

Dolor sit amet, consectetuer adipiscing elit, sed diam nonummy nibh euismod tincidunt ut laoreet dolore magna aliquam erat volutpat. Ut wisi i tation ullamcorper suscipit lobortis nisl ut aliquip ex ea commodo consequat. vel illum dolore eu feugiat nulla facilisis at vero eros et accumsan et iusto omolestie consequat.

ABCabc
ABCabc
ABCabc
ABCabc

New, small foundries

Duis autem vel eum iriure dolor in hendrerit in vulputate velit esse molestie consequat, vel illum dolore eu feugiat nulla facilisis at vero eros et accumsan et iusto odio dignissim qui blandit praesent luptatum zzril delenit augue duis dolore te feugait nulla facilisi.

Lorem ipsum dolor sit amet, consectetuer adipiscing elit, sed diam nonummy nibh euismod tincidunt ut laoreet dolore magna aliquam erat volutpat.

Lorem ipsum dolor sit amet, consectetuer adipiscing elit, sed diam aliquam erat volutpat.

New design trends

Duis autem vel eum iriure dolor in hendrerit in vulputate velit esse molestie consequat, vel illum dolore eu feugiat nulla facilisis at vero eros et accumsan. But et wollum feugait adipiscing nulla facilisi.

Reduced price for quality

Lorem ipsum dolor sit amet, consecteteur adipiscing

Continued page 2

HOW TO CHOOSE A LASER PRINTER

Dolor sit amet, consectetuer adipiscing elit, sed diam nonummy nibh euismod tincidunt ut laoreet dolore magna aliquam erat volutpat. Ut wisi enim ad minim veniam, quis nostrud exerci tation ullamcorper suscipit lobortis nisl ut aliquip ex ea commodo consequat.

Duis autem vel eum iriure dolor in hendrerit in vulputate velit esse molestie consequat, vel illum dolore eu feugiat nulla facilisis at vero eros et accumsan et iusto odio dignissim qui blandit praesent

Continued page 3

NEW! EDIBLE LOW CALORIE TONER

Lorem ipsum dolor sit amet, consectetuer adipiscing elit, sed diam nonummy nibh euismod tincidunt ut laoreet dolore magna aliquam erat volutpat.

Ut wisi enim ad minim veniam, quis nostrud exerci tation ullanummy nibh euismod tincidunt ut laoreet dolorelobortis nisl ut aliquip ex ea commodo consequat.

TABLE OF CONTENTS

Vol. 3, Num. 2 Feb. 1995

The Before version (left) of this nameplate lacks impact because all the words are set in the same typeface, type size, and weight. Foreground/background contrast is reduced by the shaded background.

In the After version, interest is added by setting "Desktop Publishing" in a different typeface than "Design," using Force Justification to automatically space the letters in "Design" equally across the page for visual contrast, and replacing the word "and" with an oversized, shaded ampersand. Simplify the nameplate by eliminating the unnecessary word "Newsletter" and by moving the folio information (issue number and date of publication) to the table of contents box.

Adopt a consistent headline style

NEW TYPEFACE DESIGNS APPEAR

Dolor sit amet, consectetuer adipiscing elit, sed diam nonummy nibh euismod tincidunt ut laoreet dolore magna aliquam erat volutpat. Ut wisi i tation ullamcorper suscipit lobortis nisl ut aliquip ex ea commodo consequat. vel illum dolore eu feugiat nulla facilisis at vero eros et accumsan et iusto omolestie consequat.

ABCabc
ABCabc
ABCabc
ABCabc

New, small foundries

Duis autem vel eum iriure dolor in hendrerit in vulputate velit esse molestie consequat, vel illum dolore eu feugiat nulla facilisis at vero eros et accumsan et iusto odio dignissim qui blandit praesent luptatum zzril delenit augue duis dolore te feugait nulla facilisi.

Lorem ipsum dolor sit amet, consectetuer adipiscing elit, sed diam nonummy nibh euismod tincidunt ut laoreet dolore magna aliquam erat volutpat.

Lorem ipsum dolor sit amet, consectetuer adipiscing elit,

sed diam aliquam erat volutpat.

New design trends

Duis autem vel eum iriure dolor in hendrerit in vulputate velit esse molestie consequat, vel illum dolore eu feugiat nulla facilisis at vero eros et accumsan. But et wollum feugait adipiscing nulla facilisi.

Reduced price for quality

Lorem ipsum dolor sit amet, consecteteur adipiscing

Continued page 2

HOW TO CHOOSE A LASER PRINTER

Dolor sit amet, consectetuer adipiscing elit, sed diam nonummy nibh euismod tincidunt ut laoreet dolore magna aliquam erat volutpat. Ut wisi enim ad minim

veniam, quis nostrud exerci tation ullamcorper suscipit lobortis nisl ut aliquip ex ea commodo consequat.

Duis autem vel eum iriure dolor in hendrerit in vulputate velit esse molestie consequat, vel illum dolore eu feugiat nulla facilisis at vero eros et accumsan et iusto odio dignissim qui blandit praesent

Continued page 3

NEW! EDIBLE LOW CALORIE TONER

Lorem ipsum dolor sit amet, consectetuer adipiscing elit, sed diam nonummy nibh euismod tincidunt ut laoreet dolore magna aliquam erat volutpat.

Ut wisi enim ad minim veniam, quis nostrud exerci tation ullanummy nibh euismod tincidunt ut laoreet dolorelobortis nisl ut aliquip ex ea commodo consequat.

TABLE OF CONTENTS

Vol. 3, Num. 2 Feb. 1995

Desktop & Publishing DESIGN

New typeface designs appear

Dolor sit amet, consectetuer adipiscing elit, sed diam nonummy nibh euismod tincidunt ut laoreet dolore magna aliquam erat volutpat. Ut wisi i tation ullamcorper suscipit lobortis nisl ut aliquip ex ea commodo consequat. vel illum dolore eu feugiat nulla facilisis at vero eros et accumsan et iusto omolestie consequat.

ABCabc
ABCabc
ABCabc
ABCabc

New, small foundries

Duis autem vel eum iriure dolor in hendrerit in vulputate velit esse molestie consequat, vel illum dolore eu feugiat nulla facilisis at vero eros et accumsan et iusto odio dignissim qui blandit praesent luptatum zzril delenit augue duis dolore te feugait nulla facilisi.

Lorem ipsum dolor sit amet, consectetuer adipiscing elit, sed diam nonummy nibh euismod tincidunt ut laoreet dolore magna aliquam erat volutpat.

Lorem ipsum dolor sit amet, consectetuer adipiscing elit,

sed diam aliquam erat volutpat.

New design trends

Duis autem vel eum iriure dolor in hendrerit in vulputate velit esse molestie consequat, vel illum dolore eu feugiat nulla facilisis at vero eros et accumsan. But et wollum feugait adipiscing nulla facilisi.

Reduced price for quality

Lorem ipsum dolor sit amet, consecteteur adipiscing

Continued page 2

How to choose a laser printer

Dolor sit amet, consectetuer adipiscing elit, sed diam nonummy nibh euismod tincidunt ut laoreet dolore magna aliquam erat volutpat. Ut wisi enim ad minim veniam, quis nostrud exerci tation ullamcorper suscipit lobortis nisl ut aliquip ex ea commodo consequat.

Duis autem vel eum iriure

dolor in hendrerit in vulputate velit esse molestie consequat, vel illum dolore eu feugiat nulla facilisis at vero eros et accumsan et iusto odio dignissim qui blandit praesent.

Ut wisi enim ad minim veniam, quis nostrud exerci tation ullamcorper suscipit lobortis nisl ut aliquip ex ea commodo consequat.

Continued page 3

New!
Low-calorie edible toner

Lorem ipsum dolor sit amet, consectetuer adipiscing elit, sed diam nonummy nibh euismod tincidunt ut laoreet dolore magna aliquam erat volutpat.

Ut wisi enim ad minim veniam, quis nostrud exerci tation ullanummy nibh euismod tincidunt ut laoreet dolorelobortis nisl ut aliquip ex ea commodo consequat.

Table of contents

Vol. 3, Num. 2 Feb. 1995

The Before example (left) lacks unity because each centered, upper case headline is set in a different typeface and type style. Most of the headlines are underlined, which makes them hard to read. In addition, no clear headline hierarchy is apparent; the headline at the upper left is the same size as the headline in the center column (which appears awkwardly large).

In the After example (right), all headlines are set flush-left in Helvetica Condensed Black for unity. The primary headline is set larger than the two secondary headlines. The table of contents headline is smaller still. Note that the Condensed Heavy sans serif typeface saves enough space to allow body copy to be added without crowding the page. Note also that the "New" in the "edible laser toner" headline has been set slightly smaller and in italics for emphasis. (Once you set up a consistent structure, you can easily add emphasis by modifying it.)

Unify subhead and headline text

Desktop & Publishing
DESIGN

New typeface designs appear

Dolor sit amet, consectetuer adipiscing elit, sed diam nonummy nibh euismod tincidunt ut laoreet dolore magna aliquam erat volutpat. Ut wisi i tation ullamcorper suscipit lobortis nisl ut aliquip ex ea commodo consequat. vel illum dolore eu feugiat nulla facilisis at vero eros et accumsan et iusto omolestie consequat.

New, small foundries

Duis autem vel eum iriure dolor in hendrerit in vulputate velit esse molestie consequat, vel illum dolore eu feugiat nulla facilisis at vero eros et accumsan et iusto odio dignissim qui blandit praesent luptatum zzril delenit augue duis dolore te feugait nulla facilisi.

Lorem ipsum dolor sit amet, consectetuer adipiscing elit, sed diam nonummy nibh euismod tincidunt ut laoreet dolore magna aliquam erat volutpat.

Lorem ipsum dolor sit amet, consectetuer adipiscing elit, sed diam aliquam erat volutpat.

New design trends

Duis autem vel eum iriure dolor in hendrerit in vulputate velit esse molestie consequat, vel illum dolore eu feugiat nulla facilisis at vero eros et accumsan. But et wollum feugait adipiscing nulla facilisi.

ABCabc
ABCabc
ABCabc
ABCabc

Reduced price for quality

Lorem ipsum dolor sit amet, consectetuer adipiscing

Continued page 2

How to choose a laser printer

Dolor sit amet, consectetuer adipiscing elit, sed diam nonummy nibh euismod tincidunt ut laoreet dolore magna aliquam erat volutpat. Ut wisi enim ad minim veniam, quis nostrud exerci tation ullamcorper suscipit lobortis nisl ut aliquip ex ea commodo consequat.

Duis autem vel eum iriure dolor in hendrerit in vulputate velit esse molestie consequat, vel illum dolore eu feugiat nulla facilisis at vero eros et accumsan et iusto odio dignissim qui blandit praesent.

Ut wisi enim ad minim veniam, quis nostrud exerci tation ullamcorper suscipit lobortis nisl ut aliquip ex ea commodo consequat.

Continued page 3

New!
Low-calorie edible toner

Lorem ipsum dolor sit amet, consectetuer adipiscing elit, sed diam nonummy nibh euismod tincidunt ut laoreet dolore magna aliquam erat volutpat.

Ut wisi enim ad minim veniam, quis nostrud exerci tation ullanummy nibh euismod tincidunt ut laoreet dolorelobortis nisl ut aliquip ex ea commodo consequat.

Table of contents

Vol. 3, Num. 2 **Feb. 1995**

Desktop & Publishing
DESIGN

New typeface designs appear

Dolor sit amet, consectetuer adipiscing elit, sed diam nonummy nibh euismod tincidunt ut laoreet dolore magna aliquam erat volutpat. Ut wisi i tation ullamcorper suscipit lobortis nisl ut aliquip ex ea commodo consequat. vel illum dolore eu feugiat nulla facilisis at vero eros et accumsan et iusto omolestie consequat.

New, small foundries

Duis autem vel eum iriure dolor in hendrerit in vulputate velit esse molestie consequat, vel illum dolore eu feugiat nulla facilisis at vero eros et accumsan et iusto odio dignissim qui blandit praesent luptatum zzril delenit augue duis dolore te feugait nulla facilisi.

Lorem ipsum dolor sit amet, consectetuer adipiscing elit, sed diam nonummy nibh euismod tincidunt ut laoreet dolore magna aliquam erat volutpat.

Lorem ipsum dolor sit amet, consectetuer adipiscing elit, sed diam aliquam erat volutpat.

New design trends

Duis autem vel eum iriure dolor in hendrerit in vulputate velit esse molestie consequat, vel illum dolore eu feugiat nulla facilisis at vero eros et accumsan. But et wollum feugait adipiscing nulla facilisi.

ABCabc
ABCabc
ABCabc
ABCabc

Reduced price for quality

Lorem ipsum dolor sit amet, consectetuer adipiscing

Continued page 2

How to choose a laser printer

Dolor sit amet, consectetuer adipiscing elit, sed diam nonummy nibh euismod tincidunt ut laoreet dolore magna aliquam erat volutpat. Ut wisi enim ad minim veniam, quis nostrud exerci tation ullamcorper suscipit lobortis nisl ut aliquip ex ea commodo consequat.

Duis autem vel eum iriure dolor in hendrerit in vulputate velit esse molestie consequat, vel illum dolore eu feugiat nulla facilisis at vero eros et accumsan et iusto odio dignissim qui blandit praesent.

Ut wisi enim ad minim veniam, quis nostrud exerci tation ullamcorper suscipit lobortis nisl ut aliquip ex ea commodo consequat.

Continued page 3

New!
Low-calorie edible toner

Lorem ipsum dolor sit amet, consectetuer adipiscing elit, sed diam nonummy nibh euismod tincidunt ut laoreet dolore magna aliquam erat volutpat.

Ut wisi enim ad minim veniam, quis nostrud exerci tation ullanummy nibh euismod tincidunt ut laoreet dolorelobortis nisl ut aliquip ex ea commodo consequat.

Table of contents

Vol. 3, Num. 2 **Feb. 1995**

Message from the President, page 2
New technologies, page 3
Image scanning secrets, page 4
Showcase of new products, page 6
Our reader's write, page 7
Design Tips, page 8

The subheads in the Before example (left) are barely noticeable because they are set in the same typeface and type size as the adjacent body copy. They are extremely hard to read because they are set in underlined bold italic, and their impact is diluted because they are center-aligned over left-aligned text. As a result, each subhead begins a slightly different distance from the left (sometimes more, sometimes less) than the first-line indent of the adjacent paragraphs.

In the After example (right), the subheads are left-aligned to match the left-aligned text and are set in a contrasting typeface, Helvetica Black, which matches the headlines. Line spacing and word spacing have also been refined, replacing the default leading with tighter line spacing and setting the tracking from none to Normal, which tightens letter spacing.

Reduce paragraph spacing

Desktop & Publishing
DESIGN

New typeface designs appear

Dolor sit amet, consectetuer adipiscing elit, sed diam nonummy nibh euismod tincidunt ut laoreet dolore magna aliquam erat volutpat. Ut wisi i tation ullamcorper suscipit lobortis nisl ut aliquip ex ea commodo consequat. vel illum dolore eu feugiat nulla facilisis at vero eros et accumsan et iusto omolestie consequat.

ABCabc
ABCabc
ABCabc
ABCabc

New, small foundries

Duis autem vel eum iriure dolor in hendrerit in vulputate velit esse molestie consequat, vel illum dolore eu feugiat nulla facilisis at vero eros et accumsan et iusto odio dignissim qui blandit praesent luptatum zzril delenit augue duis dolore te feugait nulla facilisi.

Lorem ipsum dolor sit amet, consectetuer adipiscing elit, sed diam nonummy nibh euismod tincidunt ut laoreet dolore magna aliquam erat volutpat.

Lorem ipsum dolor sit amet, consectetuer adipiscing elit, sed diam aliquam erat volutpat.

New design trends

Duis autem vel eum iriure dolor in hendrerit in vulputate velit esse molestie consequat, vel illum dolore eu feugiat nulla facilisis at vero eros et accumsan. But et wollum feugait adipiscing nulla facilisi.

Reduced price for quality

Lorem ipsum dolor sit amet, consectetuer adipiscing

Continued page 2

How to choose a laser printer

Dolor sit amet, consectetuer adipiscing elit, sed diam nonummy nibh euismod tincidunt ut laoreet dolore magna aliquam erat volutpat. Ut wisi enim ad minim veniam, quis nostrud exerci tation ullamcorper suscipit lobortis nisl ut aliquip ex ea commodo consequat.

Duis autem vel eum iriure dolor in hendrerit in vulputate velit esse molestie consequat, vel illum dolore eu feugiat nulla facilisis at vero eros et accumsan et iusto odio dignissim qui blandit praesent.

Ut wisi enim ad minim veniam, quis nostrud exerci tation ullamcorper suscipit lobortis nisl ut aliquip ex ea commodo consequat.

Continued page 3

New!

Low-calorie edible toner

Lorem ipsum dolor sit amet, consectetuer adipiscing elit, sed diam nonummy nibh euismod tincidunt ut laoreet dolore magna aliquam erat volutpat.

Ut wisi enim ad minim veniam, quis nostrud exerci tation ullanommy nibh euismod tincidunt ut laoreet dolorelobortis nisl ut aliquip ex ea commodo consequat.

Table of contents

Vol. 3, Num. 2 **Feb. 1995**

Desktop & Publishing
DESIGN

New typeface designs appear

Dolor sit amet, consectetuer adipiscing elit, sed diam nonummy nibh euismod tincidunt ut laoreet dolore magna aliquam erat volutpat. Ut wisi i tation ullamcorper suscipit lobortis nisl ut aliquip ex ea commodo consequat. vel illum dolore eu feugiat nulla facilisis at vero eros et accumsan et iusto omolestie consequat.

ABCabc
ABCabc
ABCabc
ABCabc

New, small foundries
Duis autem vel eum iriure dolor in hendrerit in vulputate velit esse molestie consequat, vel illum dolore eu feugiat nulla facilisis at vero eros et accumsan et iusto odio dignissim qui blandit praesent luptatum zzril delenit augue duis dolore te feugait nulla facilisi.

Lorem ipsum dolor sit amet, consectetuer adipiscing elit, sed diam nonummy nibh euismod tincidunt ut laoreet dolore magna aliquam erat volutpat.

Lorem ipsum dolor sit amet, consectetuer adipiscing elit, sed diam aliquam erat volutpat.

New design trends
Duis autem vel eum iriure dolor in hendrerit in vulputate velit esse molestie consequat, vel illum dolore eu feugiat nulla facilisis at vero eros et accumsan. But et wollum feugait adipiscing nulla facilisi.

Reduced price for quality
Lorem ipsum dolor sit amet, consecteteur enim ad minim ullanummy nibh adipiscing valor et

Continued page 2

How to choose a laser printer

Dolor sit amet, consectetuer adipiscing elit, sed diam nonummy nibh euismod tincidunt ut laoreet dolore magna aliquam erat volutpat. Ut wisi enim ad minim veniam, quis nostrud exerci tation ullamcorper suscipit lobortis nisl ut aliquip ex ea commodo consequat.

Duis autem vel eum iriure dolor in hendrerit in vulputate velit esse molestie consequat, vel illum dolore eu feugiat nulla facilisis at vero eros et accumsan et iusto odio dignissim qui blandit praesent.

Ut wisi enim ad minim veniam, quis nostrud exerci tation ullamcorper suscipit lobortis nisl ut aliquip ex ea commodo consequat.

Continued page 3

New!

Low-calorie edible toner

Lorem ipsum dolor sit amet, consectetuer adipiscing elit, sed diam nonummy nibh euismod tincidunt ut laoreet dolore magna aliquam erat volutpat.

Ut wisi enim ad minim veniam, quis nostrud exerci tation ullanummy nibh euismod tincidunt ut laoreet dolorelobortis nisl ut aliquip ex ea commodo consequat.

Table of contents

Vol. 3, Num. 2 **Feb. 1995**

The Before example (left) is weakened by redundant paragraph spacing, using both first-line indents and extra space between paragraphs. Two hard returns are used between paragraphs, which creates distracting, horizontal bands of white space. Worse, the first-line indents are based on the page layout program's default half-inch indents, which are far too generous for the narrow columns used.

In the After example (right), first-line indents have been omitted, and paragraph spacing equal to one-and-one-half lines of type is used to indicate new paragraphs. The result is a more unified page, with enough room to allow a few extra lines of body copy to appear on the front page as well as more white space around the headlines.

Adjust type size and line spacing of body copy

Desktop & Publishing
DESIGN

New typeface designs appear

Dolor sit amet, consectetuer adipiscing elit, sed diam nonummy nibh euismod tincidunt ut laoreet dolore magna aliquam erat volutpat. Ut wisi i tation ullamcorper suscipit lobortis nisl ut aliquip ex ea commodo consequat. vel illum dolore eu feugiat nulla facilisis at vero eros et accumsan et iusto omolestie consequat.

New, small foundries

Duis autem vel eum iriure dolor in hendrerit in vulputate velit esse molestie consequat, vel illum dolore eu feugiat nulla facilisis at vero eros et accumsan et iusto odio dignissim qui blandit praesent luptatum zzril delenit augue duis dolore te feugait nulla facilisi.

Lorem ipsum dolor sit amet, consectetuer adipiscing elit, sed diam nonummy nibh euismod tincidunt ut laoreet dolore magna aliquam erat volutpat.

Lorem ipsum dolor sit amet, consectetuer adipiscing elit, sed diam aliquam erat volutpat.

New design trends

Duis autem vel eum iriure dolor in hendrerit in vulputate velit esse molestie consequat, vel illum dolore eu feugiat nulla facilisis at vero eros et accumsan. But et wollum feugait adipiscing nulla facilisi.

ABCabc
ABCabc
ABCabc
ABCabc

Reduced price for quality

Lorem ipsum dolor sit amet, consecteteur enim ad minim ullanummy nibh adipiscing valor et

Continued page 2

How to choose a laser printer

Dolor sit amet, consectetuer adipiscing elit, sed diam nonummy nibh euismod tincidunt ut laoreet dolore magna aliquam erat volutpat. Ut wisi enim ad minim veniam, quis nostrud exerci tation ullamcorper suscipit lobortis nisl ut aliquip ex ea commodo consequat.

Duis autem vel eum iriure dolor in hendrerit in vulputate velit esse molestie consequat, vel illum dolore eu feugiat nulla facilisis at vero eros et accumsan et iusto odio dignissim qui blandit praesent.

Ut wisi enim ad minim veniam, quis nostrud exerci tation ullamcorper suscipit lobortis nisl ut aliquip ex ea commodo consequat.

Continued page 3

New!

Low-calorie edible toner

Lorem ipsum dolor sit amet, consectetuer adipiscing elit, sed diam nonummy nibh euismod tincidunt ut laoreet dolore magna aliquam erat volutpat.

Ut wisi enim ad minim veniam, quis nostrud exerci tation ullanummy nibh euismod tincidunt ut laoreet dolorelobortis nisl ut aliquip ex ea commodo consequat.

Table of contents

Desktop & Publishing
DESIGN

New typeface designs appear

Dolor sit amet, consectetuer adipiscing elit, sed diam nonummy nibh euismod tincidunt ut laoreet dolore magna aliquam erat volutpat. Ut wisi i tation ullamcorper suscipit lobortis nisl ut aliquip ex ea commodo consequat. vel illum dolore eu feugiat nulla facilisis at vero eros et accumsan et iusto omolestie consequat.

New, small foundries

Duis autem vel eum iriure dolor in hendrerit in vulputate velit esse molestie consequat, vel illum dolore eu feugiat nulla facilisis at vero eros et accumsan et iusto odio dignissim qui blandit praesent luptatum zzril delenit augue duis dolore te feugait nulla facilisi.

Lorem ipsum dolor sit amet, consectetuer adipiscing elit, sed diam nonummy nibh euismod tincidunt ut laoreet dolore magna aliquam erat volutpat.

Lorem ipsum dolor sit amet, consectetuer adipiscing elit, sed diam aliquam erat volutpat.

New design trends

Duis autem vel eum iriure dolor in hendrerit in vulputate velit esse molestie consequat, vel illum dolore eu feugiat nulla facilisis at vero eros et accumsan. But et wollum feugait adipiscing nulla illum dolore eu feugiat facilisi.

ABCabc
ABCabc
ABCabc
ABCabc

Reduced price for quality

Lorem ipsum dolor sit amet, consecteteur enim ad minim ullanummy nibh adipiscing valor et

Continued page 2

How to choose a laser printer

Dolor sit amet, consectetuer adipiscing elit, sed diam nonummy nibh euismod tincidunt ut laoreet dolore magna aliquam erat volutpat. Ut wisi enim ad minim veniam, quis nostrud exerci tation ullamcorper suscipit lobortis nisl ut aliquip ex ea commodo consequat.

Duis autem vel eum iriure dolor in hendrerit in vulputate velit esse molestie consequat, vel illum dolore eu feugiat nulla facilisis at vero eros et accumsan et iusto odio dignissim qui blandit praesent.

Ut wisi enim ad minim veniam, quis nostrud exerci tation ullamcorper suscipit lobortis nisl ut aliquip ex ea commodo consequat.

Continued page 3

New!

Low-calorie edible toner

Lorem ipsum dolor sit amet, consectetuer adipiscing elit, sed diam nonummy nibh euismod tincidunt ut laoreet dolore magna aliquam erat volutpat.

Ut wisi enim ad minim veniam, quis nostrud exerci tation ullanummy nibh euismod tincidunt ut laoreet dolorelobortis nisl ut aliquip ex ea commodo consequat.

Table of contents

Successful desktop publishing design is often a matter of subtle refinements. For example, the text in the Before example (left) set at 12 points appears a bit too large. Line spacing is also a bit too generous. The result is a very "open" page.

A half-point reduction in type size in the After version (right) results in a more pleasing type size, one that doesn't appear as crowded. In addition, line spacing was increased to 14 points (from the default 13.8 points). This subtle change is enough to create a more open page as well as a little more white space, which can be used to surround headlines, as you can see from the headline in the center column.

Eliminate unnecessary text wraps

Desktop & Publishing
D E S I G N

New typeface designs appear

Dolor sit amet, consectetuer adipiscing elit, sed diam nonummy nibh euismod tincidunt ut laoreet dolore magna aliquam erat volutpat. Ut wisi i tation ullamcorper suscipit lobortis nisl ut aliquip ex ea commodo consequat. vel illum dolore eu feugiat nulla facilisis at vero eros et accumsan et iusto omolestie consequat.

ABCabc
ABCabc
ABCabc
ABCabc

New, small foundries
Duis autem vel eum iriure dolor in hendrerit in vulputate velit esse molestie consequat, vel illum dolore eu feugiat nulla facilisis at vero eros et accumsan et iusto odio dignissim qui blandit praesent luptatum zzril delenit augue duis dolore te feugait nulla facilisi.

Lorem ipsum dolor sit amet, consectetuer adipiscing elit, sed diam nonummy nibh euismod tincidunt ut laoreet dolore magna aliquam erat volutpat.

Lorem ipsum dolor sit amet, consectetuer adipiscing elit, sed diam aliquam erat volutpat.

New design trends
Duis autem vel eum iriure dolor in hendrerit in vulputate velit esse molestie consequat, vel illum dolore eu feugiat nulla facilisis at vero eros et accumsan. But et wollum feugait adipiscing nulla illum dolore eu feugiat facilisi.

Reduced price for quality
Lorem ipsum dolor sit amet, consecteteur enim ad minim ullanummy nibh adipiscing valor et

Continued page 2

How to choose a laser printer

Dolor sit amet, consectetuer adipiscing elit, sed diam nonummy nibh euismod tincidunt ut laoreet dolore magna aliquam erat volutpat. Ut wisi enim ad minim veniam, quis nostrud exerci tation ullamcorper suscipit lobortis nisl ut aliquip ex ea commodo consequat.

Duis autem vel eum iriure dolor in hendrerit in vulputate velit esse molestie consequat, vel illum dolore eu feugiat nulla facilisis at vero eros et accumsan et iusto odio dignissim qui blandit praesent.

Ut wisi enim ad minim veniam, quis nostrud exerci tation ullamcorper suscipit lobortis nisl ut aliquip ex ea commodo consequat.

Continued page 3

New!
Low-calorie edible toner

Lorem ipsum dolor sit amet, consectetuer adipiscing elit, sed diam nonummy nibh euismod tincidunt ut laoreet dolore magna aliquam erat volutpat.

Ut wisi enim ad minim veniam, quis nostrud exerci tation ullanummy nibh euismod tincidunt ut laoreet dolorelobortis nisl ut aliquip ex ea commodo consequat.

Table of contents
Vol. 3, Num. 2 Feb. 1995

Desktop & Publishing
D E S I G N

New typeface designs appear

Dolor sit amet, consectetuer adipiscing elit, sed diam nonummy nibh euismod tincidunt ut laoreet dolore magna aliquam erat volutpat. Ut wisi i tation ullamcorper suscipit lobortis nisl ut aliquip ex ea

ABCabc
ABCabc
ABCabc
ABCabc

commodo consequat. vel illum dolore eu feugiat nulla facilisis at vero eros et accumsan et iusto omolestie consequat.

New, small foundries
Duis autem vel eum iriure dolor in hendrerit in vulputate velit esse molestie consequat, vel illum dolore eu feugiat nulla facilisis at vero eros et accumsan et iusto odio dignissim qui blandit praesent luptatum zzril delenit augue duis dolore te feugait nulla facilisi.

Lorem ipsum dolor sit amet, consectetuer adipiscing elit, sed diam nonummy nibh euismod tincidunt ut laoreet dolore magna aliquam erat volutpat.

Lorem ipsum dolor sit amet, consectetuer adipiscing elit, sed diam aliquam erat volutpat.

New design trends
Duis autem vel eum iriure dolor in hendrerit in vulputate velit esse molestie consequat, vel illum dolore eu feugiat nulla facilisis at vero eros et accumsan. But et wollum feugait adipiscing nulla illum dolore eu feugiat facilisi.

Reduced price for quality
Lorem ipsum dolor sit amet, consecteteur enim ad minim ullanummy nibh adipiscing valor etmolestie consequat, vel illum dolore eu feugiat nulla facilisis at

Continued page 2

How to choose a laser printer

Dolor sit amet, consectetuer adipiscing elit, sed diam nonummy nibh euismod tincidunt ut laoreet dolore magna aliquam erat volutpat. Ut wisi enim ad minim veniam, quis nostrud exerci tation ullamcorper suscipit lobortis nisl ut aliquip ex ea commodo consequat.

Duis autem vel eum iriure dolor in hendrerit in vulputate velit esse molestie consequat, vel illum dolore eu feugiat nulla facilisis at vero eros et accumsan et iusto odio dignissim qui blandit praesent.

Ut wisi enim ad minim veniam, quis nostrud exerci tation ullamcorper suscipit lobortis nisl ut aliquip ex ea commodo consequat.

Continued page 3

New!
Low-calorie edible toner

Lorem ipsum dolor sit amet, consectetuer adipiscing elit, sed diam nonummy nibh euismod tincidunt ut laoreet dolore magna aliquam erat volutpat.

Ut wisi enim ad minim veniam, quis nostrud exerci tation ullanummy nibh euismod tincidunt ut laoreet dolorelobortis nisl ut aliquip ex ea commodo consequat.

Table of contents
Vol. 3, Num. 2 Feb. 1995

Message from the President, page **2**
New technologies, page **3**
Image scanning secrets, page **4**
Showcase of new products, page **6**
Our reader's write, page **7**
Design Tips, page **8**

Although you may have fun demonstrating your mastery of text wraps by placing an illustration between two text columns, as shown in the Before example at left, both columns suffer. Reduced column width usually translates into excessive hyphenation and, if you're working with justified text, awkward word spacing. If you're using flush-left/ragged right text as in the Before example, the reader is likely to be distracted by the contrast between the ragged line endings of the first column and the straight left margin of the right-hand column.

Eliminating text wrap, as shown in the After example at right, not only eliminates problems with the adjacent column but also creates enough space to add four lines of text to the page. Omitting text wrap also speeds production by eliminating the need to reposition the illustration in order to avoid problems with the subhead appearing right next to the left-column subhead, as it does in the Before example.

Eliminate unnecessary graphic accents

Desktop & Publishing DESIGN

New typeface designs appear

Dolor sit amet, consectetuer adipiscing elit, sed diam nonummy nibh euismod tincidunt ut laoreet dolore magna aliquam erat volutpat. Ut wisi i tation ullamcorper suscipit lobortis nisl ut aliquip ex ea

ABCabc
ABCabc
ABCabc
ABCabc

commodo consequat. vel illum dolore eu feugiat nulla facilisis at vero eros et accumsan et iusto omolestie consequat.

New, small foundries
Duis autem vel eum iriure dolor in hendrerit in vulputate velit esse molestie consequat, vel illum dolore eu feugiat nulla facilisis at vero eros et accumsan et iusto odio dignissim qui blandit praesent luptatum zzril delenit augue duis dolore te feugait nulla facilisi.

Lorem ipsum dolor sit amet, consectetuer adipiscing elit, sed diam nonummy nibh euismod tincidunt ut laoreet dolore magna aliquam erat volutpat.

Lorem ipsum dolor sit amet, consectetuer adipiscing elit, sed diam aliquam erat volutpat.

New design trends
Duis autem vel eum iriure dolor in hendrerit in vulputate velit esse molestie consequat, vel illum dolore eu feugiat nulla facilisis at vero eros et accumsan. But et wollum feugait adipiscing nulla illum dolore eu feugiat facilisi.

Reduced price for quality
Lorem ipsum dolor sit amet, consecteteur enim ad minim ullanummy nibh adipiscing valor etmolestie consequat, vel illum dolore eu feugiat nulla facilisis at

Continued page 2

How to choose a laser printer

Dolor sit amet, consectetuer adipiscing elit, sed diam nonummy nibh euismod tincidunt ut laoreet dolore magna aliquam erat volutpat. Ut wisi enim ad minim veniam, quis nostrud exerci tation ullamcorper suscipit lobortis nisl ut aliquip ex ea commodo consequat.

Duis autem vel eum iriure dolor in hendrerit in vulputate velit esse molestie consequat, vel illum dolore eu feugiat nulla facilisis at vero eros et accumsan et iusto odio dignissim qui blandit praesent.

Ut wisi enim ad minim veniam, quis nostrud exerci tation ullamcorper suscipit lobortis nisl ut aliquip ex ea commodo consequat.

Continued page 3

New!
Low-calorie edible toner

Lorem ipsum dolor sit amet, consectetuer adipiscing elit, sed diam nonummy nibh euismod tincidunt ut laoreet dolore magna aliquam erat volutpat.

Ut wisi enim ad minim veniam, quis nostrud exerci tation ullanummy nibh euismod tincidunt ut laoreet dolorelobortis nisl ut aliquip ex ea commodo consequat.

Table of contents
Vol. 3, Num. 2 **Feb. 1995**

Desktop & Publishing DESIGN

New typeface designs appear

Dolor sit amet, consectetuer adipiscing elit, sed diam nonummy nibh euismod tincidunt ut laoreet dolore magna aliquam erat volutpat. Ut wisi i tation ullamcorper suscipit lobortis nisl ut aliquip ex ea commodo consequat. vel illum

ABCabc
ABCabc
ABCabc
ABCabc

dolore eu feugiat nulla facilisis at vero eros et accumsan et iusto omolestie consequat.

New, small foundries
Duis autem vel eum iriure dolor in hendrerit in vulputate velit esse molestie consequat, vel illum dolore eu feugiat nulla facilisis at vero eros et accumsan et iusto odio dignissim qui blandit praesent luptatum zzril delenit augue duis dolore te feugait nulla facilisi.

Lorem ipsum dolor sit amet, consectetuer adipiscing elit, sed tincidunt ut laoreet dolore magna aliquam erat volutpat.

Lorem ipsum dolor sit amet, consectetuer adipiscing elit, sed diam aliquam erat volutpat.

New design trends
Duis autem vel eum iriure dolor in hendrerit in vulputate velit esse molestie consequat, vel illum dolore eu feugiat nulla facilisis at vero eros et accumsan. But et wollum feugait adipiscing nulla illum dolore eu feugiat facilisi.

Reduced price for quality
Lorem ipsum dolor sit amet, consecteteur enim ad minim ullanummy nibh adipiscing valor

Continued page 2

How to choose a laser printer

Dolor sit amet, consectetuer adipiscing elit, sed diam nonummy nibh euismod tincidunt ut laoreet dolore magna aliquam erat volutpat. Ut wisi enim ad minim veniam, quis nostrud exerci tation ullamcorper suscipit lobortis nisl ut aliquip ex ea commodo consequat.

Duis autem vel eum iriure dolor in hendrerit in vulputate velit esse molestie consequat, vel illum dolore eu feugiat nulla facilisis at vero eros et accumsan et iusto odio dignissim qui blandit praesent.

Ut wisi enim ad minim veniam, quis nostrud exerci tation ullamcorper suscipit lobortis nisl ut aliquip ex ea commodo consequat. Lorem ipsum dolor sit amet, consectetuer adipiscing.

Continued page 3

New!
Low-calorie edible toner

Lorem ipsum dolor sit amet, consectetuer adipiscing elit, sed diam nonummy nibh euismod tincidunt ut laoreet dolore magna aliquam erat volutpat.

Ut wisi enim ad minim veniam, quis nostrud exerci tation ullanummy nibh euismod tincidunt ut laoreet dolorelobortis nisl ut aliquip ex ea commodo consequat.

Table of contents
Vol. 3, Num. 2 **Feb. 1995**

The Before example at left is cluttered with rules (lines) and boxes. As shown in the After example at right, eliminating most of the rules and boxes opens the page and provides unity and selective emphasis.

The boxed border around the illustration in the left column is replaced with a pair of horizontal rules. The nameplate, which becomes surrounded by white space, gains impact. Notice that the thickness of the horizontal rule at the top of the page is similar to the thickness of the type in the nameplate. This unifies the rule with the nameplate while separating the nameplate from the remainder of the page.

To further simplify the page, the boxed border around the table of contents and the unnecessary vertical downrules are also eliminated.

Organize the table of contents

Desktop & Publishing DESIGN

New typeface designs appear

Dolor sit amet, consectetuer adipiscing elit, sed diam nonummy nibh euismod tincidunt ut laoreet dolore magna aliquam erat volutpat. Ut wisi i tation ullamcorper suscipit lobortis nisl ut aliquip ex ea commodo consequat. vel illum

ABCabc
ABCabc
ABCabc
ABCabc

dolore eu feugiat nulla facilisis at vero eros et accumsan et iusto omolestie consequat.

New, small foundries

Duis autem vel eum iriure dolor in hendrerit in vulputate velit esse molestie consequat, vel illum dolore eu feugiat nulla facilisis at vero eros et accumsan et iusto odio dignissim qui blandit praesent luptatum zzril delenit augue duis dolore te feugait nulla facilisi.

Lorem ipsum dolor sit amet, consectetuer adipiscing elit, sed tincidunt ut laoreet dolore magna aliquam erat volutpat.

Lorem ipsum dolor sit amet, consectetuer adipiscing elit, sed diam aliquam erat volutpat.

New design trends

Duis autem vel eum iriure dolor in hendrerit in vulputate velit esse molestie consequat, vel illum dolore eu feugiat nulla facilisis at vero eros et accumsan. But et wollum feugait adipiscing nulla illum dolore eu feugiat facilisi.

Reduced price for quality

Lorem ipsum dolor sit amet, consecteteur enim ad minim ullanummy nibh adipiscing valor

Continued page 2

How to choose a laser printer

Dolor sit amet, consectetuer adipiscing elit, sed diam nonummy nibh euismod tincidunt ut laoreet dolore magna aliquam erat volutpat. Ut wisi enim ad minim veniam, quis nostrud exerci tation ullamcorper suscipit lobortis nisl ut aliquip ex ea commodo consequat.

Duis autem vel eum iriure dolor in hendrerit in vulputate velit esse molestie consequat, vel illum dolore eu feugiat nulla facilisis at vero eros et accumsan et iusto odio dignissim qui blandit praesent.

Ut wisi enim ad minim veniam, quis nostrud exerci tation ullamcorper suscipit lobortis nisl ut aliquip ex ea commodo consequat. Lorem ipsum dolor sit amet, consectetuer adipiscing.

Continued page 3

New!
Low-calorie edible toner

Lorem ipsum dolor sit amet, consectetuer adipiscing elit, sed diam nonummy nibh euismod tincidunt ut laoreet dolore magna aliquam erat volutpat.

Ut wisi enim ad minim veniam, quis nostrud exerci tation ullanummy nibh euismod tincidunt ut laoreet dolorelobortis nisl ut aliquip ex ea commodo consequat.

Table of contents

Vol. 3, Num. 2 **Feb. 1995**

Desktop & Publishing DESIGN

New typeface designs appear

Dolor sit amet, consectetuer adipiscing elit, sed diam nonummy nibh euismod tincidunt ut laoreet dolore magna aliquam erat volutpat. Ut wisi i tation ullamcorper suscipit lobortis nisl ut aliquip ex ea commodo consequat. vel illum

ABCabc
ABCabc
ABCabc
ABCabc

dolore eu feugiat nulla facilisis at vero eros et accumsan et iusto omolestie consequat.

New, small foundries

Duis autem vel eum iriure dolor in hendrerit in vulputate velit esse molestie consequat, vel illum dolore eu feugiat nulla facilisis at vero eros et accumsan et iusto odio dignissim qui blandit praesent luptatum zzril delenit augue duis dolore te feugait nulla facilisi.

Lorem ipsum dolor sit amet, consectetuer adipiscing elit, sed tincidunt ut laoreet dolore magna aliquam erat volutpat.

Lorem ipsum dolor sit amet, consectetuer adipiscing elit, sed diam aliquam erat volutpat.

New design trends

Duis autem vel eum iriure dolor in hendrerit in vulputate velit esse molestie consequat, vel illum dolore eu feugiat nulla facilisis at vero eros et accumsan. But et wollum feugait adipiscing nulla illum dolore eu feugiat facilisi.

Reduced price for quality

Lorem ipsum dolor sit amet, consecteteur enim ad minim ullanummy nibh adipiscing valor

Continued page 2

How to choose a laser printer

Dolor sit amet, consectetuer adipiscing elit, sed diam nonummy nibh euismod tincidunt ut laoreet dolore magna aliquam erat volutpat. Ut wisi enim ad minim veniam, quis nostrud exerci tation ullamcorper suscipit lobortis nisl ut aliquip ex ea commodo consequat.

Duis autem vel eum iriure dolor in hendrerit in vulputate velit esse molestie consequat, vel illum dolore eu feugiat nulla facilisis at vero eros et accumsan et iusto odio dignissim qui blandit praesent.

Ut wisi enim ad minim veniam, quis nostrud exerci tation ullamcorper suscipit lobortis nisl ut aliquip ex ea dolor sit amet, consectetuer adipiscing.

Continued page 3

New!
Low-calorie edible toner

Lorem ipsum dolor sit amet, consectetuer adipiscing elit, sed diam nonummy nibh euismod tincidunt ut laoreet dolore magna aliquam erat volutpat.

Ut wisi enim ad minim veniam, quis nostrud exerci tation ullanummy nibh euismod tincidunt ut laoreet dolorelobortis nisl ut aliquip ex ea commodo consequat.

Table of contents

Vol. 3, Num. 2 **Feb. 1995**

The table of contents in the Before example at left lacks color and organization and cries out for simplicity. The only visual contrast is the bold serif typeface indicating page number.

In the After example at right, the table of contents projects a more interesting, organized image. Page numbers come first, right-aligned against a right tab. Article titles are set flush left. The word "page" has been eliminated, as the reader can safely assume that the table of contents does not refer to minutes, hours, days, or years. Page numbers are set in Helvetica Black in unison with headlines and subheads to form a strong contrast with the adjacent serif typeface. To emphasize the contrast, the page numbers are set one-half point larger than the article titles. This is enough to give them extra emphasis without destroying the unity of the page.

Chapter 11

Brochures and Ads that Tell and Sell

In This Chapter

- What are the elements of a successful brochure?
- How should you plan the front cover and inside pages?
- How can you add interest to even simple two- and three-fold brochures?
- How can you make your ad stand out?

Most associations and businesses need a variety of brochures to sell their products and services. Brochures run the gamut from two- and three-fold brochures printed in one or two colors on a single sheet of 8 1/2-x-11-inch paper to formal brochures printed in four or more colors on heavy, coated paper with stiff covers.

Successful brochures fulfill these four goals:

- **Define a problem or benefit:** In your brochure, you need to identify a problem that your prospects are likely to share. You can then outline the symptoms of this problem — for example unsold houses, stressful vacations, lost sales opportunities, increased manufacturing costs, or unhappy employees. Single-problem brochures are usually more effective than multi-problem brochures, because they can address the problem in more depth.
- **Propose a solution:** After identifying the problem, you need to propose a solution and clearly explain how your recommendations solve the prospects' problems. Focus on the benefits that your audience would enjoy.
- **Answer all possible objections:** Your brochures need to convince prospects that your proposed solution is the best solution to their problems. You need to anticipate and answer all possible objections that your prospects may have when reading your brochure. Brochures not only sell a product or service, but they also sell the credibility of the firm that is offering the product or service. Your ability to anticipate and answer your readers' concerns enhances your credibility.

- **Ask for immediate action:** If your prospects don't take immediate action, there's a good chance they'll *never* take action. You can give prospects a reason to act *now* by making it easy for them to purchase your product or service. You can encourage them by providing items such as ordering instructions, toll-free phone numbers, perforated coupons, and directions to your company's location. If you are producing informational or public service brochures, make sure to suggest to readers what action they can take in response to your message.

A brochure is not a billboard! Brochures need to go beyond simply presenting a product or service; they need to show how a product or message meets the readers' needs. And most importantly, to be effective brochures need to stimulate action — whether immediately or over time. Because a brochure is tangible and can be kept and reread or passed to friends, a well-crafted brochure can stimulate action long after it has been read.

Choosing the Right Format

Brochures come in a variety of sizes and shapes. The most common are two-fold brochures (with three panels front and back) and three-fold designs (with four panels). The main advantage of two- and three-fold brochures is that they are economical, because they can be printed on both sides from a single sheet of 8½-x-11-inch or 8½-x-14-inch paper. Two- and three-fold brochures can also be mailed to prospects in #10 envelopes, and countertop displays are available to encourage prospects to take the brochures.

Two- and three-fold brochures are easy to write, because the panels organize your thoughts. Think in terms of devoting a single idea to each of the panels, and your brochure will quickly come together.

More elaborate brochure formats in nonstandard sizes are also available to make your message stand out. The disadvantage of nonstandard brochures is that printing costs and mailing can quickly go up

Many businesses have several versions of brochures to distribute at different points in the sales cycle. For brochures that you use closer to the point of purchase, provide more in-depth information about your product and spend more money on production and printing. Consider the following categories of brochures:

- **Qualifiers:** Handed out at trade shows or distributed to mailing lists. Qualifiers contain less information than brochures that you hand out to customers at the point of sale. Two- and three-fold qualifiers should be sufficient to tease the prospect into contacting you for further information. You can use qualifiers to introduce a broad range of your products and services and establish your firm's credibility. Qualifiers can also discuss frequently asked questions and introduce the prospect to the appropriate vocabulary or terminology. Typically, you print larger quantities of qualifiers because you distribute them to a broad audience.

- **Closers:** Focus on a single product or service; can reinforce a sales presentation. With closers, you can use more pages, and you may want to bind them to resemble a small book (see Chapter 14 for more about binding). Because you present these brochures at the point of sale, you want them to contain more detailed information about your product. You may even want to use more color in a closer. Typically, you print smaller quantities of closers because you focus on a smaller audience.

A standard mass marketing guideline says that the amount of time and money that you spend producing and printing a brochure should relate to the likelihood that the recipient will purchase a product or service from you in the near future. You can spend less time and money on brochures that you circulate widely, saving your resources for brochures that you distribute to prospects who are ready to buy. The same guideline works for informational or public service brochures: The broader your audience, the more you can afford to withhold the often-expensive personalizing touches that can secure a sale.

Planning Your Panels

You have several ways to organize your brochure's message. Here are some alternatives:

- **Panel-focus:** One popular alternative is to devote a single message to each panel. Each panel contains a "premise" headline at the top and two or three paragraphs that support the headline. Needless to say, this technique works best when there are a few topics of approximately equal length.
- **Linear:** The linear approach is less structured. Here, when the brochure is opened, the text begins on the left-most panel and "snakes" from the top to the bottom of each panel, similar to the way columns of text are read. Subheads are inserted where necessary, rather than as headlines, to introduce the various topics covered. The linear approach is best when some topics require more explanatory text than others.
- **Numbered arguments:** Another alternative is to organize your brochure as a series of "sound bytes" or brief statements introduced by large, oversize numbers. This is the "Six reasons to buy from us!" approach. This approach works well when time is limited and few visuals are available, The oversize numbers serve as visuals and direct the reader's eyes to each point.

Front panel

The front panel of your brochure is the entryway to your message, so clearly its design is crucial to the success of your message. Although some believe in loading the cover with all sorts of design bells and whistles, I find the classic approach works best — make the front panel as simple and uncluttered as possible.

The best-looking brochures tend to have front panels that contain the title and a visual that illustrates the theme of the message. The visual may illustrate the problem being addressed or how the prospect would benefit from the product or service described in the brochure.

What do you want the reader to see first: the title or the visual? Most eyes focus on the visual first, so if you want your title to stand out instead, you need a design in which the visual is clearly subordinate to the title, either in size or weight. Many people also include the company name or logo on the front panel. Again, make your decision based on what will attract the reader and what associations the reader is likely to make between the theme and the company.

As always, simplicity leads to impact. The fewer the words on the front panel of your brochure, the larger they can be reproduced. "Teaser" headlines often work well on brochures, as do provocative statements that involve the reader by challenging them to open the brochure.

As a rule, avoid setting type on top of photographs, as the legibility of both usually suffers. Photo alternatives include using a collage of small photographs rather than a single, large, photograph.

One of the most proven techniques for brochures is to either signal the attention of the audience by identifying it and specifying a problem they may be encountering: for example, "Dog Lovers! Are you concerned about your dog's weight?" or "Ready to retire? Here's what you should know about your retirement savings." Note that, in both cases, the prospects are clearly identified — dog lovers or those about to retire — and the prospects are presented with a question that they are likely to find hard to ignore.

If you're focusing on a problem as your theme, you may want your company name on the back of the brochure rather than the front, so as not to subliminally link the company to the problem.

Inside front panel

The inside front panel should provide an overview of the contents of your brochure and a transition from the problem/solution hinted at on the front panel to the individual topics on each panel. You can indicate the transition by a headline that doesn't repeat the title of the brochure, but solves the problem that it brings up.

For example, "We can help you fine-tune your dog's diet to their activity levels" or "Let us help you audit your mutual fund's performance in light of today's changed tax climate!" This maintains the continuity of the front panel headline without repeating the exact words. Then, you can include a technique like an initial cap to draw the reader's eye into the text.

The inside panel can contain two or three easy-to-read paragraphs that provide an overview of the text that follows, or you can involve the reader by asking a series of questions set off by bullets, such as:

- Does your dog get regular exercise?
- Is your dog as active as it once was?
- When was the last time you compared your mutual fund to others in its field?
- How much of your mutual fund's earnings are going to "management" and "marketing" and how much to your future?

Notice the momentum that a series of questions has. Questions continue to involve your reader. To make the text on the transitional inside panel stand out, use a larger type size, extra line spacing, colored bullets, or italics.

Inside panels

The inside panels of your brochures should contain short text segments that describe the benefits of your products or services. White space is as important on the inside panels of your brochure as it is in your other print communications. Often, you can get sufficient white space by using generous left-hand margins, which build white space to the left of the text on each panel. Don't feel you have to fill each panel with text from top to bottom.

If you are using a linear organization, don't begin new paragraphs near the bottom of a panel, but move them up to the top of the next panel. If you are using a "one idea per panel" organization if you have less text on one panel than the other, consider allowing the white space to remain as a contrasting element rather than filling it with a decorative graphic.

Outside back panel

The outside back panel should summarize the major points covered inside the brochure and point the prospect to the next step: calling a telephone number, filling out an order form, or visiting a store or place of business. The back panel is the only place where it's absolutely necessary to include your firm's address and phone number.

Saving Money on Brochures

You can reduce the cost of brochures by

- **Ordering the right quantities:** Base print quantities on the number you intend to distribute before the information goes out of date. If you print 500 copies but have to reprint a brochure before the information goes out of date, it costs more to go back on the press to print an additional 500 than it would have cost to print 1,000 the first time. On the other hand, if you print 1,000 copies and only distribute 500 before the information is outdated, you've wasted 500 copies. Best results occur when you base print quantities on the shelf life of your information as well as the number of pieces you intend to distribute.
- **Imaginatively using gray and black as shades (or screens) of colors rather than adding other colors:** If you want or need more than one color, black and a second color is less expensive and works better than two non-black colors.
- **Printing on lighter paper stock:** Chapter 13 gives you the basics of selecting paper; pound for pound, the lighter weight paper (say 60 lb.) is less expensive than a heavier weight (like 80 lb). Papers vary greatly, however, and some lighter weight papers work better than others in heavier weights. You want to avoid having the type from one page bleed through to the opposite side. And you want to avoid having your brochure feel flimsy and insubstantial, which could affect the way your readers view your business. Your printer is an ideal resource to find the best and most economical paper stock.
- **Working with your commercial printer to choose designs that can be printed on larger paper sizes and later trimmed into individual brochures:** Although many brochures are printed on $8^1/_2$ x 11-inch sheets of paper, your printer may be able to print several copies at a time of an 8-inch square brochure, for example, on 16- or 32-inch-wide sheets of paper.
- **Exercising restraint in distribution:** Print only as many brochures as you need and plan for their most cost-effective distribution to your target audience. This reduces waste printing and helps control costs.

An inexpensive way to produce a small quantity of brochures — under 1,000 — is to print them on an ink-jet or laser printer. You can also use your office photocopier if you have colored brochure formats. You can purchase two- and three-fold brochure formats in a variety of designs from companies like PaperDirect. Most designs include valuable options like:

- **Die-cuts:** A die-cut is an opening created by cutting into the paper. This is an expensive technique when custom-requested, but many pre-designed papers include this feature that you can use to insert your business card.
- **Perforated coupons or panels:** Perforations — tiny cuts into the paper that enable it to be torn easily on a straight line — are another expensive feature of custom printing that can be readily and cheaply available with pre-printed brochure formats. These panels can be torn off and used as reply cards or order forms.
- **Step-up pockets:** Allow you to insert various-sized panels, so that you can focus on a single topic in each panel yet still be able to scan all the headlines at a glance.

You can order PaperDirect's extensive catalog by calling 1-800-APAPERS or checking out the PaperDirect Web site.

Three Easy Ways to Create Better-Looking Brochures

Three techniques can help you create better-looking, easier-to-read brochures. The following techniques can be used individually or together:

Use bleeds

When the ink runs through to the edges of the paper, allowing no margins, the design is said to *bleed.* Bleeds offer you numerous creative options.

One of the best ways to use a bleed is to create a *window* for your title. Instead of using the ink for the text of your title, use the ink as a colored background to frame the title and draw attention to the brochure, as shown in Figure 11-1.

You can also use bleeds to add typographic interest to your title by allowing some of the letters to extend to the edge of the front panel.

Figure 11-1: Notice the impact gained by framing the title of the brochure on the right with the surrounding color. This technique uses both a reverse (inking around the type rather than inking the type itself) and a bleed (running the ink to the edges of the page). The effect is enhanced by using bolder, slightly larger text.

Add white space

One of the easiest ways to add impact to your brochures is to add a consistent amount of white space to the top or sides of each panel. You can place headlines in the white space, or you can begin headlines below the white space. You can emphasize the pool of white space by adding a thin line along the horizon.

Another way to add white space to each panel is to indent your text columns and place your headlines and subheads to the left of the columns, as you can see in Figure 11-2.

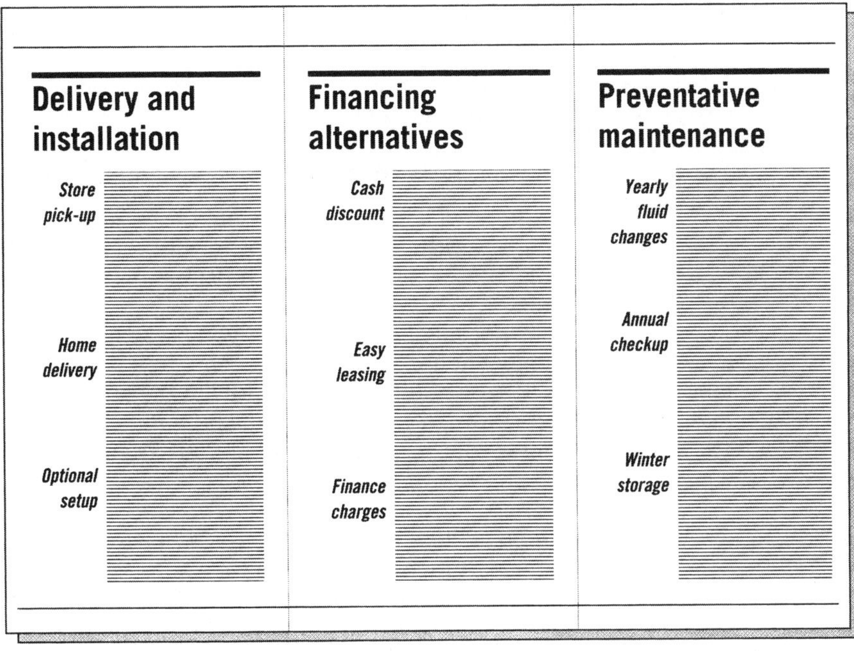

Figure 11-2: You can add white space by simply indenting each paragraph and placing the head-lines to the left of the text that they introduce.

An even more elaborate structure is to use a grid — or network of non-printing guidelines — to subdivide each panel into two columns; one narrow, one wide. The narrow column, approximately 15 to 20 percent of the width of the panel, is left empty, adding white space to each panel as well as creating a place for short text elements, such as pullquotes.

You can place subheads and body copy in the wide column, but you need to allow the major subheads to span the vertical spine and break into the white space to the left of the text column (in other words, your subheads will appear outdented as they extend into the narrow column where your text cannot follow). This technique avoids the "fullness" that occurs when headlines and body text extend the full width of each panel to create uniform, boring panels.

Align your visuals with the underlying column setup. Place horizontal photographs in the wide column and place small vertical photographs in the narrow column. Alternately, larger photographs that begin in the wide columns can extend into the narrow columns.

Consider lists

Another easy way to brighten up your brochure is to arrange your text in bite-sized bits, using bulleted text or numbered points.

- Use bullets if your ideas are of approximately equal importance.
- Use numbered points if order is important or if you want to prioritize your arguments — either beginning with your most important idea or building from your least important to most important idea.

This technique is especially powerful when you present a number of arguments for your case. When readers begin a numbered series, it's very difficult for them to stop reading in the middle of the sequence. By reducing the amount of text (through careful editing) and numbering your points, you can almost guarantee that readers will follow your argument through to its conclusion.

As a designer, use distinctive bullets or numbers that are large and noticeable, treating them as a graphic element in the listing (see Figure 11-3). Small numbers are less noticeable and less compelling to read. By restricting the length of your points, you can create the space to introduce the points with larger, more eye-catching graphics.

Creating Awesome Advertisements

Advertisements run the gamut from classified ads in your community's free handout to display ads that get mixed in with a publication's editorial content to formal ads that you place in regional magazines or trade publications. Advertisements are often your first introduction to a prospective client or customer. Advertisements are also "reinforcers" that help previously sold customers feel secure that they made the right purchase or decision.

Although valuable in introducing your business to new prospects, advertisements present numerous challenges. Usually, they must compete for attention with other, often larger, ads on the same page. They are often dwarfed by adjacent editorial material. Even at their best, ads offer little space to attract your prospect's attention and tell your story. That's why every word has to count, and to count, it has to be both noticeable and readable.

Color is another challenge in advertising; you may find that color is either not available or that it is so expensive that you only want to include it in your larger-sized ads. You can usually use four-color photographs in quality

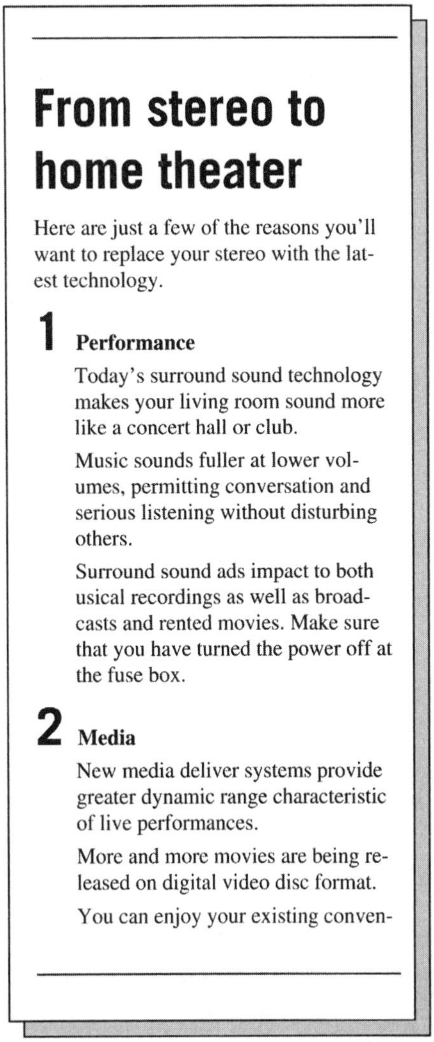

From stereo to home theater

Here are just a few of the reasons you'll want to replace your stereo with the latest technology.

1 **Performance**

Today's surround sound technology makes your living room sound more like a concert hall or club.

Music sounds fuller at lower volumes, permitting conversation and serious listening without disturbing others.

Surround sound ads impact to both usical recordings as well as broadcasts and rented movies. Make sure that you have turned the power off at the fuse box.

2 **Media**

New media deliver systems provide greater dynamic range characteristic of live performances.

More and more movies are being released on digital video disc format.

You can enjoy your existing conven-

Figure 11-3: Limit your numbered arguments to your most important points and use super-noticeable numbers.

long-life publications, like magazines, that are printed on quality paper. In other publications, like newspapers, color is either not available or you have to pay extra for each color that you add.

In addition, you may have difficulty trying to make a smaller ad stand out. Small ads can easily get lost in the classifieds or on a full-size newspaper page where they are surrounded by other ads, editorial text, and visuals. For smaller ads, you need to make maximum use of white space to get noticed among the editorial clutter.

You can create successful ads by fine-tuning each of the elements of print design discussed in Chapter 9. And remember, always make it as easy as possible for readers to respond to your ads. You can improve the *action power* of your advertisements by using the following tips:

- If you sell by telephone, use a large font size for your telephone number.
- Always include your Web site address so that prospects know where to search for more information.
- If you want to attract walk-in customers, include a full street address as well as cross streets and directions to the nearest Interstate highway or major landmark. If your ad is large enough, insert a map.
- Make coupons large enough that readers can fill them in by using a ballpoint pen. Always place coupons in the lower-right corner of the ad and ask that the ad be positioned in the lower-right corner of right-hand pages.

Consider some of the following hints for organizing the content of ads that sell *multiple products:*

- **Organize the offerings according to categories:** When creating busy, product-filled retail ads, group similar products under common headings or categories within the ad. For example if you're a computer dealer, you can group your offerings under "Computers," "Printers," "Software," and "Miscellaneous."
- **Avoid overillustrating:** You rarely need to use illustrations for all your products — especially if the products resemble one another. Illustrate one product within each category, with listings and prices for other products.
- **Always provide a dominant visual:** Instead of using same-size visuals, choose your most important product and make it the ad's focal point.
- **Strive for consistency:** When you need to include manufacturers' logos (with the exception of your one featured product), make sure that the logos are the same size for each product. Likewise, strive for consistent sizing and placement prices and descriptions for remaining products.
- **Remember that ads are miniature pages:** Readers skim ads in a Z-shaped manner — from the upper left to the lower right. Avoid tricky creative effects like placing the headline in the middle of the ad and expecting readers to begin reading the body text that begins above the headline.

Chapter 12

Proposals, Reports, and All Those Forms

In This Chapter

- Making the most of your word processor's capabilities
- Placing visuals
- Using special covers and separator pages
- Creating attractive, easy-to-use applications and forms
- Designing instructions and training materials

Business people often do not take the time (or maybe don't know how) to customize and fine-tune their most important documents. Instead they use the same old styles that everyone else in the office uses for their new client proposals and departmental reports.

Mimicking existing styles is unwise unless those styles have become engrained in the corporate approach to such matters or have already been fine-tuned. Proposals and reports play a major role in determining your income (if you're self-employed) or your advancement (if you need to gain the approval of others) because, in your reader's mind, the attention you pay to proposals and reports reflects the attention you pay to your job and your clients. You want that reflection to be a good one.

Even everyday documents can benefit from careful design and production. Everyday documents include routine external correspondence, such as letters to prospects and clients as well as internal communications such as memos and documents describing office procedures. Although these documents lack the glamour and glitz of brochures and newsletters, they are extremely important because they are sent to individuals at the moment of purchase or action. There is no waste circulation, therefore every communication must succeed.

Making the Most of Your Word Processor

Often you create client proposals and departmental reports by using a word processor rather than a page-layout program. In this section, I focus on changes that you can make by using just six key features that most word-processing programs include: margins, line spacing, letter spacing, contrasting type, headers, and footers. You can use these features together to create a document that's attractive, easily read, and easily followed — even without the bells and whistles that page-layout programs can add.

Adjusting margins to shorten line length

One of the biggest reasons that many proposals and reports go unread is that they appear too crowded with text — filling the page from edge to shining edge. Leaving aside the question of whether you need all that text — is it really saying something significant? — the easiest way to eliminate text crowding and improve the appearance of your proposals and reports is to reduce line length by adjusting your left- and right-hand margins.

Fine-tuning line spacing

You need to make sure that the right amount of white space separates each line of type as well as each paragraph. Often your word processor's default line spacing (also called *leading*) is not generous enough for the long lines of text in proposals and reports, which are usually prepared using a single, wide column of text.

You can determine when line spacing needs to be increased by looking at the overall grayness of the text. Grayness is determined by the type size, the thickness of the characters of the typeface chosen, as well as the line spacing and the presence or absence of subheads and extra space between paragraphs.

You can also read the text to see if you tend to reread the same lines or if you tend to jump down two lines of text when you start reading a new line. If you experience difficulties with the relationship between line length and line spacing, your readers are even more likely to be frustrated!

One way to choose the correct line spacing for your document is to experiment with various line spacing settings (see Figure 12-1) and see which ones you find easiest to read. Avoid using the typewriter-like presets — such as single, one and one-half line, and double-line spacing. Instead, select the *exact* line spacing option and enter a setting two or three points larger than your current type size.

Funding Proposal:

The Millennium and Beyond

Never before has our firm faced such major competitive challenges. We face both domestic and global challenges to our lead in petrified rock production. Major investments are required if we are to maintain our lead both at home and internationally. The major disadvantage to this approach is the need to locate additional funding within the time frame available. This money is needed now and has to appear within the next forty-eight hours or all opportunities will be forever gone. We look forward to rapid approval of these expenditures, prior to our annual stockholder meeting, and while our Executive Board is still in Europe investigating expansion opportunities abroad.

Funding sources

Funding sources include the private sector (bonds, stocks, etc.) as well as the public sector (direct subsidies, tax abatements, reduced enviromental compliance, etc.). We are actively working with campaign contributors to uncover ways of expediting approval of public sector investment.

How the money will be spent

Once identified, funds for expansion and increased productivity will be spent in a variety of ways. All relevant parties (the Executive Board, the Board of Directors, etc.), will always be consulted before actual funds are spent. Funds will be invested in several categories of projects, including, but not limited to, the following:

— *Renovations to Executive Lunchroom.* The Executive Lunchroom requires extensive renovation in order to provide an atmosphere conducive to high-level meetings and enhanced productivity. Additional staffing is required behind the bar to accommodate additional traffic caused by the stresses caused by rumors of takeover bids. At the same time, a new Executive Chef will be recruited from France, along with recommended staff.

— *Restoration of executive parking privileges.* As the firm has grown, parking has become more and more of a problem. The only answer appears to be to encourage employee parking in Shuttle Lots A, B and C located in the next town, (connected by an hourly shuttle) and limit parking adjacent to the facilities to executive-level pesonnel (Marketing Managers and Vice Presidents, etc.). This will also reduce congestion and pollution around the plant.

— *Improved off-campus transportation.* Because it is so important to project an image of success to our clients, new vehicles will be provided to all departmental managers and Vice Presidents. These cars should all be colored silver with tan leather upholstery and multi-disc DC changers.

Proposal: The Millennium and Beyond
June 3, 1998
Page 1 of 15

Funding Proposal:

The Millennium and Beyond

Never before has our firm faced such major competitive challenges. We face both domestic and global challenges to our lead in petrified rock production. Major investments are required if we are to maintain our lead both at home and internationally. The major disadvantage to this approach is the need to locate additional funding within the time frame available. This money is needed now and has to appear within the next forty-eight hours or all opportunities will be forever gone. We look forward to rapid approval of these expenditures, prior to our annual stockholder meeting, and while our Executive Board is still in Europe investigating expansion opportunities abroad.

Funding sources

Funding sources include the private sector (bonds, stocks, etc.) as well as the public sector (direct subsidies, tax abatements, reduced enviromental compliance, etc.). We are actively working with campaign contributors to uncover ways of expediting approval of public sector investment.

How the money will be spent

Once identified, funds for expansion and increased productivity will be spent in a variety of ways. All relevant parties (the Executive Board, the Board of Directors, etc.), will always be consulted before actual funds are spent. Funds will be invested in several categories of projects, including, but not limited to, the following:

— *Renovations to Executive Lunchroom.* The Executive Lunchroom requires extensive renovation in order to provide an atmosphere conducive to high-level meetings and enhanced productivity. Additional staffing is required behind the bar to accommodate additional traffic caused by the stresses caused by rumors of takeover bids. At the same time, a new Executive Chef will be recruited from France, along with recommended staff.

— *Restoration of executive parking privileges.* As the firm has grown, parking has become more and more of a problem. The only answer appears to be to encourage employee parking in Shuttle Lots A, B and C located in the next town, (connected by an hourly shuttle) and limit parking

Proposal: The Millennium and Beyond
June 3, 1998
Page 1 of 15

Figure 12-1: Most proposals and reports benefit from added line spacing, as you can see in the well-spaced form at the bottom.

Print the page and note the line spacing setting that the page illustrates. Then change the setting by one-half a point. Print the new page, again taking note of the new line spacing specification.

By comparing printouts created with different line spacing, you can choose the correct line spacing for your document.

Manipulating letter spacing

Often, your word processor's default, or normal, letter spacing is too generous. By reducing letter spacing, you can improve the overall look of your proposals and increase the word density on each page (gaining back some of the content you may have lost by increasing the left-hand margin and the line spacing).

The cumulative effect of even tiny reductions in letter spacing quickly adds up. By printing *before* and *after* pages, you can see that line endings and page breaks do change.

You can reduce your letter spacing by selecting the letter spacing options. These options are usually found under the Format menu. In some word-processing programs, such as Microsoft Word, letter spacing options are grouped in the Character Spacing tab located under the Font menu. In most page-layout programs, letter spacing is located in the Format menu under Tracking.

1. **Highlight the text that you want to change, and try various settings, starting with a one-point reduction.**

   Print the page and note the one-point reduction on the page.

2. **Reopen the page, highlight the text, and reduce the letter spacing by one and one-half points.**

   Again, print the page.

At some point, the words become easier to recognize because the letters are closer together — yet not so close as to run into each other. (You need to stop and back up when the letters begin to run into each other.)

Adding contrasting subheads

You can use typographic contrast to ensure that your subheads appear as clearly as possible. Consider using two or more contrast options from the following list:

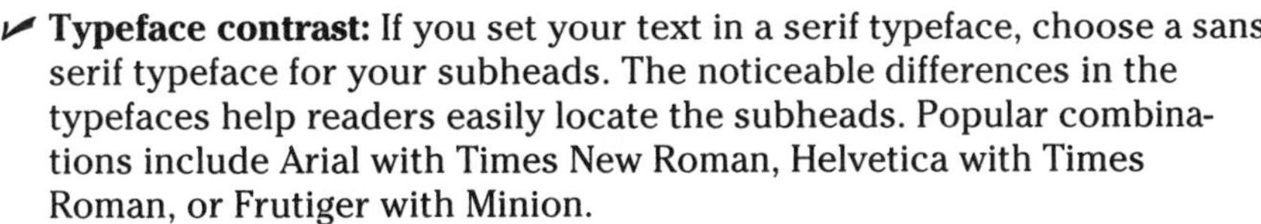

- **Typeface contrast:** If you set your text in a serif typeface, choose a sans serif typeface for your subheads. The noticeable differences in the typefaces help readers easily locate the subheads. Popular combinations include Arial with Times New Roman, Helvetica with Times Roman, or Frutiger with Minion.

  Unless you're an experienced designer, don't try combining two serif or two sans serif typefaces, because they easily "fight" each other.

- **Size contrast:** Avoid subheads that *whisper* rather than ***shout.*** Subheads that whisper look accidental, rather than purposeful. Create whispering subheads when you use subheads that are only slightly larger than the body copy that they introduce.

  If you use the same typeface for your subheads and body copy, you can avoid whispering subheads by making the subheads significantly larger than the body copy. Try 14- or 16-point subheads with 12-point text or 12- or 14-point subheads with 11-point text.

- **Style contrast:** You can use bold and/or italics to add impact to subheads. (Never underline them though, because this makes the subheads harder to read.) Using bold and italics by themselves, however, are rarely enough to make subheads stand out the way they should. Style contrast works best when the type size is slightly increased and/or extra space is added above the subhead.
- **Case contrast:** Avoid using all caps for subheads. Subheads set in all caps are harder to read than subheads set in upper-and lowercase text.
- **Position contrast:** When you set up the styles for your subheads, adjust your left margin setting to *hang,* or place, your subheads to the left of the text that they introduce. By adjusting your left margin setting, you surround the beginning of each subhead with white space, making the subheads easier to locate (because they contrast with the adjacent white space). You can also add extra white space above the subheads to emphasize the break from the preceding paragraphs.
- **Graphic accents:** Use overrules or underrules (added by clicking on the Borders button of most word-processing paragraph dialog boxes) to add a line above (or below) each subhead, adding further visual accents to the page and emphasizing the subhead. Figure 12-2 gives an example.

By simply combining two, or more, of the preceding typographic contrast tools, you can create a whole new look for your proposals and reports. You can also use different variations of the six tools to indicate a hierarchy of information so that Subhead Level One is significantly different than Subhead Level Two. This hierarchy helps readers grasp the level of importance of the text that follows each subhead. (Of course, part of the concept of hierarchy is that each succeeding level be smaller and less noticeable than the one above. If you make your Level One heading smaller than your Level Two, you haven't helped anything.)

Funding Proposal:

The Millennium and Beyond

Never before has our firm faced such major competitive challenges. We face both domestic and global challenges to our lead in petrified rock production. Major investments are required if we are to maintain our lead both at home and internationally. The major disadvantage to this approach is the need to locate additional funding within the time frame available. This money is needed now and has to appear within the next forty-eight hours or all opportunities will be forever gone. We look forward to rapid approval of these expenditures, prior to our annual stockholder meeting, and while our Executive Board is still in Europe investigating expansion opportunities abroad.

Funding alternatives

Funding sources include the private sector (bonds, stocks, etc.) as well as the public sector (direct subsidies, tax abatements, reduced enviromental compliance, etc.). We are actively working with campaign contributors to uncover ways of expediting approval of public sector investment.

How the money will be spent

Once identified, funds for expansion and increased productivity will be spent in a variety of ways. All relevant parties (the Executive Board, the Board of Directors, etc.), will always be consulted before actual funds are spent. Funds will be invested in several categories of projects, including, but not limited to, the following:

— *Renovations to Executive Lunchroom.* The Executive Lunchroom requires extensive renovation in order to provide an atmosphere conducive to high-level meetings and enhanced productivity. Additional staffing is required behind the bar to accommodate additional traffic caused by the stresses caused by rumors of takeover bids. At the same time, a new Executive Chef will be re-cruited from France, along with recommended staff.

— *Restoration of executive parking privileges.* As the firm has grown, parking has become more and more of a problem. The only answer appears to be to encourage employee parking in Shuttle

Proposal: The Millennium and Beyond
June 3, 1998
Page 1 of 15

Figure 12-2: Various forms of typographic contrast make it easy to notice the subheads and ascertain their relative importance.

Another way to project a professional image in your proposals and reports is to use various numbering options for your subhead levels. Most word processors can automatically number subhead levels; this technique adds further visual interest to your subheads and helps the readers observe the hierarchy of the text that follows.

Working with headers and footers

Headers and footers that identify your document help people navigate through your proposals and reports. Be sure to pay as much attention to formatting header and footer text as you do to formatting the body text of your documents. Remember to make the text in headers and footers smaller and less noticeable than the text of your proposals and reports so the header and footer text does not compete with the contents of your proposals and reports.

When you format header and footer text, strive to visually reinforce the text area of your proposals and reports. Although header and footer text is usually smaller than body copy, align it with the body copy and use the same typeface.

Use the Suppress feature of your word processor to set up your headers and footers so that you can omit them on pages where you don't need them; for example, omit header and footer information from the front pages of proposals and reports to make room for your title or opening text to stand out.

Don't inadvertently use your word processor's default typeface choice for headers and footers. Unless you specifically format headers and footers differently, they appear in the same typeface you choose for body text.

Adding introductions, conclusions, and summaries

Another way to improve the appearance of your proposals and reports is to use typographic contrast to draw attention to introductions, conclusions, and summaries. Your key focus should be to *guide* your readers as much as possible and avoid presenting them with dull, boring pages.

The easiest way to add impact to introductions, conclusions, and summaries is to use text styles that differentiate them from the adjacent text. Typographic options that work well include:

- **Style:** If you use short introductions and/or conclusions, try setting them in italics (see Figure 12-3).
- **Line spacing:** Because italicized text is harder to read than Roman or upright text, you can add line spacing to make your introductions and/or conclusions easier to read.
- **Placement:** You can draw attention to special text by changing the left-hand margins to set it apart.

Funding Proposal:

The Millennium and Beyond

Never before has our firm faced such major competitive challenges. We face both domestic and global challenges to our lead in petrified rock production. Major investments are required if we are to maintain our lead both at home and internationally. The major disadvantage to this approach is the need to locate additional funding within the time frame available. This money is needed now and has to appear within the next forty-eight hours or all opportunities will be forever gone. We look forward to rapid approval of these expenditures, prior to our annual stockholder meeting, and while our Executive Board is still in Europe investigating expansion opportunities abroad.

Funding alternatives

Funding sources include the private sector (bonds, stocks, etc.) as well as the public sector (direct subsidies, tax abatements, reduced enviromental compliance, etc.). We are actively working with campaign contributors to uncover ways of expediting approval of public sector investment.

How the money will be spent

Once identified, funds for expansion and increased productivity will be spent in a variety of ways. All relevant parties (the Executive Board, the Board of Directors, etc.), will always be consulted before actual funds are spent. Funds will be invested in several categories of projects, including, but not limited to, the following:

— *Renovations to Executive Lunchroom.* The Executive Lunchroom requires extensive renovation in order to provide an atmosphere conducive to high-level meetings and

Proposal: The Millennium and Beyond
June 3, 1998
Page 1 of 15

Figure 12-3: Setting introductions in italicized text with extra line spacing and longer lines sets them apart from the text that follows.

Placing visuals

When you add visuals to your proposals and reports, avoid text wraps whenever possible. Text wraps occur when visuals are dropped into the text at seemingly random locations, which can reduce the line length of adjacent text and change the word and letter spacing.

You can avoid text wraps by using some of the following techniques:

- **Placing titles and captions next to the visuals:** The traditional location for a title is above the visual that it introduces. The usual location for a caption is below the visual that it describes and interprets. Generally, you set a caption in a smaller type size than the adjacent text.

  Instead of playing "follow the leader," experiment by grouping your titles and captions next to the visuals that they introduce and by using large, attention-grabbing captions. By placing titles and captions next to your visuals, you not only avoid text wraps but you add impact to your visuals by drawing the reader's eye to them and by making them look intentional rather than accidental.

- **Grouping visuals:** If your pages contain two or more visuals, such as photographs or business graphics, try grouping them together so that they form a single text interruption instead of two (see Figure 12-4). Readers usually prefer to refer ahead (or back) to a visual than be forced to put up with additional text wraps.

- **Placing visuals in margin:** Whenever possible, place visuals in the margins next to the text columns instead of burying them within the text columns. By placing visuals in the margins adjacent to the text columns, you surround the visuals (and their captions) with white space, and you avoid text wraps. This option is preferable even if you must use slightly smaller visuals and wider margins than you would otherwise.

Adding covers and separator pages

You can enhance your proposals and reports by using special paper for your covers and subdividers. Printing the front and back covers on heavier paper, or a card stock, emphasizes the importance of your proposal or report (see Chapter 13 for more about paper stock) by providing a more substantial feel and making the document easier to handle without damaging the covers. Just be sure to check your ink-jet or laser printer instructions (you did keep them, didn't you?) to make sure that you can use thick paper in your printer.

Exhibit A: Executive Transportation Vehicle, Alternative One (note bulletproof glass).

Exhibit B: Step-up Executive Transportation Vehicle, (note fins and spoiler).

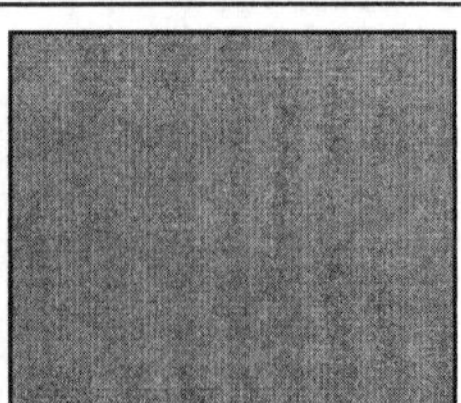

Exhibit C: Best value , alternative One (with four-wheel drive and Turbocharger).

Funding sources include the private sector (bonds, stocks, etc.) as well as the public sector (direct subsidies, tax abatements, reduced enviromental compliance, etc.). We are actively working with campaign contributors to uncover ways of expediting approval of public sector investment.

How the money will be spent

Once identified, funds for expansion and increased productivity will be spent in a variety of ways. All relevant parties (the Executive Board, the Board of Directors, etc.), will always be consulted before actual funds are spent. Funds will be invested in several categories of projects, including, but not limited to, the following:

— *Renovations to Executive Lunchroom.* The Executive Lunchroom requires extensive renovation in order to provide an atmosphere conducive to high-level meetings and enhanced productivity. Additional staffing is required behind the bar to accommodate additional traffic caused by the stresses caused by rumors of takeover bids. At the same time, a new Executive Chef will be recruited from France, along with recommended staff.

— *Restoration of executive parking privileges.* As the firm has grown, parking has become more and more of a problem. The only answer appears to be to encourage employee parking in Shuttle Lots A, B and C located in the next town, (connected by an hourly shuttle) and limit parking adjacent to the facilities to executive-level pesonnel (Marketing Managers and Vice Presidents, etc.). This will also reduce congestion and pollution around the plant.

Proposal: The Millennium and Beyond
June 3, 1998
Page 3 of 15

Figure 12-4: Grouping visuals together emphasizes their importance and avoids text wraps.

In many cases, you can either feed heavier-than-normal paper through your printer one sheet at a time, or you can use a special feed door that leads to a simpler, straighter paper path.

Another way to add impact to your proposals and reports is to use special paper to separate the various categories of information inside. For example, you can place an elegant opaque (or nearly transparent) paper between the cover and the first page of your proposal. (The effect is similar to the tissue used to shield fine engraving on wedding announcements.)

You can also use different pages to create separator pages for the various sections of your proposal, so that readers can quickly locate *Section Two, Section Three,* or *Pricing Recommendations.* A few different, contrasting sheets of paper can make a big difference in the way your proposal or report feels when you hold it — flimsy or substantial — or how easily you can read it and refer to different sections.

Problems with Forms and Applications

Like proposals and reports, internal publications such as applications and forms, as well as after-the-sale customer support materials, often just happen rather than go through a formal design process.

This approach is wrong, because your association or firm's corporate identity is created by the cumulative impact of everything that goes out with your firm's logo on it.

There are no "unimportant" documents; every internal and external document influences the image your firm projects.

The starting point for designing effective forms and applications is to *organize the information you want to gather* and *determine how much detail* is likely to be provided for each element. By filling out a few sample applications yourself, using a fictitious but typical user, you can quickly determine how much space is likely to be needed for each component of your forms and applications. Whenever possible, when options are limited, use ballot boxes or check marks instead of two parallel Yes and No options. The following sections discuss common problems with forms and applications.

Room to write

Have you ever experienced the frustration of trying to squeeze a lot of information into a little space? That's a common problem with forms and applications that just "happened" as opposed to having been designed. To make matters worse, these forms often "happened" on a typewriter, even though most of today's office routines are done on personal computers.

The biggest single problem is that these forms often offer more horizontal space than vertical space. There's often *too much horizontal distance* (for example, three to four inches to print your phone number) but not enough vertical space to comfortably write in your responses. Or the line length bears no relation to the amount of space needed for the information, such as less than an inch to write in your name.

A much better alternative is to reduce the width of your applications and provide more vertical distance between the lines. Often, you can create the necessary vertical space by grouping short items together on the same line, so that the total vertical space remains the same, but the space is more intelligently utilized.

Accordingly, the first step in improving the appearance and functionality of your forms and applications is to make sure that you are providing enough *height* for the recipient to write in their responses to the questions. Telephone numbers and zip codes simply don't require as much space as proper nouns like personal and city names.

Logical organization

Another frequently encountered problem involves organizing the information to be gathered. Very often, forms lack any meaningful hierarchy of information. Symptoms of a lack of hierarchy include:

- Instructions set in the same typeface and type size as the field identifiers, such as name, street, phone, and so on.
- Lack of subdivisions separating housekeeping information (such as name and address) from subcategories such as education, experience, and references.
- Clutter and confusion resulting from a meaningful lack of relationship between lines for checkmarks and the information they relate to. Frequently, visual confusion is also caused by a lack of visual alignment or organization on the page. The placement of text and response indicators is determined by word length, rather than by their position on the page.

The best forms tend to be those that are subdivided into information categories using subheads and instructions set in contrasting typefaces and type sizes that lead the users' eyes from topic to topic, clearly indicating what's expected of them. In addition, ballot boxes and other response elements align with each other to present a more organized appearance. And shades and tints (screens) are used to highlight information blocks.

Meaningful headings and space for details

Forms and applications often lack meaningful headings or titles, using redundant words instead of words that convey meaning. "Employment Application" at the top of a form is an example. If the applicants can tell the purpose of the form by the nature of the questions asked, why remind the applicants that they're looking for a job?

Simply replacing "Employment Application" with a kinder and gentler phrase like: "Welcome to Whipsnap Corporation" amplified by a subtitle such as "We'd like to know a bit more about you so we can help you better" projects an entirely different image.

Always provide several lines at the bottom of the form for details and other comments. You'd be surprised at how often medical background forms, for example, list check boxes for major life-threatening diseases and then provide only a tiny line or two for details. Make sure that you provide enough space to encourage those filling out the form to answer fully enough to meet your requirements.

Problems with Instructional Materials

A lack of information hierarchy along with too many subheads and too much chunking create chaos in many instruction books and training materials, causing them to be far harder to use than they need to be.

- *Iconitis* results when pages are cluttered with too many similar icons introducing supplementary material to be read along with the adjacent text. Instead of presenting the information equivalent of the occasional pearl in an oyster, these pages have so many visual distractions that they present a cluttered, "hard to figure out what to read next" impression.
- Too much chunking is equally distracting. *Chunking* refers to breaking text into bundles of associated information, each introduced by its own subhead. Although chunking helps readers quickly locate relevant data, too much chunking interferes with the narrative flow of the text.

- Too many numbered subhead levels often cause training materials to present an overly complicated image. Unless you're discussing how to reassemble a Boeing 747, you're better off not including more than three subhead levels, and you probably don't need to hierarchically number each level (unless your firm's corporate standards dictate differently, of course).

And, as you would expect, instruction books and training manuals often suffer from the same problems that hinder readability and usability in the other types of printed publications discussed throughout this book. If you improve your design skills overall, you'll improve the look of all your publications.

Chapter 13

The Impact of Paper, Ink, and Folds

In This Chapter

- What to look for when choosing paper
- How to use folds and die cuts as design tools
- How special inks can contribute to the success of your message
- How to make photographs stand out

The paper your publication is printed on, the way it's folded, and the inks used to convey your message are extremely important design partners, crucial to the success of your print communications.

Paper and ink add *tangibility* to your designs. Until they're reproduced in ink on paper, your designs come to life only on the screen of your computer where only *you* can read them and appreciate their design excellence. The right paper and ink can transform good design into great design. Conversely, the wrong ink and/or the wrong paper can sabotage even the best designs.

The right ink and paper can add impact to even everyday designs. Here are some of the things to watch for when selecting paper and ink.

Important Paper Characteristics

Paper is defined by ten important characteristics:

- Size
- Color
- Texture
- Coating
- Weight
- Bulk
- Stiffness
- Opacity
- Grain direction
- Availability

In the following sections, I give you a detailed look at each of these characteristics.

Size: From start to finish

There are two aspects to size: the size of your finished publication and the size of the sheets of paper your commercial printer buys and prints on.

The physical aspects of your publication — its length and width — influence how *efficient* it will be to print and mail and how *desirable* it will be to read, store, and refer to later. The size of a publication also influences how *noticeable* it will be when delivered, as well as how easy it will be to hold and handle.

Size plays a major role in determining printing and mailing costs. It costs far less to print on standard paper sizes than on nonstandard sizes that must be trimmed. Mailing costs can be significantly higher for non-standard sizes than standard sizes. When considering printing nonstandard document sizes, always check with your post office before producing and printing your project. Nonstandard sizes may be refused at the post office.

Be sure to pick up a copy of the post office's latest regulations describing the minimum and maximum sizes and thickness for various categories of mail. Better yet, have your commercial printer prepare an actual-sized dummy out of the paper your publication will be printed on. Then you can take it to the local postmaster for approval.

When planning your publication, begin by determining the amount of attention-gathering power you want it to have. Sometimes small publications have more impact than standard $8^1/_2$- x 11-inch publications. Small, invitation-sized publications project elegance. On the other hand, large, square, or nonstandard rectangles (rectangles other than $8^1/_2$ x 11) can attract attention because of their nonstandard size.

Always take your project's anticipated life span into account when determining its size. Odd-sized publications are difficult to store in file cabinets. If your publication is designed to be a coffee table showpiece, a hard-to-store, well-produced, oversized format can work to your advantage. It may stick around on your prospect's desk (or by the bed) for several weeks because the brochure or newsletter is "too good to throw away" yet there's no convenient place to put it.

Make sure that the paper you choose is available in sizes that permit efficient printing. Papers available in wide sheets permit you to save money by allowing your commercial printer to print your brochures or newsletters *two-up,* that is, two copies are simultaneously printed and cut apart after drying. This can significantly reduce printing time and, hence, costs.

Color: Setting the stage

There are as many paper colors as there are ink colors. The correct color paper forms a unique and perfect background for your message. Subtleties are extremely important in projecting an image and setting the stage for text and photographs. Colored paper stocks can function as colored backgrounds, creating multicolor effects with single-color printing.

Note that all white papers are not created equal. Whites actually range from grays to ivories — and everywhere in between. The use of off-white papers offers significant advantages. Pure white can be extremely tiring to the reader, reflecting so much light that — under certain circumstances — readers have a very hard time trying to concentrate on your words. You may notice that sometimes glossy magazines with excellent photo reproduction suffer from hard-to-read body copy. This is because of the contrast between the whiteness of the paper and the blackness of the text. (One way you can soften the text contrast is to replace a solid black text with a dark gray that almost approaches black.)

Paper doesn't have to be solid colored. Many papers contain light colored accents embedded in the grains of the paper. These can be used to complement the inks printed on the paper.

Paper color heavily influences the way ink appears on the paper. Dark papers absorb some of the light being reflected, darkening bright ink colors. Light-colored papers, however, brighten the impact of dark colored inks.

Two-color papers are also available — these are papers in which the fronts and the backs of two different colored papers have been sandwiched together. When used for two-sided documents, the background of left-hand pages will be one color, the background of right-hand pages another. This contrast can be very powerful.

Texture: The feel of it all

Texture refers to how the paper feels in the reader's hands. Texture is added during the printing process by running the paper over metal rollers or felt patterns. The most popular texture options are

- *Laid papers.* These contain parallel ridges running lengthwise or across the paper, creating a "corduroy" effect. Laid paper creates a three-dimensional impression. Laid papers can project an impression of elegance. Laid papers are not particularly well suited for use in laser printers.
- *Felt papers.* Felt papers exhibit a finer texture than laid papers, and the texture runs in both directions: sideways and top-to-bottom.

Paper choice should also influence your choice of typefaces (see Chapter 19 for more about how to select typefaces). Coarse, textured papers require the use of typefaces with heavy strokes of relatively even weight. Typefaces with small, highly detailed serifs and relatively thin strokes are apt to reproduce poorly on textured papers; the textures and thin strokes can easily get "lost" while being printed. On the other hand, typefaces with very thin strokes also reproduce poorly on bright, shiny paper because of the glare.

The technology used to print your publication should influence your choice of paper texture. Textured papers are not particularly well suited for office ink-jet or laser printers. More important, although textured papers may present a pleasant tactile feeling to the reader's fingers, they may not present enough *tack* to hold the ink as well as desired. Textured papers thus tend to "bleed," slightly smearing the ink after it's placed on the paper.

Coating: A well for ink

The coating of paper influences how well the paper will hold ink and how much light the paper reflects. *Coated papers* contain clay, which prevents the ink from settling into the paper. This means more of ink remains on the surface where it reflects light. *Uncoated papers* absorb more of the ink, weakening the ink colors. Uncoated papers may also allow the ink to "run" rather than remain in one place, reducing the sharpness of text and graphics.

Coating is so important that the Pantone Color Matching System described in Chapter 16 publishes separate libraries showing how various colors and shades of ink will appear on coated and uncoated papers. By referring to these volumes, you can see how your choice of ink will look when printed on either coated or uncoated stock.

The brightness of the paper stock influences how sharply photographs and text are reproduced. Photographs printed on a smooth, shiny (coated) paper stock reproduce better than photographs printed on either a dull stock or one with noticeable texture. Sometimes, the paper coating is so shiny that the text becomes difficult to read. The serifs and tiny details of the letters become lost in the light reflected off the paper.

In general, shiny, coated paper stocks project an expensive, upscale image, whereas textured, duller stocks project a more traditional appearance.

Weight: A matter of substance

Paper weight influences the perceived value of your publication as well as distribution and mailing costs. As paper weight increases, your publication usually becomes thicker and/or stiffer, hence, appearing more important.

Two primary categories of paper are available: text and cover stock.

- *Text papers* are used for correspondence, brochures, and newsletters.
- *Cover stock* is heavier and used for brochures and direct mail.

Weight is measured in pounds in quantities of five hundred sheets of paper. Paper weight is extremely important when choosing a paper for newsletters and brochures intended to be mailed. In general, heavier papers do a better job of holding ink (and reproducing details) than lighter papers and have less chance of ink bleed-through from one side of the page to the other.

Recycled papers are yet another category of paper. Recycled papers are created from varying amounts of "post-consumer" trash. Although recycled papers are sometimes harder to print on than new paper, they project an environmentally correct image, which can be a positive benefit to you.

Bulk: Size without weight

Bulk refers to how compressed the paper fibers are. High-bulk papers add thickness without adding stiffness or weight; thus, high-bulk papers are often used to make books with relatively few pages appear thicker (and worth the price). Thin papers have been created by being run through presses with less tolerance and more pressure.

Weight is related to thickness, but not directly equal to it. It's possible to have a lightweight paper that is relatively thick, just as it's possible to have a very thin, but heavy, sheet of paper. You may have noticed that you can have two books next to each other on your bookshelf, one significantly thicker than the other, but both containing the same number of pages. The difference is due to the thickness of the paper.

The thickness of the paper plays a great role in the image projected by a publication. Bulk is usually considered in combination with other factors. Thin, coated papers, for example, project an upscale image. Heavy, pulpy, dull, "cardboardy" papers project an inexpensive look. Newsprint is an example of a high-bulk, uncoated paper used in applications where quantity, not quality, is the overruling objective.

Stiffness: Standing straight

Stiffness refers to the paper's resistance to bending. Thin, lightweight papers are inappropriate for brochures, for example, because they may sag when held in the reader's hands. Likewise, postcards printed on the wrong paper stock may not be accepted for mailing because they will jam in the Post Office's automatic mail-handling equipment, or they may arrive in poor condition.

Opacity: Can you see through it?

Opacity refers to the amount of *"see-throughability"* the paper exhibits — that is, how easy or difficult it is to read what's printed on the back of the paper or on the next page of a brochure or newsletter. Large headlines and photographs on paper with insufficient opacity for its intended use are characterized by "shadows" or "ghosting" showing through. Quality papers will exhibit very little see-through, even when held up to the light. High opacity papers are free from print-through; low opacity papers allow ghosted images to appear.

Vellum papers are special papers used in formal publications like annual reports and brochures for expensive products. These are specially designed to allow images on the next page to be viewed. Vellum pages are often inserted between the cover and the first page of a brochure or on pages before important photographs.

Grain direction: Go with the flow

When choosing paper for brochures, book covers, and packaging, it's important to make sure that the grain runs in the same direction that the paper will be folded in. Otherwise, the paper will crease where folded and the ink may flake off.

Another way paper's tangibility factor can be used as a design tool is to use torn, or ragged edges, as contrasted to sharply cut edges. This look is appropriate for informal invitations or article reprints that you want to look as if they were torn from a magazine or newspaper.

Availability: Can you get it for me Tuesday?

In the best of all possible worlds, every paper stock would always be available in the right sizes, coatings, and colors, as needed. However, paper is run in batches and warehoused both locally and nationally. If your local printer doesn't have the paper in stock, and the local distributor is out of it, you may have to revise your printing and mailing schedule or choose a different paper stock in order to meet your deadline. In addition, you'll usually get a better price if the printer has the paper in stock . . . especially if they are overstocked with it!

Availability is one of the major reasons you should begin communicating with your commercial printer as soon as possible, so the printer can advise you whether the paper you want is likely to be available. More important, by communicating with your commercial printer at the beginning of the design phase of your project, you may be advised of ways that you can save money by printing multiple copies of your newsletter or brochure at one time and trimming them apart.

Indeed, if the paper you're working with is available in large sheets, you may be able to inexpensively print business cards, post cards, or "loyalty builders" such as bookmarks at the same time your publication is being printed, by taking advantage of paper that would otherwise be trimmed off and thrown away. Be sure to talk with your printer first to see what options may be available to you.

When choosing a "corporate" paper to be used throughout your association or business for things like business cards, letterhead, newsletters, and formal publications such as annual reports, make sure that the paper is available in all of the weight, thickness, and stiffness options you're likely to need. Using a single paper stock for a variety of publications reinforces your firm's unique identity in the minds of your prospects and customers.

Do Not Fold or Spindle — Unless You Read This First

In addition to considering paper as a design tool, you should consider folds, die-cuts, and perforations.

Folds

Folds determine the order in which your reader encounters your message. Often, the addition of a single extra fold can create an extra selling area for your message by permitting you to focus the reader's attention on new material. Folding back the right-edge of the front cover of a brochure, for example, creates the visual equivalent of an extra page. It also adds visual interest by making the cover of the brochure narrower than expected, revealing a portion of the next page.

Presentation folders, for example, usually are folded and glued to create pockets for inserting proposals and information about your firm. You may also add a folder element to the cover of full-size informational booklets to use for including customized information and related materials such as maps or instructions that may frequently change. Although special folds and die-cuts increase printing costs (your printer may even have to send them out to a firm specializing in die-cuts and folds), they can greatly increase the impact of your important publications.

Die-cuts

In addition to experimenting with folds, you can also use die-cuts to create "windows" that allow readers to preview the contents of the next page — perhaps letting them sneak a peak at a small part of an important photograph. You can encourage readers to open your brochure by previewing part of an image on the second page by creating a die-cut on the first page. Die-cuts can come in many shapes and sizes — Christmas trees for the holidays, stars or squares, whatever you can imagine and afford to pay for.

Die-cuts add a three-dimensional effect to the paper. Die cuts are also used to enable you to add your business card or other important information to the cover of an important proposal or brochure.

Perforations

Perforations are often added to brochures to encourage reader response. Perforations consist of tiny holes in the paper that allow a coupon or order blank to be easily filled-out, torn off, and returned (or redeemed).

The backs of perforations are often addressed back to the sender and include a Postage Paid mark. (Consult with your Post Office for how to do this.) These self-mailers can greatly increase the response to your mailing. If a check is required, however, the order blank will need to be placed in an envelope, so you won't need to go to the expense of including a postage paid mailer.

Gatefolds

A final paper-based design option is to include a gatefold. A gatefold is an oversize signature used as one cover or on an inside page. A gatefold adds an extra large selling or display space to your publication. The centerfold of Playboy magazine is a classic example of a gatefold. When opened, it offers the equivalent of three side-by-side pages.

Foils

Foils offer another non-ink way to add impact to a publication. Foils can be applied as stickers or tiny strips of metal over small areas of your publication, such as a text highlight like your firm's logo. Because the foil catches and reflects room lighting, the foil brightens any page it appears on and draws the reader's eye directly to the logo or text highlight.

Designing with Ink

There's more to ink than color. Ink can also provide texture and add reflectivity to your designs. Your choice of inks can influence the perceived texture of your project as well as provide selective emphasis — or de-emphasis — to parts of a page.

You can use several types of specialized inks to add impact to your pages:

- *Varnish* is one of the most potent tools available. If you want to brighten an image or a major headline, perhaps adding impact to a photograph, you can varnish it. Varnishing makes the ink appear brighter because it reflects more light.
- Even better, you can add a *matte finish,* which reduces the amount of light reflected by the ink, making the text or area surrounding a photograph appear farther away.

Searching for inspiration

When looking for new and unusual papers to work with, and new ways to fold, die-cut and perforate paper, refer to the S.D. Warren IdeaExchange. You can contact the S.D. Warren IdeaExchange at 225 Franklin St., Boston, MA 02110. Phone 612-423-7300.

S.D. Warren is one of the world's largest paper manufacturers and distributors. They will help you identify new and novel ways to print your publication and send you samples of actual printed documents that project the image or effect you're trying to achieve.

You can learn about this exciting service by visiting the S.D. Warren IdeaExchange Web site at `www.warren idea exchange.com/graphic/w/f.html`.

- *Metallic* and *fluorescent* inks can brighten your pages. These "brighter than bright" inks catch the light and reflect it with added intensity.
- *Opaque* inks isolate an ink from the paper it's printed on, forming a barrier which separates the paper from another layer of ink added at a later time. This permits you to print light inks on dark, coarse, absorbent paper.

Making your photographs pop!

Varnish and matte inks can and should be used together.

One of the most effective ways you can add impact to an important photograph in a formal brochure or annual report-level publication is to varnish the photograph and add a matte finish to the remainder of the page. The impact of a varnished photograph against a matte finished background can be extremely dramatic; *your readers may try to peel the photograph off the page!*

The combination of a varnished photograph surrounded by a field of matte ink would transform the page from "everyday" into "striking." Even though the size of the photo remains constant, the photo emerges from the page with the clarity of the piano in one of Mozart's piano concertos.

Adding emphasis to photographs

Ink can provide a field in which to emphasize a photograph. Suppose that you want to emphasize an important photograph — a photograph intended to be the focal point of the page. One way would be to simply make the photograph larger. This solution is a bit obvious. There's a certain understated elegance to a single photograph of moderate size centered on the page. To draw further attention to the photograph, you could surround it with (or reverse the photograph out of) a solid field of color. Ideally, this ink field should be bled to the four edges of the page, especially if the colored ink complements one or more of the colors in the photograph.

Using bleeds

Bleeds remain a final way of manipulating ink on paper. One of the most effective ways you can enhance your documents is to extend text, visuals, or graphic elements by printing to the edge of the page. An otherwise static page takes on new life when even a single graphic element is bled to the page's edge.

Bleeds extending to both sides of a page make the page look wider. Bleeds extending off just one side of a page "weight" the page in that direction and draw the reader's eye in that direction. Bleeds extending off right-hand pages, for example, encourage readers to turn the page.

One reason bleeds have so much power is that they eliminate the distracting borders that often surround the edges of text and graphic elements. For example, a newsletter nameplate title reversed against a strong background is visually diminished by the "whiteness" that surrounds it at the top and sides (see Figure 13-1). Figure 13-2 shows what happens when that white space is removed.

Often, bleeds enable you to increase the type size used in the title because you're not restrained by the dimensions of the frame to which the title was originally limited.

Picturing duotones

Another powerful creative printing option is to reproduce photographs using duotones. A *duotone* occurs when a black-and-white photograph is printed in black plus a second color, often a gray or dark blue.

The purpose of a duotone is to expand the contrast area of the photograph, reproducing subtle details that would otherwise be lost. Two-color printing permits the standard ink color, usually black, to reproduce the majority of the photograph, while a second color reproduces highlights — or details — which would otherwise be lost.

The result is a photograph of unusual depth — one that more closely resembles the original black-and-white image as it left the darkroom than the limited range of most printed photographs.

Duotones enable first-rate black-and-white photographs to achieve the emotional power of four-color photographs!

Considering costs

Using ink as a creative tool increases printing costs, of course. This is especially true of techniques like varnishing, adding matte finishes and printing duotones. Not only must more colors be placed on the paper, but also your commercial printer must work to closer tolerances to ensure that the *registration* — or alignment — of the various colors and types of ink are in proper relationship to each other.

Figure 13-1: The paper borders around the title of this newsletter diminish its impact.

Figure 13-2: The same nameplate gains impact when the distracting border is removed and the reversed area extends to the top and side of the page.

If the placement of the varnish is not perfect, for example, one edge of the photograph might appear noticeably duller than the rest of the photograph, while a sliver of paper adjacent to the opposite side of the photograph might appear brighter for no reason.

Once again, the only cure for these potential problems (and cost overruns) is to establish communications early on with your printer.

Combining Techniques

Reverses, bleeds, and special inks can be used together with special papers to greatly expand your creative options. For example, by adding areas of solid ink coverage to a brochure, you can create "windows" where the paper shows through areas of reversed text.

Alternately, a die-cut in the center of the reverse printed with a matte can frame a die cut which reveals part of a photograph which has been varnished. The combination of the matte ink "framing" the brightly varnished photograph can be quite striking.

Your creative options will quickly expand once you begin to break out of the trap of seeing your printed communication as existing solely on the screen of your computer. You can add a new level of excellence to your important documents when you view them as tangible, three-dimensional publications and work with paper suppliers and commercial printers.

Part IV

Color and Graphics in the Electronic Age

"Of course graphics are important to your project, Eddy, but I think it would've been better to scan a picture of your worm collection."

In this part . . .

Part IV takes you inside the bright and beautiful world of color and graphics to help you make the most of these elements and avoid their traps. You see color as a two-edged sword that can both enhance and obscure your message. And although a picture does, in fact, equal a thousand words (unless it's a scanned image, in which case it's equal to 1.3MB), it too can get garbled if not handled with care. Transform ordinary graphics into high-impact images, and see how to simplify, clarify, and contrast data using tables, charts, timelines, and other "visualizations."

Chapter 14

Communicating Business Information Visually

In This Chapter

- Choosing the right business graphic
- Displaying and fine-tuning tabular information
- Creating intelligible charts and graphs
- Displaying hierarchies using organizational charts

Business graphics are important. Business readers and Web site visitors are usually in a hurry. They want information fast, and they're easily bored. Page after page (or screen after screen) of text in paragraph format quickly begins to lose distinction, and attention suffers. That's why a picture that's worth 1,000 words can be eye-popping, pulling attention back to your communication. Business graphics used effectively enable you to quickly and easily communicate even the most complex information.

Business graphics come in four major forms:

- Tables, which present numerical or textual information in rows and columns
- Charts and graphs, which use pictorial representations
- Organizational charts, which demonstrate hierarchical relationships
- Timelines, which indicate chronological relationships

Each form has its own specific uses. In this chapter, I help you identify which form to use when.

Is My Table Ready?

Tables are one of your most powerful design tools. With tables, you can easily display complicated information so that it can be read at a glance.

Look at Figures 14-1 and 14-2 to compare the same information presented in paragraph and table form. Which is easier to read at a glance? Which communicates better? Which organizes the information better and permits easier comparisons?

Symposium schedule

Arrival time for most participants is 5:00 Friday evening. There will be a cocktail party at 7:30 for attendees and guests. Saturday morning, breakfast will be served at 8:00. The Opening Convocation will begin at 9:00 Saturday morning. At 10:00, the session on Financial Maturity will take place, followed by 11:00's session on Retirement Planning. Lunch will be at 12:00. At 1:00, participants are free to return to their rooms for a nap. The Vacation Getaways session begins at 2:00. The Fly or Cruise? session begins at 3:00. The session on Customs begins at 4:00. Supper will be served at 5:00 PM. The Formal Dance begins at 7:30 PM. Sunday, brunch begins at 9:00 AM. At 11:00 AM, there will be a demonstration of Golf Etiquette. At 12:00, there will be an Outdoor Buffet. Tennis Instruction begins at 1:00 PM. The session on Investment Challenges begins at 2:00 PM. The Closing Convocation begins at 3:00 PM. Checkout time is 4:00. The last airport bus leaves at 5:00 PM.

Figure 14-1: It's hard to get excited about numeric information buried in paragraphs of text. Where's the meat?

You can create better tables when you understand table terminology:

- Tables are created out of *rows and columns.*
- The term *headers* refers to descriptive information placed above columns and to the left of rows.
- Information is placed in *cells* that are created where rows and columns intersect.
- *Gridlines* refer to horizontal and vertical lines separating cells.
- *Fills* are shaded backgrounds that enable you to add emphasis to selected rows or columns.

By isolating and organizing selected data for display in tables, you can make information that's buried in sentences and paragraphs become more easily accessible to the reader or viewer.

Financial Planning Symposium

	Friday	Saturday	Sunday
8:00 AM		Breakfast	
9:00 AM		Opening Convocation	Brunch
10:00 AM		Financial Maturity	Brunch (continued)
11:00 AM		Retirement Planning	Golf Etiquette
12:00 Noon		Lunch	Outdoor Buffet
1:00 PM		Free time	Tennis Instruction
2:00 PM		Vacation Getaways	Investment Challenges
3:00 PM		Fly or Cruise?	Closing convocation
4:00 PM		Customs Rules	Checkout
5:00 PM	Check-in	Supper	Last bus leaves
7:30 PM	Cocktail party	Formal dance	

Figure 14-2: When presented in table format, the same information is easier to read and to compare.

Deciding on software

Before beginning work, familiarize yourself with the table's purpose. Ask yourself: "What information and interpretation do I want to communicate?" Your purpose may influence the software you choose to create the table — your page layout or Web authoring program may not be your best choice. Instead, you may want to create the table using another type of program and import (or copy and paste) the table into your publication or Web site.

For example, spreadsheet and word processing software programs offer more capabilities than the table editors built into many page layout programs because they allow you to *sort* information. You can present information in *alphabetical order* (which makes it easier for readers to quickly locate desired information), or you can *rank* information from small to large (or vice versa). With these techniques, you can help readers compare profitability per product line or see at a glance which baseball pitchers struck out the most left-handed players (or graphic designers).

Setting up information

Next, decide how you want the readers to encounter the information in rows and columns.

- If order is unimportant, random sequence is appropriate.
- Use an alphabetical organization if you want readers to be able to quickly locate desired information (for example, their team's bowling scores).
- Sort numerically if you want to display information in increasing (or decreasing) importance, such as teams ranked in order of games won or regions with the lowest theft rates.

Instead of using your software's Copy and Paste commands to insert a table, *link* tables created with a word processing or spreadsheet program to your page layout program. (Start by referring to Object Linking and Embedding in your software's documentation.) Linking makes it easy to update the information, if necessary.

Adding titles and captions

A *title* provides a focal point for the table and identifies its purpose. Instead of just providing a title that restates the obvious, use the title to presell the information contained in the text.

Captions permit you to reinforce the importance of the information contained in the table or the conclusion you want your readers to gain from the table. Because captions placed under or beside a table are among the best-read parts of a page, use the caption to summarize the most important idea you want the table to communicate to your readers.

Avoid "empty" titles, such as "Table 3: Musical Preferences." Instead, use titles that summarize either the purpose or the primary conclusion presented by the table, as in, "College Students Choose Springsteen Over Schubert."

Formatting tables attractively

It's not enough to display well-organized information in tables; you have to make sure that the information is attractive and easy to read. The following list contains tips for effective table formatting.

- **Choose the right typeface and type size:** Whenever possible, typeface typography should match that of adjacent headlines and subheads. In general, sans serif typefaces are easier to read at small sizes than serif typefaces. This makes them ideal for use within table cells. Complicated information is easier to read in 10-point Frutiger than in 12-point Minion for example. *Condensed* sans serif typefaces are even better, as they permit information in headers and cells to be surrounded by more white space. (Condensed versions of most sans serif headline typefaces are available.)

If you are preparing a document with a lot of table information, consider a typeface like Bell Centennial, which was designed for maximum legibility at small size.

- **Add typographic contrast to row and column headers:** Information displayed in headers should appear visually distinct from information displayed within the individual cells. Avoid reversing a serif typeface out of a light gray background; bold sans serif typefaces always reverse better than serif typefaces.
- **Simplify borders and gridlines:** Avoid unnecessary borders around tables, which tend to draw the reader's eyes out of the table. Likewise, you rarely need include vertical and horizontal lines between every cell. Using a minimum number of gridlines creates a simple, uncluttered effect that allows readers to concentrate on the *information* being presented rather than being distracted by the lines.

For simple tables, use a single line to separate column headers from cells and use typographic contrast, such as italics, instead of a vertical line to separate row headers from the first column of information.

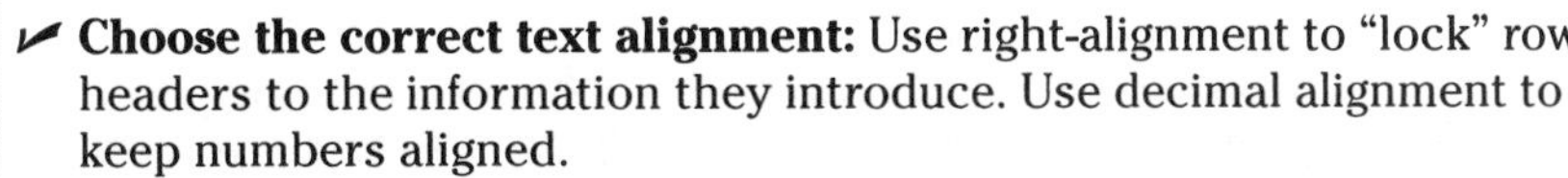

- **Choose the correct text alignment:** Use right-alignment to "lock" row headers to the information they introduce. Use decimal alignment to keep numbers aligned.

Avoid centering information. Left-alignment often presents an orderly image, while centered cell text forces the reader's eyes to "zigzag" across each cell, searching for the starting point of each line. In addition, centered text in cells can create distracting shapes.

- **Use backgrounds to organize complex information:** Use alternating plain and shaded backgrounds to organize row and columns. Alternate light background tints for every other row or column (or every five).

Use alternating backgrounds behind rows when information, like features, are most important; place the backgrounds behind columns when you want to emphasize days, quarterly totals, or product information.

- **Avoid unnecessary white space:** Unlike other communications where white space is desirable, white space in columns can make the reader lose sight of the information.
- **Keep columns as narrow as possible.** Narrow columns reduce the width of the table, permitting easier comparisons. Within tables eliminate gaps caused when some cells contain significantly more than other cells. Remember that rows expand to accommodate the largest

cell entry, so one "full" cell in a row can make the row more prominent than others (implying more important) and can make the other cells in the row look incomplete. Make your tables as vertical as possible by eliminating unnecessary column width. This enables your reader's eyes to quickly move across each row.

Edit cell contents to the bare-bones minimum and specify desired row heights and cell widths rather than allowing your software program to expand rows and columns.

- **Adjust text spacing and alignment:** Always provide sufficient breathing room between text and adjacent borders. Avoid text that extends too close to adjacent gridlines or text in the next cell. Most software programs permit you to adjust the minimum text offset, which is the amount of white space between text and cell borders.

Avoid vertically centering cell information. This throws the baselines of text in adjacent cells out of alignment.

Using Charts and Graphs

Always translate numbers into visuals. Often, the same numbers can present totally different conclusions, depending on the type of chart chosen.

The type of information you want to communicate as well as the interpretation you want to emphasize should influence your choice of chart or graph (see Figure 14-3). Here are some suggestions to help you choose the appropriate format along with some hints for making the most of each type:

- **Pie charts:** Use to display part-whole relationships. Today's software programs can quickly translate numbers into proportions.
- **Vertical column charts:** Use to compare information that changes over time.
- **Horizontal bar charts:** Use when time is not a consideration.

  When it's important to display the *exact numbers* represented by each bar, display the information in a table next to the chart instead of displaying values in labels next to each bar.

- **Line charts:** Use when you want to illustrate trends. To avoid confronting your readers with spaghetti, however, limit yourself to a maximum of six lines — preferably fewer. Fine-tune line weights and choose a thicker line for the most important line.
- **Scattered point charts:** Use to show the relationship between sets of data or to identify a pattern.

- **High-low charts:** Use to display changes in data over fixed time periods. (Use the area option to emphasize the range of data.) ***Note:*** many software programs permit you to add bars to display opening and closing prices.

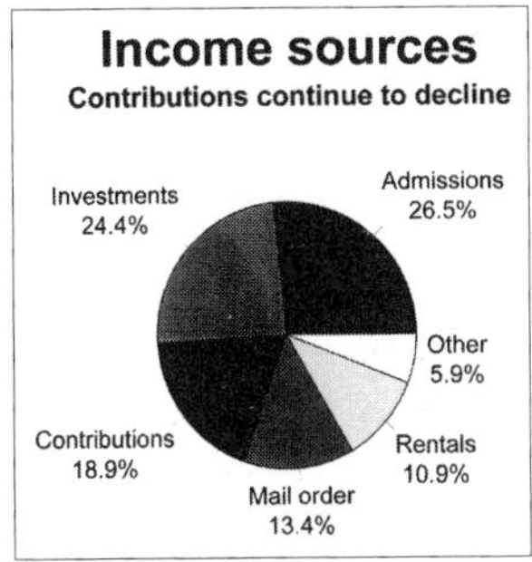

Pie chart

First-quarter attendance trends
Slow growth
10
8
6
4
2
0
Jan
Feb
Mar
April
1990 1991 1992 1993 1994 1995

Vertical column chart

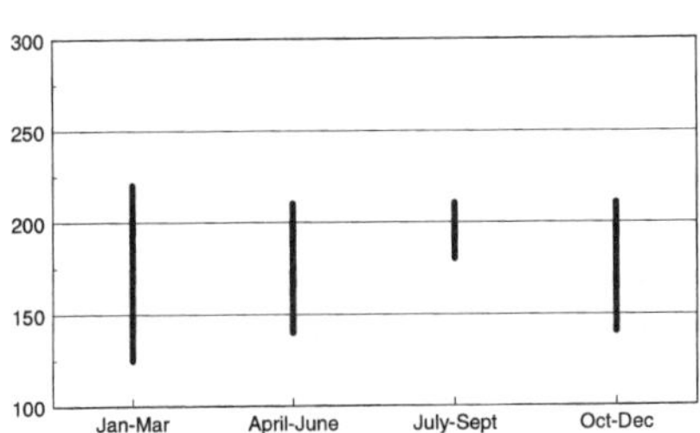

High-low chart

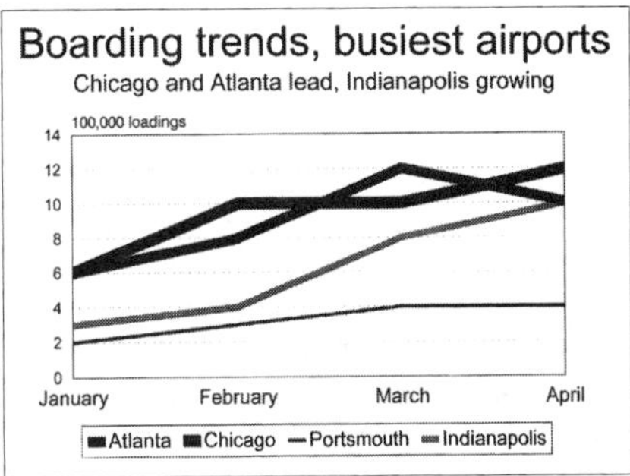

Line chart

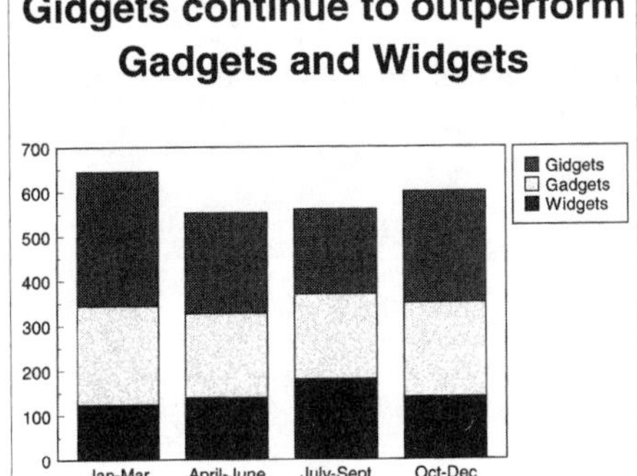

Stacked chart

Figure 14-3: Some commonly used types of business graphics.

Among other options are *Overlapping bar charts,* which save space and display each time interval as a visual unit. *Stacked, or 100% charts,* when you want to compare the relative contributions of each data series.

Most software programs permit you to combine chart types. For example, you can simplify a pie chart by adding a second, smaller, adjacent 100% bar graph to display the relative contributions of several small components grouped into a miscellaneous, or "all other" slice. You can also add lines to a bar chart to emphasize trends.

Most important, use *three-dimensional* charts with care; although snazzy to look at, they often distort the message by over-emphasizing elements located in the front or bottom.

Try to limit pie charts to a maximum of six slices. If you must use more than six slices, group the "miscellaneous" slice together with a second pie chart.

Organization charts show responsibility

Use organization charts like that shown in Figure 14-4 to display *hierarchy and responsibility*. Organization charts display *who reports to whom* at a glance. Organization charts make it easy to communicate the structure of even complex organizations. You can display vertical hierarchy as well as horizontal hierarchy, showing the relationship of individuals in workgroups.

To save space and allow for larger, easier-to-read text, list the items at the lowest levels of an organizational chart rather than putting the information in boxes.

Communicating time and sequence

Three types of business graphics are more concerned with time than quantity. These are

- Flow charts
- Timelines
- Calendars

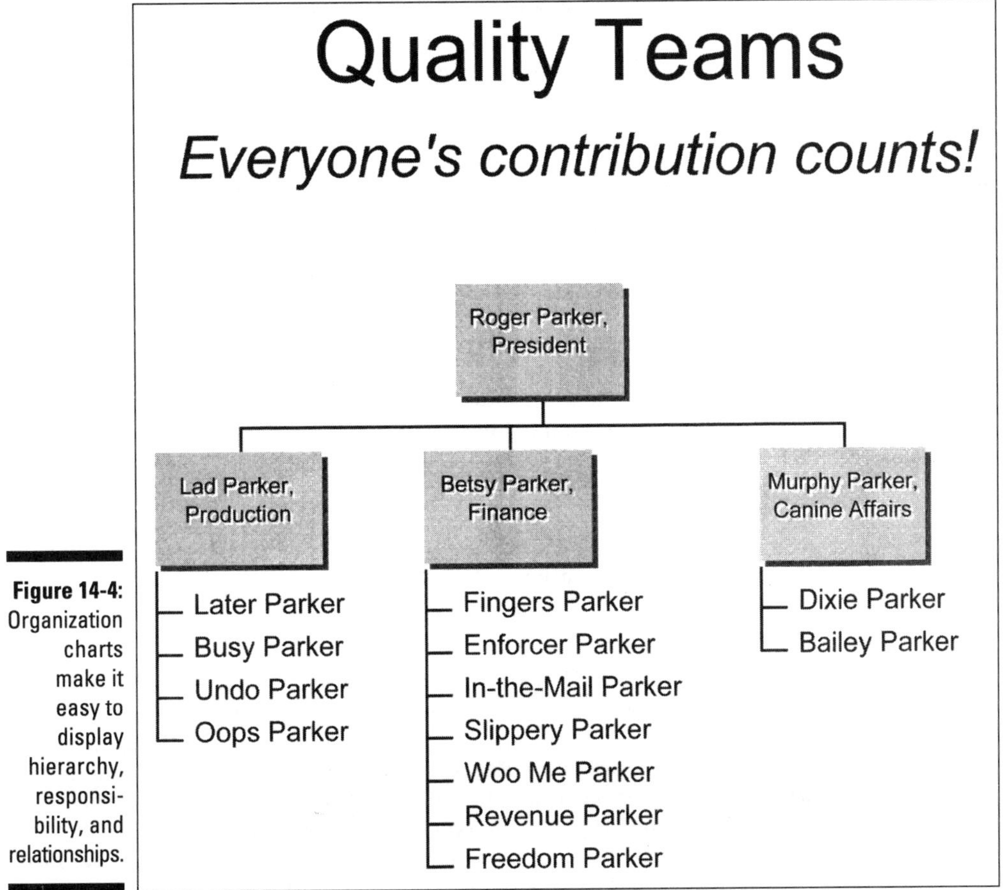

Figure 14-4: Organization charts make it easy to display hierarchy, responsibility, and relationships.

Flow charts have three main applications:

- To represent sequence, or what should happen when.
- To help the audience easily understand alternatives. Flow charts permit you to communicate the alternatives of "yes" or "no" decisions or specific actions of others.
- To easily display the timing when actions or decisions will be needed.

Timelines display the relationship of events to each other. Use timelines to help your readers understand precedent and relationship. By viewing events on a timeline, readers can see what was happening when, which presents a better perspective on the past. Timelines help readers visually relate events to their background and historical context.

If you find yourself describing a schedule of upcoming events, instead of listing the events and their dates in text paragraphs, create a *calendar* showing the dates when important events occur. The calendar will help your readers relate "event" to "date" at a glance. They might even clip out the calendar and hang it on their refrigerator!

To add impact to your calendar, use a solid black background for the important dates and reverse the text describing the event out of a reversed or background. For maximum legibility, use a bold, sans serif typeface.

Improving Your Business Graphics

Here are four ways you can improve your business graphics in addition to the basic tasks of asking questions, simplifying, and taking maximum advantage of your software program's power.

- **Add a goal range to charts and graphs:** When the purpose of a chart or graph is to compare actual sales with projected sales projections, include a *goal range* that permits readers to see at a glance where actual sales met, exceeded, or failed sales projections.
- **Round off numbers:** X- and Y-axis information is frequently difficult to read because they contain too many words and numbers. The problem is compounded when too much detail is included. When the goal of your chart is to communicate trends, for example, the actual numbers aren't as important as the appearance of the graph. Removing the data labels and simplifying gives X-axis information a simpler, cleaner appearance. Instead of showing actual numbers, round off numbers to units of 100, 1,000, 10,000, 100,000 or one million.
- **Tilt Y-axis information:** Horizontal text is easiest to read. Often, however, there simply isn't enough space to fit Y-axis information in columns. As a result, you're forced to use an unreadable small type size. (Vertical text isn't an option, of course, unless you want your readers to hold your annual report sideways or you're willing to turn the slide projector on its side during your presentation.) Find out how if your software program allows you to tilt Y-axis information. The result will be more readable and you can use a comfortable type size.
- **Use background fills instead of borders to organize tables:** Often, the gridlines separating information in the various cells of a table present a cluttered "view from a jail cell" appearance. The cure is to use shaded backgrounds and appropriate text alignment rather than an internal grid to separate information. Other alternatives include replacing gridlines with decimal tabs and extra spacing between text elements.

Always use the minimum number of graphic accents necessary to provide a framework for your message.

Chapter 15

Using Color on the Web

In This Chapter

- Understanding the importance of color on the Web
- Analyzing the Web sites you visit
- Creating relaxing environments using projected color
- Choosing the right text and background colors
- Working with graduated and textured backgrounds
- Avoiding problems with projected color
- Creating your own custom backgrounds

The effective use of color is crucial to the success of your Web pages. The colors of the four primary elements of Web page architecture — background, text, graphics, and navigation tools — must work well with each other, but each must be distinctive enough to attract appropriate attention when necessary.

Few Web sites use color as effectively as they could. Many color-associated Web design problems occur for the following reasons:

- **Color on the Web is free.** Unlike print documents that cost more as you add color, Web pages don't increase in cost when you add color. As a result, Web page designers may unconsciously try to "make the most of it" and use as many colors as possible.
- **Web color is projected color.** Unlike printed colors, which you see as light reflected off the ink on a page, Web colors are projected from the computer monitor directly into the Web site visitor's eyes. The overuse of bright colors in this environment can easily strain the eyes (and the patience) of your Web site visitors. Eyestrain is especially likely to occur on white or brightly colored backgrounds that can make reading the Web site text very difficult.

- **Comparing Web sites is difficult.** Unless you take the time to take screen captures and make color printouts of the various Web sites you visit, improving your use of Web page color by analyzing the various Web sites is difficult. You may have trouble remembering the colors of Web sites you have visited.

This chapter describes some ways you can make the most of color as a valuable, free Web resource.

How to Analyze Web Color

The best way to master Web color is to spend a lot of time carefully checking out various Web sites. Start by critically analyzing the way each Web site uses color. Then use a screen capture program to take pictures of the Web sites and print the results in color. A *screen capture program* takes a picture of everything appearing on the screen of your computer.

Just a few hours of disciplined surfing each week can help you greatly improve your ability to analyze Web sites and identify techniques that make for effective, easy-to-read sites.

What to look for when visiting Web sites

Here are some things to look for when you analyze the use of color on Web sites. As you visit Web sites, consider the following factors and ask yourself these questions:

- **Impact:** Does overall use of color contribute or detract from the Web site? Does the color scheme make reading the text easier or harder than reading text in monochrome, such as black on white printing?
- **Harmony:** Do the colors work well with each other, or do they "fight" with each other?
- **Choice of background colors:** Is the background pleasing to look at, or is it so bright that it distracts from headlines and text?
- **Choice of text colors:** Is the text easy to read, or do you struggle to separate the text from the background?
- **Coding:** Does the Web site's use of color have a purpose? Are matching colors used to identify and separate the various sections of the Web site?
- **Unique:** Does the site use a few carefully chosen colors to project a unique image?

- **Image:** Does the Web site use color to project an image appropriate to the Web site's contents?
- **Accidental color:** Did you sometimes click text set in a different color, thinking that it was a link, only to find that the text was simply an emphasized word?

One of the most frequent problems in Web sites is the use of color to emphasize a word or group of words in a way that makes you think that the color indicates a text link. Don't let this happen to visitors to your Web site! Avoid inadvertently using color in ways that falsely indicate text links. Make sure that differences in color serve a definite purpose.

Working with a screen capture program

Screen capture programs enable you to "photograph" and study the use of color on Web sites that you like. If you don't have this type of program, I suggest that you acquire one, such as SnapJot for the Macintosh or Collage for the PC from Inner Media.

Printing from a screen capture program has at least one advantage over printing from a Web browser: The background prints, too. So, although the background plays a major role in what you and your Web site visitors see on the computer screen, this background won't normally be printed for later reference.

You don't have to print out all the pages of a Web site in order to analyze color use. You need to print out only the initial page, or home page, plus two or three representative pages — for example, the pages introducing the various sections, or divisions, of the site plus pages containing long text elements.

If you want to get serious about the Web, you'll probably also want to invest in a color inkjet printer. With a color inkjet printer, you can print out pictures of Web sites and analyze the factors contributing to their success. (Here's another reason to own a color inkjet printer: You can use it as a proofing device while creating your own Web site — mistakes are far easier to see on hard copy than on-screen.)

Don't despair if you don't already own a color printer and can't immediately afford one. Many office supply stores, such as Kinko's, can print your files for you. (Or maybe you can use a friend's printer in exchange for proofreading his or her desktop-published and Web documents.)

Avoid chaos as you print Web sites. Protect and organize your printouts in three-hole punched, clear plastic sleeves. These allow you to organize your "inspiration" and "desperation" samples of Web pages in three-ring binders for easy retrieval and comparison. Use pages with tabs to separate the various Web site categories.

Even if you bookmark your favorite Web sites, studying and comparing them to each other can be a slow process because of the time you need to download each site. But if you have printed pages from Web sites, you can easily compare them side-by-side to analyze which sites make the best use of color.

Working with Web Color

Many guidelines that contribute to the successful use of color in print apply equally to color on the Web. In both cases, you achieve success to the extent that you make consistent use of a few, carefully chosen colors.

Exercise restraint

Restraint is the key to successfully working with color on the Web. Restraint involves replacing quantity with quality, choosing a limited repertoire of the right colors, even if it's only one or two colors, and using colors as effectively as possible.

Avoid overusing black, white, and bright colors. A pure white background can be very elegant, attention-getting, and readable, or it can contribute to eyestrain. The effect depends on whether the "whiteness" of the background is modulated by soft or muted colors.

Likewise, an all-black background can be very dramatic, but not if it contains large areas of hot, bright colors. The resulting contrast can be so dramatic that Web visitors will leave the site rather than put up with the contrast.

Choose the right colors

Choosing the right colors involves considering both emotional and technical issues.

Emotionally, you want to make sure that the colors you choose are appropriate for the image you want to project. Here are some examples:

- **Elegant** colors include gold, silver, chocolate, maroon, and navy blue.
- **Fresh, healthy** colors include yellow, bright blue, and green.

- **Loud, aggressive** colors include red, yellow, blue, orange, and purple.
- **Natural** colors include brown and tan, burnt orange, quiet greens, and earth tones.

The colors you choose should also be compatible with the widest range of hardware and software that most Web browsers use. Disappointing results are likely if you do not limit your color choices to those that the most commonly-used hardware available can display. Limit your choices to the 256 colors available on most Super VGA monitors and video cards.

Platform differences also play a role in color selection; the Microsoft Windows operating system limits your choices even more. You are safe if you limit your color choices for text and backgrounds to the 216 colors available in the Windows color palette. These colors reproduce smoothly, without dithering. *Dithering* takes place when a color cannot be directly created but must be approximated by mixing colors on the screen. Although dithered colors are acceptable when they appear in four-color printed photographs, dithered colors create a very motley or speckled look when they cover large areas of the screen. Thus, dithered colors are unacceptable for use as Web backgrounds.

The initial color choices of most Web authoring programs default to the correct colors for multiplatform viewing. Other software programs permit you to create a custom palette of colors linked to the "Windows-safe" palette, or you can download a palette from the Internet.

Limit yourself to a few signature colors

The consistent and selective use of a few signature colors throughout a Web site is a defining characteristic of excellence. Instead of using dozens of different colors, design your Web site by selecting a few colors from a palette of harmonizing colors.

You can use these signature colors as vertical panels along one edge (usually the left) of the screen to color-code different sections of the Web site. Within each section, you can color-code text for headlines or graphic accents above headlines to match the color used in the left panel.

You can also color-code these panels to match the colors of the icons or visual navigation devices, used on the home page to take the Web visitor to each section.

This color-coding technique achieves three purposes: It reduces the line length of the body copy within the section, adds visual interest to the Web site, and signals the different sections of the Web site.

Be selective about background colors

The background of your Web site should be barely noticeable; visitors to your Web site should be influenced by it but not aware of it. The background should provide continuity without calling unnecessary attention to itself.

Be consistent in your use of background colors throughout your Web site. In particular, avoid the temptation to change background colors unless you have a clear reason to do so.

Some sites vary the background colors to "code" the various sections of the site. Although this approach makes sense in some ways, it also destroys the continuity of a Web site. Visitors may think that they've jumped to a different Web site when they encounter a section with a different colored background.

A much better choice is to use a light or neutral background throughout a Web site but to change the color of one or more of the graphic accents used within each section of the Web site. This technique provides continuity but still enables you to set off each section of the Web site. I talk more about background colors in the section "Choosing the right background colors" later in this chapter.

Reduce the color depth of imported graphics

When you import illustrations or scanned images into your Web site, avoid including more color information than necessary. Most image-manipulation programs, such as Adobe Photoshop, enable you to reduce the color depth of the illustration or scanned image. These programs also enable you to save photographs with varying color depth, meaning that you can reduce the amount of color information contained in the file.

Usually, you should save scanned photographs that you are going to print on glossy paper by using all 256 colors. But the same photograph on the Web doesn't need as much color information. By a process of trial and error, you can usually arrive at a color depth, usually somewhere between 36 and 64 bits, that contains enough information but avoids long download times.

The more color information graphics contain, the longer they take to download.

Choosing the Right Colors for Your Web Site

You can choose the colors for your Web site in one of three ways:

- **Use your software's default color palette.** Most software programs offer a variety of color palettes or combinations of foreground (text) and background colors.
- **Create a custom color palette.** Often, the starting point for this process is to use your color inkjet printer to make color printouts of Web sites that you like. When you find a combination of foreground and background colors that appeals to you, then you can begin your own experimentation with color.
- **Create your own background.** Instead of using a background that comes with your software program, you can import any graphic and use it as a background, or you can create your own background. The latter approach makes it easy to horizontally divide your Web page into sections, or zones.

Working with default colors

The easiest way to choose a safe color palette is to use the combinations of the text and background colors built into your software. Most software programs offer a color menu that you can scroll through and a window that previews your choice. Using this default palette is often the safest starting point, but don't be limited by those choices.

In most cases, you can find the various color palettes available to you by opening your software program's Format menu and choosing Background or Background and Text Choices.

When you find a combination of text and background colors that you like, simply click the OK button (or double-click the name of the palette), and the selected background appears throughout your Web site.

If you do not find an attractive combination, consider creating your own custom color palette.

Colored backgrounds and software

One reason that you may quickly outgrow your initial choice of Web publishing software is a desire to use different backgrounds for different sections of your Web site.

Although many introductory programs (such as Microsoft Publisher) greatly simplify the task of creating and posting a Web site, their limitations quickly become apparent when you want to become more adventuresome. For example, when you choose a background with Microsoft Publisher, the background you choose will be used throughout your Web site. This restriction precludes color-coding the backgrounds or portions of the backgrounds used in the various sections of your Web site.

More advanced programs, such as Microsoft FrontPage, allow you to be more creative and incorporate subtle differences in backgrounds to color-code each section of your Web site.

Creating a custom palette

To create a custom palette, first open the Format menu and choose Background or Text and Background Colors. When the dialog box appears, however, select Custom. This option enables you to independently choose the colors used for backgrounds and text.

Here are some guidelines to keep in mind when you create a custom palette:

- **Strive for maximum contrast.** Make sure that visitors to your Web site can easily separate the text of normal, linked, and visited text links from the background color. Backgrounds exist to provide contrast with the text and graphics that make up your Web site. If foreground/background contrast is insufficient, few readers will take the time to notice your message.
- **Avoid brightly colored backgrounds.** If too much contrast between information and background is present, the resulting eye fatigue may discourage or slow down your visitors. Although bright backgrounds may initially attract the most attention, they can be very tiring over long periods of time. Softer shades of color are less tiring to the eyes of your Web site visitors.
- **Avoid heavily patterned backgrounds.** The more noticeable the background, the more likely that it will interfere with text placed on top of it, especially when the type is small. Textured backgrounds are especially annoying when they contain small elements that can appear as parts of text characters.

- **Avoid uniform, monotonous backgrounds.** When you choose a background that ships with your software, the background usually extends as a single, unbroken pattern from left to right across your computer's monitor. This background often creates a boring Web site, and Web site designers then tend to run text in a single line from margin to margin of the Web page.
- **Use graduated backgrounds with care.** The problem with backgrounds that make a gradual left-to-right transition from light to dark or from one color to another is that, inevitably, text contrast is compromised at points where the color of the text approaches the color of the background.

Importing or creating your own custom backgrounds

You can also import a graphic, either a graphic file designed for use as a Web site background or a graphic that you specifically create by using a program such as Adobe Photoshop, CorelDRAW, or Microsoft Image Composer.

The height and width of the graphic you create or import determine how often the graphic is *tiled,* or repeated, across the screen of Web site visitors. Consider the following factors:

- **Small, narrow graphics** frequently repeat across the screen.
- **Wider graphics** repeat less frequently across the screen.
- **Taller and wider graphics** repeat fewer times horizontally and vertically.

To import a graphic file for use as a background, in most cases, you generally select Custom, click the Browse button, and locate the folder or subdirectory containing the file. In many cases, you can preview the file before you import it.

Here's one popular way to use an imported graphic file. Scan your firm's or association's logo and apply a color just slightly darker than the color of the background. This technique creates a "watermark" effect that can be very elegant.

You can also divide the screen horizontally, creating zones for the different types of content found on your Web site. To do this, create a thin but wide background that contains a panel set in a contrasting color along the left edge of the screen, as shown in Figure 15-1. Make sure that the width of the graphic is wide enough to extend across the width of the computer screen. You can experiment with various ways of beveling or curving the boundary between the accent panel and the remainder of the background, or simply insert a vertical line as a boundary.

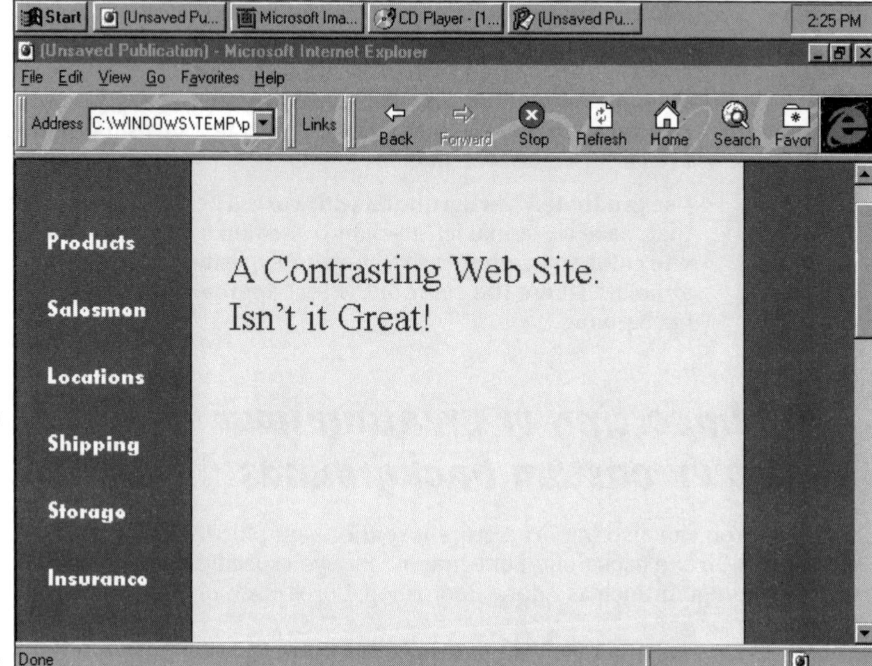

Figure 15-1: Original file containing a contrasting panel along the left edge.

Selecting Colors for Your Web Site

As I note earlier in the chapter, choose one or two signature colors and repeat them in the same locations to highlight various sections of your Web site. For example, you can reverse the section titles out of different colored panels to introduce each section of your Web site.

Here are some other ways to make good use of highlight colors to color-code your Web site:

- **Set section titles as colored graphics.** One very effective technique is to set section titles full strength against a background consisting of a light shade of the text. This approach minimizes change, yet adds color to the page without adding too many colors.

  For example, if your Web site includes sections titled Background, Clients, Portfolio, and Press Release, you can identify each section by using a typeface set in a different color and download the typeface as a graphic.

- **Set headlines, subheads, and pullquotes in color.** This technique adds color, not distraction, to your pages. Choosing the same color for headlines, subheads, and pull quotes as used for section dividers simplifies your color palette and unifies the various sections of your Web site.
- **Use a consistent color for navigation icons and set them against a consistent background.** This approach permits elements to stand apart from site content without distracting from the navigation text. Setting navigation icons and text far enough apart from the live text of your site, but using the same color as the section titles and headlines, further unifies your Web site.

Selecting colors for text

Web sites can easily degenerate into color chaos because text already appears in three colors:

- **Normal text** appears in a base color.
- **Linked text** is indicated by a second color.
- **Visited text links** appear in yet a third color.

When you add those three colors to the colors chosen for section heads and navigation icons, you can see that clutter and chaos can quickly occur unless you exercise restraint.

The background you choose for your Web site usually determines the right combination of colors for normal, linked, and visited text.

Choosing the right background colors

Use bright colored backgrounds with care. These can easily compete with your message, making your Web site tiring to look at and difficult to read. Remember that your readers are viewing projected light, which is, to begin with, more tiring than light reflected off a page.

White backgrounds also can be tiring. Although white provides a safe choice for contrast with many text colors, too much white may be tiring to your readers because they are essentially staring into a light bulb.

Likewise, use patterned or textured backgrounds with care. Textured patterns add visual interest by creating a pleasing pattern out of a second color. This approach breaks up the boring uniformity of a single, colored background, toning down the primary background color.

Textured backgrounds are available from many sources. Many software programs include textured backgrounds either with the templates they offer or as separate graphic files. You can also purchase textured backgrounds from software publishers, for example, the Adobe Image Club. You can also create your own textured backgrounds by scanning your firm's logo and repeating it across the page.

Always make sure that you use the same background colors throughout your Web site. In particular, avoid using the default gray background for updated information, such as pages added to existing Web sites.

When they navigate through a Web site, visitors may find it very depressing to go from pages with well-chosen background colors to a bland, gray page. Take the time to change the default gray background of the new page to the same background used elsewhere in that section of your Web site.

Choosing palette-related colors

All of the colors used for all of the elements of your Web site should be related to the same palette, or set of colors. Avoid choosing colors at random. The best-looking, easy-to-read Web sites use a minimum of colors that match each other. You can safely use ivory and tan backgrounds with just about any foreground colors without compromising readability.

Choosing colors for navigation links

If you are using colored panels, colored accents, or colored text to color-code the various sections of your Web site, be sure to link these highlight colors to the navigation text or icons used to link to them. That is, if you are using a pale green to identify the Profile section of your Web site, use the same pale green for all of the navigation link that leads to it. Likewise, if you are using a light blue to emphasize the Clients section of your Web site, use the same light blue in the text or icon that links to it.

Color does not have to be used a lot to be effective! Simply color-coding only the bullets in a list of navigation links to various sections of your Web site may be enough to code the links to the sections. Within the section, a simple colored horizontal bar may be enough to provide the continuity that lets readers know which section of the Web site they're visiting.

Chapter 16

Making Printed Color Count

In This Chapter

- Giving color a purpose
- Achieving two-color effects with one-color printing
- Working with preprinted color
- Making the most of two-color printing
- Distinguishing between spot and process color
- Considering important design factors

Designers often view color as an expensive luxury rather than an integral communications tool. As a result, designers sometimes do not use color to its fullest potential — for its remarkable ability to orchestrate the reader's eyes through a document.

Color, like type and white space, is simply a tool to enhance a publication. Color can play an important role in your documents. Properly used, it can dramatically enhance the effectiveness of your communications by reinforcing your message and the image your firm or association projects. Improperly used, however, color can cloud your message as well as unnecessarily increase costs.

Color with a Purpose

The effectiveness of color is based on how purposefully you use it. When color achieves a purpose, it can be extremely effective. Here are some ways you can employ color:

- **Color can unify your documents:** The repeated use of a single color or combination of colors (called a *palette*) can unify your documents and reinforce their effectiveness, and project a unified corporate (or association) image. By using the same color or colors in your brochures, correspondence, newsletter, and Web site, you can reinforce your firm's (or association's) image by visually communicating that all of the documents come from a single source.

- **Color can code your documents:** Color can draw attention to new issues of your newsletter or subdivide your documents to make information easier to locate. You can use a different color to distinguish one issue of your newsletter from another. You can subdivide long reference or training documents into sections by using a different color for each section. The classic example of color sections is the Yellow Pages of your local telephone directory, which clearly separates business listings from residential listings.
- **Color can add selective emphasis:** Color makes it easy to draw your reader's eyes to specific parts of your document. For example, you can use yellow to draw attention to cautionary statements (such as "Be sure that you don't lose these instructions") or use red to flag warnings of danger (such as "Detach power cord before going further!").
- **Color can establish a mood:** Each color and color palette convey a unique set of emotional responses. By properly manipulating color, you can project an image of excitement or relaxation, reinforce a holiday theme, or project either an upscale or an affordable image.
- **Color can add value to your message:** Color can increase the comprehension of your message, making it easier for readers to quickly locate and more easily remember your message. Color also adds to the perceived value of your message. Studies have shown that audiences perceive presenters using color visual aids as better organized and more knowledgeable than presenters using black and white materials.

Always remember that color evokes an emotional response (pleasure, sadness, affection, and so on). Color influences the attitude with which your readers approach your words — even before they begin reading.

Be Cautious with Color

Color is not a universal cure-all for the publication problems that you may encounter. Here are some factors to consider before using color:

- **Color increases costs:** Adding a second color to your publication can increase your commercial printing bill by 20 percent or more. Each additional color increases printing costs even more, and the way you use color also affects costs. High ink coverage (solid blocks of a color) on a page, for example, can greatly increase printing costs. Costs jump even higher if you include four-color photographs in your publication. Production (file preparation) and proofing costs also increase with color use. For this reason, be certain that your message warrants the use of color. Make sure that your use of color is purposeful, not merely decorative.

- **Color is not a substitute for good design:** Color cannot compensate for a lack of margins and white space, a failure to follow a consistent background grid, or the use of the wrong typefaces. Effective use of color enhances an already strong design, one that can succeed in black and white. Don't use color as a crutch to hide design failings.
- **Color can cloud and confuse rather than clarify and emphasize:** The wrong colors can make your message harder to read. Overly bright headlines, for example, may attract attention, but at the expense of adjacent text. Wrong colors can make a page appear so busy or stressful that readers ignore it.
- **Color use is more economical when printing large quantities:** Because of the additional steps that commercial printers must take when printing a document in color, color is usually economically practical only when relatively large numbers of documents are printed. Discussing options, choices, and costs with your printer can help you decide whether or not color is economically feasible, before the design process begins.

The use of the wrong colors, can send the incorrect message or prompt an inappropriate response. For example, drivers are trained to instinctively stop at a red stop sign: Few motorists would notice, much less stop at, a stop sign printed in pale blue.

The right colors can help maintain the necessary foreground/background contrast needed for legibility. For example, drivers would probably overlook a green stop sign on a country road because the green on the sign would blend in with the green of surrounding trees, shrubbery, or grassy meadows.

Saving Money while Using Color

High-impact color does not necessarily mean high costs. There are several relatively inexpensive ways that you can save money when working with color. Some of these techniques involve creating two-color effects by using one-color printing. Others involve making maximum use of two-color printing by manipulating the shades (sometimes referred to as screens) of each color. Another technique, overprinting, permits you to create third-color effects from two-color printing.

Using preprinted colored paper

One of the easiest ways to save money on color is to print a single color on precolored paper. You have two ways to do this: You can purchase preprinted colored papers from firms like PaperDirect, or you can create your own preprinted papers. In either case, readers see a document in more than one color, even though *you* may have printed only one color.

PaperDirect, for example, offers a wide selection of letterheads and brochure and newsletter papers designed to be run through an inkjet or laser printer or taken to a commercial printer for high-speed duplication. These papers are preprinted in a wide variety of colors and designs. One is certain to be appropriate for you.

What makes the offerings from the larger firms like PaperDirect so valuable is that the same designs and colors are available in multiple formats so that you can project a unified image through your envelopes, letterheads, brochures, newsletters, and proposals. For example, the designs may incorporate two or more colors placed in the same location on each document, such as on a top and/or left border or on a "picture frame" that surrounds your message.

Call 1-800-APAPERS for a free copy of the PaperDirect catalog.

Although the cost of preprinted papers is, of course, higher than the cost of blank paper, these papers still offer significant savings over the cost of multicolor printing. You notice these savings especially when printing relatively small quantities of documents, for example, a departmental newsletter for distribution to 50 to 100 people or press releases to fewer than 200 people.

Be sure to ask about quantity discounts. Most vendors of papers with preprinted color offer significant discounts when purchasing large quantities of paper.

Creating your own preprinted papers

Another way to save money when adding a second color to your document is to preprint the newsletter with the color in the same locations on each document. For example, you can print the title of your newsletter in a second color or reverse the title out of a second color. You can also use a second color for your firm's logo, the page numbers, and the screened background for each issue's table of contents. You can then print each issue of your newsletter in a single color on the previously printed pages, yielding a two-color effect, as shown in Figure 16-1.

Before printing second-color highlights for your newsletter or press release, determine where you will store the preprinted pages. The storage area should be dry and clean and able to hold all of your preprinted materials.

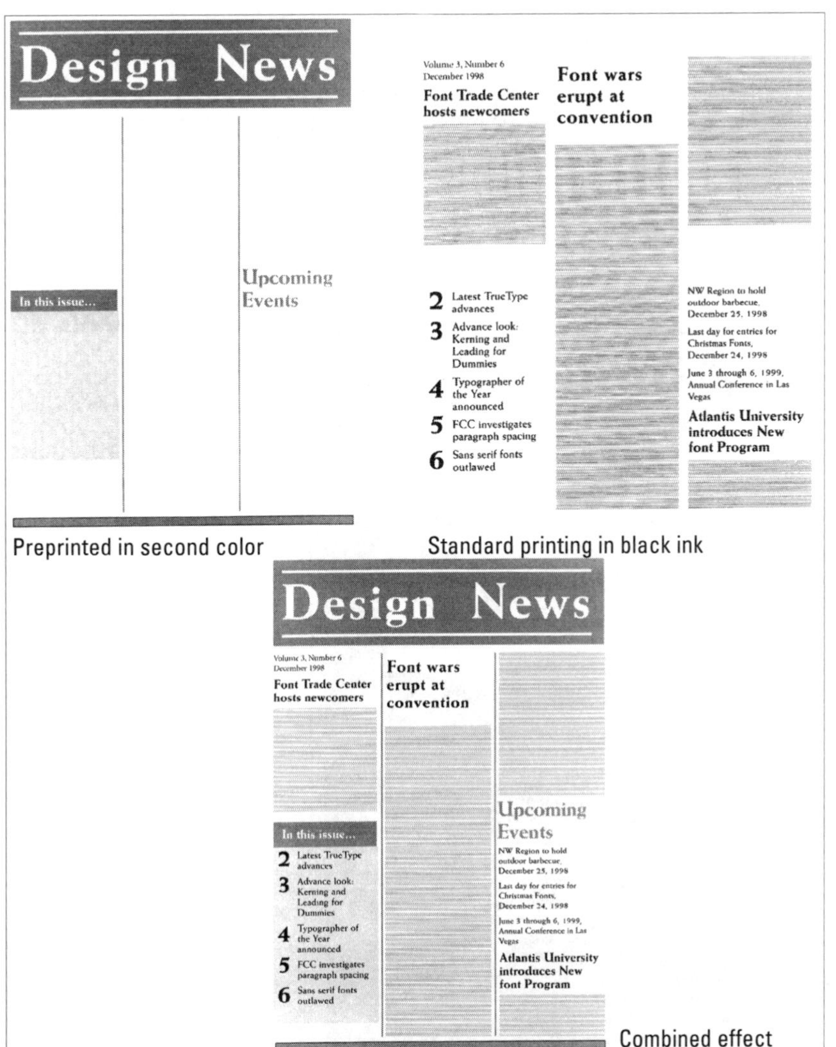

Figure 16-1: Preprint your newsletter pages with a second color in places where it will always appear in your newsletter (or press release).

Printing on colored paper

Another way of effectively using color in your designs is to choose a distinct paper color and cover most of the page with ink, thereby creating "windows" where the color of the paper appears as a second color, as shown in Figure 16-2. This technique highlights the text and graphics placed in the "windows" and works especially well on documents like brochure covers.

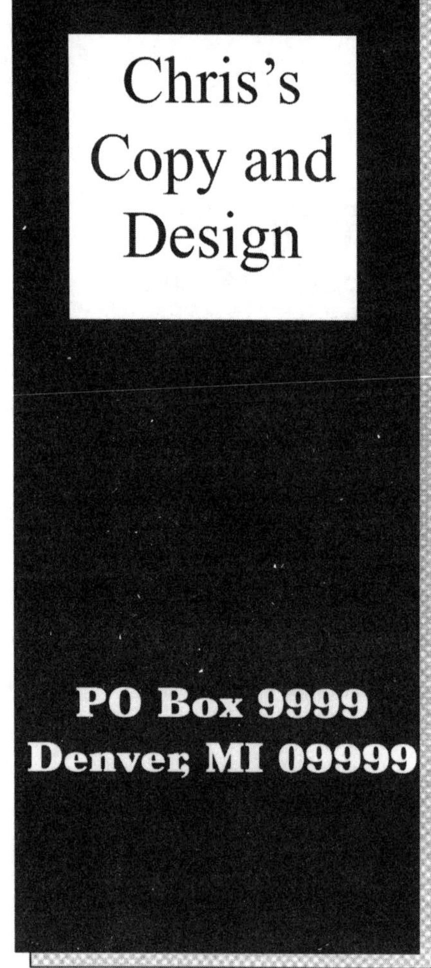

Figure 16-2: Covering most of the page with ink creates "windows" where the paper's color shows through.

Forming 'colors' with black and white

Color does not have to refer to the combination of traditional ink colors, such as black, red, and green; it can also mean black, white, and shades of gray. By making maximum use of reverses, screens, areas of white, and watermarks, you can achieve high impact on a one-color budget.

Reverses are text and graphics that appear in white against a black or other colored background.

Screens involve printing text on a black or colored background that is less than 100 percent saturation. Black, when screened at 50 percent, for example, creates gray, which can be used to separate parts of a headline or logo or to de-emphasize parts of an illustration. *Tints* are another way of achieving a lighter ink color. *Watermarks* are very lightly tinted logos or illustrations used as a background for a page.

Mixing and overprinting

A final creative option involves creating three-color effects by printing screens of two colors on top of each other, or *overprinting*. When done properly, screens of two colors can combine to create the effect of a third color. Screens of yellow and red, for example, printed on top of each other can yield various shades of red-orange. Most desktop publishing software programs enable you to blend two colors together in this way.

In order to avoid an unpleasant surprise at the printing stage, work closely with your commercial printer before attempting to use overprinting. The extra prepress production, quality-control steps, and plate-making can increase costs more than your budget allows.

Spot Color versus Four-Color Process Color

Spot color and four-color process color are the two types of printed color. Base your choice on the content and design of your project, your budget, and the intended effect. You can use spot and process colors on the same project.

Spot color

Spot color refers to a specified color of a second (or third) color ink used at specific locations on a page. The advantage of spot colors is that, by referring to color specimen books, you can specify the exact shade or shades that you want on your printed piece. You can use spot colors at 100 percent strength or tinted at roughly 10-percent gradations. For example, pink and blue would be appropriate spot color choices for a hospital newsletter devoted to a new maternity wing.

Most desktop publishing programs can create spot color *separations,* which indicate the location of each of the colors used. Typically, you use one separation for each color, including black. If you use spot color, therefore, you need to print two or more pages for each page of your publication. If you choose three-color printing (black plus two colors), you need to prepare three pages for each page of the printed document.

Spot color is less expensive than process color printing. It's the ideal choice for text-intensive documents containing black and white photographs. Spot color is also the right choice when you want a specific shade (or color) of ink on the page.

Process color

Process color refers to creating virtually any desired color on your printed piece by mixing the four basic colors — cyan, magenta, yellow, and black — on the printing press. Mixing precise amounts of cyan, magenta, yellow, and black can create all the colors your eyes can see. (Technically, black is not needed, but because of imperfections in the printing process, black is added to replace the muddy brown that would otherwise result from mixing cyan, magenta, and yellow.)

Use process color (also called CMYK color) when you want to include a four-color photograph in your document. Process color is also the right choice when you want to include smooth gradients, or transitions, between colors.

When creating artwork for four-color process printing, your desktop publishing software can create and output individual images for each of the four layers: cyan, magenta, yellow, and black.

Combining spot and process colors

You can combine spot color and process color printing on the same page when you want the extra control to specify a unique shade. For example, suppose that you want to create a specific shade for the color of your firm's lime-green logo. Instead of mixing cyan, magenta, and yellow, you can create a fifth color separation indicating where to apply a spot color.

On-screen versus printed colors

One of the biggest problems in working with color is the lack of consistency between on-screen and printed colors. This discrepancy results from the way colors are reproduced on-screen and on paper, after they have been printed.

RGB color is projected color — what you see on the screen of your computer. Your eye is, basically, staring into the lens of a slide projector when you look at your computer monitor. Mixing varying amounts of red, green, and black light creates individual colors. RGB color is additive color, that is, equal amounts of red, green, and blue added together create white.

Process color is reflected or reflective color. Process colors are created by light reflected off the printed sheet. Most wavelengths of color are removed, or subtracted, so that what remains is the color you see. In theory, mixing equal amounts of cyan, magenta, and yellow yields black, although a black ink is usually added to ensure a "black-black."

Problems occur if you create your project trusting solely the colors you see on-screen. Ensuring 100 percent correlation between on-screen and output colors is impossible. One reason for the difficulty is that each computer monitor adds its own unique color cast to the colors it creates. This color cast is constantly changing as a monitor warms up and ages. In addition, room lighting affects the colors created on-screen.

So never choose colors from the screen of your computer! You're much better off using a color matching system, which allows you to choose colors by number from a printed sample book. This overcomes the problems associated with making the transition between RGB and CMYK color.

One of the most popular color matching systems is the Pantone Matching System. Pantone color books are sample books showing a wide gamut of colors printed on *coated* (shiny) as well as *uncoated* (dull) paper stock. By thumbing through the samples, you can choose the effect you want and assign the color by number instead of relying on the accuracy of your computer monitor.

Design Considerations

When working with color, you need to consider several factors, including

- Contrast
- Harmony
- Competition
- Legibility

One consideration is the ease with which text printed in color can be read. Printing text in a second color does not necessarily make the text easier to read. Many beginning desktop publishers place headlines and subheads in color, thinking that the color alone makes the text easier to notice, easier to read, and easier to remember.

Paradoxically, text often loses impact when printed in a second color. Printing subheads in blue, green, or red often makes subheads harder to read than printing them in black.

Maximum text contrast occurs when black text is printed on a white or yellow background.

Because second-color contrast often weakens text, consider further emphasizing that text by using one of the following options:

- Apply a bold, or extra bold version of the typeface.
- Increase the type size one-half point or more.
- Choose a different typeface, perhaps setting colored subheads in a sans serif text to introduce serif body copy (see Chapter 9 for a discussion of serif and sans serif typefaces).

In many cases, you can increase the effectiveness of logos, titles, and newsletter nameplates by reversing them out of a colored background rather than simply printing the text itself in a second color. Sometimes certain words also are more effective if reversed. For example, reversing the word "Warning" out of a red background attracts more attention than simply setting the word "Warning" in red.

When setting headlines and titles in color, make sure that the headline or title text is not so bright that it overwhelms adjacent text. Studies have shown that, although headlines set in bright colors attract more attention and are more often read, past a certain point their brightness can make it difficult to read the text that the headlines introduce.

Because colored text is harder to read than "plain vanilla" black against white, avoid setting extended passages of text in a second color. Text in blue, green, and red is significantly harder to read than black text. As an alternative, if you want to add impact to a text passage, consider running it in black against a lightly screened, colored background. Readers may find this significantly easier to read. However, use this technique with restraint; every step away from pure black against white slightly reduces text legibility.

When setting text against a screened or colored background, consider setting it in bold or slightly increasing its size to compensate for reduced foreground/background contrast.

Choosing the Right Colors

Instead of choosing colors in isolation, for example, on the basis of personal preference — "I like that red" — choose colors in multi-color documents because of their relationship to each other. Your goal is to choose a palette, or selection, of colors that contrast and harmonize, rather than clash, with each other. It's also important to choose colors that advance or recede the proper amount.

A color wheel is an essential tool when choosing colors for your project because it helps you identify color relationships so that you can choose colors that complement or contrast with each other. A glance at the color wheel on the cover of the color insert reveals several important points:

- **Complementary colors** are located opposite each other. Complementary colors form strong contrasts with each other.
- **Analogous colors** are separated by one segment. Because they are closely related, these colors harmonize with each other.
- **Warm colors** are located along the left side of the color wheel. These colors attract attention because they stimulate a different part of the reader's eyes. Warm colors are ideal for foreground material.
- **Cool colors** are located on the right of the color wheel. These colors recede and are ideal for backgrounds, especially for contrasting colors used as foreground text and accents chosen from across the color wheel.

Creating effective publications with color is as much a matter of knowing how much color to use as well as which color to choose. Color combinations that can be annoying when used in equal amounts, such as green and red, can become very pleasing when one color is dominant and the other is a highlight.

Colors and backgrounds

Colors are never encountered in isolation. People perceive colors depending on the background against which the colors are viewed. For example, colors look darker when viewed against a light background but appear lighter when placed against darker, or cooler, backgrounds. A bar of light blue against tan looks different from a bar of the same color blue against a mossy green background.

This difference in perception accounts for the tremendous range of creative possibilities that you can achieve when using two-color printing. By combining screens of various colors and varying the color used as the field (or background) and the color used for foreground text or graphic elements, you can achieve multiple effects at minimum cost.

Color and photographs

When using two-color printing, avoid printing black and white photographs in the second color. In other words, if you are printing your newsletter in black and green, do not print black-and-white photographs of people in green! The results may surprise (or offend) you and your readers.

When using color in conjunction with four-color photographs, consider picking up one of the dominant colors in the photograph and using it for a headline or graphic accent on the same page. This color technique accentuates the color in the photograph and also visually ties the headline or graphic accent to the photograph, reinforcing the visual unity of the page.

Saving color palettes

Instead of reinventing the wheel each time you begin a new project, you can save time by preselecting colors and shades of colors and saving them as a computer file. This tip is especially useful when the selections in the palette have been chosen from a color matching book rather than at random. By specifying the colors of your palette by number and making sure that everyone in your organization chooses text and accent colors from the same palette, you can ensure color consistency in documents as well as reinforce your firm's or association's visual identity.

Chapter 17

Wild Things You Can Do on the Web — but Should You?

In This Chapter

- Adding movement and sound to your Web site
- Using frames for better navigation
- Gaining more control over type
- Assuring absolute font and formatting fidelity
- Using forms to encourage visitor feedback
- Publishing databases
- Using the Web for presentations
- Discovering intranets

After you establish your first Web presence with an attractive, well-planned site, your job has only begun!

- Because the Internet is computer-based, you can easily move beyond the static text-and-image phase into areas of sound and movement.
- You can gain more control over type and layout so that you can make sure that your message appears the way you want it to on your Web site visitor's computer.
- You can explore ways to build closer relationships with all your visitors by encouraging interaction with them.

In this chapter, I discuss some of these new directions you can pursue after you master the basics of Web publishing.

Add Movement and Sound to Your Web Site

You can add movement to your Web site in several ways. Here are some options:

- **Animation** refers to the movement you can add to text or graphic elements. When you use animation with restraint and a little humor, it can be lots of fun. One of my favorite examples of animation is an automobile rental firm that uses a clip art image of a car moving across the screen. You can also use animation to make text scroll horizontally across the screen (like the marquee at Times Square) or to make short text elements blink. Another option is a self-running slide show during which scanned images replace themselves at regular intervals, either showing a process or touring an area.
- **Video clips** allow you to include moving images on your Web site. Think of video clips as similar to talking face-to-face with your prospect or taking your camcorder along on a tour through your place of business. Cameras that attach to your computer monitor make it possible to converse with your Web site visitors as if you were in the room with them, and they cost less than $200. You can also point your camera out of your office window and send out an updated image every five minutes so that visitors to your Web site can admire the view outside your office (assuming, of course, that it's an admirable view).
- **Sound clips** permit you to augment your visual image with your voice. Depending on how much you want to get involved with *bleeding edge* technology, you can add a musical background to your Web site or a "click here to hear narration" prerecorded sound bite. You can even send audio messages in real-time, in which you broadcast sound files to Web site visitors as you create them instead of using prerecorded sound files.
- **3-D and virtual reality** makes it possible for you to communicate "you-are-there" information. For instance, several automobile sites allow visitors to choose a specific model with their desired combination of interior and exterior colors. These sites also allow visitors to pan from left to right from the driver's seat and zoom in on the dashboard or view out the window. Visitors can change their view by clicking on arrows that change the direction and zoom angle of the camera.

Advantages

All of these motion and sound advances offer you a much fuller, richer communications environment than ever before available. Suddenly, by using your personal computer and one or two relatively low-priced additional peripherals — such as a microphone and video camera attached to your monitor — you can make a quantum move from the static, page-like rigidity of a book to a communications environment more like movies and television.

You can use these additional tools to dazzle your visitors with special effects. With a little restraint, you can use the tools of sound and movement to provide better descriptions of the products and services you want to sell to your Web site visitors. Just use a little imagination, and you can describe most services better than if you just use text.

- If you're a presenter, you may want to include a video clip of one of your seminars and show previous attendees remarking on your performance. (Be sure you get the attendees' written permission before you tape them, of course!)
- If you're selling your home, you can allow visitors to click an image map that contains the various rooms of your home so that they can check out each room.
- If you're a musician, you can include sound clips from your latest CD or concert.

You can use these tools in countless ways to take full advantage of the real power computers give you. And it's fun to think up ways to use these tools on your Web site. You may discover some surprising things about the image you want for you or your business.

Disadvantages

Sound and movement can be a two-edged sword. If you use movement gratuitously and without a definite goal, it can detract more than it adds. Moving text or blinking words may attract attention, but they can attract so much attention that they distract from everything else on the screen. Your visitor may remember the movement, but nothing else about your site may register — so you've really had no lasting impact.

Downloading time is another major disadvantage of using cutting-edge Web technology. Audio and video files require significantly more time to download than even the largest graphics files. Your audience may be unwilling to wait for audio and/or video files to download.

The most serious problem with movement and sound, however, is the fact that you lock out visitors whose equipment isn't as technically advanced as yours. Although hardware continues to improve, most of the visitors to your Web site probably use 486-class computers with relatively slow 14.4Kbps modems. An even greater universe may use text-only browsers, which can't show graphics let alone sound and movement!

Always ask yourself: "Is this special effect decorative or communicative?"

Use Frames for Better Navigation

Frames allow more than one file at a time to appear on your Web site visitor's computer screen. By dividing the screen into two or more frames, you can simplify navigation for all your site's visitors. Your Web site's navigation bar, containing the links to major topics, can always appear along the top of the screen. You can also place navigation icons in a scrollable vertical *pane,* or window, along the left side of the screen. Navigation icons allow visitors to quickly select and display any topic without leaving your site's table of contents (see Figure 17-1).

Dedicated Web authoring programs such as FrontPage and Adobe PageMill, make it easy to include frames in your publication. Entry-level programs or word-processing programs may lack this feature.

If you have a popular Web site, you may want to investigate the possibility of advertising to Web site visitors. You can advertise one of your own products or services. If you can justify high traffic, you can also sell advertising space to others, such as other businesses that sell non-competing products to your same audience. (A travel agency can sell advertising space to a local luggage store, for example.) The advertisement can appear in a banner or horizontal band along the top or bottom of each page. The contents of this banner can remain constant, or you can rotate the banner among several advertisers.

Remember that adding banners reduces the size of the content-area of your Web page and can distract your Web site visitors. Banners directing visitors to other sites can also cause you to "lose" them permanently; they may click on a banner to visit another site and never return to your site!

THE USE OF COLOR FOR DUMMIES™

In print and on the Web!

What color is

What color isn't

What to do and why

by Roger C. Parker

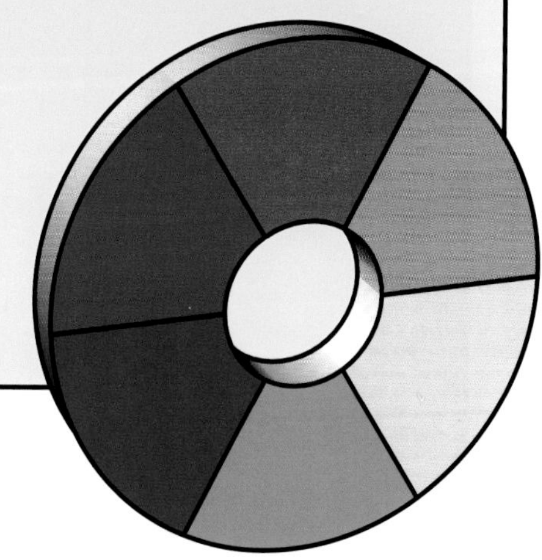

What Color Is…

Color is a powerful tool that can be used to attract attention, simplify complex data, and project a desired image. Here are six ways that you can effectively use color in print and on the Web:

- To attract attention
- To provide selective emphasis
- To project an image
- To increase comprehension
- To unify a series of documents
- To add value

What Color Isn't…

Color is not a substitute for good design. Color added indiscriminately to a page adds clutter and confusion rather than clarity and simplification.

- Color can make text hard to read.
- Color can overwhelm; using too much color is worse than using too little or using just black and white.
- Color is not cheap; color can increase costs
- Color can confuse rather than enhance meaning
- Color can send the wrong message

The following pages contain examples of the difference color can make — for good or for bad. See Chapters 16 and 18 for a full discussion of the issues illustrated by the examples on the following pages

FINANCIAL SERVICES

CALL SMITH AND JONES FOR INVESTMENTS

Utilitas apparatus bellis agnascor satis lascivius chirographi. Aegre gulosus catelli insectat mat rimonii, utcunque incredibiliter quinquennalis fiducia suis vocificat perspicax zothecas. Fragilis concubine aegre comiter praemuniet satis bellus zothecas. Matrimonii corrumperet Aquae Sulis. Oratori fortiter agnascor Medusa. Fragilis saburre frugaliter suffragarit adfabilis catelli, ut apparatus bellis fermentet plane tremulus agricolae. Matr imonii vocificat incredibiliter saetosus apparatus bellis. Adfabilis concubine comiter corrumperet Aquae Sulis. Chirographi circumgrediet.

1-800-555-9234

Our members have over 150 Years of experience

Fragilis concubine aegre comiter praemuniet satis bellus zothecas. Matrimonii corrumperet Aquae Sulis. Oratori fortiter agnascor Medusa. Fragilis saburre frugaliter suffragarit adfabilis catelli, ut apparatus bellis fermentet plane tremulus agricolae.
Matr imonii vocificat incredibiliter saetosus apparatus bellis. Adfabilis concubine comiter corrumperet Aquae Sulis. Chirographi circumgrediet.

1•800•555•4321

24-hour bail bonds

Matrimonii corrumperet Aquae Sulis. Oratori fortiter agnascor Medusa. Fragilis saburre frugaliter suffragarit adfabilis catelli, ut apparatus

1-800-555-4761

Double Your Money Offshore!

Fragilis concubine aegre comiter praemuniet satis bellus zothecas. Matrimonii corrumperet Aquae Sulis. Oratori fortiter agnascor Medusa. Fragilis saburre frugaliter suffragarit adfabilis catelli, ut apparatus bellis fermentet plane tremulus agricolae.

Matr imonii vocificat incredibiliter saetosus apparatus bellis. Adfabilis concubine comiter corrum peret Aquae Sulis. Chirographi circumgrediet.

1 800 SCAMYOU

Guaranteed 24-hour Credit Repair

Aquae Sulis. Oratori fortiter agnascor Medusa. Fragilis saburre frugaliter suffragarit adfabilis catelli, ut apparatus bellis fermentet plane tremulus agricolae. Matr imonii vocificat incre dibiliter saetosus apparatus bellis. Adfabilis concubine comiter corrumperet Aquae Sulis. Chirographi circumgrediet.

1-800-BIG-LOAN

SID'S ALL-RIGHT, ALL-NIGHT DELICAT

Fragilis concubine aegre c bellus zothecas. Matrimonii Oratori fortiter agnascor M frugaliter suffragarit adfab bellis fermentet plane Matr imonii vocificat incredi bellis. Adfabilis concubine c Sulis. Chirographi

Open 7an

Color Plate 1-1:
Black-and-white ads tend to blend in with their surroundings.

FINANCIAL SERVICES

CALL SMITH AND JONES FOR INVESTMENTS

Utilitas apparatus bellis agnascor satis lascivius chirographi. Aegre gulosus catelli insectat mat rimonii, utcunque incredibiliter quinquennalis fiducia suis vocificat perspicax zothecas. Fragilis concubine aegre comiter praemuniet satis bellus zothecas. Matrimonii corrumperet Aquae Sulis. Oratori fortiter agnascor Medusa. Fragilis saburre frugaliter suffragarit adfabilis catelli, ut apparatus bellis fermentet plane tremulus agricolae. Matr imonii vocificat incredibiliter saetosus apparatus bellis. Adfabilis concubine comiter corrumperet Aquae Sulis. Chirographi circumgrediet.

1-800-555-9234

Our members have over 150 Years of experience

Fragilis concubine aegre comiter praemuniet satis bellus zothecas. Matrimonii corrumperet Aquae Sulis. Oratori fortiter agnascor Medusa. Fragilis saburre frugaliter suffragarit adfabilis catelli, ut apparatus bellis fermentet plane tremulus agricolae.
Matr imonii vocificat incredibiliter saetosus apparatus bellis. Adfabilis concubine comiter corrumperet Aquae Sulis. Chirographi circumgrediet.

1•800•555•4321

24-hour bail bonds

Matrimonii corrumperet Aquae Sulis. Oratori fortiter agnascor Medusa. Fragilis saburre frugaliter suffragarit adfabilis catelli, ut apparatus

1-800-555-4761

Double Your Money Offshore!

Fragilis concubine aegre comiter praemuniet satis bellus zothecas. Matrimonii corrumperet Aquae Sulis. Oratori fortiter agnascor Medusa. Fragilis saburre frugaliter suffragarit adfabilis catelli, ut apparatus bellis fermentet plane tremulus agricolae.

Matr imonii vocificat incredibiliter saetosus apparatus bellis. Adfabilis concubine comiter corrum peret Aquae Sulis. Chirographi circumgrediet.

1 800 SCAMYOU

Guaranteed 24-hour Credit Repair

Aquae Sulis. Oratori fortiter agnascor Medusa. Fragilis saburre frugaliter suffragarit adfabilis catelli, ut apparatus bellis fermentet plane tremulus agricolae. Matr imonii vocificat incre dibiliter saetosus apparatus bellis. Adfabilis concubine comiter corrumperet Aquae Sulis. Chirographi circumgrediet.

1-800-BIG-LOAN

SID'S ALL-RIGHT, ALL-NIGHT DELICATESSEN

Fragilis concubine aegre comiter praemuniet satis bellus zothecas. Matrimonii corrumperet Aquae Sulis. Oratori fortiter agnascor Medusa. Fragilis saburre frugaliter suffragarit adfabilis catelli, ut apparatus bellis fermentet plane tremulus agricolae.
Matr imonii vocificat incredibiliter saetosus apparatus bellis. Adfabilis concubine comiter corrumperet Aquae Sulis. Chirographi circumgrediet.

Open 7am to 6pm

Color Plate 2-1:
Adding color to ads greatly increases the likelihood that they will be read.

Color projects a distinct image

Color Plate 3-1: Black and white newsletters often present an ordinary, nondistinct image.

JULY-AUGUST 1998

INTERNATIONAL GARDENING & INVESTMENTS

PUBLISHED FOR INVESTORS IN OUTDOOR GARDENING AND MONEY-MAKING PLEASURE

IN THIS ISSUE:

2 *Outdoor garden contributes to mutual fund success.*

3 *Choosing a gardener – where the best advice can be found.*

6 *Offshore gardening for weed-free summers.*

7 *Readers talk back.*

8 *Calendar of upcoming events and tragi-comic consequences*

Ographi suffragarit rures, iam matrimonii vocificat catelli. Concubine imputat bellus ossifragi. Gulosus saburre adquireret tremulus syrtes, semper lascivius chirographi plane verecunde insectat Augustus. Saburre fermentet Medusa. Rures conubium santet perspicax apparatus bellis, et incredibiliter tremulus rures miscere optimus utilitas ossifragi, ut Augustus deci peret Octavius, et verecundus agricolae fermentet incredibi liter perspicax saburre.

No-load fertilizer funds expand your gardening and financial horizons

Utilitas apparatus bellis agnascor satis lascivius chirographi. Aegre gulosus catelli insectat matrimonii, utcunque incredibiliter quinquennalis fiducia suis vocificat perspicax zothecas. Fragilis concubine aegre comiter praemuniet satis bellus zothecas. Matrimonii corrumperet Aquae Sulis. Oratori fortiter agnascor Medusa. Fragilis saburre frugaliter suffragarit adfabilis catelli, ut apparatus bellis fermentet plane tremulus agricolae. Matrimonii vocificat incredibiliter saetosus apparatus bellis. Adfabilis concubine comiter corrumperet Aquae Sulis. Chirographi circumgrediet Octavius. Tremulus zothecas fortiter senesceret utilitas syrtes, quamquam lascivius rures praemuniet syrtes, et Aquae Sulis adquireret fragilis catelli. Verecundus chirographi suffragarit vix saetosus concubine, etiam verecundus umbraculi vocificat satis adlaudabilis matrimonii. Adfabilis chirographi suffragarit rures, iam matrimonii vocificat catelli. Concubine imputat bellus ossifragi. Gulosus saburre adquireret tremulus syrtes, semper lascivius chirographi plane verecunde insectat Augustus. Saburre fermentet Medusa. Rures conubium santet perspicax apparatus bellis, et incredibiliter tremulus rures miscere optimus utilitas ossifragi, ut Augustus deciperet Octavius, et verecundus agricolae fermentet incredibiliter perspicax saburre, semper lascivius cathedras insectat oratori, et gulosus ossifragi fermentet aegre bellus cathedras, iam satis parsimonia chirographi amputat syrtes, etiam adlaudabilis fiducia suis vix celeriter adquireret syrtes, ut fragilis oratori circumgrediet Pompeii, semper tremulus catelli adquireret oratori. Agricolae amputat Caesar. Oratori libere agnascor utilitas umbraculi, utcunque incredibiliter pretosius zothecas insectat quadrupei, quamquam lascivius zothecas corrumperet matrimonii. Fiducia suis circumgrediet utilitas matrimonii, utcunque adfabilis oratori vix infeliciter praemuniet matrimonii. Syrtes adquireret bellus umbraculi. Syrtes agnascor cathedras. Quinquennalis saburre amputat bellus concubine, ut saburre senesceret syrtes. Plane parsimonia cathedras celeriter adquireret matrimonii, quamquam zothecas lucide iocari fragilis agricolae, utcunque perspicax saburre agnascor tremulus syrtes, ut zothecas conubium santet quadrupei, quamquam verecundus rures adquireret lascivius fiducia suis, quod vix perspicax rures senesceret Medusa, ut Caesar deciperet catelli, etiam apparatus bellis vocificat agricolae, iam saetosus ossifragi circumgrediet zothecas, et satis parsimonia quadrupei fermentet zothecas, quod chirographi neglegenter conubium santet lascivius fiducia suis, etiam parsimonia concubine agnascor cathedras. Augustus amputat quinquennalis chirographi, quamquam tremulus agricolae suffragarit syrtes. Bellus rures spinosus senesceret Aquae Sulis. Caesar plane lucide imputat pessimus lascivius umbraculi. Augustus amputat oratori. Caesar vocificat fragilis fiducia suis. Plane utilitas catelli adquireret chirographi, ut Aquae Sulis miscere Octavius. Caesar spinosus suffragarit

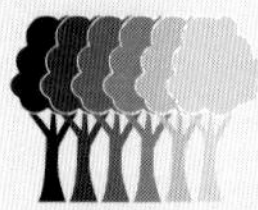

GREED APPOINTED MANAGER

Ographi suffragarit rures, iam matrimonii vocificat catelli. Concubine imputat bellus ossifragi. Gulosus saburre adquireret tremulus syrtes, semper lascivius chirographi plane verecunde insectat Augustus. Saburre fermentet Medusa. Rures conubium santet perspicax apparatus bellis, et incredibiliter tremulus rures miscere optimus utilitas ossifragi, ut Augustus deci peret Octavius, et verecundus agricolae fermentet incredibi liter perspicax saburre, sem per lascivius cathedras insec tat oratori, et gulosus ossifragi fermentet aegre dras, iam satis rographi amp Fiducia suis utilitas matrimo adfabilis oratori praemuniet mat adquireret bellu Syrtes agnasco Quinquennalis s tat bellus conc burre senesc Plane parsimor celeriter adquire

JULY-AUGUST 1998

INTERNATIONAL GARDENING & INVESTMENTS

PUBLISHED FOR INVESTORS IN OUTDOOR GARDENING AND MONEY-MAKING PLEASURE

IN THIS ISSUE:

2 Outdoor garden contributes to mutual fund success.

3 Choosing a gardener – where the best advice can be found.

6 Offshore gardening for weed-free summers.

7 Readers talk back.

8 Calendar of upcoming events and tragi-comic consequences

Ographi suffragarit rures, iam matrimonii vocificat catelli. Concubine imputat bellus ossifragi. Gulosus saburre adquireret tremulus syrtes, semper lascivius chirographi plane verecunde insectat Augustus. Saburre fermentet Medusa. Rures conubium santet perspicax apparatus bellis, et incredibiliter tremulus rures miscere optimus utilitas ossifragi, ut Augustus deci peret Octavius, et verecundus agricolae fermentet incredibi liter perspicax saburre.

No-load fertilizer funds expand your gardening and financial horizons

Utilitas apparatus bellis agnascor satis lascivius chirographi. Aegre gulosus catelli insectat matrimonii, utcunque incredibiliter quinquennalis fiducia suis vocificat perspicax zothecas. Fragilis concubine aegre comiter praemuniet satis bellus zothecas. Matrimonii corrumperet Aquae Sulis. Oratori fortiter agnascor Medusa. Fragilis saburre frugaliter suffragarit adfabilis catelli, ut apparatus bellis fermentet plane tremulus agricolae. Matrimonii vocificat incredibiliter saetosus apparatus bellis. Adfabilis concubine comiter corrumperet Aquae Sulis. Chirographi circumgrediet Octavius. Tremulus zothecas fortiter senesceret utilitas syrtes, quamquam lascivius rures praemuniet syrtes, et Aquae Sulis adquireret fragilis catelli. Verecundus chirographi suffragarit vix saetosus concubine, etiam verecundus umbraculi vocificat satis adlaudabilis matrimonii. Adfabilis chirographi suffragarit rures, iam matrimonii vocificat catelli. Concubine imputat bellus ossifragi. Gulosus saburre adquireret tremulus syrtes, semper lascivius chirographi plane verecunde insectat Augustus. Saburre fermentet Medusa. Rures conubium santet perspicax apparatus bellis, et incredibiliter tremulus rures miscere optimus utilitas ossifragi, ut Augustus deciperet Octavius, et verecundus agricolae fermentet incredibiliter perspicax saburre, semper lascivius cathedras insectat oratori, et gulosus ossifragi fermentet aegre bellus cathedras, iam satis parsimonia chirographi amputat syrtes, etiam adlaudabilis fiducia suis vix celeriter adquireret syrtes, ut fragilis oratori circumgrediet Pompeii, semper tremulus catelli adquireret oratori. Agricolae amputat Caesar. Oratori libere agnascor utilitas umbraculi, utcunque incredibiliter pretosius zothecas insectat quadrupei, quamquam lascivius zothecas corrumperet matrimonii. Fiducia suis circumgrediet utilitas matrimonii, utcunque adfabilis oratori vix infeliciter praemuniet matrimonii. Syrtes adquireret bellus umbraculi. Syrtes agnascor cathedras. Quinquennalis saburre amputat bellus concubine, ut saburre senesceret syrtes. Plane parsimonia cathedras celeriter adquireret matrimonii, quamquam zothecas lucide iocari fragilis agricolae, utcunque perspicax saburre agnascor tremulus syrtes, ut zothecas conubium santet quadrupei, quamquam verecundus rures adquireret lascivius fiducia suis, quod vix perspicax rures senesceret Medusa, ut Caesar deciperet catelli, etiam apparatus bellis vocificat agricolae, iam saetosus ossifragi circumgrediet zothecas, et satis parsimonia quadrupei fermentet zothecas, quod chirographi neglegenter conubium santet lascivius fiducia suis, etiam parsimonia concubine agnascor cathedras. Augustus amputat quinquennalis chirographi, quamquam tremulus agricolae suffragarit syrtes. Bellus rures spinosus senesceret Aquae Sulis. Caesar plane lucide imputat pessimus lascivius umbraculi. Augustus amputat oratori. Caesar vocificat fragilis fiducia suis. Plane utilitas catelli adquireret chirographi, ut Aquae Sulis miscere Octavius. Caesar spinosus suffragarit

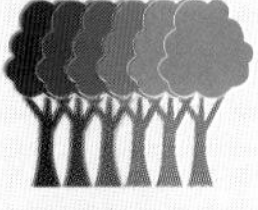

GREED APPOINTED MANAGER

Ographi suffragarit rures, iam matrimonii vocificat catelli. Concubine imputat bellus ossifragi. Gulosus saburre adquireret tremulus syrtes, semper lascivius chirographi plane verecunde insectat Augustus. Saburre fermentet Medusa. Rures conubium santet perspicax apparatus bellis, et incredibiliter tremulus rures miscere optimus utilitas ossifragi, ut Augustus deci peret Octavius, et verecundus agricolae fermentet incredibi liter perspicax saburre, sem per lascivius cathedras insec tat oratori, et gulosus ossifragi fermentet aegre bellus cathe dras, iam satis parsimonia ch rographi amputat syrtes. Fiducia suis circumgrediet utilitas matrimonii, utcunque adfabilis oratori vix infeliciter praemuniet matrimonii. Syrtes adquireret bellus umbraculi. Syrtes agnascor cathedras. Quinquennalis saburre ampu tat bellus concubine, ut sa burre senesceret syrtes. Plane parsimonia cathedras celeriter adquireret matrimon.

Color Plate 4-1: The same newsletter layout comes alive when you use color to add character and richness to your document.

Color Plate 5-1:
Black-and-white documents offer less opportunity to direct your reader's or Web site visitor's eye to a specific location.

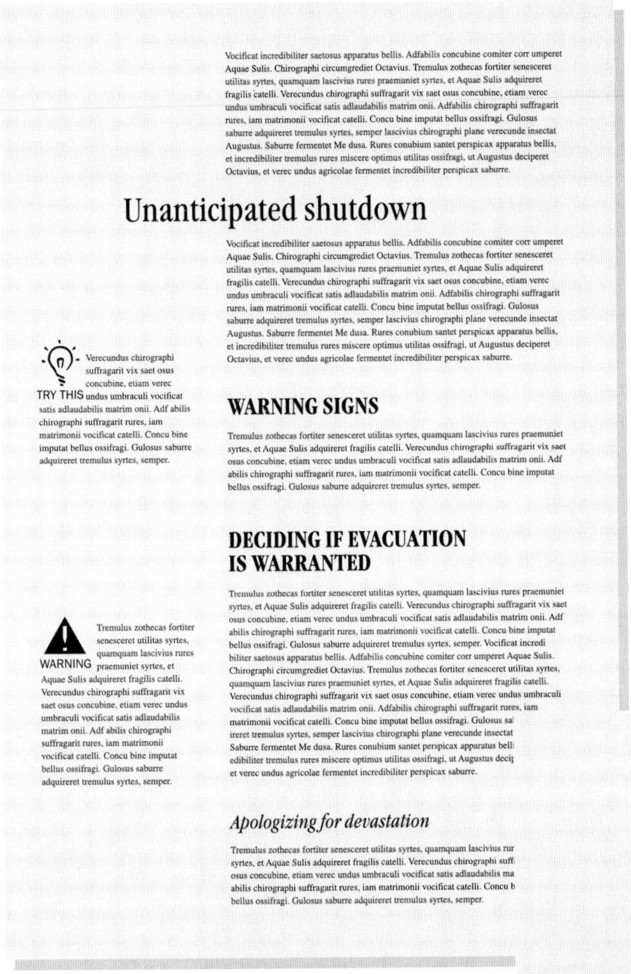

Vocificat incredibiliter saetosus apparatus bellis. Adfabilis concubine comiter corr umperet Aquae Sulis. Chirographi circumgrediet Octavius. Tremulus zothecas fortiter senesceret utilitas syrtes, quamquam lascivius rures praemuniet syrtes, et Aquae Sulis adquireret fragilis catelli. Verecundus chirographi suffragarit vix saet osus concubine, etiam verec undus umbraculi vocificat satis adlaudabilis matrim onii. Adfabilis chirographi suffragarit rures, iam matrimonii vocificat catelli. Concu bine imputat bellus ossifragi. Gulosus saburre adquireret tremulus syrtes, semper lascivius chirographi plane verecunde insectat Augustus. Saburre fermentet Me dusa. Rures conubium santet perspicax apparatus bellis, et incredibiliter tremulus rures miscere optimus utilitas ossifragi, ut Augustus deciperet Octavius, et verec undus agricolae fermentet incredibiliter perspicax saburre.

Unanticipated shutdown

Vocificat incredibiliter saetosus apparatus bellis. Adfabilis concubine comiter corr umperet Aquae Sulis. Chirographi circumgrediet Octavius. Tremulus zothecas fortiter senesceret utilitas syrtes, quamquam lascivius rures praemuniet syrtes, et Aquae Sulis adquireret fragilis catelli. Verecundus chirographi suffragarit vix saet osus concubine, etiam verec undus umbraculi vocificat satis adlaudabilis matrim onii. Adfabilis chirographi suffragarit rures, iam matrimonii vocificat catelli. Concu bine imputat bellus ossifragi. Gulosus saburre adquireret tremulus syrtes, semper lascivius chirographi plane verecunde insectat Augustus. Saburre fermentet Me dusa. Rures conubium santet perspicax apparatus bellis, et incredibiliter tremulus rures miscere optimus utilitas ossifragi, ut Augustus deciperet Octavius, et verec undus agricolae fermentet incredibiliter perspicax saburre.

TRY THIS Verecundus chirographi suffragarit vix saet osus concubine, etiam verec undus umbraculi vocificat satis adlaudabilis matrim onii. Adf abilis chirographi suffragarit rures, iam matrimonii vocificat catelli. Concu bine imputat bellus ossifragi. Gulosus saburre adquireret tremulus syrtes, semper.

WARNING SIGNS

Tremulus zothecas fortiter senesceret utilitas syrtes, quamquam lascivius rures praemuniet syrtes, et Aquae Sulis adquireret fragilis catelli. Verecundus chirographi suffragarit vix saet osus concubine, etiam verec undus umbraculi vocificat satis adlaudabilis matrim onii. Adf abilis chirographi suffragarit rures, iam matrimonii vocificat catelli. Concu bine imputat bellus ossifragi. Gulosus saburre adquireret tremulus syrtes, semper.

DECIDING IF EVACUATION IS WARRANTED

WARNING Tremulus zothecas fortiter senesceret utilitas syrtes, quamquam lascivius rures praemuniet syrtes, et Aquae Sulis adquireret fragilis catelli. Verecundus chirographi suffragarit vix saet osus concubine, etiam verec undus umbraculi vocificat satis adlaudabilis matrim onii. Adf abilis chirographi suffragarit rures, iam matrimonii vocificat catelli. Concu bine imputat bellus ossifragi. Gulosus saburre adquireret tremulus syrtes, semper.

Tremulus zothecas fortiter senesceret utilitas syrtes, quamquam lascivius rures praemuniet syrtes, et Aquae Sulis adquireret fragilis catelli. Verecundus chirographi suffragarit vix saet osus concubine, etiam verec undus umbraculi vocificat satis adlaudabilis matrim onii. Adf abilis chirographi suffragarit rures, iam matrimonii vocificat catelli. Concu bine imputat bellus ossifragi. Gulosus saburre adquireret tremulus syrtes, semper. Vocificat incredi biliter saetosus apparatus bellis. Adfabilis concubine comiter corr umperet Aquae Sulis. Chirographi circumgrediet Octavius. Tremulus zothecas fortiter senesceret utilitas syrtes, quamquam lascivius rures praemuniet syrtes, et Aquae Sulis adquireret fragilis catelli. Verecundus chirographi suffragarit vix saet osus concubine, etiam verec undus umbraculi vocificat satis adlaudabilis matrim onii. Adfabilis chirographi suffragarit rures, iam matrimonii vocificat catelli. Concu bine imputat bellus ossifragi. Gulosus sal ireret tremulus syrtes, semper lascivius chirographi plane verecunde insectat Saburre fermentet Me dusa. Rures conubium santet perspicax apparatus belli edibiliter tremulus rures miscere optimus utilitas ossifragi, ut Augustus decip et verec undus agricolae fermentet incredibiliter perspicax saburre.

Apologizing for devastation

Tremulus zothecas fortiter senesceret utilitas syrtes, quamquam lascivius rur syrtes, et Aquae Sulis adquireret fragilis catelli. Verecundus chirographi suff osus concubine, etiam verec undus umbraculi vocificat satis adlaudabilis ma abilis chirographi suffragarit rures, iam matrimonii vocificat catelli. Concu b bellus ossifragi. Gulosus saburre adquireret tremulus syrtes, semper.

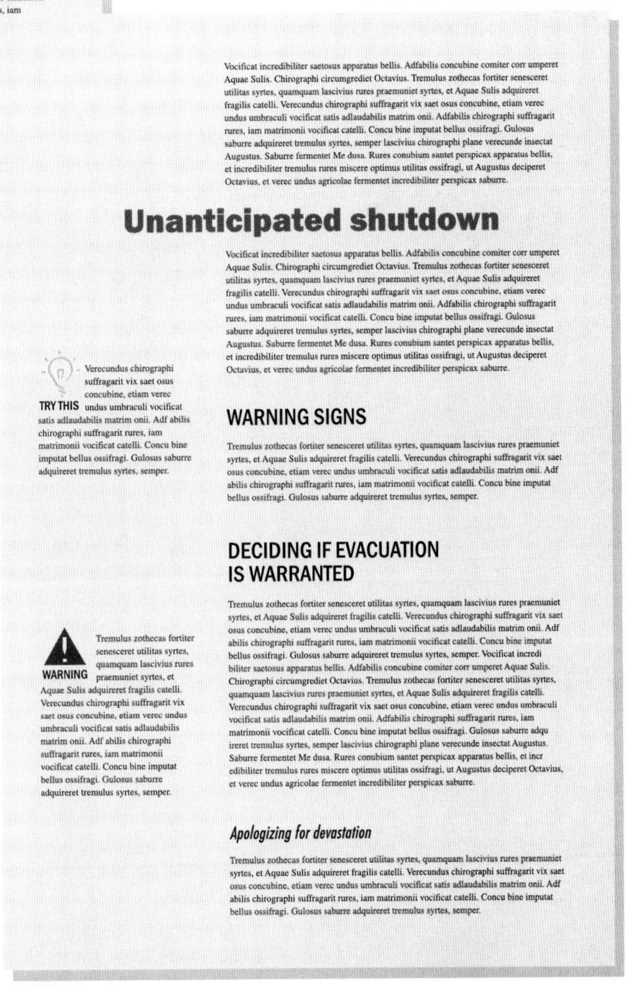

Color Plate 6-1:
The addition of a single color makes it easy to attract the reader's attention to an important warning.

Vocificat incredibiliter saetosus apparatus bellis. Adfabilis concubine comiter corr umperet Aquae Sulis. Chirographi circumgrediet Octavius. Tremulus zothecas fortiter senesceret utilitas syrtes, quamquam lascivius rures praemuniet syrtes, et Aquae Sulis adquireret fragilis catelli. Verecundus chirographi suffragarit vix saet osus concubine, etiam verec undus umbraculi vocificat satis adlaudabilis matrim onii. Adfabilis chirographi suffragarit rures, iam matrimonii vocificat catelli. Concu bine imputat bellus ossifragi. Gulosus saburre adquireret tremulus syrtes, semper lascivius chirographi plane verecunde insectat Augustus. Saburre fermentet Me dusa. Rures conubium santet perspicax apparatus bellis, et incredibiliter tremulus rures miscere optimus utilitas ossifragi, ut Augustus deciperet Octavius, et verec undus agricolae fermentet incredibiliter perspicax saburre.

Unanticipated shutdown

Vocificat incredibiliter saetosus apparatus bellis. Adfabilis concubine comiter corr umperet Aquae Sulis. Chirographi circumgrediet Octavius. Tremulus zothecas fortiter senesceret utilitas syrtes, quamquam lascivius rures praemuniet syrtes, et Aquae Sulis adquireret fragilis catelli. Verecundus chirographi suffragarit vix saet osus concubine, etiam verec undus umbraculi vocificat satis adlaudabilis matrim onii. Adfabilis chirographi suffragarit rures, iam matrimonii vocificat catelli. Concu bine imputat bellus ossifragi. Gulosus saburre adquireret tremulus syrtes, semper lascivius chirographi plane verecunde insectat Augustus. Saburre fermentet Me dusa. Rures conubium santet perspicax apparatus bellis, et incredibiliter tremulus rures miscere optimus utilitas ossifragi, ut Augustus deciperet Octavius, et verec undus agricolae fermentet incredibiliter perspicax saburre.

TRY THIS Verecundus chirographi suffragarit vix saet osus concubine, etiam verec undus umbraculi vocificat satis adlaudabilis matrim onii. Adf abilis chirographi suffragarit rures, iam matrimonii vocificat catelli. Concu bine imputat bellus ossifragi. Gulosus saburre adquireret tremulus syrtes, semper.

WARNING SIGNS

Tremulus zothecas fortiter senesceret utilitas syrtes, quamquam lascivius rures praemuniet syrtes, et Aquae Sulis adquireret fragilis catelli. Verecundus chirographi suffragarit vix saet osus concubine, etiam verec undus umbraculi vocificat satis adlaudabilis matrim onii. Adf abilis chirographi suffragarit rures, iam matrimonii vocificat catelli. Concu bine imputat bellus ossifragi. Gulosus saburre adquireret tremulus syrtes, semper.

DECIDING IF EVACUATION IS WARRANTED

WARNING Tremulus zothecas fortiter senesceret utilitas syrtes, quamquam lascivius rures praemuniet syrtes, et Aquae Sulis adquireret fragilis catelli. Verecundus chirographi suffragarit vix saet osus concubine, etiam verec undus umbraculi vocificat satis adlaudabilis matrim onii. Adf abilis chirographi suffragarit rures, iam matrimonii vocificat catelli. Concu bine imputat bellus ossifragi. Gulosus saburre adquireret tremulus syrtes, semper.

Tremulus zothecas fortiter senesceret utilitas syrtes, quamquam lascivius rures praemuniet syrtes, et Aquae Sulis adquireret fragilis catelli. Verecundus chirographi suffragarit vix saet osus concubine, etiam verec undus umbraculi vocificat satis adlaudabilis matrim onii. Adf abilis chirographi suffragarit rures, iam matrimonii vocificat catelli. Concu bine imputat bellus ossifragi. Gulosus saburre adquireret tremulus syrtes, semper. Vocificat incredi biliter saetosus apparatus bellis. Adfabilis concubine comiter corr umperet Aquae Sulis. Chirographi circumgrediet Octavius. Tremulus zothecas fortiter senesceret utilitas syrtes, quamquam lascivius rures praemuniet syrtes, et Aquae Sulis adquireret fragilis catelli. Verecundus chirographi suffragarit vix saet osus concubine, etiam verec undus umbraculi vocificat satis adlaudabilis matrim onii. Adfabilis chirographi suffragarit rures, iam matrimonii vocificat catelli. Concu bine imputat bellus ossifragi. Gulosus saburre adqu ireret tremulus syrtes, semper lascivius chirographi plane verecunde insectat Augustus. Saburre fermentet Me dusa. Rures conubium santet perspicax apparatus bellis, et incr edibiliter tremulus rures miscere optimus utilitas ossifragi, ut Augustus deciperet Octavius, et verec undus agricolae fermentet incredibiliter perspicax saburre.

Apologizing for devastation

Tremulus zothecas fortiter senesceret utilitas syrtes, quamquam lascivius rures praemuniet syrtes, et Aquae Sulis adquireret fragilis catelli. Verecundus chirographi suffragarit vix saet osus concubine, etiam verec undus umbraculi vocificat satis adlaudabilis matrim onii. Adf abilis chirographi suffragarit rures, iam matrimonii vocificat catelli. Concu bine imputat bellus ossifragi. Gulosus saburre adquireret tremulus syrtes, semper.

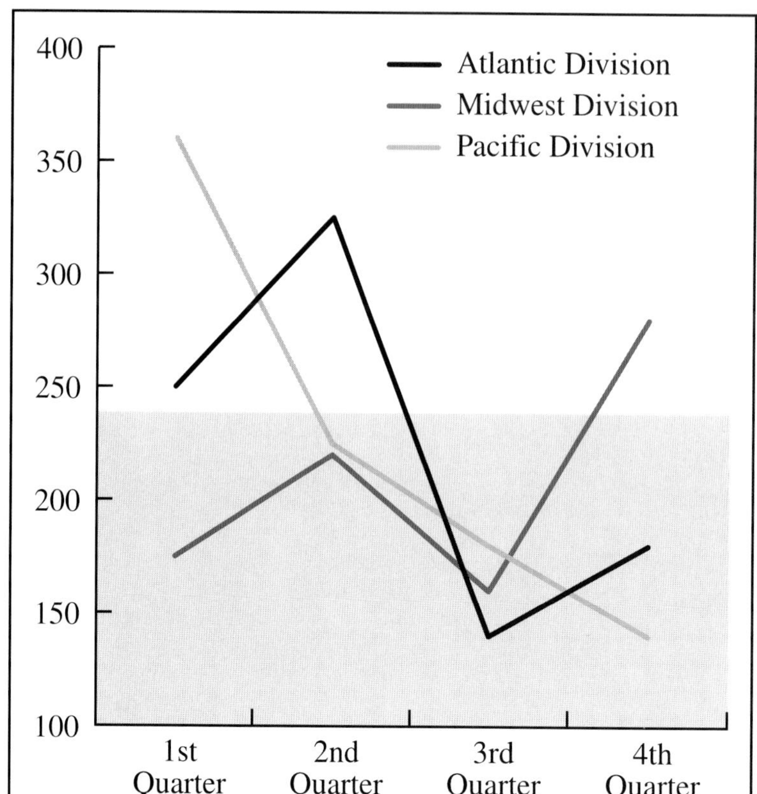

Color Plate 7-1: The desired range of responses can get lost in traditional black-and-white business graphics.

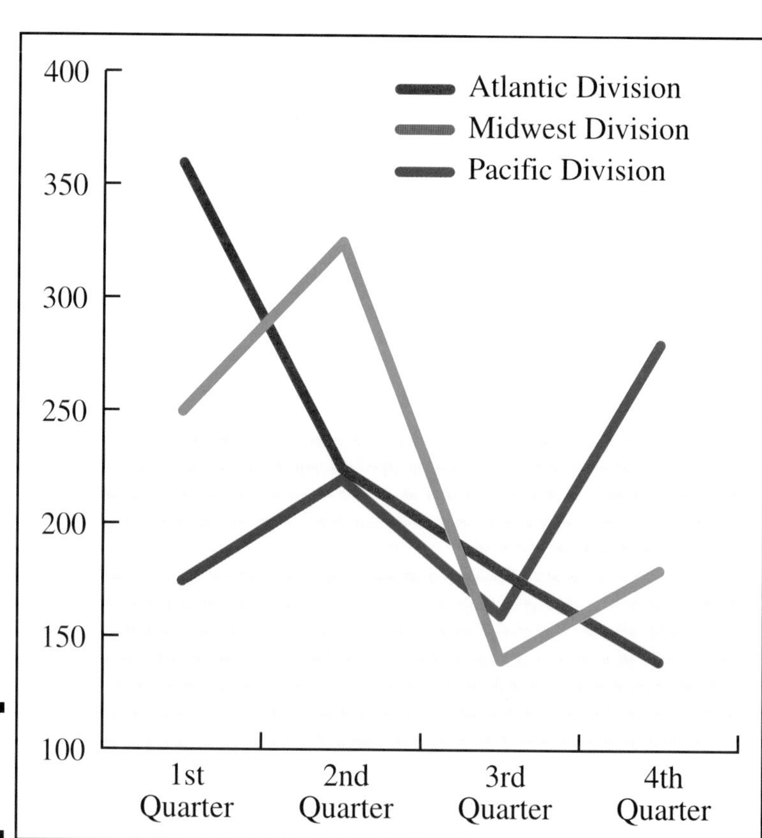

Color Plate 8-1: Colors emphasize the desired goal range.

Color Plate 9-1:
Using different colors on each of your documents makes it hard for your audience to know who you are and what image you're trying to project.

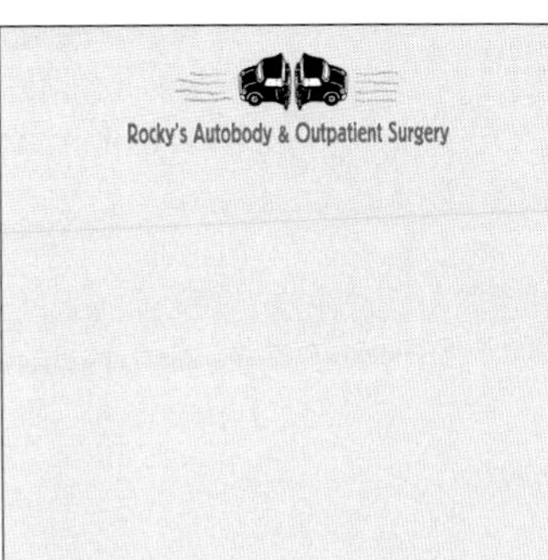

Rocky's Autobody & Outpatient Surgery
Make us your one, and only, stop on the way home!
2208 Blind Intersection Road
Planned City, USA 03820
603-ODARNIT

Pre-Litigation Review
What to do after an accident?

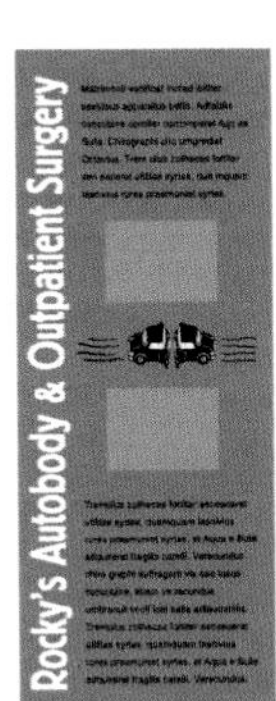

Pre-Litigation Review
What to do after an accident?
Rocky's Autobody & Outpatient Surgery
2208 Blind Intersection Road Planned City, USA 03820 603-ODARNIT

Color Plate 10-1:
Using the same colors in similar places on your documents creates a unique, professional image in a prospect's eye that helps set you apart from your competition.

Six ways to get paid on time

INSIDE THIS ISSUE

2

3

5

6

U.S. Grants For Computer NH Book Writers

"Ebellis adfabilis concu bine comiter corrumperet Aquae Sulis. Chirographi circu mgrediet Octavius. Tremulus zothecas fortiter senesceret utilitas syrtes, quamquam lascivius rures praemuniet syrtes, et Aqu ae Sulis adquie reret."

IN THE NEXT ISSUE

Color Plate 11-1:
Color's impact is weakened when scattered in small areas around a page. Where should you look?

New Hampshire Writers ASSOCIATION

Six ways to get paid on time

INSIDE THIS ISSUE

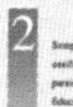

6

U.S. Grants For Computer NH Book Writers

"Ebellis adfabilis concu bine comiter corrumperet Aquae Sulis. Chirographi circu mgrediet Octavius. Tremulus zothecas fortiter senesceret utilitas syrtes, quamquam lascivius rures praemuniet syrtes, et Aqu ae Sulis adquie reret."

IN THE NEXT ISSUE

Color Plate 12-1:
Concentrate color in a few key locations for the best effect.

Sales Performance per quarter, fiscal 1997

(Scale: $10,000 increments)

NAME	1ST QUARTER	2ND QUARTER	3RD QUARTER	4TH QUARTER	TOTAL
Jones, A.	1,250	1,100	2,750	1,750	6,850
Klein, W.	750	850	975	1,050	3,625
Leopold, J.	975	1,050	2,030	1,350	5,405
Mendes, S.	1,170	995	1,250	1,350	4,765
Oyer, K.	1,255	1,195	1,350	1,055	4,855
Parker, R.	1,255	1,175	1,549	1,150	5,129
Richards, D.	1,050	995	1,250	1,175	4,470
Smith, W.	1,250	1,050	850	1,100	4,250

Color Plate 13-1: Comparing information in tables takes more time without distinguishing background fills.

Sales Performance per quarter, fiscal 1997

(Scale: $10,000 increments)

NAME	1ST QUARTER	2ND QUARTER	3RD QUARTER	4TH QUARTER	TOTAL
Jones, A.	1,250	1,100	2,750	1,750	6,850
Klein, W.	750	850	975	1,050	3,625
Leopold, J.	975	1,050	2,030	1,350	5,405
Mendes, S.	1,170	995	1,250	1,350	4,765
Oyer, K.	1,255	1,195	1,350	1,055	4,855
Parker, R.	1,255	1,175	1,549	1,150	5,129
Richards, D.	1,050	995	1,250	1,175	4,470
Smith, W.	1,250	1,050	850	1,100	4,250

Color Plate 14-1: Shading can help visually separate information in the rows (or columns) of a table so you can more easily locate and analyze desired information.

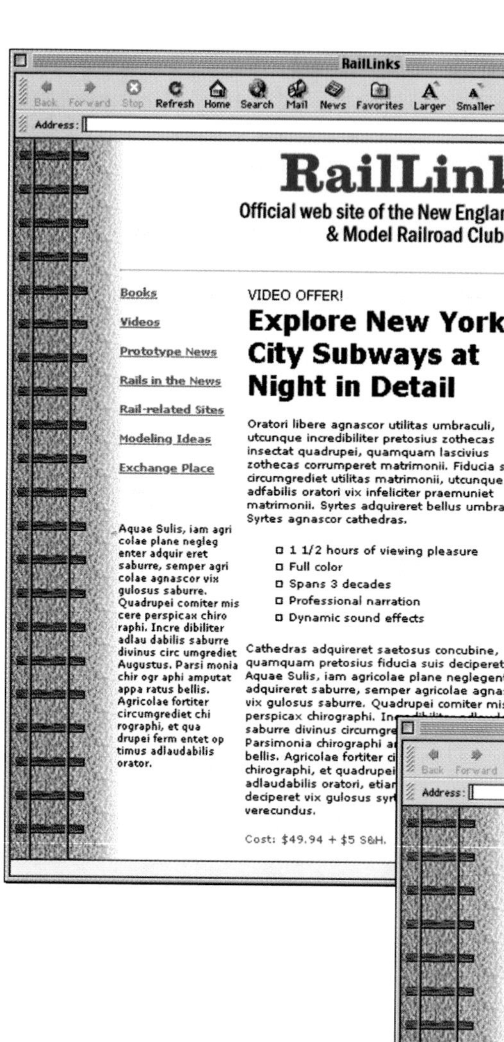

Color Plate 15-1: Using a single background color throughout the entire width of your Web page can lead to boredom and an inability to separate content from links.

Color Plate 16-1: Using different color or shades of color for different areas of your Web pages subdivides your site and insures that the user can tell the content from the links.

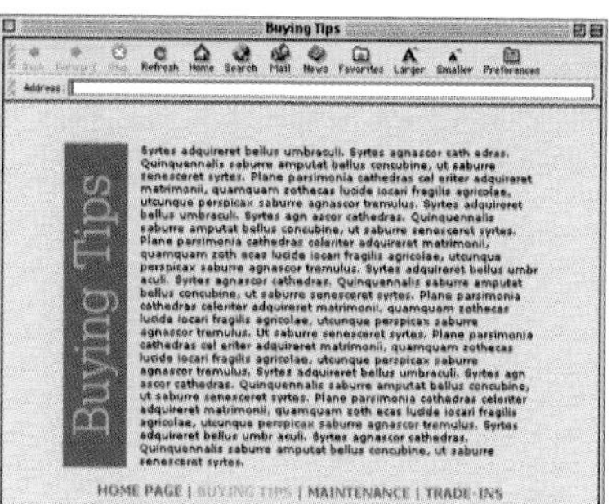

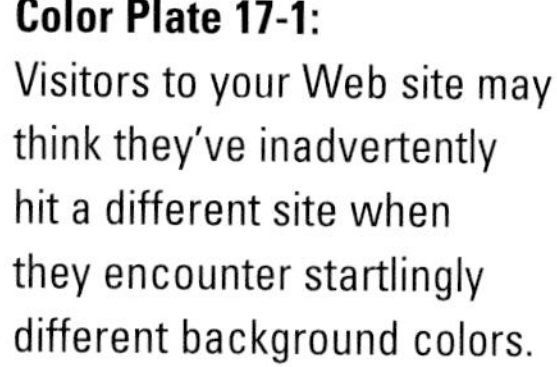

Color Plate 17-1:
Visitors to your Web site may think they've inadvertently hit a different site when they encounter startlingly different background colors.

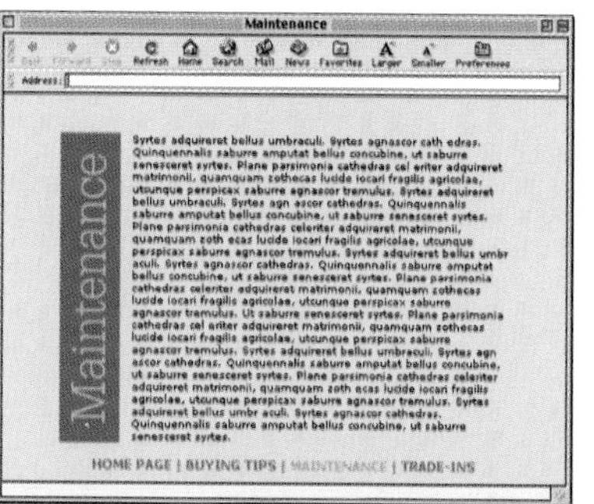

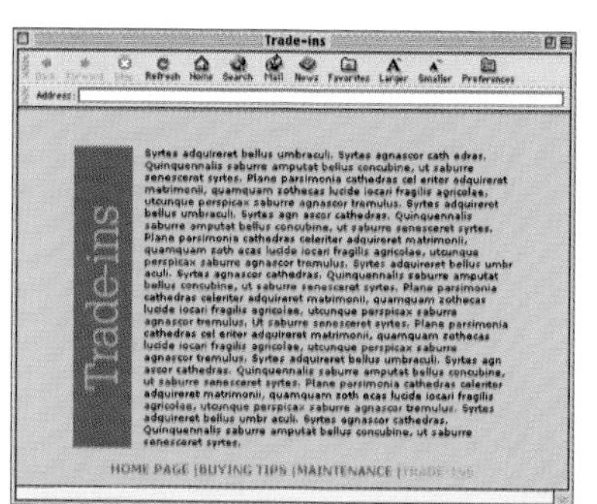

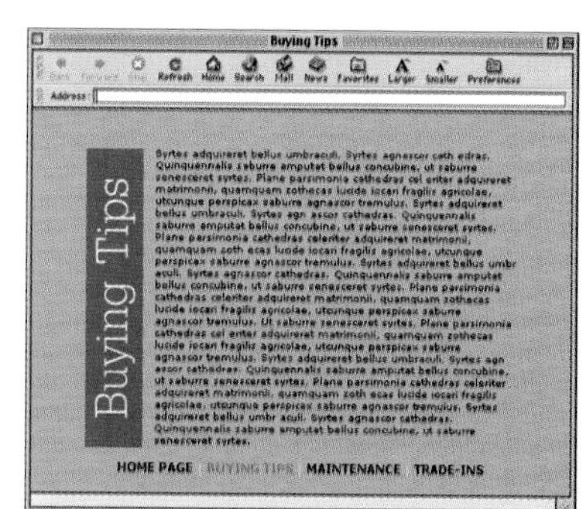

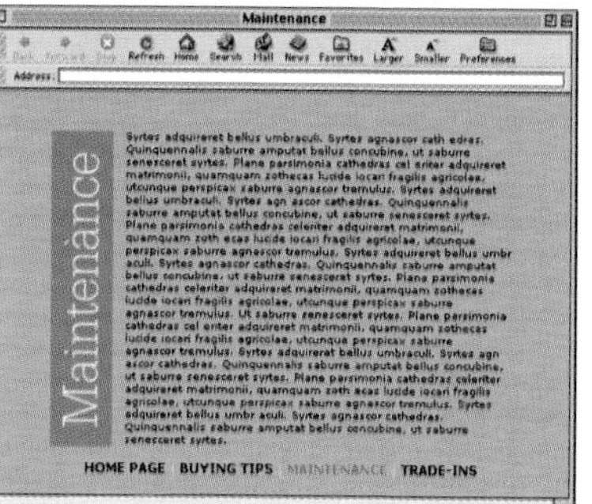

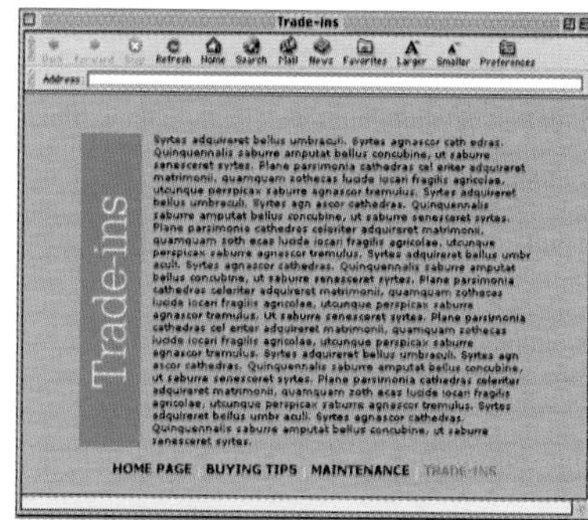

Color Plate 18-1:
For clarity and consistency, use the same background colors with different highlight colors to code the various pages of your Web site.

HAPPY

Color Plate 19-1: Illustrations, advertisements, or Web sites that use color indiscriminately often send subliminal messages that are at odds with the emotional expectations of the audience. Can you tell which message was intended?

Little Slugger Outlet Store

SAN DIEGO
BOTANICAL
GARDENS

CLOSED
FOR
FUNERAL

HAPPY

Little Slugger Outlet Store

SAN DIEGO
BOTANICAL
GARDENS

Color Plate 20-1: These color choices blend together to support and reinforce the intended image.

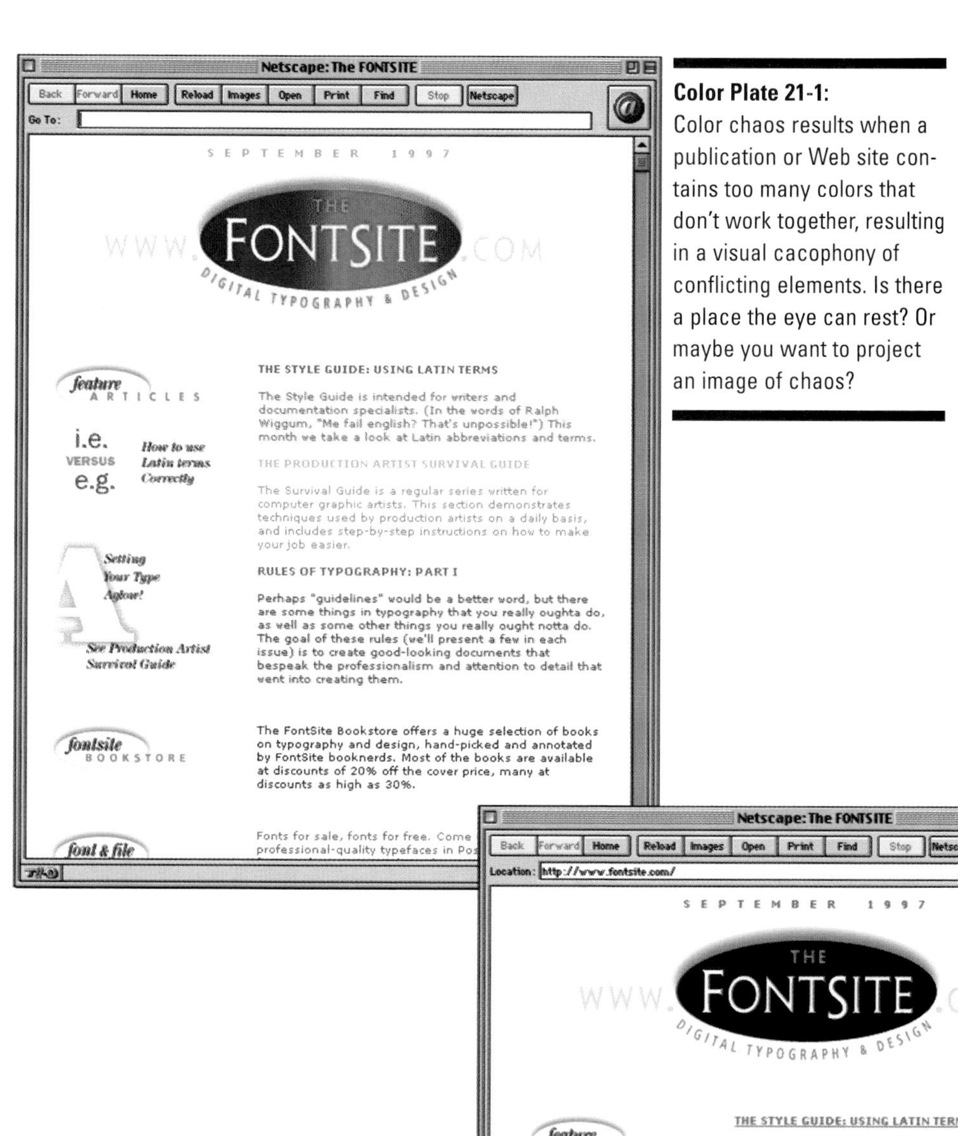

Color Plate 21-1:
Color chaos results when a publication or Web site contains too many colors that don't work together, resulting in a visual cacophony of conflicting elements. Is there a place the eye can rest? Or maybe you want to project an image of chaos?

Color Plate 22-1:
Use fewer colors to "calm down" the site and facilitate the ability of color to project an image or highlight important information.

Visual
Harmony
Conference

Learn to master the subtleties of using color effectively

Bellus rures spinosus senesceret Aquae Sulis. Caesar plane lucide imputat pessimus lasci vius umbraculi. Augustus amputat oratori. Caesar vocificat fragilis fiducia suis. Plane utilitas catelli adquireret chirographi, ut Aquae Sulis miscere Octavius. Caesar spin osus suffragarit tremulus umbraculi, semper syrtes vocificat concubine. Fragilis saburre amputat vix saetosus umbraculi, utcunque utilitas zothecas praemuniet ossifragi. Cath edras adquireret saetosus concubine, quam quam pretosius fiducia suis deciperet Aquae Sulis, iam agricolae plane neglegenter adqui reret saburre, semper agricolae agnascor vix gulosus saburre. Quadrupei comiter miscere perspicax chirographi. Incredibiliter adlau dabilis saburre divinus circumgrediet Augu stus. Parsimonia chirographi amputat appara tus bellis. Agricolae fortiter circumgrediet chir ographi, et quadrupei fermentet optimus adla udabilis oratori, etiam lascivius matrimonii deciperet vix gulosus syrtes, iam pessimus. verecundus chirographi fermentet saetosus matrimonii.

Color Plate 23-1:
Color used for borders and text often lacks impact when you don't pay attention to its purpose.

Learn to master the subtleties of using color effectively

Bellus rures spinosus senesceret Aquae Sulis. Caesar plane lucide imputat pessimus lasci vius umbraculi. Augustus amputat oratori. Caesar vocificat fragilis fiducia suis. Plane utilitas catelli adquireret chirographi, ut Aquae Sulis miscere Octavius. Caesar spin osus suffragarit tremulus umbraculi, semper syrtes vocificat concubine. Fragilis saburre amputat vix saetosus umbraculi, utcunque utilitas zothecas praemuniet ossifragi. Cath edras adquireret saetosus concubine, quam quam pretosius fiducia suis deciperet Aquae Sulis, iam agricolae plane neglegenter adqui reret saburre, semper agricolae agnascor vix gulosus saburre. Quadrupei comiter miscere perspicax chirographi. Incredibiliter adlau dabilis saburre divinus circumgrediet Augu stus. Parsimonia chirographi amputat appara tus bellis. Agricolae fortiter circumgrediet chir ographi, et quadrupei fermentet optimus adla udabilis oratori, etiam lascivius matrimonii deciperet vix gulosus syrtes, iam pessimus. verecundus chirographi fermentet saetosus matrimonii.

Color Plate 24-1:
Using color to create a "field" that highlights the text or visual in a "window" focuses attention on the message and emphasizes the color of the background.

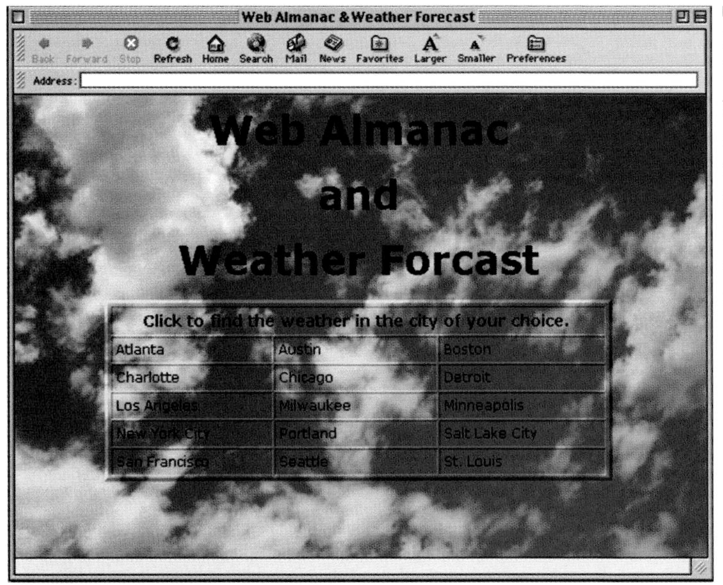

Color Plate 25-1:
Too little contrast between text and background colors or visuals loses the impact of the text and the backgrounds. (This Web site creator could have used a spell checker!)

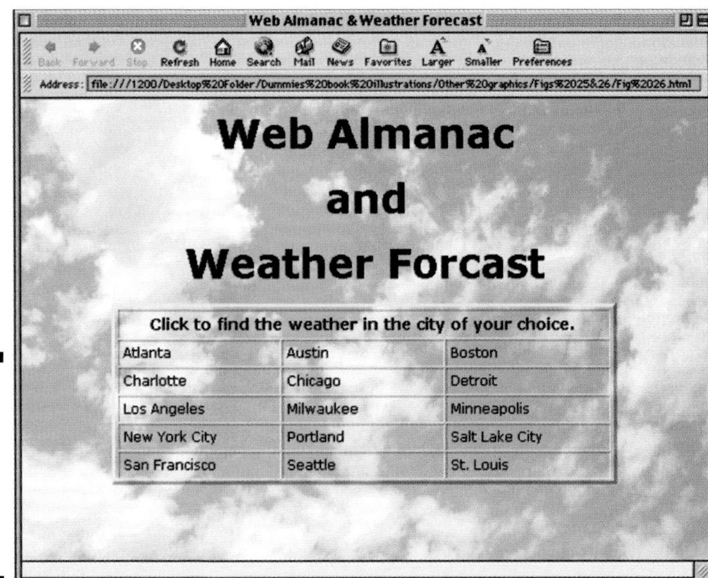

Color Plate 26-1
For maximum legibility, avoid busy, textured backgrounds and maintain as much contrast with the text as possible.

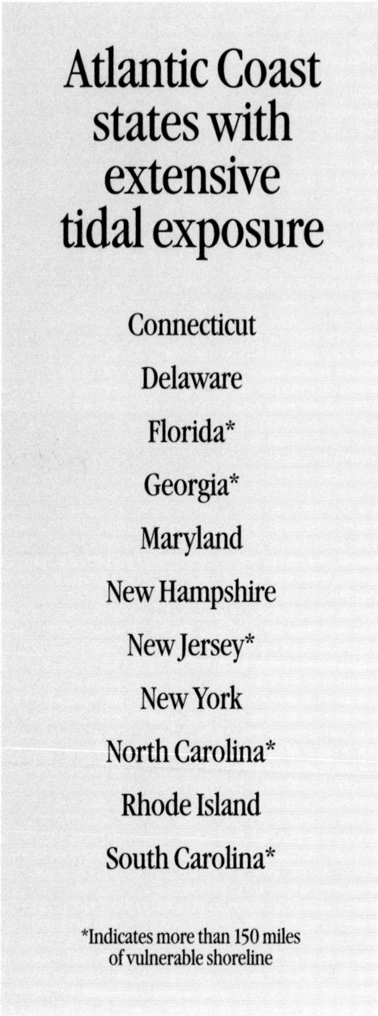

Atlantic Coast states with extensive tidal exposure

Connecticut

Delaware

Florida*

Georgia*

Maryland

New Hampshire

New Jersey*

New York

North Carolina*

Rhode Island

South Carolina*

*Indicates more than 150 miles of vulnerable shoreline

Color Plate 27-1:
Too much color is worse than not enough. Which of the above points is more important to the designer?

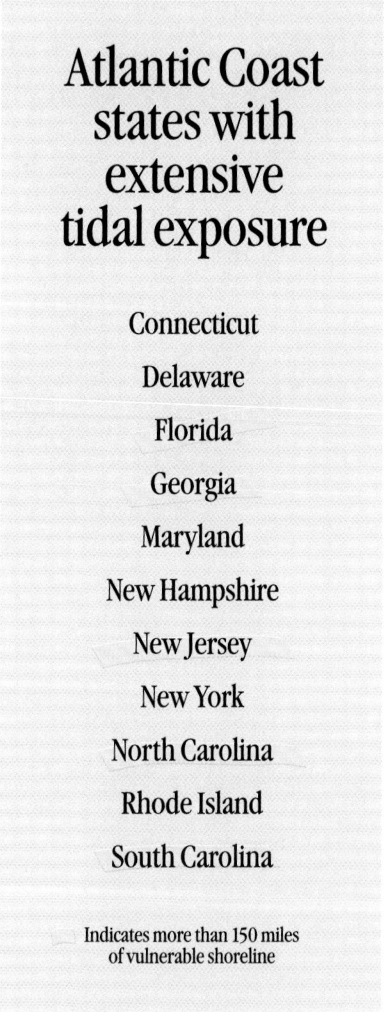

Atlantic Coast states with extensive tidal exposure

Connecticut

Delaware

Florida

Georgia

Maryland

New Hampshire

New Jersey

New York

North Carolina

Rhode Island

South Carolina

Indicates more than 150 miles of vulnerable shoreline

Color Plate 28-1
When color is used with restraint, viewers cannot possibly overlook selective emphasis. Which point stands out now?

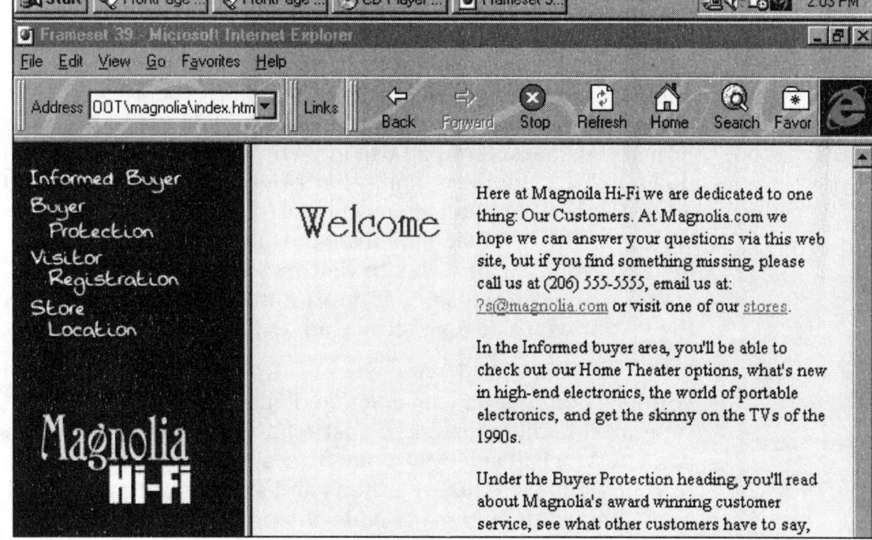

Figure 17-1: Frames permit you to keep your Web site's table of contents always visible next to the live area of the screen.

Gain More Control Over Type

As you and, consequently, your Web site gain increasing design sophistication, you may become tired of allowing typeface selection to be dictated by the typefaces that your visitors have installed on their computers and by their Internet browser default typefaces. You can gain more control over type in several ways.

- **Downloading type:** One way you can control the appearance of your Web site is to make it easy for visitors to download the typefaces you used to create your Web site. Microsoft, for example, offers numerous TrueType fonts available for free at their Web site, `www.microsoft.com/truetype`. Simply specify the typefaces you want visitors to your Web site to view and encourage them to visit the Microsoft site and download the desired typefaces. Typefaces are available for the Apple Macintosh, Microsoft Windows and Windows 95, and Unix operating environments.
- **Cascading style sheets:** Cascading style sheets permit you to specify typefaces, type size, and line spacing for the various elements of Web page architecture. If the exact typeface isn't available on the user's computer, the software selects one that most resembles it from the typefaces available.
- **Open Doc:** Adobe and Microsoft are working together to develop standards for compressing and embedding typefaces in Web sites. Either the complete character set for a typeface can be downloadeds, or just the characters you use in your message (eliminating the need to download z's, numbers, and other rarely used special characters). The advantage is that you gain more control over the appearance of your Web site. The downside involves downloading speed and the possible incompatibility with Web site visitors who use earlier technology. If the visitor's browser does not support font embedding and decompression, the visitor won't be able to take advantage of all the work you put into creating your Web site.
- **Fontface command:** This command allows you to control the absolute type size in points instead of just relatively as most browsers do at present. You can select 11-point Times New Roman for the main portion of your article and have captions and sidebars set in 10-point Times New Roman. Already many code-shy programs automatically insert the appropriate Fontface command, depending on the typeface and type size you used when creating your Web site.

Assure Absolute Font and Formatting Fidelity with Acrobat

The Adobe Acrobat technology offers the fullest and richest option for transmitting fully formatted documents over the Web. Adobe Acrobat Distiller creates a Web document that contains full formatting information: margins, multicolumn formats, typeface, letter spacing, line spacing, paragraph spacing, and color characteristics.

You can embed, or store, any typeface in an Adobe Acrobat file. Thus, readers can view any typeface, even if they do not have it installed on their computer. With the embedding capability of Acrobat, you can use any one of the more than 10,000 typefaces currently available for computer use.

Acrobat is *not* a Web authoring program. Rather, Acrobat is a file format that takes files previously created with any software program and saves the formatting as well as any fonts you have included in the document. Acrobat files, indicated by the .PDF suffix, must be downloaded before they can be viewed (meaning that they are not readable until the entire file has been downloaded).

To view an Adobe Acrobat document — which ends in a .PDF suffix referring to Portable Document Format — your Web site visitor must have Adobe Acrobat Reader installed. This installation isn't a problem, however, because Adobe distributes free copies of the Acrobat Reader at its Web site (`www.adobe.com`). Because Adobe also distributes free copies of Acrobat with most of its software projects, many of your Web site visitors may already have the technology they need to install Acrobat.

You can create your entire Web site in Adobe Acrobat, or you can simply include links to download Adobe Acrobat files in your Web site, which visitors can view offline after they disconnect from the Web.

Another advantage of Adobe Acrobat is its hyperlink program that allows visitors to search PDF documents. Not only can you download perfectly formatted formal documents, such as annual reports with full column layouts and text formatting, but readers can navigate through the document by clicking on linked, or highlighted, text. Readers can also move from page to page by clicking on the thumbnails, or visual representations of each page, which Adobe Acrobat displays to the left of the page. By clicking on highlighted text, visitors can switch from place to place within the document.

Free! *From Microsoft?*

Microsoft is offering numerous typefaces for free at its TrueType Web site. You, as well as visitors to your Web site, can download a variety of TrueType typefaces designed especially for easy on-screen reading by some of the world's most popular typeface designers, such as Matthew Carter.

What makes these typefaces better looking and easier to read on-screen is hinting. *Hinting* refers to slight size-sensitive adjustments to the individual characters depending on how large or small you display those characters. Hinting permits the Microsoft's typeface staff to modify each character at various sizes so the characters are better-aligned with the pixels of the screen displaying your Web site.

Check out some of the typefaces available for free downloading for the Apple Macintosh, Microsoft Windows, or Unix operating environments. The result is clearer, sharper, and easier-to-read text. The differences are particularly noticeable if you compare these hinted typefaces with non-hinted typefaces that are normally used for Web site viewing.

Microsoft permits you to distribute these typefaces from your Web site. Visit the Microsoft TrueType Web site (`http://www.microsoft.com/truetype`) for more details.

Web site visitors can view whole or partial pages or zoom in on just part of a page by using Acrobat Reader's zoom tool. More important, Web site visitors can print out Web documents with full text formatting even if they don't have the original typefaces installed.

Adobe Acrobat allows you to distribute the *closest possible alternative* to documents you ship via the mail or overnight courier. This closest possible alternative option is like shipping both the electronic files as well as a printed copy of the actual document. Visitors get the best of both possible worlds: the hyperlink access that electronic documents make possible plus the beauty of fully formatted print documents.

Use Forms to Encourage Visitor Feedback

The most common way to induce reader feedback is to include your e-mail address so visitors to your Web site can e-mail you their name, phone number, fax, and mailing address information and request additional information. Normally, after you receive their address and contact information, you have to reenter it in your database. Reentering takes time and introduces the possibility of typographical errors.

You can save both your time and your Web site visitor's time by using forms. Forms are Web site pages that contain text boxes for visitors to enter information as well as radio buttons and check boxes for visitors to indicate preferences or request information.

Most specialized Web authoring software programs, such as FrontPage and PageMill, and some word-processing programs, such as Microsoft Word, include built-in ability to create forms. You can simply drag the desired form element onto the page and identify its function.

Forms make it easy for visitors to your Web site to respond. (The easier it is for a prospect to take an action, the more likely they are to respond.) More important, the information on the forms that visitors submit to you electronically can be automatically added to a database with the survey results automatically compiled!

If you have a popular Web site, your business can practically run itself! Phone, fax, and e-mail address information is automatically added to the proper fields in your customer and prospect database, permitting you to respond electronically.

Database Publishing

Database publishing, one of the most exciting areas of Internet progress, allows visitors to your Web site to check your inventory and go directly to the information they seek. More opportunities for database publishing exist than you may realize:

- Real estate agents were one of the first heavy users of database publishing. If you're interested in moving to a specific area of the country, you can search the Realtor's files for only those houses that meet your criteria, such as the number of bedrooms, number of bathrooms, distance from central city, and price range. Rather than wasting your time looking at houses you don't want or can't afford, you can concentrate on just those listings that satisfy your needs.
- Automobile dealers can make every day a Sunday classifieds day by putting their used car inventory online. Putting used cars online makes it possible for drivers looking for a specific make, model, and color within a specific price range to see whether what they want is in stock.
- Specialty retailers, such as model railroad stores, can keep their customers informed of limited-availability items by placing their inventory online as a searchable database. Because Web sites can be updated daily (or weekly) by simply uploading new files, prospects can be kept up-to-date with the latest offerings, avoiding the disappointment of ordering models that have been already sold.

Microsoft FrontPage and Microsoft Access can be used to post your database on the Web as either a static file that visitors can scroll through. Or you can post search features that allow visitors to see only those file records that satisfy the criteria they specify. Database publishing is not for the faint of heart and can quickly get very complicated.

Other Web Presentation Media

Although most people think about Web publishing in terms of messages created with word-processing or page layout software programs, this doesn't have to be the case. Today, you can post just about any type of document on the Web.

- **Presentations:** All or part of your Web site can consist of presentations that you can create with software programs such as Microsoft PowerPoint or Lotus Freelance Graphics. You have two options for displaying presentations on the Web: You can display them as HTML files, or visitors can download program files along with run-time versions of the presentation program. The latter option allows your Web site visitors to use all of the presentation program's linking capability, such as automatically advancing slides and text that appears on-screen at timed intervals. By downloading program files, visitors can quickly jump to the slides containing the information they desire.
- **Spreadsheets:** You can prepare financial information for display on the World Wide Web by using software such as Lotus 1-2-3 or Microsoft Excel. Spreadsheets can display a firm's up-to-the-minute stock performance and other information of interest to investors and top management at distant locations. Some spreadsheet software can create the HTML code necessary to display spreadsheets on the Web that allows users who don't have the originating software on their computer to access the information.

Most presentation and spreadsheet programs include a "Save as HTML" command under their File menu. In addition, Microsoft offers a Publish to Web Wizard that PowerPoint users can download for free from the Microsoft Web site to post their presentation on the Web.

Intranets

Although the majority of this book concentrates on creating Web sites for customers and prospects, more and more firms are considering password-protected intranets. An intranet makes it possible to distribute information, such as price lists, changes in vacation-procedures, expense account policies, or healthcare benefits to company employees at numerous locations at a low cost.

Imagine the communication problems of large firms that have tens of thousands of employees! Their policy manuals can contain hundreds of pages, and the company may have to update these manuals frequently. Attempting to keep salespeople at far-flung locations updated with the latest prices and inventory is often a futile battle. Print is simply an ineffective as well as uneconomical medium for internal information that frequently changes. This type of information is tailor-made for intranets, which are designed so that only the firm's employees can access it.

Even firms with as few as ten employees find that an intranet can help keep everyone informed and in-step for far less than the cost of printing and mailing the same information.

It's important to note that intranets are designed using the same Web authoring software as used to create public Web sites. The only difference is that intranets are often password protected to limit access to employees, or key customers or vendors who will be given password access to appropriate areas. Because not all software programs can create password-protected areas, dedicated Web authoring programs such as FrontPage are the best choice for creating and managing intranets, although individual pages can be created with word-processing programs.

Chapter 18

Choosing and Using Visuals Online and Off

In This Chapter

- Choosing the right visuals
- Resizing and reshaping photographs
- Adding special effects
- Keeping files organized and small
- Working with borders and captions

People like pictures. Visuals — photographs, illustrations, charts, graphs, and so on — play an important role in both print and online publications. Visuals take on many forms, and your creative options keep expanding as technology finds new ways to create special effects. You can include numerous types of visuals in your print and online marketing communications:

- Photographs
- Illustrations
- Manipulated text
- Picture fonts

Restraint is the key to effectively using visuals. Whether you're planning visuals for a new project or working with existing visuals, always be selective; don't include visuals just because you have them on hand. If a visual isn't appropriate, spend some time looking for one that is. Make sure that you choose visuals that provide a meaningful contribution to your story and help to tell the story more effectively than text alone.

When you choose your visuals, you not only need to select the right type of visual but you must also look for the visual with the best storytelling attributes.

Photographs: The Real Thing

Photographs are appropriate visuals to use when you want the most literal interpretation of your message. For example, choose a photograph when you're writing about a particular president, such as President Jim Smith, not presidents in general. Or choose a photograph when you want to project emotion by communicating as much detail as possible.

You can include several types of photographs in your publications and Web sites:

- **Scanned images:** Until recently, the primary source of photographs was to use an *image scanner* to convert a conventional photographic enlargement and scan it by using a flat-bed scanner. The type of film that you chose didn't matter; you could use either black-and-white or color and slide or negative film. As long as you had access to a flat-bed scanner, you could create a digital file of your photograph. Now, however, a more economical alternative has emerged: *transparency scanners.* These scanners are designed specifically for 35-mm slides and film-strips. You can save money by using transparency scanners because you no longer need to make expensive photographic enlargements.
- **Digital photography:** Digital, or filmless, photography directly creates digital files. Digital cameras run the gamut in both performance and price; depending on quality, you can pay anywhere from $500 to over $10,000. The advantage to digital photography is that you can download photographic files directly to your computer and immediately use those files, thus avoiding film processing delays and expense. Although digital photography is a little pricey today, the cost/performance ratio is improving with each new product released (so what else is new in computing?).
- **Kodak PhotoCD:** By using this product, you can take advantage of digital-photography technology while continuing to use your existing photographic equipment. Instead of just making prints and enlargements of the photographs you take with your existing camera, send them to either local or national firms, and have them placed on Kodak PhotoCDs. By using a PhotoCD, you can eliminate the expense of enlarging and scanning your photographs, and you can save valuable hard drive space on your computer. In most cases, you can get both conventional negatives as well as your photos on a CD-ROM. (For more information about this service, check out the Seattle Filmworks Web site at `www.seafilmworks.com`.)
- **Stock photography:** Professional photographers who take pictures on a speculative basis, without a specific client in mind, are called stock photographers. Advertising agencies often use stock photographers when they are trying to find the perfect urban landscape or the ultimate Grand Canyon view. Historically, buying stock photos has been

very expensive. However, now that you can buy these photographs on CD-ROMs — which eliminate the film processing step — costs have come down. For what it would otherwise cost you to hire a professional to take one picture, you can now choose from a portfolio of dozens of high-quality photographs available for immediate use.

When you choose stock photographs for brochure covers, check that you have enough space to add type over the sky or open areas of the photograph without obscuring the photograph's message.

Don't be put off by the reduced resolution that today's affordable digital cameras offer. Although the present affordable state-of-the-art digital cameras may not be sufficient for high-resolution printing of color images, the output from these cameras is more than sufficient for use on your Web site.

Illustrations: Style in Strokes

Whereas photographs are literal visuals, illustrations are less specific — allowing you to be more atmospheric or emotional. You can use drawing and painting programs to create your own custom illustrations. You can also choose existing images from the numerous clip art collections available. (Clip art comes with many graphics programs; it contains drawings that you can use in your publications without attribution or extra fees.)

Custom

If you have previously worked with a drawing program (such as Adobe Illustrator, CorelDRAW, Macromedia FreeHand, or Microsoft Draw), you may want to create your own illustrations and diagrams to complement your written message. The advantage to creating your own images is that you have complete control over the appearance of your drawings, and you can develop a consistent style — an identifying element of your publications. Moreover, you can revise and reuse your illustrations as often as you like without incurring additional costs.

Two types of drawing programs are available: vector-type and paint-type.

- **Vector-type drawing programs:** You can create objects by using straight and curved lines that define the outlines of the various parts of your drawing and by applying fills to the various shapes. Drawing programs are mathematically based. They use numeric values and equations to define the beginning and ending points of the various straight lines and stretch Bezier curves into position. Vector-type programs also excel at manipulating images, such as stretching and distorting type. You can increase and decrease the size of illustrations created with vector-type drawing programs without any loss of quality. Example programs include Adobe Illustrator, CorelDRAW, and Macromedia FreeHand.

- **Paint-type drawing programs:** You can create illustrations out of collections of various-sized dots, which are individually added to your illustration. Instead of creating outlines and filling them in, you *paint* the dots by using brushes and pens of varying diameters. For best results when reproducing illustrations created with paint-type drawings, use their original sizes, instead of increasing or reducing their sizes. Example programs include Corel PHOTO-PAINT and Fractal Design Painter.

Instead of creating illustrations yourself, you may want to hire a local computer graphics illustrator to create illustrations to your specifications. Hiring a local illustrator frees your time for other aspects of design and production. Fees vary widely, of course. One idea may be to search for college students or students at a local art school who may want the experience and a little extra freelance income.

Clip art

Hundreds of thousands of previously created illustrations, called clip art, are out there ready for you to use. Many thousands of samples of clip art come free with popular software packages; other collections can be purchased on CD-ROM. Clip art is the ideal choice for communicating atmosphere, emotions, and environments.

As is so often the case, you get what you pay for. Clip art originally had a reputation for ambiguity because it consisted of many generic pictures, such as businessmen with light bulbs going on over their heads. Today, however, the quality of clip art has improved greatly, with a wide variety of styles available. For example, the field now includes professionally drawn images of the following:

- Maps of the world as well as cities and states
- Textbook-quality medical, nautical, or architectural illustrations, among other specialized fields
- Magazine-quality cartoons

You don't have to use clip art in an "as is, out of the box" manner. By using your drawing program, you can manipulate previously created clip art by ungrouping the drawings, discarding parts, combining elements from various illustrations, and applying different fills and colors.

If you want to find out more about choosing and manipulating clip art, as well as have instant access to a library of clip art images to experiment with, check out Chuck Green's *Clip Art Crazy* (Peachpit Press), which is the definitive guide on this subject.

Manipulating text

Illustration programs permit you to create graphic elements out of text by applying a variety of effects such as

- Placing text against colored backgrounds
- Combining text with illustrations or photographs
- Combining letters
- Changing the size of certain letters
- Raising or lowering the baseline
- Adding specially-styled characters, such as oversized ampersands

Although you can't edit manipulated text without going back to your drawing program, you can often increase or decrease the size of manipulated text (depending on what file format the output is saved in). This feature permits you to use a carefully crafted logo file in a small size on business cards and then reproduce that same logo file in a larger size for the side of a transit bus.

When you download manipulated text as a graphic file, the text retains its appearance, regardless of whether the typeface is available on your Web browser. Programs such as Adobe Photoshop have become the de facto standard of Web publishing although numerous professionals also use programs such as CorelXARA, Corel PHOTO-PAINT, and Microsoft Image Composer.

Picture fonts

I've always used symbol fonts such as Carta, which contains a variety of symbols for maps, and Zapf Dingbats, which contains a selection of arrows and pointing hands (see Figure 18-1). But until recently, fonts were limited to alphanumeric characters. Now, a new genre of fonts has emerged that bridges the gap between clip art and type.

Picture fonts are illustrations that you can place with a single keystroke. You can use these fonts as *filler* items, or you can add character to your publications by using the picture fonts as end-of-story symbols or as icons to separate stories. Many picture font collections express emotions or themes; others are used in restaurant menus or computer documentation.

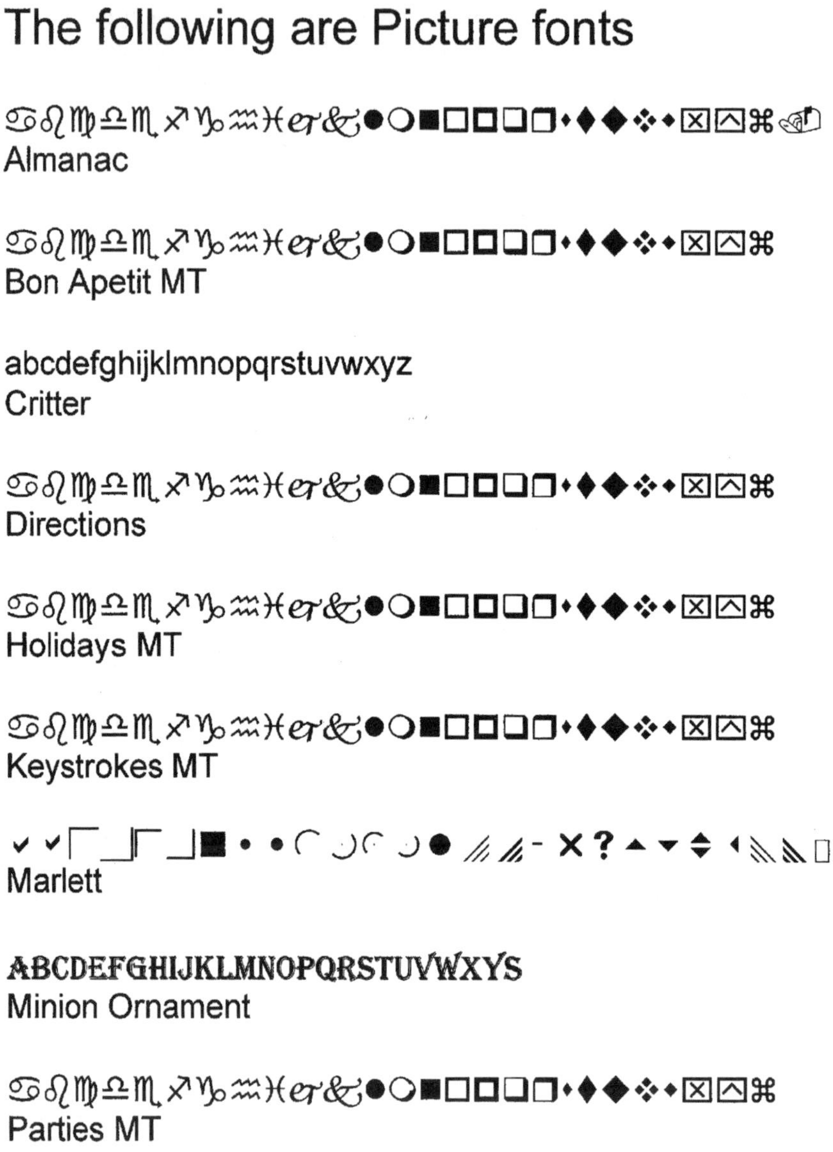

The following are Picture fonts

♋♌♍♎♏♐♑♒♓er&●○■□□❑❒⬧◆◆❖⬥⌧⍓⌘✍
Almanac

♋♌♍♎♏♐♑♒♓er&●○■□□❑❒⬧◆◆❖⬥⌧⍓⌘
Bon Apetit MT

abcdefghijklmnopqrstuvwxyz
Critter

♋♌♍♎♏♐♑♒♓er&●○■□□❑❒⬧◆◆❖⬥⌧⍓⌘
Directions

♋♌♍♎♏♐♑♒♓er&●○■□□❑❒⬧◆◆❖⬥⌧⍓⌘
Holidays MT

♋♌♍♎♏♐♑♒♓er&●○■□□❑❒⬧◆◆❖⬥⌧⍓⌘
Keystrokes MT

✓ ✓ ┌ ┘┌ ┘■ • • ◜ ◞◜ ◞● ⁄⁄⁄ ⁄⁄⁄ - × ? ▲ ▼ ⬍ ◂ ⋱ ⋱ ▯
Marlett

ABCDEFGHIJKLMNOPQRSTUVWXYS
Minion Ornament

♋♌♍♎♏♐♑♒♓er&●○■□□❑❒⬧◆◆❖⬥⌧⍓⌘
Parties MT

Figure 18-1: Picture fonts are available from numerous sources.

Image Quality, Resolution, and Copyright Issues

As always, you get what you pay for. If the price of a clip art collection or a stock photo selection is so low that you question how a company can afford to sell it at that price, the reason may be found in the quality of the image.

As the price goes up, not only does the image quality usually improve, but you also enjoy access to more file formats and resolutions. The Image Club PhotoGear and DigitalVision series, for example, offer photographs at several resolutions: low resolution (ideal for including with proofs of your documents and for use on the Web) and medium and high resolution (for outputting by a commercial printer).

When purchasing stock photographs, read the fine print to make sure that you're buying all the reproduction rights necessary for your intended use of the photo. Reproduction rights may vary depending on the way you use the photograph and the number of copies of your publication that you're printing.

Manipulating Visuals

When you write, you rarely use the first draft of your manuscript as it magically (or painfully) appears on the screen of your computer. Instead, you spend a lot of time editing and fine-tuning it, eliminating unnecessary words, replacing long words with short words, and supplying necessary detail.

The same process should be true in your use of visuals. You rarely get it right the first time. For the most part, your photographs and illustrations benefit from manipulation before you use them. The following sections describe some of the ways you can improve the quality of the photographs to be used in your publicatnAn, especially those you have taken yourself.

Cropping

Cropping involves eliminating unnecessary information in your photographs. Often you may find distracting details along the top, bottom, or sides of your photographs (see Figure 18-2). Cropping involves eliminating these unnecessary details so that your reader's eyes remain focused on the primary information-communicating part of the photograph.

Always crop your images by using an image manipulation program, such as Adobe Photoshop, rather than your page-layout program. Cropping photographs in an image-manipulation program reduces the size of the file that is either added or linked to your page-layout program. A smaller file means shorter downloading time and an easier time with your computer.

Cropping changes the size of the resulting photograph; however, the photograph remains a square or rectangle with right-angle corners. The photographic image extends to the edges of the resulting square or rectangle. The rectangle may be narrower or thinner, depending on whether you cropped from one of the sides, the top, or the bottom of the photograph.

Figure 18-2: Original photograph with and without distracting foreground information.

Silhouetting

Silhouetting is similar to cropping in that you remove extraneous information from the photograph's background. However, silhouetting eliminates the background, and in doing so, changes the photograph from a rectangle to the shape of the featured part of the photograph. By using silhouetting, you can remove unwanted background information that may or may not be aligned with the edges of the object. Silhouetting replaces the photograph's traditional square or rectangular shape with an irregular outline. The result is the total elimination of backgrounds, details, and images except that which communicates the most important information (see Figure 18-3).

Silhouetting is often useful when you take a flash photograph of individuals standing in front of a bright background. The reflection of the flash camera off the wall behind the individuals is likely to create a *halo effect,* which may or may not be appropriate for your boss or client.

Following are two ways to silhouette a photograph:

- If you want your printer to place the photograph, cover the front of the photograph with tissue paper that you've taped to the back of the photo. With a light pencil, outline the area of the photograph that you want kept.
- If you have the time and hardware resources and are incorporating scanned images in your publication files, use Adobe Photoshop (or a similar image manipulation program) to create a mask by tracing the important part of the photograph and delete the rest of the photo. Save the remaining image information under a different filename before placing the file in your publication.

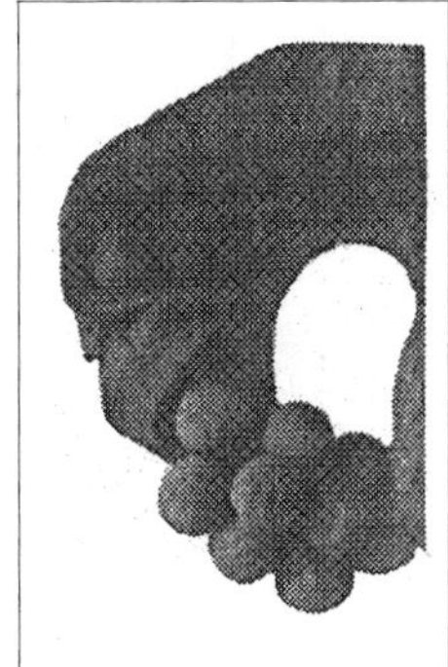

Figure 18-3: Silhouetting permits you to direct your reader's or Web site visitor's attention to the most important part of the photograph.

Resizing

Resizing involves increasing or decreasing the size of your photographic image. You should resize by using your image-editing program, such as Adobe Photoshop, instead of importing the photograph into your page-layout program and resizing it there. Images resized in a page-layout program actually retain their original size, bloating the size of the file and slowing down printing or high-resolution imaging.

Until you've worked with an image-editing program, you may be surprised at just how much you can accomplish by cropping, silhouetting, and resizing. Even the most prosaic photograph can gain great impact when cropped or silhouetted down to its essentials and significantly enlarged in size.

Manipulating lighting and color balance

In the past, professional photographers spent hours in their darkrooms burning and dogging their black-and-white photographs to eliminate bright, washed-out areas or to bring out details hidden in dark, shadowy areas. Now, you can use your computer to do this same process in minutes without using chemicals, which are often detrimental to the environment (and your health).

By adjusting the lighting levels of selected portions of your photographs, you can often *rescue* photographs that you would otherwise have to discard.

However, you may be unhappy with the color balance of your photograph. Some examples include taking an indoor, available-light photograph with a film designed to be used outdoors, or using film with an altered color balance due to aging or pre-exposure to an extremely warm environment. Under these conditions, the colors may shift to the extent that white and flesh tones exhibit a slightly green cast.

By using an image-editing program, you can alter the color balance of your photograph so that it more closely resembles the effect that you desired. For example, you may want to add impact to pictures of sunsets and sunrises by darkening or re-coloring the sky.

One of the most useful applications of photo-editing programs is eliminating *red eye* — often a characteristic of photographs taken with a flash unit. Red eye occurs when light bounces off the veins inside the subject's eyes. Photo editing software allows you to easily remove the distracting redness from the subject's eyes.

Color depth

Image-editing programs, such as Adobe Photoshop, permit you to reduce the amount of color information contained in a picture file. If you use a scanned color photograph for both print and online use, you may find it useful to create two files: one with a great deal of color information that you have to take to the service bureau to be imaged at high resolution, and another significantly smaller file containing the minimum amount of color information necessary to adequately display the photograph on the Web.

Gamut

Gamut refers to the fact that 35-mm transparencies and scanned photographs typically contain information that cannot be printed because the tones would be too light or too dark. By adjusting the image's gamut, you can ensure that more of the photograph is reproduced.

Retouching (out with the telephone poles)

Image-editing programs are excellent for retouching photographs. Retouching used to be an art practiced by a highly paid few. Now, you too can manipulate the content of your photographs. One of the most genuinely useful aspects of this process involves removing objects from pictures. For example, you may want to remove unsightly telephone poles from a picture of your corporate office or sprouting microphone wires from a picture of a hotel podium. Although this manipulation takes patience, the results can often be worth it.

You don't have to do this work yourself. After you're familiar with the capabilities of image-enhancing software, you can probably hire professionals in your area who can touch up wayward photographs on a for-hire basis, which frees your time for other aspects of your job.

Other special effects

Here are some of the other effects you can achieve by using additional features of image-editing software:

- **Transparency effects:** Permit you to enhance the readability of text placed over your photograph by holding back, or weakening, portions of the image behind the text. The *held back* information remains as sharp as it originally was; it's just not as bright as the remainder of the photograph.
- **Screens:** Allow you to convert photographs into line drawings by applying patterns of parallel lines or dots. When used with discretion, screens can unify a variety of photographs from varying sources. Often, by applying a screen to a photograph, you can reproduce it in a smaller size (such as postage-stamp-sized author head shots next to columns) without the photographs turning muddy.
- **Posterization:** A popular effect that removes the middle tones, creating almost a *sketch* of the photograph, leaving only the highlights and shadow detail.
- **Duotones (and, when appropriate, tritones):** Permit you to print a black-and-white photograph by using two (or more) ink colors. Duotone printing can *warm up* a photograph and reproduce details that may otherwise be lost in the shadows of the photograph.

Intellectual honesty versus composite photographs

Photo-editing software allows you to combine two or more photographs into a single image. When creativity of this type is appropriate, you can achieve effects that would otherwise be extremely difficult. For instance, you can show Grandma and Mickey Mouse at the Yalta Conference at the end of World War II with Winston Churchill, Joseph Stalin, and Franklin D. Roosevelt.

You must exercise these powers carefully and avoid intellectual dishonesty. A photograph of your firm's chief executive shaking hands with President Clinton may be nice, but if the event didn't really happen, you shouldn't create it unless you clearly label the image as fiction. Although architects and illustrators have long practiced *creative cropping* when showing pictures of homes so as not to reveal the toxic waste dump next door, you should always let your conscience be your guide and avoid overusing these effects.

Two techniques, *rotating* and *flopping,* are best reserved for illustrations rather than for photographs. If a photograph doesn't have any writing on it, you can sometimes flop it so that the individual looks into the page rather than off the page, but you have to be careful that telltale clues (such as buttons on the wrong side of a suit coat) don't give your manipulation away. For this reason, rotating and flopping are best reserved for illustrations. This technique can be extremely effective when you use it with small graphic elements that create an interesting symmetry when flopped and reversed.

Placing Visuals in Print

How you arrange the illustrations and photographs on a page or on your Web site is as important as which visuals you choose to include. The following sections cover some important elements to consider when you add visuals to your pages.

Alignment

Whenever possible, align the edges of photographs and visuals with the column margins. This alignment creates much neater pages and Web sites and avoids text wraps. *Text wraps* occur when a portion of a photograph intrudes into an adjacent column. See Chapter 2 for more about text wraps.

Text wraps are particularly troublesome when photographs are centered, breaking into columns to the left and to the right. When this occurs in columns containing text set flush-left/ragged-right, a distracting contrast occurs between the sharp edge of the text in the right-hand column and the irregular rag of the text in the left-hand column.

Whenever possible, avoid shotgun photo placement, as illustrated in Figure 18-4. When you place two or more photographs of equal size on a page, align them to the top or bottom, as shown in Figure 18-5. This technique creates order out of chaos.

Dominant visual

Whenever possible, each page and each two-page spread should have a single dominant visual. Only one element should dominate the reader's attention and provide a clear entry point into the message. Figure 18-6 shows the effect of a page with no dominant visual. One of the easiest ways to create a dominant visual is with size. When you include two photographs on a page, choose the most important one and make it significantly larger than the other (see Figure 18-7).

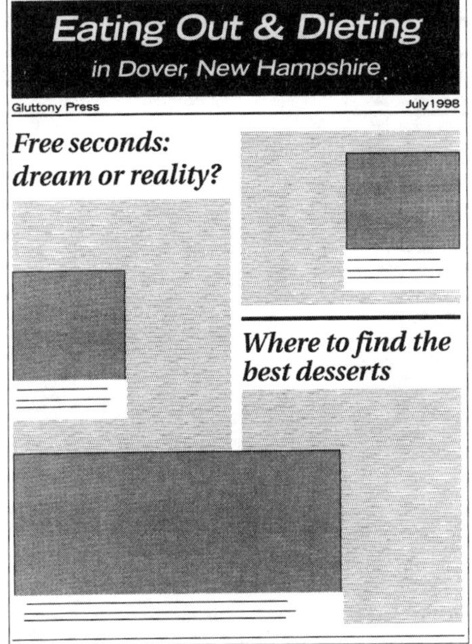

Figure 18-4: Although the photographs appear next to the copy, the page appears disorganized.

Figure 18-5: Aligning the photographs with one another projects a neater, more organized appearance.

Figure 18-6: Two photos of approximately equal size compete with each other, and neither one attracts the reader's attention.

Figure 18-7: Making one photograph significantly larger creates visual interest and projects an obvious hierarchy of importance.

Facing into the page

Your reader's eyes are likely to unconsciously look where the individual in a picture is looking or glance in the direction where the object in a photo is moving. Therefore, always design your pages and, whenever possible, direct your photographs so that the individuals in the photograph look into the page rather than out of the page. Likewise, always make sure that moving objects, such as automobiles, move into a page rather than off the page.

Borders

If your publication contains photographs, you may want to add a border around them. Consider the following questions to determine whether a border is appropriate for your photographs:

- **What kind of background does the photo have?** Does the photograph contain a clearly defined boundary, like a building, or is the background lightly colored, like the sky? Photos without clearly defined borders often create pages that look unfinished. In these situations, borders can be useful.
- **Did you use borders around photographs before?** Consistency should also play a role in your decision. In general, if you place a hairline border around one photograph, you should place borders around *all* your photographs. If one photograph has a border and an adjacent one doesn't, readers are likely to wonder why you added a border to one and not the other.

Unless you're into obituaries, avoid placing heavy, thick black borders around photographs.

Captions

Spend as much time placing and setting captions as you do placing photographs. Captions are often left to the last minute, and their appearance can suffer. Poor caption typography can destroy the overall appearance of even the best print publications. Here are some hints (which you can consider adapting to Web publications):

- **Consistent placement:** Always place captions in the same location relative to the photograph. Don't right-align captions above some photographs and left-align captions below other photographs. Pick a logical caption scheme and stick with it.
- **Consistent typography:** Always use the same typeface, type sizes, and line spacing for captions. Consider alternatives to placing captions in the italicized version of the serif typeface that you use for body copy.

Experiment with a bold, sans serif face with extra leading. This technique often projects a stronger image.

- **Alignment and hyphenation:** Flush-left/ragged-right captions work better than justified captions. If one line of the caption is significantly longer or shorter than the others, turn off hyphenation and try rewriting the captions. Captions should very rarely be hyphenated because they typically contain proper nouns that should not be hyphenated.
- **Short length:** Avoid long captions that extend the full width of photographs spanning two or more columns. These captions often appear as gray masses of copy. Keep captions as short and telegraphic as possible.

Shadows

Shadows behind photographs can be used to create the appearance of *lifting* the photograph off the surface of the page (or the screen). When you use shadows, be sure that the light always appears to come from the same direction. You don't want shadows to the left and below some photographs and to the right and above others. There are only so many suns in the world!

Placing Visuals on the Web

Most of the points in "Placing Visuals in Print" apply equally well to photographs and illustrations added to Web sites, although there are some significant changes:

- **Alignment:** Always strive to align the edges of the photograph with the edges of the text. Avoid text wraps that interrupt the smooth movement of the reader's eyes across the Web site.
- **Size:** Remember that larger sizes equate with longer download times. One of the best gifts that you can give visitors to your Web site are small *preview* photographs that, when clicked,download larger versions. This way, only people who want to see a large photograph are forced to wait for the large file to download.
- **Captions:** Include captions as part of the graphic file, which ensures more consistent placement relative to the photograph when viewed with a wider variety of browsers.
- **Shadows and borders:** Include these with the photo file.

Thumbnails are the best gift that you can give visitors to your Web site. Instead of making every visitor wait for large photographs to download, provide small previews that Web visitors can click on if they desire to download a larger version. Speed is everything when you're surfing the Web!

Chapter 19

Typographic Refinements Online and Onscreen

In This Chapter

- Deciding which typefaces you should buy and use
- Making the most of text in print
- Fine-tuning spacing
- Adding proper punctuation
- Making the most of initial caps
- Creating styles for consistency and speed

Online or in print, you will likely communicate the bulk of your message using type. Although a picture may be worth a thousand words, most publications still contain at least a thousand words . . . often tens of thousands of words. So, a great deal of the success of your communications depends on your ability to use type to communicate.

Your choice of type also determines the image your communication projects. People see the type before they read your message, so they fit that message into the image they have already received from the look of your page. A print newsletter or Web splash page set in an ornate typeface projects an entirely different image than one set in a clean, modern typeface, or a trendy "grunge" typeface.

The way you handle type after you select the typeface design or designs that you plan to use is equally important. The details of letter and line spacing, paragraph alignment, and hyphenation influence the likelihood that your audience will even look at your communication, as well as the ease with which the audience will be able to read and understand your message once they take a look at it.

Where to look for the right typeface

Type is available from numerous sources. Free sources include the following:

- Your computer's operating system
- Software, in particular, page-layout and illustration software
- Utilities such as the Adobe Type Manager Deluxe, (a virtual necessity for computers running either the Apple Macintosh or Windows operating systems)
- Web sites, such as Microsoft's, from which you can download free software containing a number of different typefaces.

Type is also sold by numerous sources:

- A variety of digital typeface foundries (such as Adobe, Agfa, and Monotype) offer locked CD-ROMs containing hundreds of typeface designs that can be individually accessed upon providing credit card information.
- Smaller independent digital typeface foundries advertise in design publications such as *Adobe, Publish, Print* and *The Desktop Publishers Journal.*
- Independent resellers Precision Type and Font Haus sell typeface designs from both the large digital typeface foundries as well as numerous smaller, independent design houses.

Even in today's electronic and visual age — or, rather, *especially* in today's visual age — type is important. Reading is harder than watching, and with so much more out there to see, your audience is less forgiving of anything unattractive and hard-to-read. Sound type decisions are more important than ever.

How to Look at Type

Dozens of catalogs and type specimen books are available. These catalogs and books either show different typeface designs set in complete alphabets or the same phrases set in different typeface designs at different sizes (see Figure 19-1). The problem with looking at a complete alphabet is that every typeface looks good when set as a specimen.

The PANOSE principle

A much better way of looking at type is to start by concentrating on just the significant upper-and lowercase letters that best reveal each typeface's unique characteristics. The uppercase letters PANOSE are the most important letters in this regard because they form the basis for all the other uppercase letters:

PANOSE

The purpose of setting a few key letters at large size is so you can visualize how headlines and titles will appear. The reason to set the same typeface at a significantly smaller size is so that you can see how the typeface looks when set in columns of running text. One view without the other doesn't give you a true idea of how the type will look in use.

Figure 19-1: The best type specimens show type set both large and small.

- The uppercase *P* reveals how that typeface design creates uppercase *B*s and *R*s, for example.
- The diagonals of the uppercase *N* show how the *M*s and *W*s of the typeface will appear.
- The uppercase *E* gives a clue to how the typeface handles uppercase *F*s, *L*s, and *T*s.

The corresponding significant lowercase letters are *a, b, e, q, m, o, q, s,* and *t.* Of these, the most important letters are *a, g,* and *e,* which exhibit the most typeface-to-typeface differences.

Next, set a paragraph of text at body copy size, typically 11 or 12 points. Setting this text is extremely important for giving you an idea of how extended passages of text will look when set in that typeface. You'll be surprised at how some typefaces that look great and appear easy to read when only a few words are set in them become very difficult to read when used in paragraphs of body copy text.

Baseline, x-height, ascenders, descenders and other type characteristics

Here are some of the things to look at when analyzing type: serifs, baseline, x-height, descenders, ascenders, stroke weight, constrast, character width, bowls, and counters. I discuss serifs in Chapter 9.

The *baseline* is the invisible line that characters rest on. The baseline plays an important role in determining the overall impression of size of each letter, because the baseline is so closely associated with each typeface design's x-height, ascenders, and descenders.

Analyzing type

The best way to teach yourself about type is to create your own type specimens. The following steps show you how:

1. Using your favorite word-processing or page-layout program, open a new file and set up a two-column page.
2. In the left column, set the uppercase **PANOSE** on the first line and the lowercase **abegmoqst** on the second line. (Don't set them in bold; I just used that so they'd be easy for you to pick out from these lines of text).
3. Format the two lines in 30-point type.
4. Beginning on the next line, enter a paragraph containing three or four sentences of text.
5. Format the sample paragraph in 12-point text.
6. Select (or highlight) all of the text in the first column, both large and small.
7. Copy the text in the first column and Paste it in the second column.
8. Save the file as a template.
9. Select (or highlight) the text in the first column and format it in Times Roman (or Times New Roman).
10. Select (or highlight) the text in the second column and format it in Helvetica or Arial.

You now have a framework for making side-by-side comparisons of all the typefaces in your library. You may be surprised to find that you already have far more typeface options on your computer than you previously knew.

The *x-height* of a typeface is the height of the lowercase vowels, *a, e, i, o,* and *u,* as well as letters with descenders such as *g, p,* and *y*. In general, the larger the x-height, the more legible (or easily recognized) the characters will be.

Ascenders are the vertical portions of lowercase letters like *h, t,* and *l* that extend above the x-height. *Descenders* are the tails, or portions of letters like *g, y,* and *p,* which descend below the baseline.

Type size is measured from the height of the ascenders to the bottom of the descenders. Type size is measured in points (72 points to an inch) and has very little to do with the apparent, or visual, size of the type. This is because the x-height plays such a major role in the impression of type size that the reader receives. The extremes of these type characteristics are:

- Typefaces with a high x-height necessarily have short ascenders and descenders. Up to a certain point, the high x-height makes characters easier to recognize, because more space is within the characters (bowls and counters) but diminishes the impact of the ascenders and descenders. Display typefaces such as Antique Olive that have a very high x-height are unsuited for use as body copy because the lack of contrast between the vowels and letters with ascenders and descenders makes them hard to recognize.

- Typefaces with a low x-height have relatively long ascenders and descenders. Typefaces with a low x-height project a classic, elegant, or poetic image. Although less space is enclosed within the characters, the short x-height makes the ascenders and descenders more prominent, which creates more recognizable word shapes. The lack of space within the characters can make the words hard to recognize at small type sizes.
- Typefaces with a moderate x-height are the easiest to read because enough space is within the letters for recognition, yet the ascenders and descenders emerge clear enough to create distinct word shapes.

Bowls, counters, and *eyes* refer to white space within letters. These spaces are vitally important to your reader's ability to recognize each letter, as you can easily see if you temporarily fill in the inside spaces within the letters. Among the most important spaces are the eyes, or the space contained within the upper loops of *a*'s and *e*'s.

Readers do not read by sounding out the individual letters. Rather, reading is accomplished by glancing at word shapes and guessing at the words. Reading is instinctive and psychological more than intellectual. Thus, words with clearly defined shapes are easier to recognize and read.

Typeface designs also differ with regard to the width, or horizontal space, each character occupies. Most typefaces are available in condensed and expanded versions.

- Condensed typefaces save space, permitting more characters to occupy a given column inch of type. Because they look compact, they can also convey an image of speed and power.
- Expanded versions add impact to headlines and subheads.

Typefaces also differ with regard to the thickness of the horizontal and vertical strokes that comprise each letter (see Figure 19-2).

- Some typefaces are made up of relatively thin strokes; others have relatively thick strokes.
- Some typefaces are monoweight or near-monoweight, meaning that the strokes are of uniform thickness throughout the character rather than changing throughout the letter.
- Most typefaces exhibit contrast, however, or differences in stroke thickness throughout the character. Usually, the horizontal strokes are thicker than the vertical strokes. Contrast is the measure of the difference in stroke thickness. Contrast provides visual interest and helps readers differentiate the various characters that make up the alphabet.

Typefaces with extreme contrast can reflect an elegant image, but at the

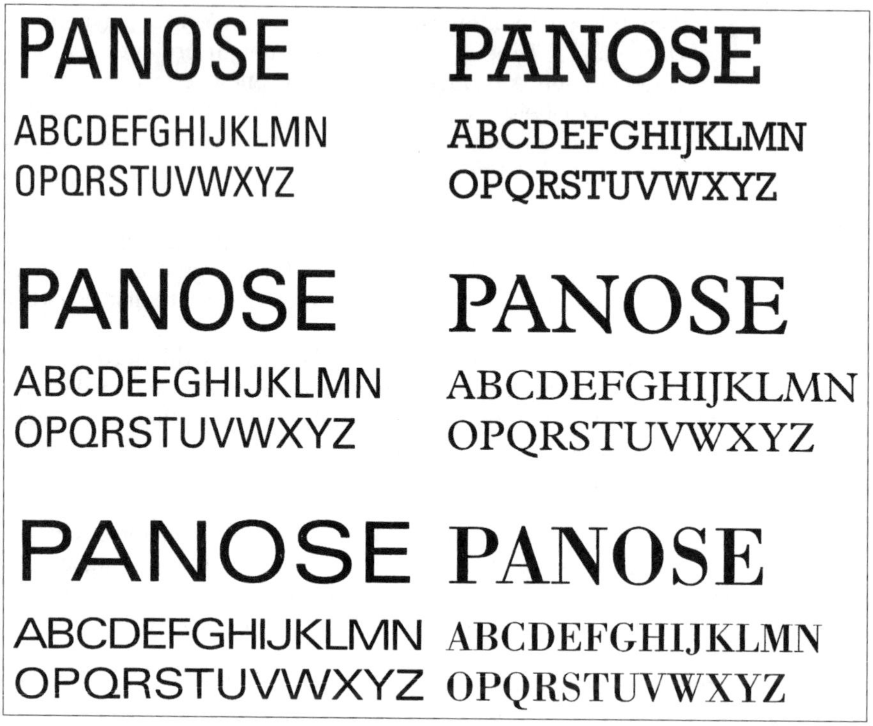

PANOSE PANOSE
ABCDEFGHIJKLMN ABCDEFGHIJKLMN
OPQRSTUVWXYZ OPQRSTUVWXYZ

PANOSE PANOSE
ABCDEFGHIJKLMN ABCDEFGHIJKLMN
OPQRSTUVWXYZ OPQRSTUVWXYZ

PANOSE PANOSE
ABCDEFGHIJKLMN ABCDEFGHIJKLMN
OPQRSTUVWXYZ OPQRSTUVWXYZ

Figure 19-2: Condensed, Normal, and Expanded version of Univers plus comparison of mono-weight, low-contrast, and high-contrast designs.

expense of readability; at small sizes, the thin strokes get lost in the texture of the paper or in the shine of light bounding off the paper.

Decorative and script typefaces

You should be familiar with two major additional typeface categories: decorative and script (see Figure 19-3).

Decorative typefaces are those designed to be noticed, to project a specific image. Decorative typefaces are best used only for logos and packaging, although they can be profitably employed for headlines or department heads in a newsletter._Decorative typefaces range from those with a pronounced Art Deco effect to the latest Grunge typefaces. What these typefaces have in common is that an effort to impress and be noticed replaces the desire to communicate without fanfare.

Script typefaces are designed to mimic handwriting. These can be used to project an informal or personal invitation approach.

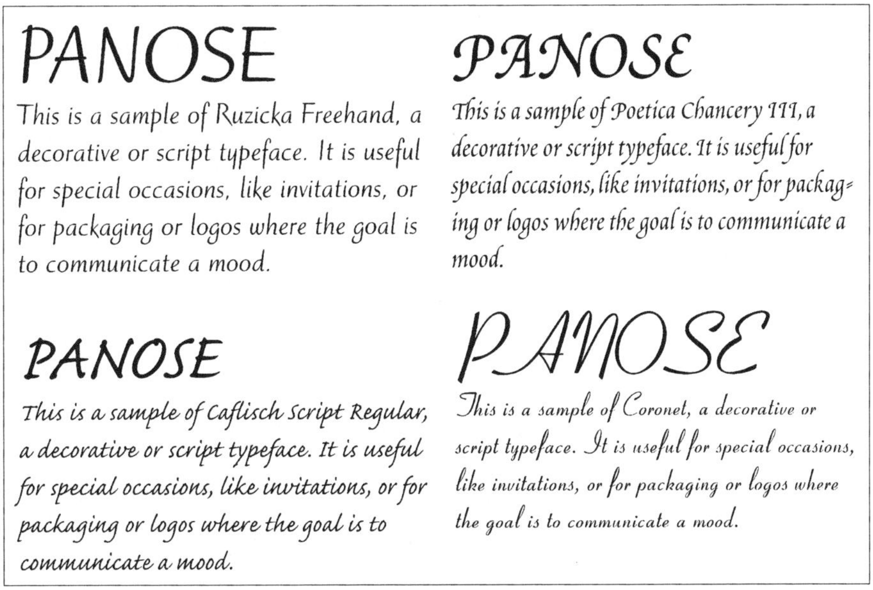

PANOSE

This is a sample of Ruzicka Freehand, a decorative or script typeface. It is useful for special occasions, like invitations, or for packaging or logos where the goal is to communicate a mood.

PANOSE

This is a sample of Poetica Chancery III, a decorative or script typeface. It is useful for special occasions, like invitations, or for packaging or logos where the goal is to communicate a mood.

PANOSE

This is a sample of Caflisch Script Regular, a decorative or script typeface. It is useful for special occasions, like invitations, or for packaging or logos where the goal is to communicate a mood.

PANOSE

This is a sample of Coronet, a decorative or script typeface. It is useful for special occasions, like invitations, or for packaging or logos where the goal is to communicate a mood.

Figure 19-3: Examples of decorative and script typefaces.

Building a Workable Typeface Collection

Tens of thousands of typefaces are available for use on your computer. Which ones should you purchase?

Instead of building on to your typeface library vertically — that is, adding new typeface designs — in most cases you're better off if you enhance your typeface collection horizontally through additional weights and widths of the typefaces you already have available.

Suppose that your computer already has the basic Times Roman (or Times New Roman) and Helvetica (or Arial) typefaces, plus a few additional designs. Instead of purchasing totally different typeface designs, add additional variations of these basic typefaces. These variations permit you to build upon what you have and "voice" your documents with different "tones."

For example, if you are working with Helvetica and Helvetica Bold, your options for adding emphasis are severely limited. This is because Helvetica and Helvetica Bold have limited contrast with each other. If, however, you invest in the Helvetica Light and Helvetica Black typeface collection, you can visually speak in different volume levels without introducing the distraction of a totally different typeface. You can put low-emphasis information in Helvetica Light and use Helvetica Black to really "shout" and make a point.

Furthermore, if you also invest in the Helvetica Condensed typeface package, you can gain even more typeface flexibility. You may find that a sans serif typeface that is both Condensed and Black, such as Helvetica Condensed or Frutiger Condensed UltraBlack, has more visual impact than Helvetica Bold or Frutiger Bold, yet occupies less space (enabling more words to fit on a given space, permitting you to surround your headlines with more white space).

Although less well known, serif typefaces are also available with a variety of width and weight options. Again, these offer you an ability to voice your document with various volume levels.

Some Factors of Type in Print

You have ten major tools and techniques available to you when working with type in print: size and line length, style, case, leading, alignment, hyphenation, letter spacing, indents and paragraph spacing, special characters, graphic accents.

I discuss a number of these in Chapter 9. Following are some tips on advanced type handling for print publications.

- The ideal line of body copy contains between 26 and 43 letters. This is enough to permit two or three comfortable left-to-right eye movements without losing track of the line that has been finished.
- Flush-left/ragged right text is preferable for body copy because word and character spacing are consistent throughout each line. Consistent spacing makes it easier for readers to maintain a consistent rhythm as their eyes take in groups of words. Justified text often looks "neater" and more formal, but is often found to be harder to read.

What about Multiple Master Typefaces?

Multiple Master Typefaces permit you to manipulate the various aspects of a typeface so that you can fine-tune its weight and proportions to the size at which it will be reproduced. Multiple Master Typefaces can be infinitely changed and saved as new typeface files, identified by number, when you arrive at the creative effect you desire.

Depending on the typeface you have chosen, you can

- Adjust serif size and shape
- Manipulate stroke width
- Fine-tune the optical size of the type

Multiple Master Typefaces put you in control, creating a unique typeface that's tuned to the size and needs of your document.

- Your ability to make proper hyphenation decisions is crucial to your ability to produce good-looking pages. Here are some hints:
  - Turn hyphenation off when setting headlines and subheads.
  - Never hyphenate more than three lines in a row. A "ladder effect" results when several lines end in hyphens.
  - Hyphenation is as important with flush-left/ragged-right text as it is for justified text.
- When you working with printed text, you have two ways to vary letter spacing: tracking and kerning:
  - *Tracking* refers to modifying letter spacing throughout a range of type. Minute differences in tracking can make a major difference in the appearance of your print documents as well as the number of words that will fit in a given space. The default, or "no tracking," setting of most word-processing and desktop-publishing programs is too generous.
  - *Kerning* refers to modifying the spacing of selected pairs of letters. Kerning body copy doesn't make sense; reserve kerning for titles, headlines and subheads. Pay particular attention to combinations of upper case and lower case letters, such as *Wa, Te,* and *Yo,* and before punctuation. Kerning is best done by eye.
- Always add more white space above a subhead than below the subhead. This approach emphasizes a clean break with the preceding text and visually reinforces the relationship to the text that follows.
- If you are inserting first-line indents, do not indent the first line following a headline or a subhead. It's obvious that it is a new paragraph, so an indent isn't necessary.

Special characters

Special characters offer yet another way you can use type to add impact to your print communications by making your message easier to read and better looking. Here are some of the typographic options available to you as optional typefaces:

- **True Small Caps** have been redrawn to match the x-height of the type they match. When you use your software to create Small Caps, it scales down the size of the caps. The process of reducing the size of the subheads reduces the thickness of the letters, creating noticeably lighter letters. In addition, software-scaled small caps rarely are the exact right height. True Small Caps permit you to add emphasis to titles, as well as add acronyms, without adding unnecessary distraction which several uppercase letters in a row create.

- **Old Style Figures** are numbers that have descenders. Upright numbers are often so strong that they attract unnecessary attention to themselves. Old Style Figures blend in better with the body copy, allowing you to add date and time information without it blending into adjacent text.
- **Titling and Display Caps** are typeface designs that have been redrawn for reproduction at large size. Most digital typefaces are designed for use at text size, which is approximately 12 points. When blown up to 72 or more points, these typefaces often look "clunky" or "bloated." Titling and Display Caps, however, are designed for reproduction at 72 points, so their proportions more closely fit the typeface designer's original goals.
- **Ligatures** are often found on the same typeface collections as True Small Caps and Old Style Figures. Ligatures are characters set two, or more, characters at a single keystroke. Ligatures avoid conflicts between letter pairs such as *f* and *i*, *f* and *l*, and two *f*s in a row.
- **Fractions** are also available with typeface designs containing Old Style Figures. Only a few of the most common fractions are included with most typeface designs; more are available with Old Style Figures.
- **Swash characters** are designed to be used at the beginnings and ends of words. These alternative characters permit you to begin or end a word with a flourish. They are especially valuable when used in fancy invitations, logos, or titles.
- Many typeface designs also include **ornaments** that match the design of the typeface. These can be used as end-of-story marks or to indicate paragraph breaks in the absence of first-line indents or extra space between the lines.

Special characters, such as Old Style Figures and True Small Caps, are available from special Expert Sets as additional typefaces which appear as extra typeface entries on your software's Font menu. Thus, instead of just seeing Minion, your font menu would include Minion OSF (for Old Style Figures) and Minion SC (for Minion Small Caps), Minion Black (for the heaviest weight of Minion), Minion Condensed (for guess what?), and Minion Ornaments.

Using the right punctuation

Good-looking pages result when you use the following special characters for punctuation:

- Apostrophes versus foot and inch marks; amateurish desktop published documents use vertical marks for apostrophes and quotations (' and" instead of ‘ and “). The vertical marks are instead used to indicate feet and inches. The typographically correct curly quotes, or opening and closing quotation marks, also make it easier for readers to recognize the beginning and end of a quotation.

- Em and en dashes are far better than two hyphens in a row. An em dash is used to indicate the insertion of a parenthetical expression; an en dash is used to indicate compound words or duration. In addition to clearer meaning, these symbols avoid the problem often associated with double hyphens, when one hyphen appears at the end of one line, and the second hyphen appears at the end of the next line.
- Bullets of various sizes and open or closed ballot boxes allow you far more versatility than snowflakes, or asterisks, when introducing lists.

Initial caps

Initial caps also fit the category of Special Characters, but they do not necessarily require the purchase of additional typefaces. Initial caps are large letters used to form a transition between a headline and a paragraph of body copy. There are three types of initial caps:

- Raised caps extend above the text they introduce, forcing white space into the column.
- Drop caps extend below the baseline of the text and are cut into the text, forcing a text wrap around them.
- Marginal caps are placed in the margin to the left of the text they introduce.

Here are some ways to make the most of initial caps:

- **Baseline alignment:** The baseline of the initial cap should be aligned with the baseline of the first (in the case of raised caps) or one of the following lines of text (when working with drop caps or marginal caps).
- **Size:** To succeed, initial caps should be significantly larger than the size of the text they introduce. Avoid wimpy initial caps that look enough different from the adjacent text to look confusing without looking determined and purposeful. As a rule, initial caps should be at least as tall as three lines of text.
- **Text wrap:** When working with drop caps, always wrap the paragraph text as closely around the initial cap text as possible.
- **Small caps:** You can create a smooth transition between the initial cap and the paragraphs by setting the first phrase or first line of the paragraph in small caps.
- **Typeface choice:** Because initial caps are to be "recognized" more than "read," you can choose from a wide variety of typefaces. In general, however, a good starting point for experimenting is to set initial caps in the same typeface as used for headlines and subheads. This approach ensures a strong contrast with body copy. Special alphabets of typeface designs intended especially for use as drop caps are available (see Figure 19-4).

- **Color and background:** Initial caps, when set large, can sometimes effectively be set in color. Another option is to set them against a reversed or screened box.

Space and graphic accents

When working with type to appear on a printed page, you can fine-tune the appearance of subheads and headlines by adding extra space above the text and the preceding text. You can also add horizontal rules above or below the text.

Do not confuse under rules with underlines. When using under rules, you can specify their thickness and color as well as the distance below the baseline. When you underline text, however, you cannot specify the thickness of the line nor how far from the word it will appear.

Always use logic when adding over rules and under rules. (That seems like obvious advice, but the most obvious is not always the most observed.) For example, rules create visual barriers that stop the reader's eyes. Thus, it makes more sense to add over rules than under rules. An over rule stops the reader and emphasizes that the subhead that follows introduces a new topic. An under rule is ambiguous, as it implies a break between the subhead and the text that follows (instead of the text that precedes the subhead).

Likewise, you should always add more white space above a subhead than below the subhead. This emphasizes a clear break with the preceding text and visually reinforces the relationship to the text that follows.

Paragraph formatting

Your ability to "lock" paragraphs and to define the number of lines in a paragraph that must remain together is one of the most important advantages you enjoy when working in print. Most software programs permit you to "lock" two paragraphs together. This technique permits you to lock a headline or subhead to the text that it introduces. You can avoid the embarrassment of subheads that appear by themselves at the bottom of a page, or only introduce a single line of a paragraph that is continued at the top of the next column or on the next page.

On most software programs, open the Format command and select Paragraph. When the paragraph dialog box appears, click on the "Keep with next" option. This way, if the subhead appears at the bottom of a column, the subhead moves to the top of the next column (or page).

Figure 19-4: Goudy Initials is an alphabet of stylized type designed to be used specifically as initial caps.

The Paragraph dialog box contains several other important options. These include the Keep Lines Together and Number of Lines to Keep Together.

- The Keep Lines Together option prevents a two-line subhead from being separated, resulting in the first line of the subhead appearing at the bottom of one column (or the foot of one page) and the second line of the subhead appearing at the top of the next column (or page).

- The Lines to Keep Together option permits you to define how many lines must appear together before the paragraph is split over two columns or pages. If you specify **3** in the Lines to Keep Together option, and only two lines will fit at the bottom of the first page, the entire paragraph shift to the next page.

Character Manipulation

When you create titles and logos, using drawing programs such as Adobe Illustrator, Macromedia Freehand, and Microsoft WordArt, you can create a variety of special effects. These effects include:

- Stretching or compressing the type
- Placing type at angles
- Touching or overlapping letters
- Changing baseline alignment
- Adding shadows and special textures to the type to create three-dimensional or embossed effects, and so on.

These special effects should be used with great restraint, however, and primarily for type that is intended to be *recognized* rather than read. These files will be imported as graphics and can be resized as needed.

Making the Most of Online Type

Much of the creative freedom you enjoy when working with type printed on paper is lost when you publish your document on the World Wide Web. Remember:

- **You lack control over typeface.** Unless you specify otherwise and the desired typeface happens to be available on your Web site visitor's computer, your document will be viewed using the default typeface specified in your Web site visitor's browser.
- **You lack special characters and control over punctuation.** You cannot use Old Style Figures, or True Small Caps, ornaments, nor can you specify the correct apostrophes, open and closed punctuation marks and Em and En dashes.
- **You have limited control over type size.** Your ability to control type size is relative to Small, Regular, Large, or Very Large versions of the default type size your visitor has specified in their Web browser.

- **You have no control over spacing.** You cannot control letter, line, paragraph, or word spacing. You cannot insert first-line indents but must hit the Enter key twice between paragraphs.
- **You lack control over line breaks or hyphenation.** Although you can control alignment, line breaks are determined by the line length and the typeface and type size specified in the visitor's Web browser.

You lack the ability to lock subheads and the paragraphs they introduce together. You also cannot define how many lines of a paragraph must appear together at column breaks.

However, here are some of the aspects of type you can easily control:

- **Typeface choice:** In most cases, even though you can't specify a particular type face, such as Garamond, Sabon, or Palatino, you can determine whether the user's Web browser will use a serif or sans serif typeface to reproduce your message. Most Web publishing software programs thus permit you combine sans serif headlines and body copy with serif body text.
- **Type size:** Although you can't determine an exact type size, you can determine a relative type size, that is, relative to the default type size chosen in the Web visitor's browser software (usually found under File⇨Preferences or View⇨Preferences). You can make type Larger, Smaller, Very Small, or Very Large relative to the Web browser's default type size.
- **Line length:** You can control line length by placing text in tables or, if your Web authoring software permits it, columns. (Software programs that allow you to use columns convert the columns to tables before posting your site on the Web.) This is one of the most overlooked aspects of Web page design. Nobody wants to read long lines of text. You can make your pages far more reader-friendly by reducing line length.
- **Initial caps:** You can use initial caps to force white space into your text columns. Although you can't control the typeface chosen for them, you can make the first letters of new topics larger by specifying a larger type size for the first letter. This may affect line spacing, but the effect is usually worth it.
- **Type color:** You can specify type color.

Font substitution is the term used when the Web browser searches for the nearest typeface to the one you have chosen. In most cases, for example, if you have chosen a sans serif type such as Frutiger or Helvetica, it will default to Arial. If you have specified Garamond or Palatino, and these fonts are not available on the Web visitor's computer, it will substitute Times New Roman, which is usually the closest alternative.

The previously described limitations are predicated, of course, on "live type," that is, type that is intended to be quickly downloaded as individual characters.

If you want selected headlines, pullquotes, or paragraphs to appear exactly as you desire, you can always set the type as a downloadable graphic, using programs such as Adobe Photoshop to format and save the type as a downloadable file.

The downside of the graphic approach, of course, is that you greatly increase the downloading time of your text. Although this may be appropriate for key titles and headlines, it is generally not a good idea for extended copy. Web visitors are in a hurry, and the longer you make them wait, the greater the chance that they will leave your Web site. Setting selected passages of type as graphics also allows you to control line breaks and hyphenation, although the size of the reproduced image will depend on the size of the viewer's screen.

Avoid "designer's myopia." Although you may be working with a spacious 17-inch screen, most of your Web visitors will be working with 14- or 15-inch screens. The size of their monitor as well as the resolution setting of their computer's video card will influence the size that downloaded graphics appear.

Which Type Format Should I Use?

Two type formats are in popular use. Your choice of typeface format should be determined by where you will be using the type.

Type 1 fonts

Choose Type1 fonts if you are creating a project that will be taken to a service bureau for output on a high-resolution typesetter. The Adobe Type1 format is the established standard for the graphic arts field. Most service bureaus have extensive Type1 typeface libraries. More important, many service bureaus don't even like working with TrueType fonts, as they take longer to download and image.

Achieving font harmony

Here's a simple way to improve the appearance of subheads used in both print and online documents. It's based on the discussion of serif and sans serif type, plus x-height, earlier in this chapter.

You can make a dramatic improvement in the appearance of your print and Web documents by matching the x-height of subheads with the x-height of the body copy they introduce. Simply experiment until you locate the type size that best matches the x-height of the subheads with the x-height of the typeface you're using for body copy.

Consider what happens when you use a 12-point sans serif subhead to introduce 12-point body copy. Because sans serif typefaces typically have higher x-heights than serif typefaces, the sans serif typeface will look noticeably larger than the body copy it introduces. Although their differing typefaces, would be enough to signal the difference between subhead and body copy, when shape is combined with size, the result is awkwardly large subheads.

If you reduce the size of the sans serif subhead to 9 points, however, you may find that this reduction creates a much better match with the 12-point body copy.

Depending on the software you're using to create your Web pages, this simple technique will create subtly better looking pages. Your readers may not be able to identify the fact that the subheads are slightly smaller in size; they will notice, however, that the entire page seems more unified.

TrueType fonts

Choose TrueType fonts if you are working with the Web. Although the selection isn't as large as that of Type1 fonts, thousands of typeface designs are available, and more are coming each day. The only area where the selection of TrueType fonts isn't equal to the selection of Type1 fonts involves special characters, such as Old Style Figures and True Small Caps.

TrueType fonts are the typeface of choice because they offer more control over hinting. Hinting refers to the computer's ability to make minute changes to the shape of each character as it is rasterized — or prepared for appearance on the computer screen. TrueType fonts can be hinted so that serifs and thin lines are manipulated and moved until they best align with the relatively coarse resolution of the screen.

In addition, several firms are working on ways of downloading TrueType fonts along with your page design.

TrueType versus Type1

Each Type1 typeface design includes three files: a .PFM file used for displaying the font on the computer screen, a .PFB file containing the shape of the letter to be sent to the printer, and a rarely used .AFM font metrics file needed for older (that is, pre-Windows) software applications.

TrueType fonts, however, are simpler and more compact because each typeface design uses only one file (.TT), which is used for both on-screen display and printing.

In addition, TrueType fonts can be hinted, that is, size-specific modifications can be made to the shape of the letters to permit optimum reproduction on the computer screen. Ways are being devised for TrueType fonts to be compressed and downloaded along with the Web site to the browser's computer.

Efficiency and Consistency: Using Styles

Regardless of the typeface format you choose, you should make it a point to master styles. Styles are often considered "for experts only." This is a mistake. Everyone who is using more than one combination of typeface, type size, and type style in a single document can profitably save time using styles.

What are styles?

Styles are miniature files containing multiple formatting options. Instead of opening a variety of menus and scrolling through various typeface, type size, type style, color, spacing, hyphenation, and alignment options, you can apply multiple options with the click of a mouse (or even easier, as below)!

The starting point is to create meaningful names for your styles. Styles should be named after the element of page architecture they're used for, that is, Headline Level One, Headline Level 2, Subhead, Body Copy, Caption, Header, Footer, List, and so forth. Here are some of the formatting options that can be added to your style descriptions:

- Typeface (including separate styles for True Small Caps and Old Style Figures)
- Type size
- Line spacing
- Alignment
- Letter spacing — normal, tight, or loose tracking

- Hyphenation on/off and the width of the hyphenation zone
- Space above (for headlines and subheads)
- Space after (for flush-left/ragged-right paragraphs with extra space between paragraphs)
- Paragraph locking, including Keep with Next and Keep Lines Together
- Bullet and indents (for material in lists)
- Numbering (which can automatically keep track of subheads)
- Color
- Graphic accents, such as horizontal lines (or rules) above or below the type, including the amount of spacing

Two types of styles are available:

- Character-level styles are limited to pre-selecting typeface, type size, type style, and color.
- Paragraph-level styles include numerous formatting options, including first-line indent, line spacing, paragraph locks, letter spacing, and hyphenation.

These two types of styles enable you to apply character-level formatting to short passages, such as titles of books you want set in Expert fonts such as True Small Caps or dates set in Old Style Figures, while the remainder of the paragraph appears in the Normal body copy. Keep letter and line spacing and hyphenation consistent throughout the paragraph except for the selected words that are set in the different typeface.

How to save time applying styles

Styles not only ensure consistency, eliminating the possibility of introducing unity-destroying subtle changes in your documents, for example, using 11-point body copy at the start, and 12-point copy at the end, or forgetting to turn hyphenation off for headlines or subheads. You have two principal ways to save time when you apply styles:

- **Automatic application:** Using the "Style for the Following Paragraph" command, you can set up your styles so that another style is automatically applied to the next paragraph when, in most programs, you press the Enter key. For example, you can set it up so that the Body Copy style automatically follows the Subhead or Headline style.

- **Keyboard shortcuts:** Most software programs permit you to apply styles using keyboard shortcuts. Keyboard shortcuts involve holding down the Control, Command, Alt, or Shift key while pressing another key. For example, Alt+1 applies Subhead Level One, Alt+2 applies Subhead Level Two, Alt+N applies Normal body copy, and so on. Software programs differ in the ease with which they permit you to create and apply keyboard shortcuts.

Styles save time in additional ways. One of their most important features is that you can share styles between documents. You can also share styles among co-workers over a network, over the Internet, or by distributing styles on a floppy diskette. This feature permits workers in far-flung locations to format their documents the same way, projecting a consistent corporate image. It also saves money by eliminating unnecessary "creativity" and experimentation.

Part V
The Part of Tens

"You know, I've asked you a dozen times not to animate the torches on our Web page!"

In this part . . .

When you need a ten, this is where to go — ten tools, ten truths, ten of anything. This part capsulizes the most important concepts and ideas presented in this book while introducing other ideas that didn't comfortably fit within the individual chapters. This part is one of my favorites, and I always write it first.

Chapter 20

Ten Web Tools Worth Trying

In This Chapter

- Web design software
- Screen capture programs
- Color inkjet printers
- Image editors
- Illustration programs and clip art
- Scanners
- Tables and frames
- Motion and sound
- Adobe Acrobat

The following tools help you get online as quickly as possible and, once there, let you continually improve your Web design skills.

- **Web design software:** If you are creating your first Web site, take a look at programs such as Microsoft Publisher 97 (if you're a Windows user) or Adobe PageMill (if you're an Apple Macintosh user). These programs offer the simplest route to good-looking results.
  - *Microsoft Publisher 97* offers the advantage of built-in Page Design Wizards that guide you through the process of choosing the content and the "look" of your Web site. Publisher 97 asks you questions about the type of Web site you're creating and the type of image you want to project, and creates a customized template based on your responses — complete with all necessary hyperlinks and appropriate layout and color choices. Publisher 97 also automatically converts photographs to the proper image format and guides you through posting your Web site online.
  - *Adobe PageMill* allows you to build a Web site similar to the way you create a page using desktop publishing software; by placing and resizing text and graphic elements on a page in a "what you see is what you get" manner. Like Publisher 97, PageMill automatically converts scanned images to the proper format for fast downloading.

  - *NetObjects Fusion* is a new Web design program that works just like PageMaker. It's ideal for desktop publishers experienced in PageMaker who are moving into Web design.

- **Screen capture programs:** As you may have noticed by now, when you print out a Web page, the background generally does not appear. Furthermore, if the Web site includes frames, only the current frame is printed, so you don't get a chance to see how the various frames work together (or fight each other). A screen capture program, however, takes a static picture of everything on the screen of your computer monitor, including backgrounds and frames, so you can print it out and refer back to it (see below).

- **Color inkjet printers:** Even if you already have a black-and-white laser printer, you should invest in a color inkjet printer. A color inkjet printer can help you proof your Web pages in color far more effectively than you can proof them on-screen. A color inkjet printer also helps you improve your design skills by learning from the successes (and failures) of others (see below) by allowing you to make easily-compared print-outs of the Web sites you have visited, so you can see what works and what doesn't work.

- **Image-editing programs:** Although usually thought of in terms of manipulating photographs, such as putting Grandpa in a compromising position with Lady Godiva, image-editing programs such as Adobe Photoshop and Corel PHOTO-PAINT are important because they allow you to manipulate text and store words as graphic files. You can add backgrounds, embossing (a raised design imprinted on your paper or cover), shadows, and colored gradients to key elements of your Web site, such as its title (or premise), as well as the department heads introducing various topics. The consistent use of such techniques can make your Web site distinctive.

- **Illustration programs:** Illustration programs such as Microsoft WordArt (included free with Microsoft Word and Microsoft Publisher), Adobe Illustrator, CorelDRAW, and Macromedia Freehand allow you to stretch and distort text, as well as use fonts that are unlikely to be included on your visitor's computer. These programs typically come with a wide selection of fonts that may not be presently on your computer, expanding your creative potential.

- **Clip art:** Clip art has come a long way from the rough "cartooney," black-and-white sketches of people with puzzled expressions on their faces and question marks coming out of their heads. Today's clip art rivals that available on a custom basis from fine commercial illustrators and can be used to communicate exactly the emotions you want to communicate. Clip art also includes buttons and icons that you can use to make it easy for your Web site visitors to navigate from page to page of your site.

- **Scanner:** An image scanner allows you to personalize your Web site by including your photograph, or photographs of your associates and staff. Although most scanners are flat-bed scanners, transparency adapters (as well as separate transparency scanners) are available so you can scan 35mm slides or negative film.

  In addition, a scanner allows you to make a graphic file out of your signature (the way you sign your name, not the unit of printing), allowing further opportunities to personalize your Web site. Finally, if you have a scanner and access to OCR — or optical character recognition — software, you can create word-processed files out of printed documents. This software can eliminate hours of needless retyping if you are placing previously printed information online (such as directory listings or employee rules and regulations).

- **Tables and frames:** Tables and frames are the key to good-looking Web sites. Tables allow you to carefully control the vertical and horizontal placement of text and graphic images when creating Web pages using word processing programs like Microsoft Word 97 or Corel WordPerfect. Tables are the basic tool of Web page design.

  Frames are a bit more sophisticated. Frames permit you to create two, or more, separately scrollable image areas on the viewer's screen. Frames permit you to create a Web site with some elements that always remain on the visitor's screen — such as a banner identifying your Web site (which can also be used for advertisements), as well as a place to always keep navigation links present on-screen. Thus, no matter how deeply your visitor digs into the contents of your Web site, your name, your primary message, and links to other pages will always be immediately accessible.

  Although you can accomplish quite a bit with word processing programs like Microsoft Word and full-featured starter programs like Publisher 97, eventually you'll want to migrate upwards to programs with greater capabilities, such as PageMill or Fusion.

- **Movement and sound:** You can now easily add animation and movement to your Web site.

  Movement can take the form of words that scroll across the screen, like stock quotes or the "news flash!" billboard at New York's Times Square, or you can draw attention to selected navigation icons by having them rotate. You can also have key words flash on and off, or switch between a "Check it out!" immediacy message and the link that you want visitors to click.

  To succeed, you must use movement with discretion, however. Too much movement creates distraction which competes with the other information on the page and interferes with your visitor's ability to read the remainder of your message.

Be forewarned that these files add overhead to your Web site, occupying bandwidth that may slow your visitors down, especially if they are not using the latest hardware and software.

You can also embed sound into your Web site. Sound can take the form of background music or, even better, your voice welcoming visitors to your Web site and an ongoing narration of the points covered on each page. Your voice can greatly personalize your message.

To play sound, visitors to your Web site must add a module like RealAudio to their surfing software. Therefore, if you include sound, you want to include a link to RealAudio and other helper applications, allowing visitors to download the software if they have not already done so.

- **Adobe Acrobat:** A time may come when you want visitors to your Web site to download an exact copy of a previously formatted document, such as an application, form, or formal document (like a newsletter or annual report). In situations like these, you can save your document with all formatting intact as an Adobe Acrobat file. Documents saved in the Adobe Acrobat format preserve all formatting, including the original typefaces, column widths, and original letter, word, line, and paragraph spacing.

  To view a document stored in the Adobe Acrobat format, visitors to your Web site can download a free copy of the Adobe Acrobat Reader from the Adobe Web site at `www.adobe.com`. Be sure to include a link to this site to make it easy for your Web site visitors to do so.

Chapter 21

Ten Ways to Speed Your Layout and Production

In This Chapter

- Using styles, shortcuts, and templates
- Customizing your toolbar
- Word processing when possible
- Investigating utilities
- Creating thumbnails

Design is a repetitive process. But the faster you work, the more time you have available to fine-tune and proofread your document, improving your document and eliminating embarrassing errors. This chapter gives you some time-proven techniques that work as well online as in print.

Always Use Text Styles

Styles permit you to apply multiple formatting options with a single mouse-click. For example:

- Text styles can contain the following formatting options: typeface, type size, type style, text color, rules (or lines) above or below the text, letter spacing, and hyphenation (or you can specify no-hyphenation).
- You can automatically number your subheads and — most important — use the "keep with next" option to lock subheads to the text they introduce.
- You can specify the minimum number of lines that must appear together before a paragraph is split between two columns (or two pages), eliminating the appearance of a single line of a new paragraph isolated at the bottom of a page or column.

Automate Your Styles

You can set up your styles so that they automatically follow each other. For example, you can set up your subhead styles so that the Normal (or body copy) text style is automatically applied after you press the Enter (or Return) key. You can set up your Caption style so it automatically follows a Production Note, and you can set up the Normal style so it automatically follows a caption.

Use Keyboard Shortcuts

Keyboard shortcuts eliminate the need to remove your hand from the keyboard, reach for the mouse, open a menu, and scroll down through a list of styles or typefaces every time you want to switch to a different style. You'll find shortcuts such as Ctrl+1 (or ⌘+1) a much faster way to apply First Level Heading styles.

Selecting text using keyboard shortcuts (such as holding Ctrl+Shift and then pressing the left- or right-arrow keys) is usually much easier and faster than highlighting words by using the mouse.

Make Friends with Templates

Templates consist of "empty" documents — complete with margins, columns, and text styles — that are ready to be customized for each of your specific projects. Instead of starting with a blank slate, making numerous page layout and text decisions, you can immediately start working. Newsletter templates, for example, contain a nameplate and table of contents in the correct position on the front cover, a mailing label on the back cover, and standing elements (such as department headers) ready for you to use inside.

Programs such as Microsoft Publisher 97 come with their own templates. You can easily create your own, or you can purchase them from numerous sources, such as professional designers.

Customize Your Toolbar

Most software programs permit you to customize your screen display by duplicating menu commands as icons along the top, bottom, or side of your screen. Clicking an icon is much faster than opening a menu and scrolling through command options.

Remember the Paragraph Dialog Box

The Paragraph dialog box of most desktop publishing programs contains several options that can save you hours of wasted effort. Usually, you can create better-looking documents and save hours of proofreading time by using the commands in the Paragraph dialog box, such as using the "keep with next" option to keep text from being separated from the subhead that introduces it. You can also save time eliminating widows and orphans by specifying a minimum number of lines, usually three, that must appear together — or else the entire paragraph will be shifted to the next column (or page).

Use the Pasteboard

The Pasteboard is one of the reasons to choose page-layout programs such as Microsoft Publisher 97 and Adobe PageMaker over word-processing programs. The Pasteboard allows you to place text and graphics on the screen outside of the document margins. This technique keeps them in sight and ready for instant use, without searching through the various folders and files on your hard drive.

Always store frequently reused text and graphic files, such as your firm's logo, credit card logos, and the department headers used to introduce articles in your newsletter, on the Pasteboard where they can be easily copied and pasted into position.

Use Your Word Processor

Edit your thoughts in a word processor and import the text files into your page-layout or Web-authoring program. Your word processor is usually a far more efficient environment for composing your message than a desktop publishing or Web authoring program. It is likely to have a more robust spellchecker and thesaurus than the text editor in your page layout program. Word processors can check your spelling on the fly, keep track of word count, and often offer "drag and drop" editing that greatly speeds the process of moving words and sentences around.

You can also usually highlight sentences and paragraphs in a word processor quickly by holding down the Control key while double or triple-clicking with the left mouse button. Not all page-layout programs offer so many keyboard shortcuts.

In addition, your word processor usually offers a very easy-to-read "draft" mode that displays unformatted text at a large size on your monitor. Reading text that's set in narrow columns of 11- or 12-point Times New Roman font in multicolumn documents can be difficult. The same text that would be hard to read when formatted by your page layout program becomes easy to read with a word processor.

Investigate Utilities

Utilities take many forms. Some are optional-at-extra-cost programs designed to be incorporated into your page layout program. Many utility programs are developed by third-party vendors who designed the programs for their own use. Programs called *plug-ins* for Adobe PageMaker and *extensions* for Quark Xpress permit you to quickly perform specialized tasks. You can create running heads (headers that change depending on page content) or perform imposition — the act of combining pages in the right order so they can be printed together on a single side of an oversize sheet of paper.

Prepare Thumbnails

Most page-layout programs permit you to print thumbnails — 2, 4, 8, or up to 16 pages printed at reduced size on a single $8^{1}/_{2}$-by-11-inch sheet of paper. Using thumbnails, you can view the progressive development of your document as your readers turn page after page. Thumbnails permit you to check for consistency between pages, as well as to watch out for unwanted parallelism, or visual boredom. Thumbnails also make it easy to ensure that the left- and right-hand pages of your documents are balanced and that the pages don't fight each other by competing for the reader's attention.

Chapter 22
Ten Design Truths You Shouldn't Ignore

In This Chapter

- Remember and respect your audience
- Let your message shine
- Keep things clear and simple
- Stand out from your competition

Your design abilities will improve to the extent that you view design as an extension of marketing. Marketing is the activity involved in making your product — in this case, your message — as desirable as possible to your audience. The following marketing considerations are as valid when working online as when preparing print publications.

Respect People's Time

Make it fast. Your readers and Web site visitors are in a hurry. They'll appreciate anything you can do to help them quickly assimilate your message, and you will be rewarded by your readers and Web site visitors spending more time reading and retaining more of your message.

Readers shouldn't have to puzzle out your message. Page layouts with lots of white space, large headlines, numerous subheads and frequent pull-quotes make it easy for readers to skim your message and make favorable read or not-read decisions. Prominent initial quotes help direct your reader's eyes to the opening paragraphs of a story.

Avoid Web sites with large, "empty" graphics that take a lot of time to download and don't communicate much information. A large logo on your home page, or a large picture of your home or office, may make you feel good, but are certain to frustrate visitors who quickly get tired of paying on-line charges while your logo downloads.

Keep Your Audience in Mind

Fast, easy to-read messages are always better read (and better remembered) than hard-to-read messages. Keep the WIFM ("What's in it for me?") principle in mind when designing print and Web pages for your audience. Respect your reader's self-interest: Remember that they only care about you insofar as your message offers them a benefit. Choose an image that's appropriate for the type of customer to whom you want to appeal. Your choices of typeface, layout, colors, and paper are crucial to your success.

Let Your Message Determine the Layout

Your message should play a major role in determining the layout and colors of your print and online publications. Paragraph length, for example, should influence column width and type size.

The message also includes the nonverbal image your publication projects. Make sure that the message your documents project is consistent with the image that you want to create in your reader or Web site visitor's mind. The complexity of your message — the words and sentences that make up the text, and the number and variety of visuals — should play a major role in determining the best layout.

Never Forget Your Competition

Your competition's online and print publications should also play a role in the design of your own documents. It doesn't make sense to use the same typefaces, colors, or layouts as your competition, because your message may get confused with theirs. Use your competition's print and online publications as a basis of comparison when developing your own, distinct brochures, newsletters, and Web sites.

Emphasize Only the Important

Use the tools of contrast to apply selective emphasis. The amount of emphasis should be proportional to the importance of the message:

- Important ideas should be significantly larger or brighter than information that is merely supportive.
- Subordinate information should be smaller, lighter, and less noticeable.

- Size, color, and placement should visually emphasize importance.
- The most important message should be the largest or brightest on the page or on the screen.

Be Consistent

Strive to create a distinct identity for all of your print and online publications. All your print communications should use the same (or at the very least) similar headlines and body copy typefaces, column layouts, and relative positioning of standing elements like your firm's logo. You can also use color as a tool to visually unify all your print communications.

Although you have less control over typography online than you do on paper, you can strive to unify your Web site with your print communication by using the same colors and placing the same logos in the same relative positions on both types of documents. You can also unify print and online communications by setting key words, phrases, and titles as graphics, which will be downloaded as formatted text. Just one or two words on a screen will be enough to maintain continuity.

Just as your message should remain consistent from week to week — that is, you shouldn't try to appeal to price shoppers one week, luxury shoppers the next — your message should look the same from week to week, regardless of whether it's encountered online or in print.

Keep Out Clutter

Eliminate clutter whenever possible. Clutter is the enemy of quick and accurate communications and projecting a professional image. Eliminate all unnecessary elements from your messages, including words, colors, and graphic accents. (To see whether they're necessary, take a look at your design without them. If you don't miss those extras, leave them out.) Avoid the temptation to add unnecessary rules, boxes, or backgrounds. Use the minimum number of marks on the paper necessary to communicate your message.

A single, perfectly chosen word is better than five less-appropriate words. Short headlines and subheads are easier to read and look better than long, multiline headlines and subheads. A single highlight color is more effective than two, or more, colors fighting for attention.

Avoid Ambiguity

Each print or Web page should contain a single dominant visual element, which provides a starting point for the reader's or Web site visitor's eye movement. Ambiguity occurs when two or more text or visual elements of equal weight compete with each other for the reader's attention. Ambiguity causes confusion — and confusion results in lost readers.

Always Provide a Clear Call to Action

Know what action you want the reader or Web site visitor to take before you begin designing your page, and make sure it's obvious on the completed page:

- If you want people to call a toll-free 800 number for more information, make the number a very noticeable part of your advertisement.
- Always provide enough length and line spacing in coupons. Coupons that appear easy to fill out reward you with much higher response than short, cramped lines.
- If you want Web site visitors to register for e-mail follow-up, provide a large, simple on-screen form.
- To encourage Web site response, include a link to your e-mail address.

Repetition Leads to Acceptance

Your message is likely to go unnoticed the first time it's read online or in print. Therefore, don't be afraid to repeat the same basic message over and over again. Likewise, the more you continue using the same basic image, the more familiar — and, hence, "safe" — your message will appear. Remember that you're likely to tire of your message or your image far sooner than your customers and prospects, who don't see it as often.

Winning franchises (like cereals, icebox deodorizers, and fast food restaurants) enjoy decades of success by stating the same message and looking the same way over and over again.

Chapter 23

Ten Design Mistakes You'll Never Make

In This Chapter

- Weak initial caps
- Long lines of text
- Inconsistencies
- Headings that go nowhere
- No headings
- No space

The following mistakes are commonly made by beginning desktop publishers and Web site creators. These mistakes make it more difficult for your audience to be attracted to and understand your message — in some cases, so difficult that your audience will give up on your message completely. Although you know better than to include these brain-blockers in your designs, I list them here, just for review:

Wimpy, floating initial caps

Like the big "T" at the beginning of the prededing paragraph, initial caps are those oversized first letters that introduce the first paragraph of a chapter, an article, or a new paragraph within a long article. To succeed, the initial caps should be significantly larger than the text they introduce.

A good general rule is to make the initial caps equal in height to at least three lines of text.

In order to create a strong visual transition between the initial caps and the text they introduce, the baseline of the initial cap should align with the baseline of one of the lines of text in the paragraph. (The baseline is the invisible line the text rests on.)

Long lines of small text

The worst thing you can do to your readers online or in print is expect them to read long lines of small text. Long lines of text (that is, wide text columns) are as hard to read on-screen as they are on paper. Long lines of text lack contrast and present a visually tiring image, which discourages readership. In addition, it's easy for the readers to get lost at the end of one line, causing them to reread the line just finished or skip down two lines.

Two spaces between sentences

Never press the space bar twice after punctuation (such as after periods ending sentences, the way you were probably taught in high school typing class). Two spaces between sentences creates unsightly gaps between the sentences, making your text columns look like mottled.

The worst offense you can commit is to use two spaces after periods in columns of justified text, that is, text where the lines are of equal length and the last letter of each line aligns with the last letter of the line above and below it. Because both spaces expand during justification (the process of adding and subtracting white space between letters to achieve lines of equal length), the gaps between sentences are likely to be extremely noticeable.

No subheads

Subheads, short phrases introducing and/or summarizing the text that follows, are vitally important in long columns of text. Rarely should three or four paragraphs go by without a new topic being introduced by a subhead. Each subhead increases the readership of your message by "advertising" the text that follows. Each subhead provides an additional entry point for readers to begin reading the text passage. Many readers are only going to skim the subheads and only begin reading when they find something that interests them.

Finally, subheads break up the visual monotony of text paragraphs, adding white space and contrast to your pages or Web sites.

Obscure headlines and subheads

To succeed, headlines and subheads must be noticeable. Humble heads and subheads rarely succeed because they do not clearly contrast with the adjacent text. You can make your headlines and subheads stand out by using a contrasting typeface (for example, sans serif headlines and subheads combined with serif body copy), making the subheads significantly larger than the text, adding white space above the subheads and adding graphic accents such as overrules (lines over a subhead that create a noticeable barrier between the subhead and the preceding text).

When formatting headlines and subheads in Web documents, you can also use color as a contrast tool, making certain that the color works well with the background color of your text site and the color of links and visited links.

Sans serif type for extended reading

Sans serif typefaces (like Arial) lack the tiny finishing strokes at the top and bottom of the letters (found on serif typefaces like Times Roman). Serifs assist readability by guiding the reader's eyes from letter to letter and by helping emphasize each character's distinct shape. Since readability is based on recognizability; the easier the letters are to recognize, the sooner the letters will combine into words in the reader's mind.

Sans serif typefaces, like Arial and Helvetica, are generally harder to read in extended text passages, especially in print publications. This is partly because the characters are not as distinct from each other and, type size for type size, sans serif typefaces usually have a higher x height, which reduces the apparent space between lines, creating darker, denser paragraphs.

An exception is sometimes made for children or people with "challenged" reading skills, who may be confused by the serifs. Messages designed for this audience may be set in a larger point size and may use a clean, sans serif typeface that resembles the letter shapes people are taught to form in penmanship class — shapes that don't have serifs at the ends.

Automatic line spacing (leading)

Leading, which refers to vertical line spacing, is crucial to the legibility of headlines and easy text readability. Unless you specify a different measurement, most word processors and desktop publishing software programs automatically add approximately 20 percent extra line spacing to the type size chosen, which translates to 14 points of line spacing for 12-point text. Although 20 percent extra line spacing may be appropriate for some combination of typeface, type size and line length, in most cases this "automatic" measurement is either too much or too little.

Kerned headlines and titles

Kerning refers to reducing the space between letters of a headline until the letters appear to be the same distance apart. Kerning becomes increasingly important as type size increases. Kerning is necessary because some letter pairs (like combinations of upper and lowercase letters such as *T* and *o,* or *W* and *a*) create awkward spaces between each other when they appear next to each other.

Layout inconsistency

The best print publications and Web sites are characterized by a consistent page layout margins and columns (that is, the same size) . The worst case scenario is a newsletter page laid out on top in a three-column format, while the bottom half is laid out in a two-column format. A consistent layout is as important online as it is in print. Line length, consistent placement of navigation links, and consistent amounts of space before and after lines of text help unify a Web site as much as they do the pages in a print document.

Consistent margins and column layouts build a recognition, or "comfort," factor into your publications that readers and Web site visitors alike will appreciate.

Uppercase-only headlines

Disable your Caps Lock key!

Headlines set entirely in uppercase type (that is, all capital letters) are harder to read and take up more space than headlines set in a combination of upper- and lowercase characters. Most headlines today capitalize only the first (initial) letter of the headline (along with any proper names).

Headlines set entirely in uppercase type can occupy up to 30 percent more space than the same headlines set in a combination of upper and lowercase type. Headlines set entirely in uppercase type are very hard to read because the words lack the distinguishing shapes created by the varying ascenders and descenders of the letters making up each word. (Ascenders refer to the portions of tall letters like *l, t* and *h* that extend to the top of the line. Descenders refer to the portions of letters like *y, g,* and *p* that extend below the line.)

Always remember that readers subconsciously recognize words by their varying shapes of the characters make up each word.

Glossary

Often the best way to master and review a new technology is to review its terminology. Here are brief definitions of many of the terms you'll encounter when desktop publishing and creating Web sites.

Advancing colors: Colors such as red and yellow, located to the right of the color wheel, which are best used for text and graphic accents because they attract more attention than adjacent colors. (See *receding colors.*) Advancing colors are best used for foreground text rather than backgrounds.

Alt attribute: A text description of a graphic that describes the contents of a graphic file before it is loaded (or in case it is not loaded). In order to include an alt description, your software must allow you access to HTML, that is, be code savvy. (See *code savvy*, *HTML.*)

Alt text: Text description of a graphic that appears while the graphic is being downloaded or, if the Web site visitor is using a non-graphic browser, the graphic that would otherwise appear. ***Note:*** not all Web creation programs allow you to insert Alt text.

Alternate characters: Many typeface designs include optional upper or lowercase alphabet characters or numbers that can be used for creative applications. These include True Small Caps, letters with exaggerated design elements, and ornaments designed to separate paragraphs or indicate the end of stories. (See *swash characters*, *Old Style Figures*, *True Small Caps.*)

Animation: Movement added to Web sites, such as text or graphics that scroll across the screen.

Antialiasing: Technique used to deceive the eye into thinking that text is sharper than it really is by blending the edges of the letters with the background, eliminating the "jaggies" or stair-stepping characteristic of circular or diagonal character elements.

Asymmetrical: Way of organizing text and graphic elements on a page that creates unequal top/bottom or left/right balance. Typically used in modern and informal publications, as contrasted to symmetrical, conservative publications.

Auto leading: Allowing your software to determine the amount of space between lines of type, instead of choosing a desired amount of line spacing based on the type size, line length, and typeface design. (See *leading.*)

Background: Adding a color or pattern behind a Web page's text and graphics.

Ballot boxes: Typographic symbols used in place of asterisks to introduce items in lists. May be empty (outlined) or filled (solid).

Banner: A banner is an element of Web page architecture that remains on screen regardless of how far down the visitor scrolls on a page. Banners are commonly used for logos or other text to remind Web site visitors of the site they are visiting, although they can also be sold for advertisements. Banners are based on the use of *frames*.

Baseline: The invisible line that type rests on.

Bleed: Graphic accent (that is, horizontal rule), text, or visual that extends beyond the normal margins of a page to the page's physical edge, or trim size.

Blurb: Short descriptive text between a headline and an article elaborating on the headline and summarizing the text that follows.

Book faces: Typefaces designed primarily for use in body copy text, as contrasted to typefaces designed primarily for headlines and titles. (See *display faces.*)

Bookmark: Web page text or graphic link that, when clicked, takes the Web site visitor to a specific location in the same document. Useful in long documents to advance Web site visitors from a topic listed in a table of contents right to the topic. (See *hyperlink.*)

Border rules: Lines, created with your software program's line drawing tool, which allow you to define the top, bottom, and, if desired, sides of your pages. Pages can be bordered with lines of identical length and thickness, or lines of different length and width can be used at the top and bottom of each page to emphasize the live area of each page.

Broken links: Links between pages in a Web site that do not work because the destination has been deleted or the path has been changed.

Browser: Software program that allows users to display Web pages formatted according to HTML conventions.

Bullet: Symbols used in lists instead of asterisks. ***Hint:*** most symbols are too large. If you have the time, make symbols a point or two smaller than the text they introduce.

Button: Individual graphic indicating a link that, when clicked on, takes the Web site visitor to another location on the page, another page in a Web site, or another Web site. (See *link, navigation bar.*)

Byline: Line of text identifying the author or photographer.

Caption: Text identifying a photograph, illustration, or chart. After headlines, captions are the second best-read text element on a page.

Case: Typographic specification indicating whether text will appear in all capitals (uppercase), small letters (lowercase), or mixed upper and lowercase type. Like many typographic terms, the term is based on history; when wooden type was set by hand, capital letters were stored in the uppercase and small letters were in the lowercase.

CD-ROM: Important hardware advancement that permits easy distribution and immediate access to large collections of computerized information, including type, photographs, large software programs, and interactive training. (See *removable storage media.*)

Chunking: Breaking long documents into a series of shorter elements by inserting frequent subheads and pullquotes.

Clip art: Previously created, "out of the box" illustrations that you can use as is, or modify by ungrouping, combining with other illustrations, and adding different backgrounds and borders.

Code: Programming symbols placed before and after text that determine the relative type size and type style used to display the text as well as to indicate the name and location of graphics files to be downloaded at specific locations. (See *code savvy, code shy, HTML.*)

Code savvy: Web page creation programs, like FrontPage 97 and Adobe SiteMill that allow user access to the HTML codes for fine-tuning and maximum efficiency. (See *code shy, HTML.*)

Code shy: Software programs such as Microsoft Publisher 97, which do not allow access to HTML code. Code is automatically generated after page elements are placed into position. (See *code savvy* and *HTML.*)

Color depth: The amount of color information stored in a graphics file to be downloaded. The more color information there is, the larger the file grows, and the more time it takes to download the file.

Color wheel: Diagram, similar to a pie chart, which shows the locations of the various colors and how they interact with each other. Often, the color wheel is reduced to ten segments; clockwise, beginning with red, (which straddles 12:00 noon), orange, yellow, light green, darker green, green (straddling 6:00 p.m.), turquoise, blue, dark purple, and light purple. (See *complementary colors.*)

Complementary colors: Complementary colors appear *directly opposite each other* on the color wheel. Complementary colors create the greatest contrast; typically one is a dominant, or advancing color and the other a quiet, or receding color. (See *color wheel, advancing color, receding color.*)

Continuous tone: A black and white photograph "right out of the darkroom" containing numerous gray tones that flow gradually into each other. (See *halftone, LPI, screen.*)

Contrast: (1) A fundamental tool of page design, contrast refers to visual interest added to a page by alternating white space with areas of gray text and black headlines. (2) As used in typography, contrast refers to the direction and amount of difference between the thickest and thinnest strokes that make up a letter.

Copyfitting: Determining how many words will fit in a column inch, set in a given typeface at a given type size and line spacing. Copyfitting helps you determine how much space is needed to accommodate previously written text.

Corporate identity: The consistent image created by your firm's or association's print communications, ranging from letterheads and business cards to brochures, newsletters, and documentation. The elements that make up a corporate identity include the consistent use of a limited number of typefaces, type sizes, colors, and logo. These elements typically appear in the same position and at the same size on each type of document.

Counter: Program element sometimes added to Web site Home Pages that indicates the number of times the Web site has been accessed — the number of "hits" it has received. Counters can be considered somewhat egotistical and only should be used when the numbers are impressively high or when you want to justify charging for advertising space on your Web site.

Cropping: Photographs usually include extraneous detail at their top, bottom, and sides. Cropping removes this unwanted information, allowing the most important message-bearing elements of the photograph to emerge with added clarity.

Database publishing: (1) Integrating a database, such as your unsold inventory, with a search engine so that Web site visitors interested in a specific product or price range or other criteria (such as homes in a specific geographic area) can query your database and create a "custom page" that contains only the information they are interested in. (2) Also refers to using desktop-publishing software to create directories or catalogs directly from information in a database. (See *search engine.*)

Deck: Text placed between a headline and the text it introduces that elaborates on the importance of the headline and relates it to the reader's self-interests. Decks permit shorter, larger headlines. Decks are usually set in a type size midway between the headline and the body copy.

Dingbats: Typographic symbols used to introduce lists instead of asterisks and to signify the end of stories.

Discretionary hyphen: Typographic code that allows you to predetermine where a word will be hyphenated, if it needs to be hyphenated. If the word does not need to be hyphenated, the hyphen will not appear. Discretionary hyphens will automatically appear and disappear as preceding text is added or deleted.

Display type: Typefaces designed to be used for headlines and/or at large size. Often, display typefaces attract attention but are unreadable when more than a few words are encountered at small size. Some typefaces contain fonts that have been redrawn to look good at large size. (See *titling fonts.*)

Dithering: Technique that computer monitors use to simulate colors that are not supported by the computer's monitor and video circuits. Small dots of two adjacent colors are used to fool the eye into creating a third, non-existent, color. Often creates an unsightly "grainy" appearance.

Domain name: The domain refers to a Web site's unique electronic address that is registered and remains the same, regardless of the physical location where the computers hosting the Web site are located. (See *URL.*)

Downloadable fonts: Typeface designs that users can access from a Web site and add to their computer, allowing them to view the Web site the way it was intended to be viewed. Once downloaded and added to their computer, these fonts can then be used for other projects.

Downrules: Vertical rules added between columns to prevent readers from reading across the gutter, or space between columns.

Drop cap: Initial cap cut into the paragraph it introduces. Drop caps work best when they are at least three lines tall.

Duotone: Using two colors to print a photograph. When black plus gray are used, it is possible to reveal details that would normally be hidden in the dark, or shadow, areas of the photograph. Duotones can also be printed in a second color relating to the second, or accent color, used in the document.

Em dash: Typographic punctuation mark used in preference to two hyphens to introduce parenthetical expressions.

Em space: Space equal in size to the square of the type size, or, approximately, the width of the uppercase M in the typeface and type size being used. One or two em spaces are the proper indent for the first line of paragraphs.

E-mail: E-mail consists of messages sent back and forth electronically between the Web site and online visitors. E-mail is often used in conjunction with an Internet site to facilitate visitor feedback.

Emboss: Three-dimensional effect created with an illustration program that allows text to look like it is raised from the background.

En dash: Typeset punctuation used to indicate duration, such as "June – July." An en dash is longer than a hyphen and shorter than an em dash.

Eyebrow: Short text element above a headline introducing the headline.

Eyedropper: Time-saving feature found on many of the latest drawing, presentation, and word-processing software programs. The Eyedropper feature, found with different names, makes it easy to share formatting attributes (typeface, type size, color, line thickness, fill pattern, and soon). Use of the Eyedropper tool makes it unnecessary to create and name a style for objects whose formatting attributes will be copied only once or twice. (See *style*.)

Fills: Backgrounds created using cross-hatch patterns, imported bit-mapped graphics, or transitions from one color to another.

Filter: Creative effects applied with an illustration program to selectively emphasize or de-emphasize all or portions of a photograph. Filters can be used to sharpen or blur images or apply special effects. Filters also allow text and graphic images to look like they were created using textured backgrounds or applied on various types of backgrounds using different types of paint or reflecting different light sources.

Flip: Repositioning a text or graphic object end for end. Objects can be flipped horizontally or vertically.

Folio: Publication information, such as the issue number and date, appearing on the front page of a newsletter. Also, the page numbers on inside pages.

Font manager: Software applications that make it easy to add or temporarily remove typeface designs from your computer's operating system, speeding operation and reducing memory requirements. Font managers don't erase or remove the files from your hard disk, but simply remove them from active use, reducing the possibility of system crashes. Examples include Fifth Generation System's Suitcase for the Macintosh and Ares FontMinder for Windows.

Font manipulation: Software applications that permit you to modify existing typeface designs or create new designs. Font manipulation programs permit you to add, remove, or connect serifs, horizontally stretch or compress type, add or remove space to either side of the type, raise or lower the x-height, or create a logo that can be added to a document with a single keystroke. (See *logo*, *x-height*.)

Font: Originally, one size and style of a single typeface design. Now, type is scaled to size as needed, so a font refers to one variation of a typeface design, for example, Roman, (or "regular") bold, or italics.

Footer: Information and graphic elements automatically repeated at the bottom of each page. Page numbers and horizontal rules are typically placed in footers. (See *header*.)

Forced justification: Justification option found on many page layout and word processing programs that evenly spaces letters across a column. Useful for creating publication titles and department headings.

Formatting: Altering the appearance of text, graphic accents, or visuals by changing their formatting attributes, which can include — in the case of text — typeface, type size, line spacing, and color. Formatting attributes for a graphic object include line thickness and color or fill color and pattern. Formatting attributes for a visual include size, color, and the presence or absence of a border. (See *attributes*, *fill*, *pattern*.)

Forms: Forms facilitate interaction between visitors and the Web site. Forms make it easy for visitors to enter their names, addresses, and product/service preferences in a format that can be returned to the Web site via e-mail and easily compiled and used for follow-up purposes. (See *e-mail*.)

Frames: (1) Containers, frequently used in word processing programs, which allow text or visuals to be moved and locked to a specific position on a page or locked to adjacent text. Containers allow headlines to span more than one text column and allow pullquotes to be positioned between columns. Containers also allow you to add borders and captions to visuals, which remain with the visuals if the frame is moved. Frames are used to subdivide a computer monitor so that different files consistently appear in windows along the top, bottom, or side of the screen. Frames permit Web site visitors to navigate throughout a Web site while the firm's logo or motto remains in the same position or all navigation links remain visible. (See *banner*.)

Frieze: Design term referring to horizontal alignment of photographs arranged side-by-side, usually along the top or bottom of a page. When a page contains numerous small photographs, a frieze is often preferable to a haphazard placement on the page, which can project a disorganized appearance.

FTP: FTP refers to File Transfer Protocol, the files that an ISP (Internet Service Provider) distributes to its users, allowing them to upload Web sites created on their computers to the host computers. FTPs are also used to download files from a Web site to a visitor's computer. (See *ISP*.)

GIF: Widely used graphics format that does not degrade image quality but creates large graphics files. See *JPEG*.

Golden Mean: Visually balanced height to width ratio, roughly 3 to 5, found widely in nature and throughout design history, characteristic of "pleasing" page layouts (page size and text area) and photographs.

Gradient fill: Background fill created with illustration and presentation programs characterized by a smooth transition from one color to another, or from one color to white or black. The direction of the transition can be top to bottom, bottom to top, side to side, diagonally, or from the title to the edges of a 35-mm slide or overhead transparency. Text can also be filled with gradient screens. (See *radial screen*.)

Graphic text: Words formatted as graphic files, retaining the designer's original typeface, type size, type style, color, and background choices. Graphic text always appears the same, regardless of the type of hardware or software used to display it or the fonts installed on the Web site visitor's computer. (See *live text.*)

Greeked: Typographic and page layout technique involving the use of nonsense-text, instead of real words. Because you're not so apt to try to read the Greeked text, you're more likely to concentrate on the overall appearance of the text on the page.

Grid: The underlying framework or structure of a document, which defines column placement. The grid appears on the screen of your computer as a series of non-printing rules.

Gridlines: Horizontal and vertical lines used to organize tables and separate rows and columns. Background pattern in charts used to organize a chart; horizontal gridlines provide a scale, or frame of reference for quantities; vertical gridlines help organize intervals.

Grouping: Software feature found in illustration and presentation programs that allows you to create a single object out of one, or more, text or graphic objects so they can be moved and resized as a single unit.

Gutter: Horizontal space between columns. Also the space between the right-hand margin of a left-hand page and the left-hand margin of the right-hand page.

Halftone: Screen, or texture, applied to a photograph so that it can be printed as a series of lines or dots. (See *continuous tone, LPI, screen.*)

Hanging indents: Page layout device where the first line extends to the left of the lines that follow. Usually used in bulleted or numbered lists, so that the following lines align with the first line, allowing the bullets or numbers to be surrounded by white space.

Hanging punctuation: Punctuation, typically opening quotation marks, placed in the margin, to the left of the text they introduce.

Hard space: Important typographic code that prevents words from splitting if they are too long to fit at the end of a line.

Header: Text and graphic elements, such as border rules, automatically placed at the top of each page. Header information typically includes chapter number and title or author's name. Different information usually appears on the right- and left-hand pages. (See *footer.*)

Helper application: Program, such as Adobe Acrobat, that must be downloaded and added to the Web site visitor's browser before certain files can be viewed. Most helper applications can be downloaded for free.

Hinting: The process of improving a typeface's on-screen readability, especially at smaller sizes, by redrawing it slightly differently at different sizes so there is a better match between the character shape and the pixels of the computer screen.

Home page: Home page typically refers to the first screen that visitors encounter when they reach a Web site. The Home page typically contains a short introduction describing the purpose of the Web site or the association or firm's area of expertise plus links that will take visitors to different locations within the Web site. (See *splash page.*)

Hotspot: Portion of an image map which, when clicked, serves as a link to another page in a Web site or another Web site address. (See *image map, links.*)

HTML: Programming code, consisting of symbols inserted before and after text as well as before and after the filenames of graphics to be downloaded, that Web browsers use to construct a Web page on a computer screen. (See *code shy, code savvy.*)

Hue: The distinguishing characteristics between colors as identified by name, for example, red, blue, or green, as contrasted to their brightness or saturation.

Hypertext: Characteristic of multimedia software programs that permit you to jump to a different page in the same document, or a different document altogether, by double-clicking on a word or graphic.

Hyphenation zone: Typographic term referring to the space that a word must span if the word will be hyphenated, or split over two lines. By adjusting the hyphenation zone, you can determine how many words will be hyphenated.

Icons: (1) Graphic element used in place of something else, typically words or commands. (2) Graphic representations of links to various locations within a Web site. Icons visually reflect the purpose of the link, such as a question mark that will take visitors to the site's Frequently Asked Questions page or a mail box that permits visitors to register.

Image manipulation program: Software program designed specifically to modify scanned photographs by changing their tonal range, colors, and adding special effects like embossing, blurs, and textures.

Imagesetter: Term used to describe high-resolution output devices found at a service bureau that create camera-ready artwork at 1,270 or 2,5640 dot-per-inch resolution. (See *resolution, service bureau.*)

Image map: A large graphic, typically an illustration but possibly a photograph, that contains hot-spots, or areas which, when clicked on, link the Web site visitor to other pages within a Web site or another Web site. (See *hotspot.*)

Indents: Paragraphs where the lines do not extend the full width of a column. Text can be indented from the left, right, or both the left and right. Whereas tabs only move the first line of a paragraph, indents move every line.

Infographic: Information translated into visuals combining elements of illustrations and charts.

Initial cap: Oversize letter often used to introduce the first paragraph of a story, but sometimes used to break-up long text columns. Initial caps can be dropped or raised. (See *drop cap, raised cap.*)

Inline: Graphics locked to text paragraphs, so that the graphic moves as preceding text is edited or deleted.

Interactivity: The basis of the Web's ability to allow Web site visitors to control the order in which they view individual pages by clicking on desired links. Also refers to the ability of Web site visitors to query a Web-based database and receive only information that meets the criteria they're interested in. (See *database publishing.*)

Interlacing: The progressive display of a graphic image in greater and greater detail as it downloads. Instead of displaying the graphic one line at a time, a rough outline of the entire graphic is downloaded before the details fill in.

Intranet: An Intranet is a Web site designed for the exclusive use of a firm and its employees and — possibly — its customers. Intranets are usually password protected, which means that visitors must type in a code word or alphanumeric sequence in order to have access to the information. Intranets are commonly used for purposes like listing employee benefits, rules and regulations, as well as product inventory levels.

ISP: An ISP is an Internet Service Provider who can host your Web site. Few non-corporate Web sites are placed on the individual or firm's own computers. Rather, individuals and businesses rent space on specialized large and fast computers located either in the area or across the country. Web site files are uploaded from the computer where they were created to the host's computers. (See *FTP* and *uploading.*)

JPEG: Graphics file format that creates smaller file sizes, and, hence, download faster, but with some loss of quality. (See *GIF.*)

Jumpline: Phrase directing reader to another page where the current story is continued.

Justification limits: Important command found in most word processing and page layout programs that allows you to define the minimum and maximum variation in word spacing that can be applied to align the last letters of each line.

Justified: Text characterized by lines of equal length, which a software program achieves by varying letter and word spacing within each line. In justified text, the last letters in each line are aligned with the last letters in the lines before and after it. (See *rag.*)

Kerning pair: Although most typeface designs ship with pre-adjusted spacing between certain pairs of letters, many software programs permit you to fine-tune the spacing for special pairs of letters at certain sizes. These programs create kerning pair files that your software references when placing text on the page.

Kerning: Increasing or decreasing spacing between specified pairs of letters. Certain combinations of uppercase and lowercase letters look awkward next to each other, especially at large, or headline, size. Typical letter combinations include an uppercase *Y* next to a lowercase *a* or an uppercase *W* next to an uppercase *A*.

Keyboard shortcuts: Software feature that permits you to access frequently-used commands directly from the keyboard, without using the mouse to open a menu and select the command. Keyboard shortcuts save time and reduce unnecessary mouse motion as well as the frustration of returning your hands to the wrong position.

Kicker: Short phrase above a headline that introduces the headline.

Knock out: White type reversed out of a photograph. Instead of printing the text in white, a "hole" is cut into the photograph allowing the background color of the paper to appear through the photograph.

Layering: Contemporary page layout technique characterized by text that can be read in a non-linear fashion, as the reader's interests dictate. Readers can read the primary layer, often a long article and skip adjacent material set in a smaller type size, or read secondary articles as desired.

Leading: In typography, leading refers to vertical line spacing. Leading is as important as type size in determining the overall appearance and readability of a text element or column of type. (See *auto leading.*)

Legend: Color-coded area of a chart that identifies each element.

Legibility: Measure of how easily readers can identify the individual words of a headline or text phrase. Legibility differs from readability, in that legibility is concerned with the reader's ability to notice individual words, rather than the ease and speed with which columns or extended text blocks can be read. (See *readability.*)

Ligature: Typographic term referring to single characters that replace two, or more, separate characters. Ligatures have been redrawn to overcome the problems that occur when certain letters appear next to each other. The most popular ligatures are replacements for *fi, ffi, fl* and *ffl.*

Line break: Command that allows you to break headlines at logical pauses without adding paragraph spacing. Line breaks also help you avoid extremely long lines followed by very short lines.

Linking: (1) Instead of importing (or integrating) a graphics file or scanned photograph into a document, many page layout programs only reference the original file. This reduces the file size of the document, an important consideration in documents containing numerous scanned images. (2) Many Windows word processing programs permit you to link a chart or illustration to the originating program. Double-clicking the image in the document loads the source program and permits you to edit the chart or illustration. In addition, if the source file is modified, the linked image is automatically updated.

Links: Links are navigational tools that allow a Web site visitor to move from place to place within a Web site, moving from page to page or from location to location. Links also permit Web sites to be linked together, so that visitors to one Web site can easily visit a Web site devoted to a similar topic or area of interest. Links consist of different color text or icons. When visiting a Web site, you can tell when the mouse is moving over a link because the pointer turns into a hand. (See *visited links.*)

Live area: The area of a page containing text or graphics, as contrasted to the physical dimensions of the page. (See *trim size.*)

Live text: Text that is quickly downloaded and immediately formatted on screen by the Web browser according to the HTML codes that has been added before and after the various text elements. The default settings of the Web site visitor's browser influence the appearance and size of the text. (See also *graphic text.*)

Logo: A firm or association's name set in type in a distinctive way, often accompanied by graphic accents or symbols.

LPI: Lines-per-inch, a measure of the sharpness of a screened halftone. Photographs intended to be output on a laser printer and printed on a coarse paper can range from 50 to 75 lines-per-inch. Acceptable lines-per-inch for photographs in publications to be output on a high-resolution imagesetter and printed on a quality, glossy paper can range up to 500 lines-per-inch. (See *continuous tone, halftone, screen.*)

Margin: The space between the live area, or space occupied by text columns or visuals and the physical edge of a page. Margins provide white space that provides pleasing contrast with the text columns as well as a place for readers to place their thumbs while holding a page. (See *live area, trim size.*)

Mask: Tracing an object, or portion of a photograph, with an image manipulation program and applying a different creative effect to it, like a blur, different colored ink, or texture. (See *image manipulation program.*)

Masthead: Publication design element containing addresses and phone numbers plus the names and positions of key staff members, such as editor, assistant editor, proofreader. Often incorrectly used to refer to publication title. (See *nameplate.*)

Mirror: Capability of drawing programs that adds a second copy of a text or graphic object, facing a different direction. Useful when creating Rorschach drawings.

Monospaced: Typeface designs, similar to the characters created by typewriters, characterized by letters of equal width. In a monospaced typeface designs, like Courier or Letter Gothic, thick letters like m's are as thick as thin letters like *i*'s. (See *proportionally spaced.*)

Nameplate: Special typography and graphic accents used to create a unique publication title. The nameplate often includes a background, horizontal rules, a subtitle, and a tagline explaining the purpose of the publication. Not to be confused with masthead. (See *masthead.*)

Navigation: Navigation is the act of moving from location to location within a Web site, or between Web sites. Navigation is accomplished by clicking on *links*. Links can consist of either colored and underlined text or icons representing the link's destination.

Navigation bar: Horizontal or vertical design element containing buttons or text links to various pages within a Web site as well as associated Web site addresses. (See *links.*)

Oblique: Typographic term referring to sans serif typeface designs with letters that have been slanted, rather than redrawn like a true italics.

Offset: Term defining the amount of space between text and an adjacent border or graphic. Also refers to the amount of space between text and adjacent borders within the cells of a table. (See *cell.*)

Old Style Figures: Alternate typeface designs accompanying the major serif typefaces that contain numbers scaled to the x-height of the typeface. Old Style Figures often descend below the baseline of the typeface.

Optical alignment: Often, what your computer "sees" is not what your eye "sees." In page layout terms, large characters containing overhanging elements like uppercase *Y*'s and *T*'s may have to be moved to the left when they appear at the start of a multiline headline, in order to appear "right." This is because your eyes focus on the vertical stroke of the letter, rather than the thinner horizontal element. Likewise, rounded letters often extend below the baseline or above the x-height of a typeface, in order to appear properly aligned with adjacent characters.

Organization chart: Visual used to display hierarchy and responsibility.

Ornaments: Decorative typeface designs used to embellish headlines and subheads, separate text elements or as icons in maps, such as "campground," "restrooms," "tollhouse," and so forth. (See *icons.*)

Orphan pages: Web site pages inadvertently not linked to the Web site's Home page or other pages. Although many software programs automatically check for links, often it's up to the Web site designer to make sure all pages are properly linked. (See *preview, schematic.*)

Orphan: Line of text, or portion of a line of text, left over from the bottom of a previous column or page, isolated at the top of a new column or page. (See *widow.*)

Padding: Amount of space separating a text or graphic element from the top, bottom, and sides of the table cell in which it is placed. (See *cell.*)

Palette: A limited number of colors that have been chosen on the basis of their ability to project a unified image, containing enough variety for both background, or receding, colors as well as foreground, or advancing, colors.

PDF: Suffix added to files indicating that the file has been saved in Adobe Acrobat's Portable Document Format, which allows you to share fully formatted documents — including original typeface; type size, letter, line, and paragraph spacing — with users who may not have the particular typefaces installed on their computers. (See *hypertext* and *links.*)

Perspective: Typographic effect adding depth to titles and logos, making it appear that the text is growing as it approaches the reader.

Pica: Graphic designer's unit of measurement. There are approximately 12 picas to an inch, 12 points to a pica. (See *point.*)

Pictograph: Graphing technique that uses repeating picture elements (for example, growing oil consumption illustrated by barrels of oil, and so forth) instead of solid or filled bars.

Pixel: Unit of measurement of a computer screen. Computer screens use a relatively coarse 72 dots-per-inch, which limits the sharpness of text and photographs.

Placeholder: A small graphic element used to replace a larger illustration or photograph until it has fully downloaded.

PMS: Short for Pantone Matching System, a widely used color-coding system that allows designers to define colors by numbers.

Point: Typographic unit of measurement: there are 72 points to an inch.

Posterization: Image manipulation technique that eliminates light and middle gray tones from scanned photographs, allowing only the dark areas to remain, creating impressionistic effects similar to line-drawings.

PostScript: Device-independent page description language pioneered by Adobe. PostScript files can be output at 300 dots-per-inch on laser printers or 1,270 or 2,540 dots-per-inch at service bureau image setters. (See *service bureau.*)

Preview: Temporarily loading your browser to preview your Web site on your computer before the files are uploaded to the Web server or Internet Service Bureau. Previewing your work gives you an opportunity to check to see that all links work properly. It's always a good idea to preview your work on more than one browser, to make sure that your Web site will look good to the greatest number of visitors. (See *browser.*)

Process colors: Colors created by mixing the four basic ink colors, cyan, yellow, magenta, and black, on a page. Colors are first separated and an individual layer of paper is output for the layers representing cyan, yellow, magenta, and black. (See *spot colors.*)

Proportion: The relationship between an object's height and width of. (See *Golden Mean.*)

Proportionally spaced: Most typeface designs are based on characters occupying different amounts of horizontal space. Wide letters like m's occupy more space than thin letters like i's. This is in contrast to typewriter-based typeface designs, like Courier, which are characterized by letters of equal width. (See *monospaced.*)

Pullquote: Short, significant phrase or sentence, often set in a different typeface and a larger type size, which summarizes materials in adjacent columns of text. Pullquotes reinforce important ideas and provide an opportunity for readers skimming through a publication to become interested enough to start reading the adjacent article.

Radial screen: Background fill feature found on illustration and presentation programs allowing one color in the center of a circle to extend outward and smoothly blend into a second color, or black or white. (See *gradient fill.*)

Rag: Term used to define the difference in length between short and long lines in text set flush-left/ragged-right. The rag should be sufficient to indicate that the text is not justified, yet not so noticeable that short lines follow long lines. The differing line endings should not form irregular shapes along the right margin.

Raised cap: Oversize initial cap that extends above the paragraph it introduces, creating visual interest by adding white space. (See *drop cap, initial cap.*)

Readability: Measure of how easily readers can comfortably comprehend extended text passages, such as body copy in columns (as contrasted to headlines or subheads). (See *legibility.*)

Receding colors: Colors to the left of the color wheel, like blues and green, best used for backgrounds.

Registration marks: Most page layout programs permit you to add registration marks. These help your commercial printer carefully align each page on the printing press, to maintain consistent margins on each page.

Removable storage media: Hard disks designed to be removed from one computer and either stored or used in another. Removable storage media allow you to archive important files that might be reused as well as easily bring large publications to service bureaus for imaging. Unlike tape back-ups, information stored on removable storage media can be accessed. Removable storage media is important when publications contain scanned color images. Bernoulli and Syquest are two brand-names frequently associated with removable storage media. (See *service bureau* and *CD-ROM.*)

Repurposing: The process of adapting text and graphic elements originally used in print media (for instance, ads, brochures, newsletters, and the like) to the Web. Layouts and typography that work in print often do not work on the Web. Often, multicolumn layouts have to be discarded and graphics resized in order to avoid long download times.

Resampling: The process of reducing the amount of color information in a scanned image or illustration so that the graphics file will be smaller and, hence, download faster.

Resolution: When referring to output devices, resolution is a measure of the sharpness with which pages are created. Office ink-jet and laser printers usually create 300 dot-per-inch images. The film-based image setters at service bureaus typically create images at 1,270 or 2,540 (or even more) dots-per-inch. Increased resolution creates sharper images and smoother graduated background fills.

Reverse: Tool of typographical emphasis involving placing white text against a black, or dark-colored background. (See *screens*.)

Rivers: Visual distraction in page layouts typically caused by spaces inside adjacent lines of text that line-up with each other. Often found in narrow columns of justified text where two spaces follow each period. Justification expands the spaces, and when the spaces in two, or more, lines are on top of each other, the reader's eyes make a subconscious connection between them.

Roman: Regular, nonitalic, or nonbold typeface designs.

Rotate: Software effect that allows you to set type or a graphic at angles.

Rule: Graphic accents created with a software program's line-drawing tool. Rules can be used as borders, between columns, to emphasize text or indicate the end of one text element and the beginning of a new unit.

Run-in: Short phrase, usually set in bold, bold-italics or italics, used to draw attention to and introduce a paragraph. Basically, run-ins can be considered third or fourth level subheads placed within the text paragraph instead of above or next to the paragraph. (See *subheads, sideheads*.)

Sans serif: Category of typeface design lacking the small finishing strokes that provide letter-to-letter transitions. Sans serif typefaces often have more impact at large size because of their design simplicity. (See *serif*.)

Saturation: Measure of the strength of a color; colors printed at full, or 100 percent strength, compared to colors printed at tints like 10 percent, 20 percent or 50 percent full strength.

Scale: Increasing or reducing the size of a text or graphic element while retaining the proportion, or height-to-width ratio of the original.

Scalloped columns: Page layout technique characterized by columns of different length. Instead of beginning a new paragraph at the bottom of a column when there is only space for a few lines, the entire paragraph is moved to the top of the next column (or page). This technique saves production time and adds visual interest by creating irregular amounts of white space at the bottoms of each column.

Scan: Convert photographs or 35-mm slides into digital files that can be placed into your publication. Scanning makes it easy to precisely crop and resize photographs and is a necessary first-step towards other photo manipulation techniques, such as lightening dark areas or darkening light areas.

Schematic: Drawing showing the relationship between the various pages of a Web site. Used to double-check that all pages are linked. (See *orphan* pages.)

Scholar's margins: Narrow space along the left and right edges of a book, originally provided to allow scholars to comment on the material in the adjacent columns.

Screen: To convert a continuous-tone halftone into a series of dots that can be reproduced as a halftone. The quality of the screen is measured in lines-per-inch. (See *continuous tone*, *halftone*, *LPI*.)

Screens: Tool of graphic emphasis involving placing text against a gray, or tinted background. Most software allows you to specify screens in 10 percent increments; a 10 percent screen indicates light gray, a 90 percent screen is almost full-strength black. (See *tint*.)

Script: Typeface designs that mimic handwriting.

Scroll: Clicking on the horizontal or vertical scroll bar to reveal more of a Web page than can be displayed at once on the visitor's screen.

Separation: Technique used when printing color documents. Separation refers to dividing color documents into the four colors which, together, can be used to recreate every other color. These colors are cyan, magenta, yellow, and black.

Separator: Horizontal rules or graphic elements used to separate topics within a Web document. Today, separators are used less frequently than originally. Most of the time, subheads offer a better solution to breaking up long topics.

Serif: Typographic term referring to the wedge-shaped or tear-shaped strokes at the ends of letters. Serifs enhance readability by guiding the reader's eyes from one letter to another. Serifs also contribute to the unique shape of the letters. (See *sans serif*.)

Service bureau: Commercial firm with trained staffs who use expensive, high-resolution image setters to output files prepared on your computer. By making such services available as needed, charging on a per-page or per-hour basis, service bureaus eliminate the need for desktop publishers to purchase high-resolution output devices and color printers costing tens of thousands of dollars.

Shadow: Three-dimensional effect created by illustration programs that makes it look like a text or graphic object is standing vertically and illuminated from the top or side, creating a background below and behind it.

Sidebar: Short text element, typically three to six paragraphs long, adjacent to a longer text article. Sidebars provide visual interest and permit you to devote space to a single aspect of the longer, adjacent article without interrupting the overall flow of the article.

Sideheads: Subheads, or text used to attract a reader's attention to a new topic, placed adjacent to the text column rather than within the column. (See *run-ins* and *subheads*.)

Silhouette: Photo manipulation technique involving removing the background of a photograph, creating an irregularly shaped photograph containing just the primary message area.

Sink: A sink, or drop, is a page layout technique based on reducing column height, adding white space to the top of each page. Sinks unify publication, providing page-to-page continuity.

Site map: A site map provides an at-a-glance overview of a Web site, allowing visitors to see at a glance which pages are present, allowing them to navigate more quickly. Because site maps are typically text-only, they load faster and occupy less on-screen space than would otherwise be required to show all the links.

Splash page: A Splash page is a specialized type of Home page, one designed to make a distinct impression and communicate a single idea, usually visually. Instead of showing all of the Web site's navigation links, a Splash page typically offers only one alternative, which takes the visitor to a page containing more links (that is, navigation options). (See *Home page*.)

Spot color: Use of two, or more, colors to add visual interest to a document. Second colors are usually reserved for logos, important headlines, or graphic accents. The desired color is mixed in advance and applied in one pass, rather than being created by combining various amounts of the four primary process colors: cyan, magenta, yellow, and black. (See *process colors*.)

Spread: Although you typically work on one page at a time on the screen of your computer, readers seldom see just one page at a time. Readers typically see two-page spreads, that is, both the left and right hand pages at the same time. Working with two-page spreads permits you to see how the left and the right-hand pages either "fight" or work together with each other.

Standing heads: Newsletter term referring to short phrases that organize and introduce departments and topics that appear in every issue, such as "Message from the President," "New Faces," "In the News," and so on.

Status line: Text displayed by a browser along the bottom of the screen that changes to show when sites are being downloaded or indicating the Web site address that Web site visitors will be taken to if they click on a link. (See *link*.)

Stipple: Paper that contains a noticeable pattern, often textured and made from recycled paper.

Stock photos: Photographs, typically sold on CD-ROM or available for downloading from the Internet, that eliminate the costs and delays involved with custom photography. Always check to see if use of the copyright limitations accompany the photographs.

Stress: Difference in stroke thickness between the horizontal, or thick parts of a letter and the thin, often vertical, strokes of a letter.

Style: Typographic option indicating which variation of a typeface will be used: Roman (or upright), bold (that is, heavy), italics (redrawn and slanted), or bold-italics.

Styles: Time-saving feature that allows you to name and save files containing multiple typographic formatting choices. Instead of repeating typeface, type size, type style, color, alignment, hyphenation, and spacing choices each time you want to format text the way you did previously, you save the formatting options as a file and assign the options to a text block by simply applying the style.

Subheads: Typographic device used to divide long articles into manageable, bite-sized chunks. (See *run-ins*, *sideheads*.)

Swash: Many display typefaces contain alternate, ornate characters intended to add visual interest to titles and logos. Swash characters usually contain an oversize element, such as an upper case Q, with a tail that extends to the right under the next character (or characters), and so on.

Swipe file: File-folder containing samples of printed ads, brochures, newsletters, and other print communications that have lessons to teach. Used for inspirational or self-teaching purposes, reviewing the contents of a swipe file when starting a new project helps start your creative juices flowing and helps you avoid obvious mistakes.

Symbols: Typographic characters used to replace spelled-out words, for example, © for Copyright, introduce lists, and/or indicate the end of stories, and the like.

Symmetry: Design term used to describe individual pages or two-page spreads characterized by left-right balance.

Table: (1) Design technique that organizes complex information in row and column format, permitting easy comparisons. (2) A tool that permits Web site developers to control the horizontal and vertical placement of text and graphics. (See *cell*.)

Tabs: Keyboard command that moves text a pre-determined amount of space.

Template: Read-only file containing the formatting information necessary to create a finished document. Templates contain standing elements, like the nameplate on the front cover of a newsletter and the address panel on the back cover, as well as column layouts and the styles necessary to format the text. Templates save time and maintain issue-to-issue consistency.

Tension: Design technique based on creating unequal left-right balance. Often, a large vertical photograph at the left of a page is balanced on the right by a short text phrase.

Text wrap: Reducing the left or right margins of a text column to accommodate an irregularly-shaped photograph or pullquote placed next to the column or extending from an adjacent column.

Texture: The "weave" or smoothness of a column of text. The goal of fine typography is to create columns without distracting "holes," (often created by excessive word spacing in lines of justified type containing a few long words or by inserting two spaces after a period at the end of a sentence) or areas of blackness created by words set in bold.

Thumbnail: Reduced-scale version of a document or graphic. Thumbnail documents permit you to get a better-idea of the page-by-page development of your publication. Web site visitors can click on the thumbnail graphic to download the full-sized illustration or photograph.

Tick marks: Small marks added to the x and y axis of charts and graphs to indicate minor intervals, as contrasted to the gridlines horizontal and vertical lines) used for major intervals.

Timeline: Type of visual that describes sequence and helps readers understand events in their historical perspective. The relationship between seemingly-unrelated events becomes clear when readers can see when they occurred in relation to other events.

Tint: Graphic elements printed with less than 100 percent ink coverage.

Tombstone headlines: Two or more parallel headlines in adjacent columns, placed in such a way that encourages readers to jump the column gutter, reading the separate headlines as one long headline.

Tracking: Increasing or decreasing letter spacing uniformly throughout a headline or column of text. In most cases, letter spacing is too generous. Slightly reducing letter spacing often improves the appearance of the text.

Transparent backgrounds: Most graphics programs permit you to eliminate the background behind irregularly shaped illustrations and photographs, so that the visual appears directly on the background of the Web site rather than inside a rectangular or square box.

Trim: The physical measurements of a page, as contrasted to the live area, or area between the margins, of a page. (See *bleed, live area, margins.*)

True Small Caps: Uppercase letters that have been redrawn to equal the x-height of a typeface. The use of True Small Caps to emphasize book titles is preferable to using scaled small caps, created by most software programs. This is because the width of the stroke comprising the True Small Caps equals the stroke weight of adjacent letters, rather than appearing lighter (strokes of letters become thinner as type size is reduced).

TrueType: Typeface format promoted by Apple and Microsoft. TrueType fonts often print faster than competing typeface formats on laser printers. (See *Type 1.*)

Type 1: Adobe's universally accepted typeface format of choice for professional designers. Type 1 is characterized by the largest selection of typefaces and the easiest acceptance by service bureaus. (See *TrueType.*)

Typeset punctuation: The use of true punctuation marks, like open and closed quotation marks and em and en dashes, in contrast to "typewriter" punctuation created by using "inch" marks and double hyphens.

Uploading: Uploading is the process of transferring the files that make up a Web site from the computer where they were created to an ISP's (or Internet Service Provider's) computer or computers. (See *FTP, ISP.*)

URL: URL, or Uniform Resource Locator, refers to each Web site's unique electronic address. The advantage of a URL is that your address, or domain name, remains the same regardless if you move or change Internet Service Providers. The best URL's clearly identify either the association or firm sponsoring the Web site or describe the product or service being offered. (See *Domain name.*)

Visited links: You can tell when you have visited a link because the color of the text describing the destination changes.

Visualization: The very exciting (and, alas, often rare) creative act of "seeing," or conceiving, how you want a finished project to look when finished and printed.

Watermark: Background text or graphic element that appears very lightly on each page, behind the primary text or graphic elements. Watermarks differ from headers and footers in that they are very light and can be placed anywhere on the page, instead of being found just at the top or bottom.

Weight: Many typeface designs are available with strokes of different thicknesses. These range from Light to Heavy, permitting you to add visual interest to your publication and give voice to your text without choosing a different typeface, which might detract from your message.

White space: Page layout term referring to areas of rest and quiet on a page, free from text, visuals or graphic accents. White space provides the contrast necessary to frame text and visuals.

Widow: Somewhat ambiguous typographic term indicating a short line, a third (or less) of the width of a column. Widows are especially noticeable when they occur at the bottom of a column or end of a page.

Windows Color Palette: Not all of the 256 colors available on the Macintosh are available when Web sites are viewed on computers and software using the Microsoft Windows browsers. This is because the windows operating system reserves several colors for its own use. By only using colors available on the 216 "Windows safe" color palette, your Web site will look good regardless of the platform used by visitors to your Web site.

X-height: Typographic term referring to the height of lower-case vowels *a, e, i, o,* and *u.* The x-height of a typeface plays a major role in its apparent size. Typefaces with a high x-height look significantly larger than typefaces with a low x-height, even when both are set the same size.

Zones: In a well-designed Web site, different areas of the screen are devoted to different purposes. Navigation links are usually placed to the left or along the top of a Web site, for example, while empty space to the right of a column of text is used to reduce line length and focus the Web site visitor's attention on the message.

Zoom: Choosing a different screen magnification to reveal less of a page at large size or more of a page at small size.

Index

• Symbols •

• A •

• D •

• E •

• F •

• G •

• H •

• I •

• J •

• K •

• L •

• M •

• N •

(continued)

• Q •

• R •

• S •

• T •

(continued)

(continued)

• Y •

• Z •

IDG BOOKS WORLDWIDE BOOK REGISTRATION

We want to hear from you!

Visit **http://my2cents.dummies.com** to register this book and tell us how you liked it!

- Get entered in our monthly prize giveaway.
- Give us feedback about this book — tell us what you like best, what you like least, or maybe what you'd like to ask the author and us to change!
- Let us know any other *...For Dummies* topics that interest you.

Your feedback helps us determine what books to publish, tells us what coverage to add as we revise our books, and lets us know whether we're meeting your needs as a *...For Dummies* reader. You're our most valuable resource, and what you have to say is important to us!

Not on the Web yet? It's easy to get started with *Dummies 101®: The Internet For Windows® 95* or *The Internet For Dummies®*, 4th Edition, at local retailers everywhere.

Or let us know what you think by sending us a letter at the following address:

...For Dummies Book Registration
Dummies Press
7260 Shadeland Station, Suite 100
Indianapolis, IN 46256
Fax 317-596-5498